Japanese Monograph No. 154

RECORD OF OPERATIONS AGAINST SOVIET RUSSIA, EASTERN FRONT

(AUGUST 1945)

PREPARED BY
MILITARY HISTORY SECTION
HEADQUARTERS, ARMY FORCES FAR EAST

DISTRIBUTED BY
OFFICE OF THE CHIEF OF MILITARY HISTORY
DEPARTMENT OF THE ARMY

Published by Books Express Publishing
Copyright © Books Express, 2011
ISBN 978-1-78039-070-3

Books Express publications are available from all good retail and online booksellers. For publishing proposals and direct ordering please contact us at: info@books-express.com

This manuscript may not be reproduced
without the permission of the Office
of The Chief of Military History

RECORD OF OPERATIONS AGAINST SOVIET RUSSIA,

EASTERN FRONT (AUGUST 1945)

PREFACE   I - II

Table of Contents

                                                                  Page

Monograph No 154-A

CHAPTER I   Kwantung Army Operations in Manchuria
             (9-15 August 1945)

    Preliminaries to Invasion   1
    First Reports of the Soviet Invasion   3
    First Estimate of the Situation   8
    Change in Plan for the Western Front   10
    Transfer of General Headquarters   13
    Situation on 12 August   15
    The War Ends   19
    Cancellation of Operational Missions   23
    Dissolution of the Kwantung Army   25

                         MAPS   Following page

No 1   Deployment of Japanese and Known Soviet Forces   3
            9 August 1945
No 2   Progress of Operations, 2400 9 August 1945   8
No 3   Progress of Operations, 2400 10 August 1945   10
No 4   Progress of Operations, 2400 11 August 1945   15
No 5   Progress of Operations, 2400 12 August 1945   16
No 6   Progress of Operations, 2400 13 August 1945   18
No 7   Progress of Operations, 2400 14 August 1945   19
No 8   Progress of Operations, 2400 15 August 1945   19
No 9   Depth of Soviet Penetration, 15 August 1945   19

                        CHARTS

No 1   Kwantung Army Divisions, 10 August 1945   8
No 2   Organizational Chart of General Headquarters
            Kwantung Army   20

Monograph No 154-B   Page

CHAPTER II   The First Area Army in Eastern Manchuria

		Page
Military Geography of Eastern Manchuria		26
Operational Planning		30
Operational Plans		33

CHAPTER III   Composition of Major Units

General Structure	39
Third Army	43
Fifth Army	44

CHAPTER IV   Status of Preparations

Fortifications	46
Revisions in Logistical Planning	48
Communications	50
Training	53
Border Garrisoning	53
Changes in Strength and Materiel	55
Combat Effectiveness	56

CHAPTER V   First Area Army Operations on Eastern Front

Opening of Hostilities	59
Operations - 10 August	62
Operations - 11 to 14 August	63
Estimate of Losses	69
Situation at the End of Hostilities	70
Cease Fire Measures	71
Negotiations with the Soviet Army and Disarmament	72
Civil Affairs	75

MAPS

		Following Page
No 1	Army Boundary Changes, Eastern Manchuria	26
No 2	Deployment of Tactical Units of First Area Army 9 August 1945	43

CHARTS

No 1	Organization Chart, First Area Army September 1944	39
No 2	Organization Chart, First Area Army 8 August 1945	45

SKETCHES

		Page
No 1	Type of Fortifications on Eastern Front	28
No 2	Eastern Front Fortifications (Approximate Location) August 1945	29
No 3	Terrain Analysis, Eastern Front	32
No 4	Major Defense Lines of First Area Army	34
No 5	Major Signal Communications of First Area Army 9 August 1945	50

Monograph No 154-C

	Page
CHAPTER VI The Third Army	
Composition of Third Army	80
Preliminary Operational Planning	82
The Hsinking Conference	83
The Final Operational Plan	85
Construction and Improvement of Defense Installations	88
Logistical Plan	89
Status of Training and Other Preparations	90
CHAPTER VII Third Army Operations	
Situation at the Start of the War	93
Situation from 10 to 13 August	96
Situation from 14 to 16 August	98
Summary of Movements and Disposition of Zone of Communications Units	102
The Cessation of Hostilities	104
Civil Affairs	106

MAP

		Following Page
No 1	Deployment of Tactical Units of Third Army August 1945	86

SKETCHES

No 1	Third Army Main Resistance Areas, July - August 1945	85
No 2	Disposition of Supply Depots of Third Army, Early 1945	89
No 3	Disposition of Supply Depots and Munition Dumps of Third Army, August 1945	89

Monograph No 154-D

CHAPTER VIII The 79th Division

	Page
Origin of the 79th Division	110
Third Army Commander Announces New Plan	111
Organization of Division into Engineer Sector Units	114
Operational Preparations	118
Training, and Changes in Organization	121
Status of Preparations	122
Opening of Hostilities	123
Progress of Operations	125
The Attack on the Mayusan Positions	129
The Enemy Crossing near Tumen	131
Cease-fire Order	133
Negotiations with the Soviet Army	134
Japanese Residents in the 79th Division Area	137

MAPS

		Following Page
No 1	Construction Sector, 79th Division	117
No 2	Progress of Operations, 79th Division (Showing Part of 112th Division's Sector) August 1945	118

CHART

No 1	Construction Sector Units 79th Division	116

Monograph No 154-E

CHAPTER IX The 127th Division

	Page
Organization and Source of Personnel	139
Deployment of 127th Division	140
Operational Preparations	142
Status of Preparations Prior to the Outbreak of Hostilities	143
Situation at the Outbreak of Hostilities	145
Situation After the War	147

MAP

		Following Page
No 1	Operations in 127th Division Sector August 1945	141

Monograph No 154-F

	Page
CHAPTER X The Fifth Army	
Organization	148
Operational Preparations	153
Fortifications	159
Logistical Planning	163
Communication	166
Training	168
Intelligence	171
Border Garrisoning	173
Status of Supplies and Equipment	176
Status of Preparations Immediately Prior to the War	179
CHAPTER XI Fifth Army Operations	
Opening of Hostilities	181
Operations of Border Garrisons on the 124th Division Front	184
Operations of Border Garrisons on the 126th Division Front	186
Operations of Border Garrisons on the 135th Division Front	187
Operations of the 15th Border Garrison Unit	190
CHAPTER XII Operations in the MLR	
Operations of the 124th Division Near Muleng	193
Operations of the 126th Division Near Tzuhsingtun	199
Operations of the 135th Division South of Linkou	200
CHAPTER XIII Fifth Army Operations Near Yehho	
Preparations for the Defense of Yehho	202
Operations of the Kobayashi Detachment Near Motaoshih	204
Operations of the 126th Division Near Ssutaoling	205
Operation near Aiho	206
Operations of the 135th Division South of Hualin	207

CHAPTER XIV   The Withdrawal to Hengtaohotzu

	Page
Withdrawal Orders from the First Area Army	209
Occupation of Hengtaohotzu Positions and Disarmament	213
Losses Suffered by Both Sides	214
Situation at the Time the War Ended	215
Negotiations with the Soviet Army	217

CHAPTER XV   Civil Affairs

Japanese Residents and Cultivating Parties	221
Manchukuoan Government Agencies	222
The Manchukuoan Army and Police	223
Attitudes of Manchurians, Koreans, and White Russians	224

MAPS

		Following Page
No 1	Fifth Army Deployment, March 1944	148
No 2	Deployment of Fifth Army Elements Prior to 9 August 1945	176
No 3	Progress of Fifth Army's Operations From 9 August to beginning of September 1945	181
No 4	Defense of Fifth Army's MLR Positions 10 - 13 August 1945	193
No 5	Defense of Fifth Army's Yehho and Hengtaohotzu Positions, 13 - 17 August 1945	202

CHARTS

No 1	Order of Battle of the Fifth Army	154
No 2	New Fortification Constructions in 1944	161
No 3	Actual Strength of Infantry Divisions June - August 1945	170

SKETCHES

No 1	Fifth Army Main Resistance Areas, August 1945	157
No 2	Main Supply Depots and Dumps of Fifth Army	166
No 3	Operational Roads in Fifth Army Sector	167

Monograph No 154-G

	Page
CHAPTER XVI The 124th Division	
Organization	225

	Page
Fortifications in the MLR	227
Communications	229
Training	230
Intelligence and Border Garrisoning	230
Status of Preparations Immediately Prior to the Outbreak of War	232
Outbreak of Hostilities	232
Attack on the MLR	236
Civil Affairs	244

MAPS

		Following Page
No 1	124th Division's Defense of Border 9 - 11 August 1945	236
No 2	124th Division's Defense of MLR 10 - 22 August 1945	239

Monograph No 154-H

CHAPTER XVII   The 126th Division

	Page
Organization	246
Intelligence and Estimate of the Soviets	247
Operational Preparations for Border Defense	250
The Pingyang Line	250
The Pamientung Line	252
The Lishan and Chingkulingmiao Positions	253
Opening of Hostilities	253
Engagement in Pingyangchen	255
Engagement in the Pamientung Area	256
Engagements Along the Pamientung Line	257
Engagement Near Tzuhsingtun	260
Plan for the Withdrawal of the Division's Main Force from Tzuhsingtun	262
Plan for Occupying Positions Near Yehho	263
Engagements Near Hill 371 and Ssutaoling Hill	266

MAP

		Following Page
No 1	Operations in 126th Division Area 9 - 12 August 1945	251

Monograph No 154-I

	Page
CHAPTER XVIII The 135th Division's Preparations	
Organization	274
Operational Planning	276
Status of Fortification Construction	277
Signal and Road Communication	278
Training	279
Intelligence	280
Border Garrisoning	281
Status of Preparations	282
CHAPTER XIX 135th Division Operations	
Opening of Hostilities	285
Engagements of Border Garrison Units	287
The Army Commander Revises the Defense Plan	289
Engagement of Division's Main Body Near Yehho	292
Engagement on 14 August	294
Engagement of 15 August	296
Engagement of Division Headquarters Near Hualin	297
Withdrawal of the 135th Division Toward Hengtaohotzu	299
Disarmament of the Division's Main Body	300
Losses on Both Sides	302
Post Hostilities Status	302
Negotiations with Soviet Forces	303

MAP

		Following Page
No 1	Defense of 135th Division's Positions Near Yehho 13 - 16 August 1945	292

Monograph No 154-J

	Page
CHAPTER XX The 128th Division	
Organization	306
Redeployment	308
Status of Preparations	310
Opening of Hostilities	311
Operations of the 132d Independent Mixed Brigade	315
Division Operations	317
Operations Near Huapitientzu and Taipingling	320

	Page
Battle Near Tahsingkou	322
Situation Near Tachienchang	322
Estimated Losses to Both Sides	323
Negotiations with the Soviet Army	325
Civil Affairs	328

MAP

		Following Page
No 1	Operations in 128th Division's Sector 9 - 16 August 1945	308

Monograph No 154-K

CHAPTER XXI   The 132d Independent Mixed Brigade

	Page
Organization	331
Status of Supplies and Training	333
Opening of Hostilities	334
Engagements During the Withdrawal	338
Losses	344
Civil Affairs	344
Situation at the End of the War	345

MAP

		Following Page
No 1	Withdrawal of Main Body of 132d Independent Mixed Brigade, 9 - 15 August 1945	337

NB

The Representative Fraction is not to be used with reproduction. However, the Graphic Scale can be used to measure distances on the sketches

Preface to Monograph No 154

Monograph No 138, which preceded this monograph, dealt with the preparations of the Kwantung Army in Manchuria for operations against the Soviet Union. This monograph (No 154) as well as its sequel (No 155) deal with actual operations.

Monograph No 154, except for the first chapter which covers operations of the Kwantung Army throughout Manchuria, deals exclusively with the eastern front under the jurisdiction of the First Area Army. It covers preparation for operations as well as the operations themselves.

This monograph actually consists of eleven monographs. Aside from the Kwantung Army and the First Area Army, the units covered are Third Army, Fifth Army, the following divisions: 79th, 127th, 124th, 126th, 135th, 128th, and the 132d Independent Mixed Brigade. The monograph is the product of twelve former officers in the Japanese Army. All served in Manchuria during the brief war that lasted from 9 August to 15 August 1945, all were taken captive by the Soviets, and all were subsequently repatriated to Japan.

Each of the contributing authors has dealt with his subject separately, following a prescribed outline, and providing as much detail as was available to him through notes or memory. Naturally, the quantity of detail varies with each author. The burdensome repetition inevitable in accounts of operations in the same area and under the same command characterized the original translation. In eliminating much of this repetition, the editor felt that to excise too much would run the risk of denying to the historian and military student the different points of view presented by each author. Furthermore, the editor recognized that when the historian can get confirmation of statements from different sources, he feels freer and more confident in assessing facts and in condensing his material.

The consultants who assisted the editor believe that the monograph is the best that could be compiled from the source material now available. Its weaknesses are that it was compiled mostly from the notes of a limited number of participants, supplemented by their memories. Furthermore, no participants other than the authors checked the manuscript (a weakness partially remedied in editing), and many of the leading participants, still in captivity, were unable to express their views. The outstanding omissions in the monograph are accounts of the operations of the 134th Division in Chiamussu and of the 112th Division; no survivors of these two operations were available for the preparation of these accounts, although 112th Division operations are partly covered in the section on the 79th Division.

In a sense this monograph had to be almost completely re-written. It must be remembered that the losing side during military operations is always too preoccupied with tactical matters to devote much attention to the preparation of records. From such circumstances very little precision writing can be expected. Hence, although voluminous, the monograph had many omissions. Gaps had to be filled, inconsistencies reconciled and, where the author jumped headlong into a subject, prefatory notes had to be inserted by the editor. Still, the historian will not find all the answers here. For example, in view of the short duration of operations in Manchuria, the editor felt that the time element was of great importance. But the time is often missing. Instead, such generalities as "morning," or "early evening" occur. Nevertheless, enough information is provided to give the reader a fairly accurate picture of what took place. Furthermore, the editor has attempted to retain Japanese mentality throughout the monograph.

The original Japanese monograph, written between 1949 and 1951 by the Japanese former Army officer whose names appear at the beginning of each sub-monograph, was prepared under the supervision of the Report and Statistical Division of the 1st (Army) Demobilization Bureau in Tokyo at the direction of the Supreme Commander for the Allied Powers. The untranslated manuscript was turned over to the Army Translator Intelligence Service on 29 May 1951. The translated manuscript was edited early in 1954 by the Military History Section, Headquarters Army Forces Far East. Assistance to the editor was provided by ex-Colonel Muraji Yano and ex-Lieutenant Colonel Ko Takahashi.

The wide range of map scales used in this monograph was dictated by the fact the sub-monographs deal with organizations vastly different in size. For an over-all picture of Kwantung Army operations on all fronts in Manchuria a scale of 1/9,000,000 was used; for the operations of two regiments near Yehho on the eastern front a scale of 1/100,000 was used. Intermediate size maps were used for the area army, armies, divisions, and smaller units.

If one lesson stands out above all others in this monograph it is that the best antitank weapon is a tank. Japanese attempts to stop Soviet tanks with suicide squads, though heroic, were futile. Their lack of adequate antitank defenses left them at the mercy of Soviets tanks.

6 April 1954

Monograph No 154-A

CHAPTER I

Kwantung Army Operations in Manchuria[1]
(9-15 August 1945)

Preliminaries to Invasion

During May 1945 the Intelligence Section of Kwantung Army Headquarters, reporting on the Soviet build-up along the border, estimated that war with the Soviets during 1945 was unlikely. Nevertheless, it recommended close surveillance of Soviet actions particularly after August 1945.

On 14 June Kwantung Army Headquarters furnished each area army and army under its direct command with a copy of the outline of its new operational plan calling for delaying operations on all fronts, and set the latter part of September as the deadline for the completion of major preparations.[2] The fact was, however, that the completion of necessary preparations in 1945 was impossible and, in view of the growing tension caused by Soviet preparations, Kwantung

---

1. The information in this chapter about the over-all operations of the Kwantung Army was furnished by the following former staff officers of Kwantung Army Headquarters: Lt Col Genichiro Arinuma (air), and Major Kyoji Takasugi (operations).
2. Kwantung Army Headquarters had earlier notified each major subordinate command of the new plan, informally during March 1945 and officially during May. The major subordinate commands were First and Third Area Armies and the Fourth and Thirty-fourth Armies (the latter was transferred to Kwantung Army, from China on 17 June 1945). The other armies were under one of the area armies--the Third and Fifth under the First Area Army, and the Thirtieth (established 31 July 1945) and Forty-fourth under the Third Area Army. (A Japanese army is equivalent to a US corps; a Japanese area army is equivalent to a US army.)

Army leaders could not help but feel impatient and uneasy.

Following the Potsdam Conference in July, the Intelligence Section amended its May estimate. The possibility of war with the USSR in the early fall, it stated, was extremely great.

By late July the Soviets had virtually completed the build-up of ground combat troops in eastern Siberia. Thereafter they accelerated the build-up of aircraft and antiaircraft gun units. Intelligence concluded from this that the Soviet Army would be capable of attacking Manchuria during August.

Meanwhile, border incidents occurred with increasing frequency. Toward midnight on 6 August, one company of Soviet troops crossed the eastern Manchurian border near Kanhsiatun (south of Hutou) and attacked a lookout position there. Fifth Army was alerted. But Soviet troops withdrew on the following night and the incident ended without mishap. From the brazenly provocative attitude displayed by the Soviets during this incident, Kwantung Army Intelligence concluded that hostilities were close at hand. The scale of the incident convinced Intelligence that it was more than a simple reconnaissance. Kwantung Army Headquarters instructed all commands to give increased attention to surveillance along the borders.

The army areas and armies, however, regarded this latest incident merely as a prolongation of the earlier series of incidents and felt that with prudence and patience it would pass without difficulties. (See Monograph 138, pp 82-87.)

None of them drew the conclusion that the opening of hostilities was imminent. Hence, they did not take adequate emergency measures to meet the situation.

Kwantung Army Headquarters, however, felt the growing tension sharply and cautioned the Commander in Chief against taking a scheduled trip to Dairen. He refused to cancel the trip, however, and departed Hsinking on the 8th.

First Reports of the Soviet Invasion (See Map No 1.)

At about 0100 hours on 9 August, a telephone report from the First Area Army stated: "The enemy in front of Tungning and Suifenho has launched an attack," and then, "the city of Mutanchiang is being bombed by the enemy."

These reports came in to a Headquarters which for years, pursuant to Japan's national policy of maintaining peace with the USSR, had sought not only to prevent war but to prevent border disputes as well. Standing orders of the Kwantung Army strictly forbade untoward acts in the border areas. Frontline commanders, frequently admonished to localize incidents instigated by the Soviets, were submitting these reports. It became necessary, therefore, for Kwantung Army Headquarters first to remove these restrictions and cautions and second to direct commanders to offer resistance.

At about 0130 hours Hsinking, site of Kwantung Army Headquarters, and Kuanchengtzu, a suburb to the north of the city, were bombed by several enemy planes. Members of Kwantung Army Headquarters hurried

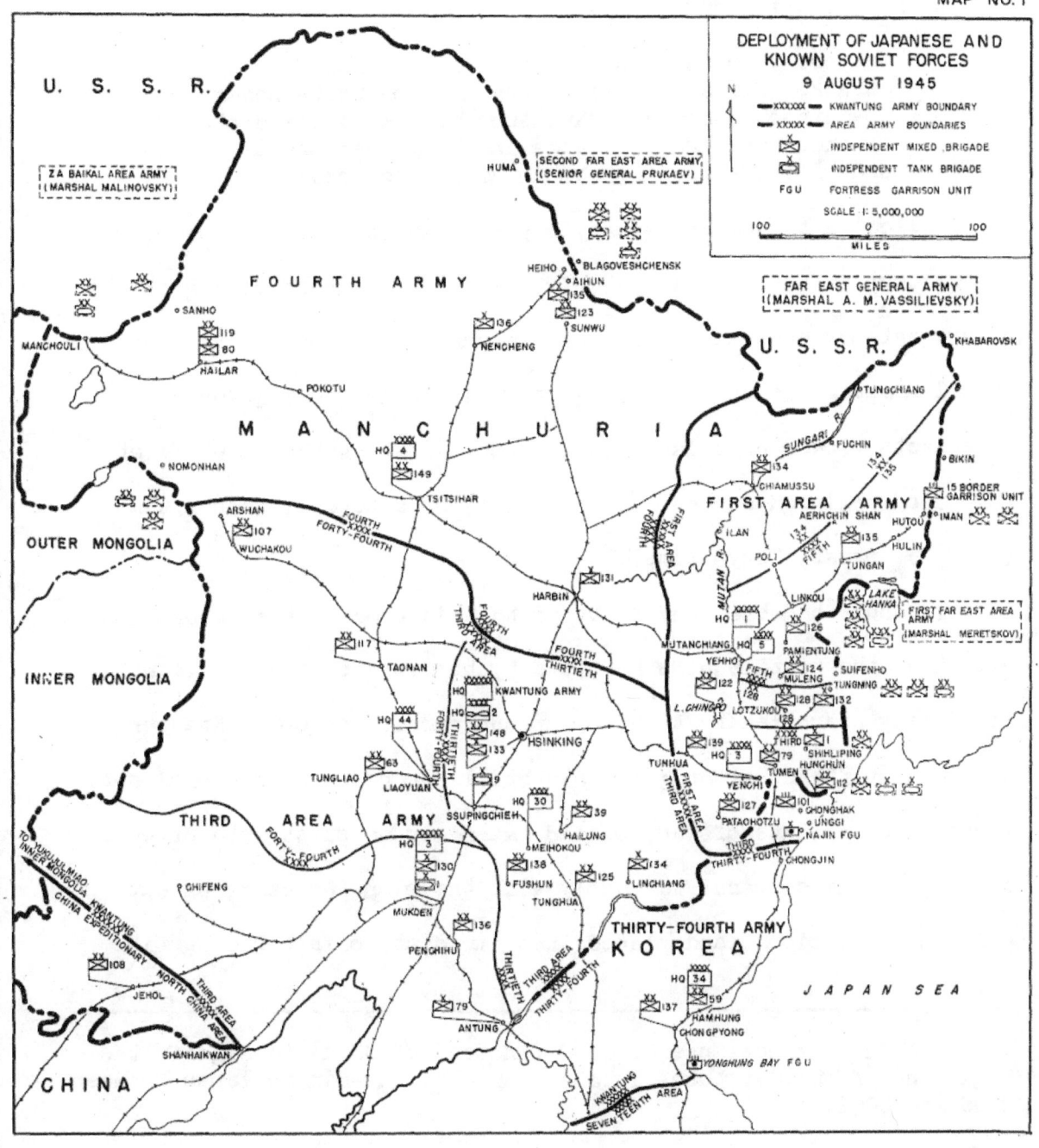

to their offices. At 0200, although it had not as yet received official instructions that a state of war existed, Headquarters issued the following order:

> The enemy on the eastern front has launched an attack. All area armies, armies, and units under the direct command of Kwantung Army will immediately check the enemy advance in the border areas, and will prepare for war in all other areas.

Following these preliminary reports, which were confined to the eastern front, word was received from other areas making it clear that Soviet armed forces had launched an all-out offensive on all fronts. At 0400 Kwantung Army radios monitoring Moscow broadcasts picked up a Tass Agency report stating that the Soviet Union had declared war on Japan as of 1700, 8 August, Moscow time (0000, 9 August, Tokyo time).[3]

If there had been any doubt up to this time of the nature and extent of the hostile acts reported by the various fronts, it was completely dispelled by the Tass announcement. At 0600, Kwantung Army Headquarters, although it had still not received official notification of a state of war, placed emergency measures into effect: it ordered all commands to comply with the plan for carrying out delaying operations, and placed into immediate effect the Wartime

---

3. The Japanese use of 0000 (instead of 0001) to signify the beginning of the day takes into account the one-minute lapse between 2400 and 0001.

Defense Regulations, and the Manchukuo Defense Regulations.[4] At the same time it rescinded the Guide for the Defense of the Manchukuoan-Soviet-Mongolian Border, drawn up in August 1944 to prevent the spread of border incidents.[5]

Placing into effect the 30 May 1945 plan for delaying operations was the signal for the Second Air Army to search for and attack enemy armored units on the western front, to conduct strategic reconnaissances on the eastern front, and to assign some "direct-cooperation" planes to the First and Third Area Armies and the Fourth Army. Another matter clarified by placing the plan into effect was that control of line of communications units and supply depots would shift from the Kwantung Army Headquarters to the area armies or armies in whose areas they were located.

In view of the danger that Hsinking might again be bombed after dawn, Kwantung Army Headquarters ordered its command post removed to Nanling, a southeast suburb.[6] In the evening, however, when General Yamada returned from Dairen, he went direct to the Hsinking head-

---

4. The Wartime Defense Regulations outlined emergency measures to be taken at the outbreak of hostilities, such as added protection for key communications centers, railroads, and reservoirs. The Manchukuoan Defense Regulations empowered the Commander in Chief of the Kwantung Army to assume control of Manchukuoan Army troops, and also to assume limited control over the civil administration.
5. The Guide for the Defense of the Manchukuoan-Soviet-Mongolian Border had been adopted following the Wuchiatzu and Mongoshile Incidents. These incidents are described in Monograph 138.
6. This emergency command post had been constructed in 1942. It had fallen into disrepair, however, and was found unsuitable at this time. It was closed on 10 August mainly because of poor communication facilities.

quarters.

In Tokyo, meanwhile, Imperial General Headquarters first learned of the existence of hostilities from the Domei News Agency which had picked up the Tass 0400 broadcast. Kwantung Army Headquarters transmitted word of the Soviet attack to Imperial General Headquarter, including the action it had taken, but the latter did not receive the message until after it learned of the Tass broadcast.[7]

In view of the Kwantung Army report and the Tass broadcast, Imperial General Headquarters issued emergency orders to commanders of all theaters involved. Besides the Kwantung Army in Manchuria, these included the Seventeenth Area Army in Korea, the China Expeditionary Army, the Fifth Area Army in Hokkaido, and homeland armies. These orders, the first issued by Imperial General Headquarters after the Soviet attack, were signed by the Emperor early in the afternoon of the 9th and transmitted promptly. The text follows:[8]

> The Soviet Union declared war on Japan and launched attacks at several places along the Soviet-Japanese and Soviet-Manchukuoan border at 0000, 9 August. However, the scale of these attacks is not large.

---

7. When Foreign Minister Shigenori Togo was aroused from sleep to be given the news of the Soviet invasion be expressed complete astonishment in view of the fact that the Soviets knew that Japan was then considering whether to accept the terms of the Potsdam Declaration. The formal note of a declaration of war was not handed to the foreign minister until 1115, 10 August by Ambassador Jacob Malik.

8. IGH ADO No 1374, 9 Aug 45. (Soviet-Japanese border here means the border in Sakhalin.)

Imperial General Headquarters will make immediate preparations for all-out military operations against the Soviet Union, while checking the enemy's advance with troops stationed in the border areas.

The Seventeenth Area Army will enter the order of battle of the Kwantung Army, the transfer to be effective at 0600 hours on 10 August.

The Commander in Chief of the Kwantung Army will immediately prepare to carry out all-out military operations against the Soviet Union; using troops stationed in the border areas he will check the enemy's advance for the time being. The principles to be followed in these operations are: the Kwantung Army will direct its major operation against the Soviet Union in such a manner so as to defend the Japanese territory of Korea; meanwhile, a minimum number of troops required to check a US invasion will be stationed in the South Korea area.

The Commander in Chief of the China Expeditionary Army will immediately make preparations to transfer a part of his troops and munitions to the South Manchuria area, while checking a possible Soviet invasion of his own area of responsibility utilizing troops stationed there.

The demarcation line of the operational area between the Kwantung Army and the China Expeditionary Army is as follows: Shanhaikwan, Tachengtzu, the eastern end of Lake Taerhhu, and the Yukujuru Mausoleum. The area falling on the boundary line shall be under the jurisdiction of the China Expeditionary Army.

The Commander in Chief of the Kwantung Army will place under the command of the Commander in Chief of the China Expeditionary Army all units stationed in the area newly assigned to the China Expeditionary Army.

This order had the effect of changing the primary mission of the Kwantung Army to one of defending "the Japanese territory of Korea." The object of placing the Seventeenth Area Army under the

MONOGRAPH NO. 154-A
CHART NO. 1

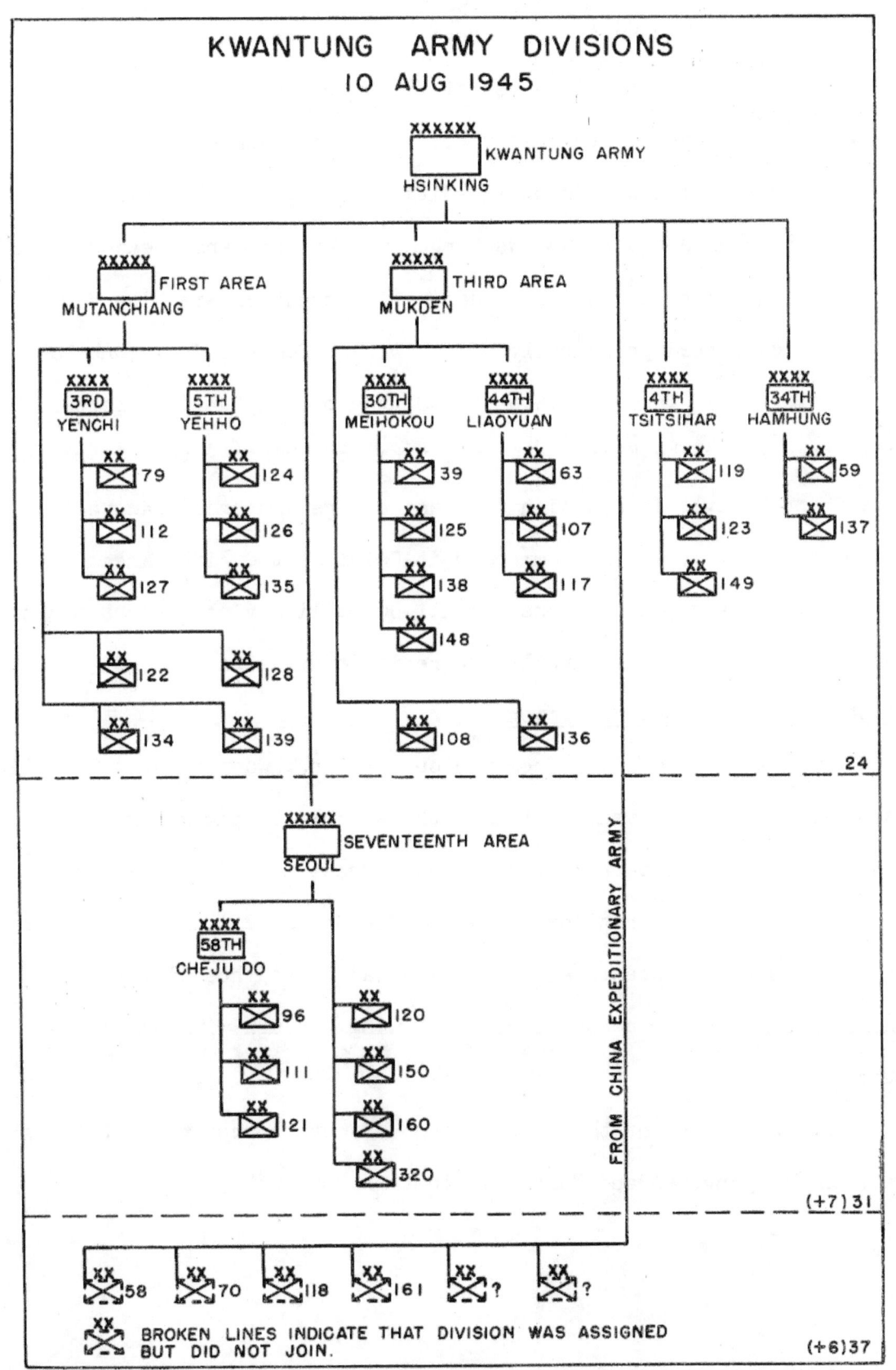

Kwantung Army was to establish a unified structure for the conduct of operations in Manchuria and Korea. By this action the Kwantung Army acquired the seven divisions of the Seventeenth Area Army, bringing to thirty-one the number of divisions under its control.

The units which the China Expeditionary Army was to transfer to South Manchuria under the Kwantung Army were one army headquarters, about six divisions and six brigades. (The munitions mentioned in the order consisted principally of ammunition for the divisions to be transferred.) These additions, had they been actually effected, would have given the Kwantung Army a total of thirty-seven divisions. (See Chart No 1.) In addition to these orders, Imperial General Headquarters directed the Commander in Chief of the Fifth Area Army to make immediate preparations for all-out military operations against the Soviet Union and, meanwhile, to resist enemy attacks.

First Estimate of the Situation

From reports received from various fronts, Kwantung Army General Headquarters on the evening of the 9th was able to piece together the situation on the eastern, northern, northwestern, and southwestern fronts, and in the north Korea area. (See Map No 2.)

In the north Korea area, the enemy had opened hostilities by shelling the Wuchiatzu positions, following through with small scale attacks.

The main force of the enemy on the eastern border was attacking between Pingyangchen and Tungning (in front of Fifth Army and the

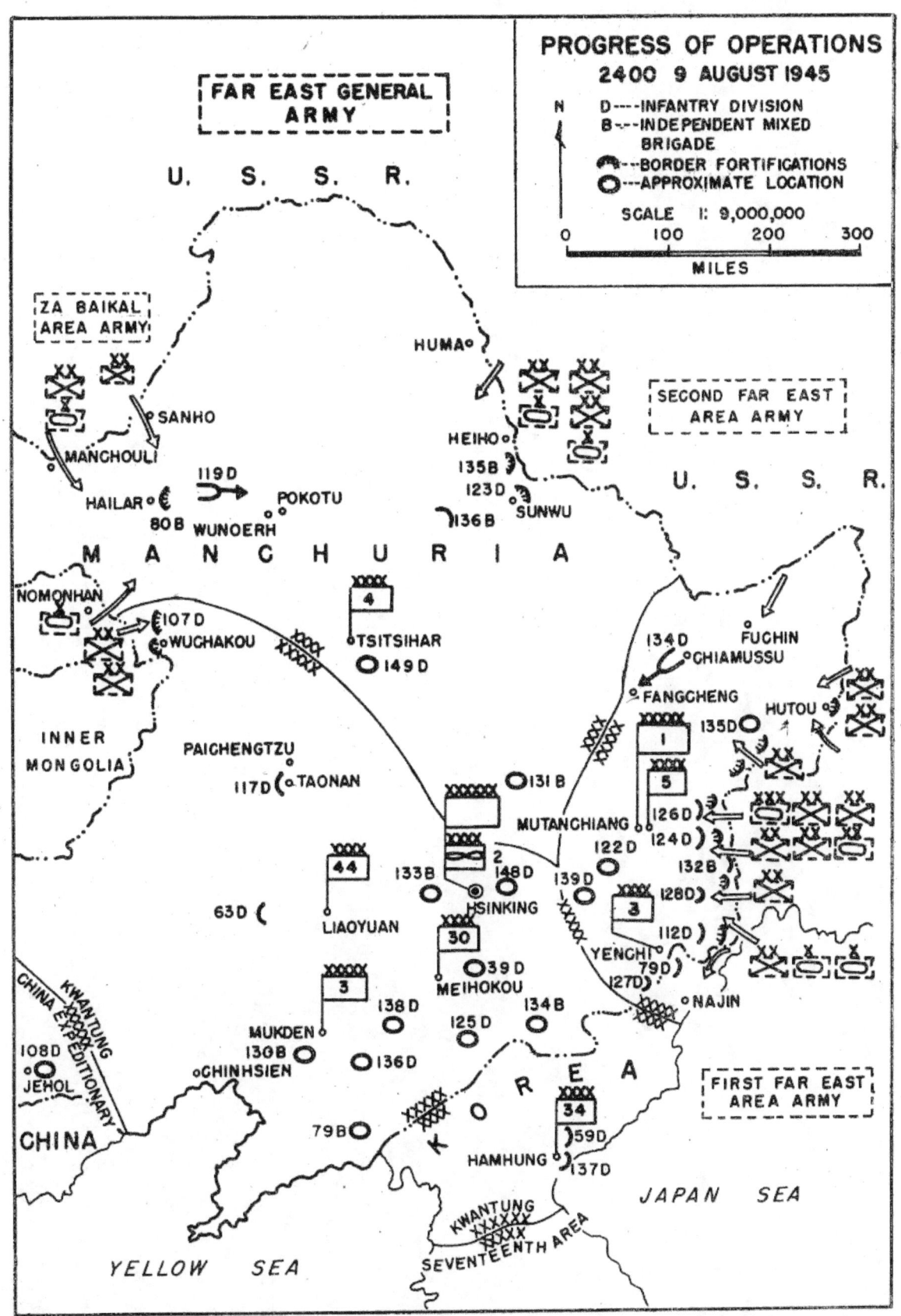

128th Division.)[9] The Soviet force attacking this front was estimated at the time to be three infantry Divisions, and between two and three armored brigades, although later the estimated number of infantry divisions was revised upward to five, and the number of armored brigades to five. The enemy facing the Third Army in the southern sector was not active as yet. In the northern sector, the 134th Division at Chiamussu was withdrawing toward Fangcheng as planned, having set fire to Japanese houses in the city. Several border observation units seemed to have been totally destroyed while defending their assigned posts. Conditions in the Hutou area remained unknown.

On the northern front an enemy force of undetermined strength crossed the Amur River south of Huma. No enemy troops were observed crossing the river in the Heiho or Sunwu areas, however, where the initial attack was expected, and our troops there seemed to be launching operational actions in comparatively good order. The enemy force in this area was estimated to be three infantry divisions and two armored brigades. Hailar, which on the morning on the 9th had been bombed heavily by enemy planes, by evening had become the objective of enemy tanks rushing from the Sanho, Manchouli and Nomonhan areas. The 80th Independent Mixed Brigade was ordered by the 119th Division to defend the positions at Hailar as planned. The 119th Division itself began leaving Hailar by train in the morning for Wunoerh, and

---

9. By a pre-arranged plan, the 128th Division had come under the direct control of the First Area Army at the outbreak of hostilities. At the same time, the 132d Independent Mixed Brigade was assigned to the 128th Division.

the last train departed in the evening when enemy tanks were in the outskirts of Hailar. Conditions in the Manchouli area remained unknown.

Reports from the western front indicated that the enemy was attacking Wuchakou. However, no confirmation of these reports could be obtained since reconnaissance planes sent to this area on the 9th had not yet returned. On the 10th, observation planes located a powerful enemy armored unit which had crossed the border and was advancing eastward in the direction of Paichengtzu. Our air force could not attack this column on the 10th because of incomplete preparations.

The southwestern front had not yet been attacked. In this sector, however, the redeployment of the 108th Division began according to plan. One regiment passed to the control of the China Expeditionary Army, while the remainder of the division prepared to concentrate in the Chinhsien area. (See Map No 3)

Change in Plan for the Western Front

The Kwantung Army's plan for operations on the western front was to occupy important points (chiefly towns, villages, and natural obstacles) on the enemy's anticipated route of advance and, with air support, to delay the enemy. This was to be accomplished by establishing guerrilla positions in depth and by conducting continuous large-scale attacks against enemy armored units.

General Jun Ushiroku, Commander of the Third Area Army, was

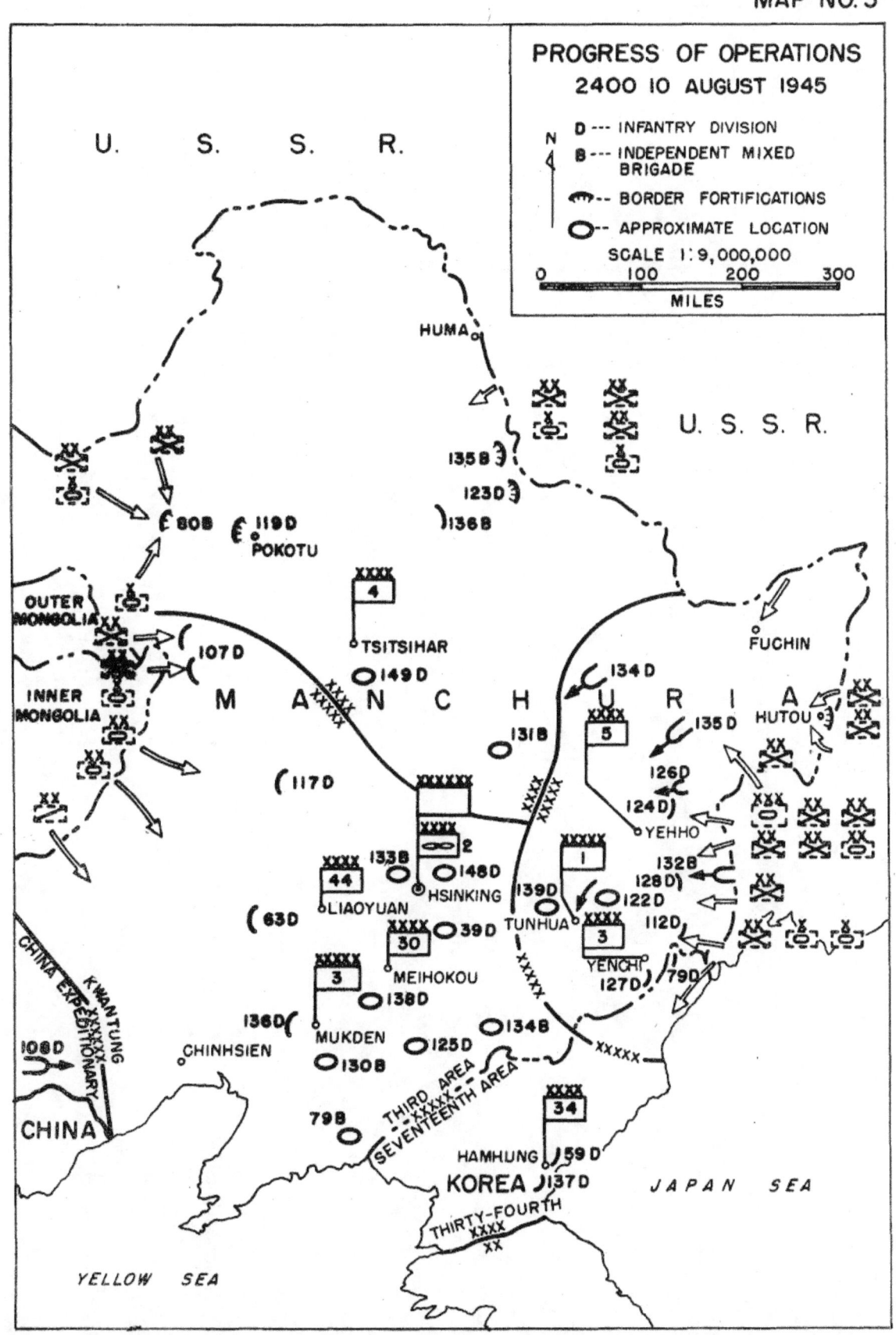

opposed to this plan.[10] First, his Forty-fourth Army was not prepared for guerrilla warfare: the 63d and 117th Divisions which composed this Army had only recently arrived from the China area where their experience consisted principally of offensive-type operations. Second, Kwantung Army's plan requiring the dispersal of troops over a wide area far to the west would mean committing troops in small numbers and would result, General Ushiroku felt, in their piecemeal destruction. Furthermore, General Ushiroku did not wish to leave the approximately 1,100,000 Japanese residents along the Dairen-Hsinking line to their fate, nor did he believe that withdrawing both military and civilian personnel to the redoubt was practicable from the standpoint of housing or supply.

General Ushiroku therefore recommended that the Forty-fourth Army be pulled back to the line of the Dairen-Hsinking Railway, stationing the main force at Mukden with elements at Hsinking, and counterattacking after the enemy had extended his supply lines to the limit. On the morning of 10th, General Ushiroku acting independently ordered the Forty-fourth Army to withdraw to the Dairen-Hsinking line, and advised Kwantung Army Headquarters of this action.

---

10. General Ushiroku was a classmate of Premier Tojo at the military academy. When Tojo was chief of the Army General Staff in 1944 he created the position of 1st Deputy to the Chief of the Army General Staff, superimposing it on the long-standing position of Deputy Chief of the Army General Staff. The newly created position was given to General Ushiroku. (During November 1953, when this monograph was being edited, word was received in Japan that General Ushiroku was scheduled for early repatriation by the Soviets.)

Confronted with this illegal order, Kwantung Army Headquarters promptly held a staff conference, during which the following opinions were voiced: a sudden change in pre-arranged plans would inevitably cause confusion; an attempt to counterattack after the withdrawal would end in failure if the enemy's advance were rapid; the early abandonment of forward airfields would allow the enemy to advance at will. To most conferees, General Ushiroku's decision appeared to strike a fatal blow to the Kwantung Army Headquarters' over-all direction of operations. However, since the Forty-fourth Army had already begun the withdrawal ordered by General Ushiroku, Kwantung Army Headquarters was confronted with a fait accompli, and therefore upheld the decision of the Third Area Army Commander. This action was approved by General Yamada.

On 10 August, Imperial General Headquarters followed up its orders of the preceding day by announcing to the Commander in Chief of the Kwantung Army that:[11]

> The plan of Imperial General Headquarters is to bring about a successful completion of the war against the United States, its main enemy, and at the same time to destroy the Soviet Army by launching all-out military operations against the Soviet Union to frustrate its inordinate ambition and thus preserve our national polity and protect Imperial territory. The Commander in Chief of the Kwantung Army will direct his main operation against the Soviet Union and will protect Korea by destroying the invading enemy everywhere.

---

11. ADO No 1378, 10 Aug 45. This order was signed by the Emperor on the morning of the 10th.

This order was followed by a directive the same day authorizing General Yamada to transfer his headquarters to other areas within his zone of operation at any time to keep pace with the progress of operations.[12]

At the same time, Imperial General Headquarters ordered the Commander in Chief of the China Expeditionary Army (General Yasuji Okamura) "to carry out a protracted war against the US, the Soviet Union, and China, thereby contributing toward the operations of the whole army on the mainland." Operations against the Soviet Union, it informed General Okamura, would have the object of facilitating in every way the operations of the Kwantung Army in South Manchuria and North Korea. In this connection he was instructed to send troops and munitions to these areas as quickly as possible.

Transfer of General Headquarters

On 11 August the Intelligence Section, reporting on the tactical situation, stated that enemy armored units in the west were making an unexpectedly swift advance and could be expected to arrive in Hsinking on the 14th or 15th. Standing plans called for the transfer of General Headquarters to Tunghua, approximately forty miles from the Korea border, immediately upon the outbreak of hostilities with the Soviets. By 11 August, reconnaissance and field investigation of the Tunghua area and (also of the Linchiang area) which

---

12. AD No 2539, 10 Aug 45 (p 186, Imperial General Headquarters Army Directives, Vol III, hereafter referred to as IGH AD Vol III).

was to be the site of the final stand, had been completed. General Headquarters therefore ordered the transfer to begin. The entire headquarters except for the general staff and other essential personnel was directed to move by rail on the 12th.[13]

The transfer to Tunghua, however, did not mean that Hsinking was to be abandoned. This city was the capital of Manchukuo, and had many strong buildings suitable for street fighting. General Ushiroku, in connection with his plan to defend the Dairen-Hsinking line, on the morning of the 10th pulled the Thirtieth Army Headquarters out of the redoubt area and ordered it to move to Hsinking to direct its defense. He also ordered several tactical units to move to Hsinking to support the 148th Division there.

On the evening of the 11th, the Intelligence Section summarized the progress of operations on the various fronts. An enemy force of approximately brigade size had carried out an amphibious assault against Najin in northern Korea, and was advancing southward. On the eastern front proper the enemy's strength was estimated to be eight infantry divisions and four to five tank brigades; in the Fifth Army sector the enemy had advanced to positions near Muleng after destroying our advance forces in the border area; in the northern sector, an enemy unit proceeding up the Sungari River was attacking our garrison unit in the Fuchin area; the Third Army area had been

---

13. The Emperor of Manchukuo together with the ministers of the Manchukuoan Government had left for Linchiang by train on the 10th, escorted by the Kempei-tai Training Unit of the Kwantung Army. Vice ministers and other officials, however, remained in Hsinking.

penetrated and the enemy was occupying a hill west of Hunchun in front of the 112th Division. The First Area Army Headquarters had moved to Tunhua on the preceeding night. On the northern front the enemy had crossed the river near Aihun and near Shengwutun, but had not yet launched a full-scale attack. No report was received from Hailar because of the interruption of communications with the 80th Independent Mixed Brigade. On the western front, enemy armored columns had reached a speed of 100 kilometers a day, and leading elements were approaching Lichuan. The 107th Division had withdrawn from the Wuchakou area and was engaged in close fighting with enemy armored units south of the Paichengtzu-Arshaan railway line. (See Map No 4)

Situation on 12 August

By 12 August problems confronting the Kwantung Army began to mount. General Yamada feared that the counterattack which General Ushiroku had decided to launch from the Dairen-Hsinking line might develop into a decisive battle there, completely upsetting the over-all plan for Kwantung Army operations. On this basis, be made several appeals to General Ushiroku to reconsider, but the latter remained adamant.

Meanwhile, General Yamada flew to the new headquarters at Tunghua in company with his deputy chief of staff and his operations chief. The Intelligence Section remained in Hsinking because communitions in the Tunghua headquarters were not adequate for its operations. The Civil Affairs (Fourth) Section also remained in

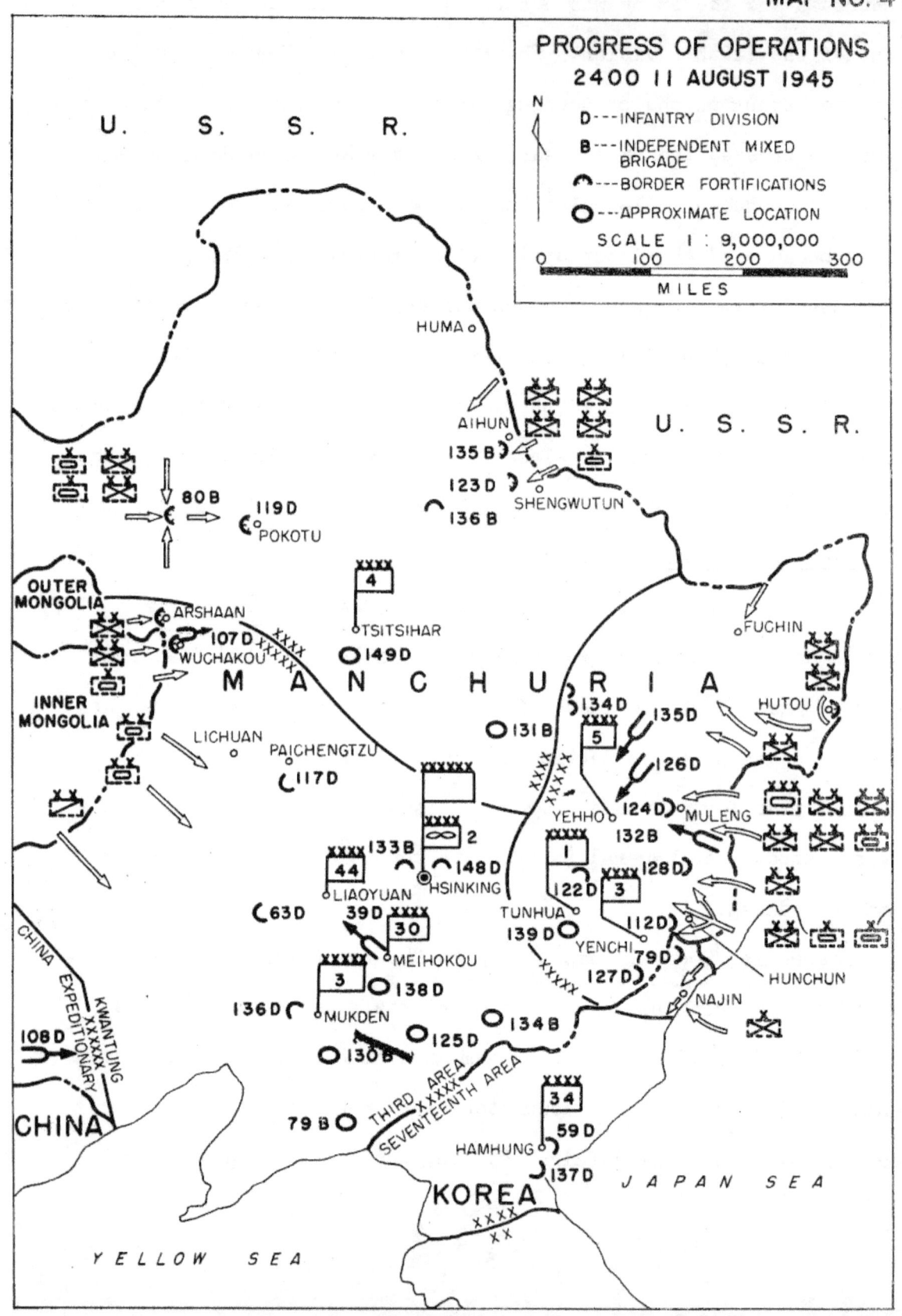

Hsinking and continued liaison activities with the Manchukuoan vice ministers. On the evening of the 12th, the commander and key staff officers of the Thirtieth Army arrived in Hsinking to direct the defense of that city.

The Intelligence Section's estimate of the tactical situation on the evening of the 12th was substantially as follows. On the eastern front, although reports were fragmentary, it appeared that the Fifth Army was engaged in a fierce battle at the Muleng positions. On the northern front the situation remained unchanged in the Sunwu area; in the Pokotu area, where the 119th Division was in position, the enemy had not yet commenced his attack. On the western front the speed of the enemy armored column advancing toward Lichuan was slowed down by the Second Air Army whose 15th Independent Air Brigade had attacked the armored unit in the Linhsi area while its 101st Air Training Brigade was striking in the Lichuan area. Altogether, fifty-six planes were flown and succeeded in destroying twenty-seven guns and forty-two vehicles. (See Map No 5)

The drive of the enemy armored columns in the west was hampering the evacuation of Japanese nationals. On the 10th Kwantung Army had asked the Manchukuoan Government to evacuate Japanese residents in Hsinking and vicinity and directed the Continental Railway Command to place ten trains at its disposal, scheduling the first train to leave Hsinking that day. The Manchukuoan Government found it quite impossible to carry out the withdrawal promptly, however, and

was able to transport only the families of officers and civilians attached to the army. These families had to flee with only a few hours notice and with practically only the clothes they wore on their backs. On the 12th, there was a great deal of confusion in Hsinking. The advance of the enemy armored columns and the withdrawal of the main force of the Forty-fourth Army, together with the evacuation of the capital by Kwantung Army General Headquarters and the arrival of the first refugee trains with Japanese evacuees from the west border areas spread alarm among the local residents, many of whom promptly rushed to the crowded train station.

Compared with the enemy advance in the west, his advance in the north against the Fourth Army was relatively slow. The arbitrary decision of General Ushiroku to make the Hsinking-Mukden area the major battlefield meant that a counterattack structure had to be established there. The Thirtieth Army which at first had been designated as a counterattack force in the Meihokou area in the redoubt, had already advance to Hsinking as ordered and was preparing to defend the capital. In consequence of these moves, Fourth Army Headquarters, which on the night of the 10th had been ordered to fall back from Tsitsihar to Harbin, was now ordered by Kwantung Army to withdraw to Meihokou to take up the positions left vacant by the Thirtieth Army's removal. In the southwest the main body of the 108th Division assembled at Chinhsien and established contact with the Third Area Army.

The situation on the 13th was as follows. At about noon the enemy carried out a second amphibious operation, this time at Chongjin where a battalion-size infantry unit made an assault landing. On the eastern front, Mutanchiang was shelled by enemy tanks. On the northern front an enemy force in the Hailar area advanced to the front of the outpost positions of the 119th Division. On the western front, only one element of the 101st Air Training Brigade sallied forth on this day, owing to bad weather, and the enemy armored column which had been slowed down in the vicinity of Lichuan resumed its advance and was approaching the Paichengtzu area. On the following day, however, air strikes were resumed and resulted in damage to forty-three armored vehicles. (See Map No 6.)

On 14 August a Kwantung Army staff officer was sent to Mukden to urge General Ushiroku to reconsider his determination to wage a decisive battle along the Dairen-Hsinking line. The staff officer pointed out that General Yamada, while upholding the arbitrary order, felt that the consequences of it might jeopardize the over-all operations of the Kwantung Army. General Ushiroku, swallowing bitter tears, responded that he would submit to the opinion of the Commander in Chief of the Kwantung Army. As a result Third Area Army Headquarters began formulating a new plan providing for a withdrawal toward the Hunjen area, a plan which because of the adrupt end of the war was never carried out.

On the 14th, the tactical situation on all fronts became critical. In the afternoon the Manchurian News Agency reported that the war might shortly be terminated and that an important announcement

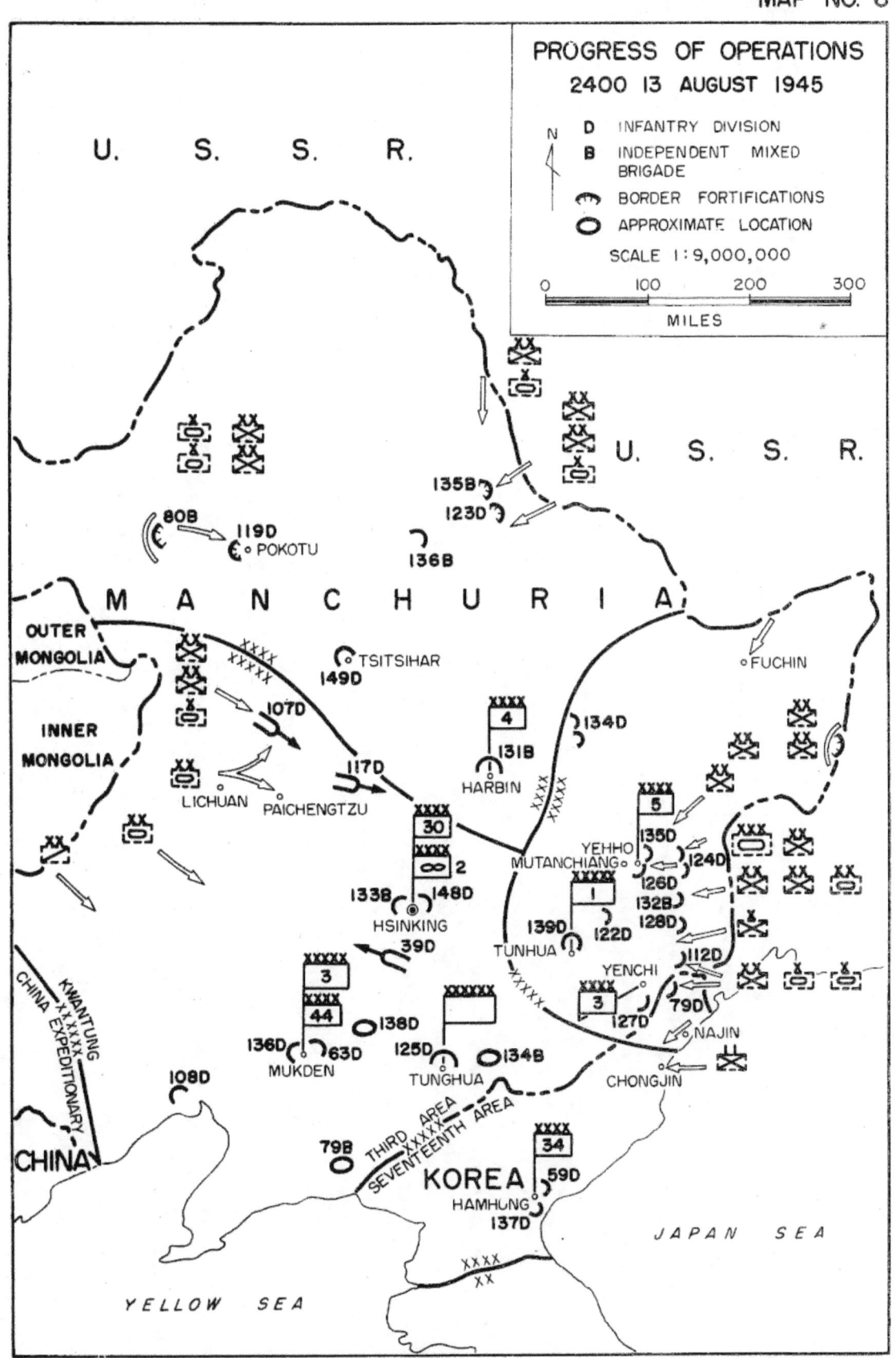

would be broadcast at noon on the following day. In the evening, General Yamada, accompanied by his deputy chief of staff and important staff officers, returned to Hsinking from Tunghua. Third Area Army Headquarters, meanwhile, misunderstanding a message from Tunghua, had issued orders to cease hostilities; later in the day, however, on the advice of Kwantung Army General Headquarters, it rescinded the order.

On the night of the 14th the enemy followed up the earlier amphibious operation at Chongjin by landing approximately one infantry division. This was the third enemy amphibious operation along the north Korea coast. (See Map No 7)

The War Ends

At noon on the 15th, Kwantung Army Headquarters listened to the Emperor broadcasting the Imperial Rescript Terminating the War. Staff officers still at Tunghua promptly began to depart for Hsinking by air, while other personnel entrained for the capital.

Meanwhile, during the morning of the 15th, the Second Air Army carried out thirty-nine sorties against enemy armored and air units in the Paichengtzu area, damaging three planes and 135 vehicles. After receiving the Imperial Rescript, however, it withheld further assaults. (See Maps No 8 and No 9.)

By the 16th no cease-fire order had been received from Imperial General Headquarters in Tokyo. Having heard the Imperial Rescript, however, Kwantung Army Headquarters was in a dilemma. A staff conference was held to discuss possible courses of action. The majority of the conferees felt that we should offer resistance to the last ditch, win or lose, thus leaving in the hearts of the people a flame to be kindled in the future for the reconstruction of our nation.

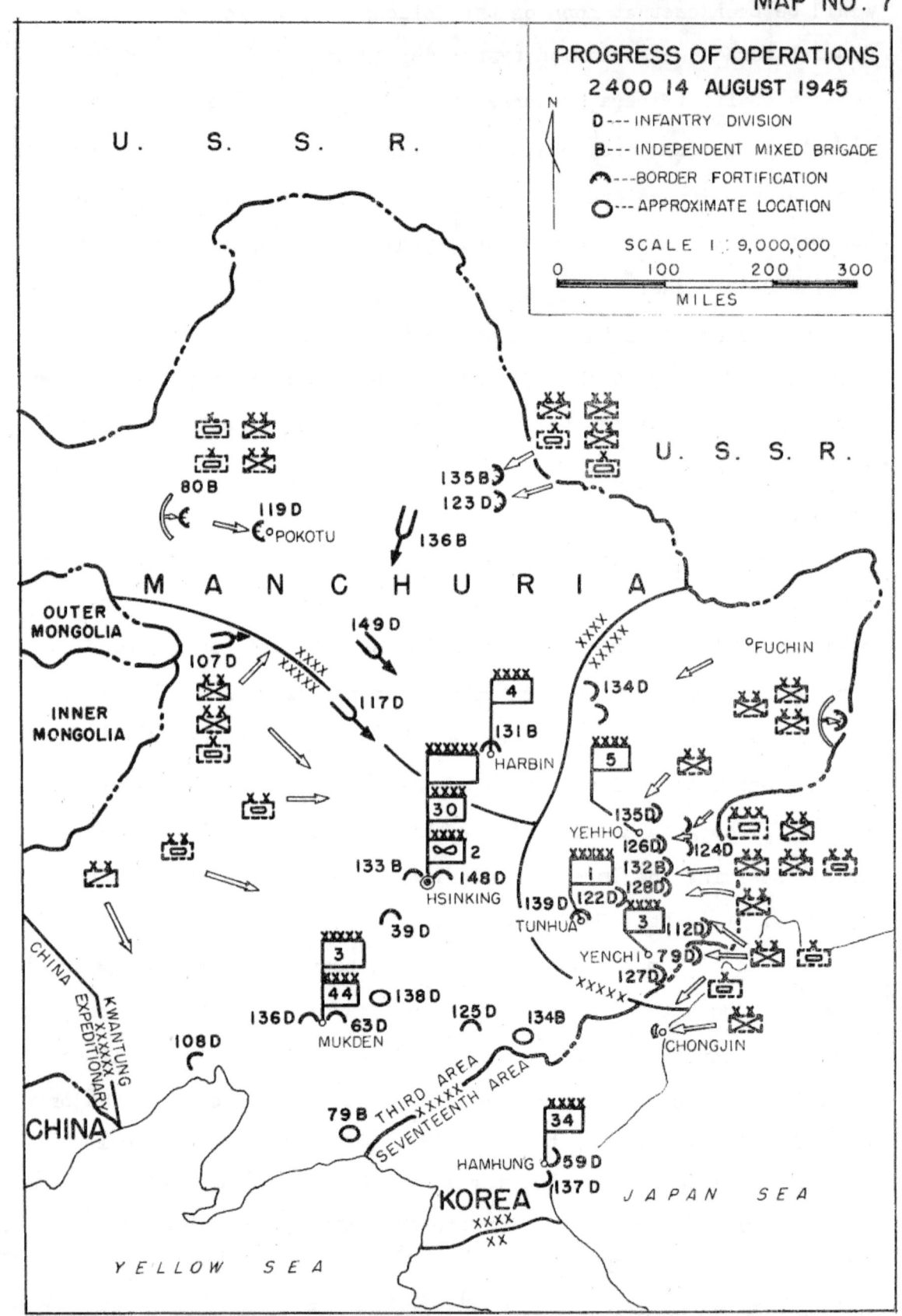

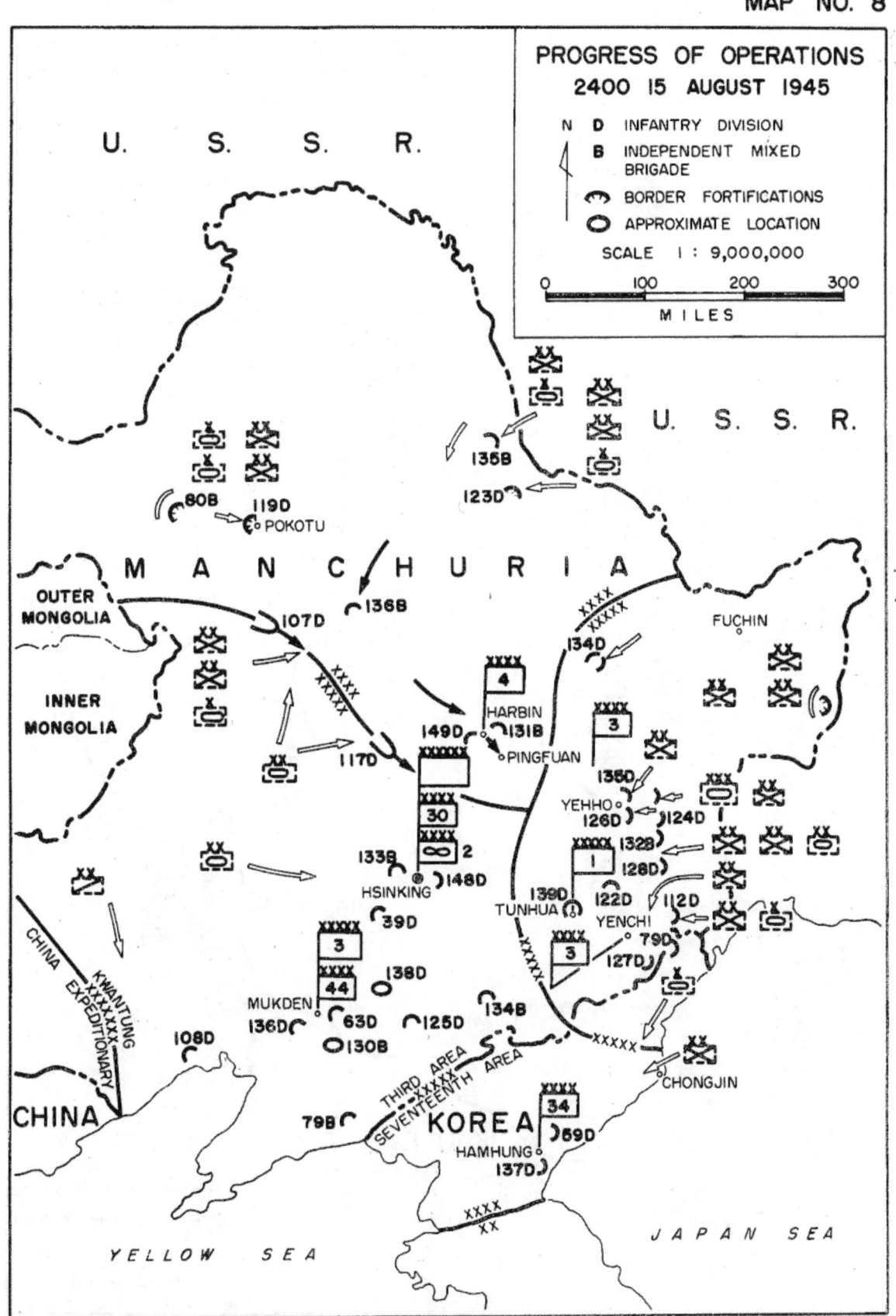

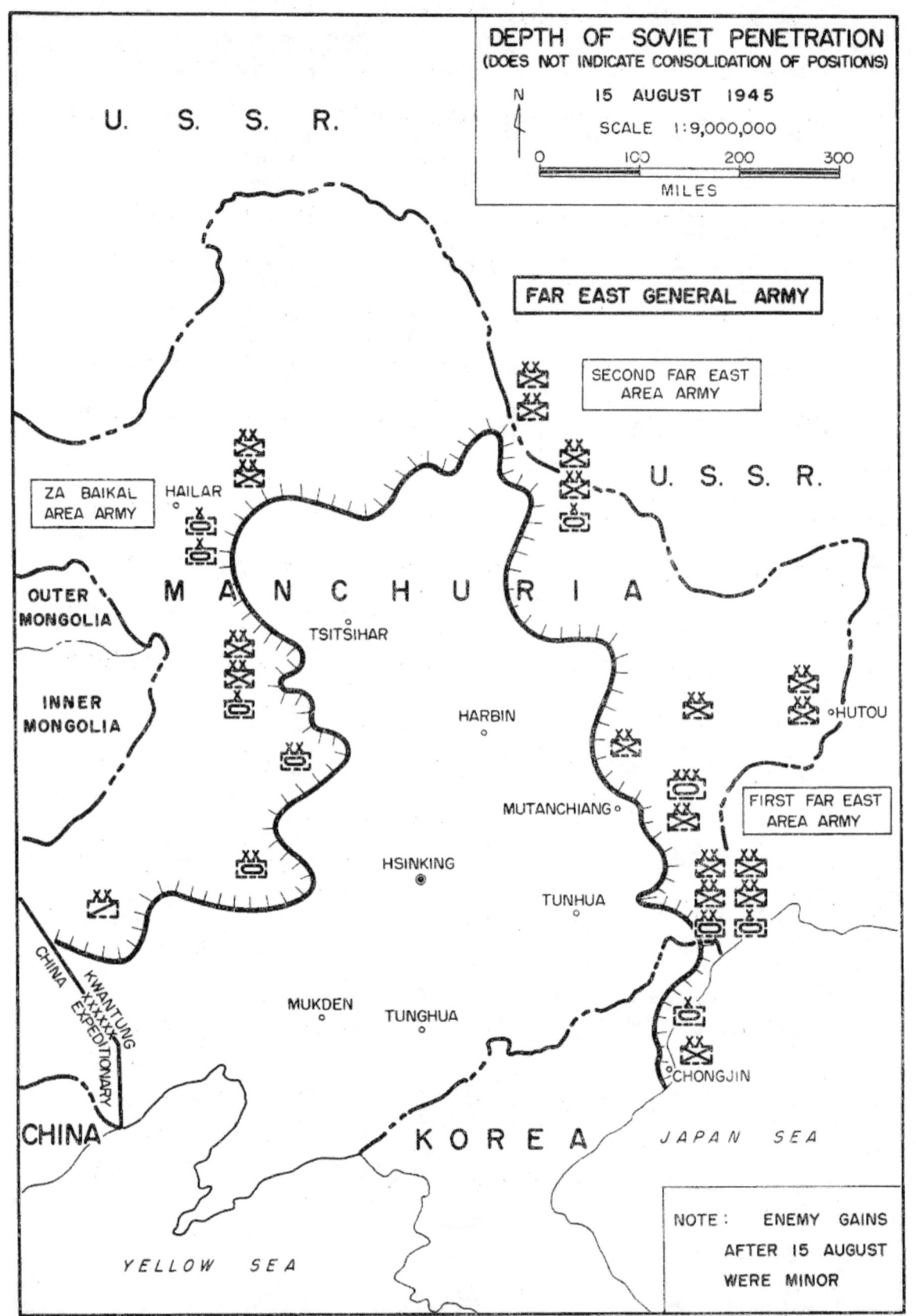

On the other hand, some staff officers, including the chief of the Operations Division of the Operations (First) Section, Colonel Teigo Kusaji, opined that since things had come to this end and since the Imperial Rescript had already been issued terminating the war, they had no alternative but to obey the Rescript respectfully.[14] As for the reconstruction of Japan, these officers declared, that was a matter which only future policies could realize.

A grave discussion ensued, both factions adhering stoutly to their opinions for a long time. Finally, the deadlock was broken when the Chief of Staff, General Hikosaburo Hata, with hot tears in his eyes, ruled: "We the military men have no alternative if we are to retain our loyalty but to obey the command issued by His Majesty the Emperor. Those who disobey the Imperial Rescript will be branded traitors for all time. Therefore, those who stubbornly insist upon continuing the operations of the Kwantung Army may do so only after killing us." The Commander in Chief, in obedience to His Majesty's wishes, also decided to exert every effort to terminate hostilities. In this way, the policy of the Kwantung Army was settled.

On 17 August, His Imperial Highness Prince Tsunenori Takeda, on behalf of His Majesty the Emperor, flew from Tokyo to Hsinking to

---

14. The Operations Section of Kwantung Army Headquarters was divided into four divisions--operations, logistics, railway, and signal communication. Other sections of the Headquarters were: Intelligence (Second), Training (Third), and Civil Affairs (Fourth). See Chart No 2 for Organizational Chart of Kwantung Army General Headquarters.

ORGANIZATIONAL CHART
GENERAL HEADQUARTERS, KWANTUNG ARMY
AUGUST 1945

LEGEND:
- - - - STAFF SUPERVISION

- **Commander in Chief**
  - **Chief of Staff**
    - **Deputy Chief of Staff**
    - **Personnel Affairs Division**

GENERAL STAFF

1st Section (Operations)
Divisions
1. Operations
2. Logistics
3. Railway
4. Signal Communication

2d Section (Intelligence)
Divisions
1. Intelligence
2. Military Geography

3d Section (Training)
(Abolished 9 Aug 45)

4th Section (Civil Affairs)
Divisions
1. Political
2. Economic

SPECIAL STAFF

Adjutant Department

Ordnance Department
1. General Affairs
2. Arms
3. Ammunition
4. Vehicle
5. Implement

Intendance Department
1. General Affairs
2. Accounting
3. Clothing & Provisions
4. Supply
5. Construction

Medical Department
1. Medical
2. Medical Supply

Veterinary Department

Judicial Department

Military Advisory Department

Public Information Department

MONOGRAPH NO. 154-A
CHART NO. 2

deliver a message to the Army pertaining to the Imperial Rescript.[15] The message was ready by Prince Takeda in a ceremony held at Kwantung Army General Headquarters

Imperial General Headquarters orders to terminate "active offensive operations," though issued on the 15th, were not received by Kwantung Army Headquarters until the 17th. The orders, addressed to all major theater commanders, stated:[16]

> Imperial General Headquarters intends to carry out completely the purport of the Imperial Rescript of 14 August.
>
> All armies will continue their present mission until further orders. Active offensive operations, however, will cease. Strict military discipline and strong esprit will be maintained in order to insure coordinated action.
>
> Every effort will be made in the homeland, Sakhalin, Korea, and Formosa to prevent disturbances of the public peace.

On the same day, Kwantung Army Headquarters also received Imperial General Headquarters Army Department Order No 1382, dated 16 August 1945, which directed all army commanders to cease hostilities immediately and to report the time of the cessation. This

---

15. A lieutenant colonel, Prince Takeda had served with Kwantung Army Headquarters as assistant operations officer until March 1945 when he was transferred to Imperial General Headquarters.
16. Though read by the Emperor at 1200 on 15 August, the Imperial Rescript was signed by the Emperor at 2300 on 14 August, was immediately transmitted to the four major powers, through the Swiss, and normally carries that date. See ADO No 1381, 15 Aug 45.

order did not, however, cancel operational missions. It stipulated that the cessation did not apply to unavoidable acts of hostilities carried out in self-defense during enemy attacks made before the completion of armistice negotiations.

Also received on the 17th was Army Directive No 2544, dated 16 August, which stated:

> The Commander in Chief, Kwantung Army, is authorized to conduct on-the-spot negotiations for armistice with the Russian Army, and to surrender arms and equipment.

Similar orders issued to the Commander in Chief of the China Expeditionary Army and the Commander of the Fifth Area Army directed them to maintain liaison with the Kwantung Army regarding negotiations with the Russian Army.

On 18 August the chiefs of staff of the First Area Army, the Third Area Army, the Fourth Army, the Second Air Army, and Seventeenth Area Army were called to Hsinking to be informed of His Majesty's wishes, and were given Kwantung Army's orders relating to the cease-fire and disarmament.

On the same day, the Kwantung Army Chief of Staff, accompanied by several staff officers, flew to the advance command post of General Headquarters of the Soviet Far East Army at Zharkovo in compliance with a demand transmitted through the Soviet Consul-General in Harbin. There they held an interview with Marshal A.M. Vassilievsky, supreme commander of the Far East Army. After conferring on procedures for disarmament, protection of Japanese nationals in Manchuria, and other related matters, they returned to Hsinking.

Meanwhile, Kwantung Army Headquarters made extensive efforts to transmit to its subordinate commands as much information as it had on the termination of hostilities and disarmament, using all possible means of communications. It was hampered in these efforts by the wide dispersal of its forces and also because Soviet troops while disarming our units failed to observe the standards of discipline agreed upon at Supreme Headquarters of the Soviet Army.

Cancellation of Operational Missions

On 18 August Imperial General Headquarters advised the Commander in Chief of the Kwantung Army together with other army commanders that at a time to be announced later all operational missions were cancelled and all military actions were to cease. At the same time, it cautioned that:[17]

> None of the Japanese Army personnel and civilian employees coming under the control of enemy forces after the promulgation of the Imperial Rescript will be considered prisoners of war. All subordinates down to the last private will be immediately cautioned against rash actions and will be made to realize the necessity for fortitude with a view to the future prosperity of Japan.

On the 19th, Imperial General Headquarters announced the effective date for the cancellation of missions and the cessation of military actions in the Kwantung Army as 0000, 25 August 1945.[18]

---

17. IGH ADO 1385, 18 Aug 45. (P 238, Vol III).
18. For homeland areas the time set was 0000, 22 Aug 45.

On the same day, a delegation of the Soviet Army arrived at Hsinking and directed Kwantung Army Headquarters to assemble in the suburb north of Hsinking all Japanese forces in the general vicinity, and to disarm all troops. The Soviet delegation also forbade the Japanese forces to use any means of communication. At this point, General Headquarters of the Kwantung Army ceased to function. Late in the day Major General Tomokatsu Matsumura, the Kwantung Army deputy chief of staff, together with several staff officers went to GHQ Far East Army by Soviet airplane.

In Hsinking, the buildings of the Kwantung Army General Headquarters were taken over by the Soviet Army. In order to maintain liaison with the Soviet Army, several staff officers, including the Chief of the Intelligence Section, retained space in the western building. Personnel of the General Headquarters were moved to the office of the Resident Naval Officer.

Severed communications prevented Kwantung Army Headquarters from transmitting the cease-fire order and military actions were still in progress in the sector northeast of Hsingan. The 107th Division had not been heard from since its retreat from Wuchakou. The Thirtieth Army, in compliance with a Soviet demand, dispatched one of its staff officers in a plane of the Manchurian Air Transport Company to stop the fighting. The division was located near Chalaitochi, and the plane made a forced landing between it and the opposing Soviet force, whereupon the staff officer delivered orders terminating hostilities in that sector.

On 5 September all generals in Hsinking, including General

Otozo Yamada, Commander in Chief of the Kwantung Army, and some staff officers were taken to the Soviet Union by air. Other personnel of Kwantung Army Headquarters were interned at the Nanling Concentration Camp after disarmament.

Dissolution of the Kwantung Army

On 22 August Imperial General Headquarters removed the Seventeenth Area Army from the order of battle of the Kwantung Army, but authorized the Commander in Chief of the Kwantung Army to retain control of this area army for the purpose of terminating hostilities with the Soviet Army. The effective time of this transfer of command was 0000 hours, 25 August.[19]

On 13 September orders were issued by Imperial General Headquarters dissolving the order of battle of the Kwantung Army effective 0000 17 September. The same orders dissolved the China Expeditionary Army, the Southern Army, and other major commands of the Japanese Imperial Army.[20]

---

19. ADO No 1388, 22 August 45.
20. Army Department Order Special No 3, 13 Sep 45.

Monograph No 154-B

CHAPTER II

The First Area Army in Eastern Manchuria[21]

Military Geography of Eastern Manchuria

Until March 1945 the territory under the jurisdiction of the First Area Army consisted of the four administrative provinces in eastern Manchuria.[22] From north to south these were Sanchiang, Tungan, Mutanchiang, and Chientao. The rear boundary of the Area Army conformed generally with the province boundaries. During March, in preparation for the transition from a holding operational plan to a delaying operational plan, Kwantung Army authorized the First Area Army to expand rearward. The rear boundary of the Area Army was consequently extended to include the eastern parts of the Pinchiang and Chilin provinces. This gave the Area Army approximately 100,000 square miles to defend. (Map No 1 shows Army boundary changes from 1943 to 1945.)

In planning military operations on the eastern front, as on other fronts, it was necessary first to determine what might be

---

21. The information in this chapter about the operations of the First Area Army was furnished by Colonel Hiroshi Matsumoto.
22. Kwantung Army jurisdiction over the northern part of Hamyong Pukto (north Korea) had not been clearly established at this time. The Commander in Chief had been given authority on 18 Sep 44 to issue orders to the Commander of the Korea Army in those "areas which will become Kwantung Army operational zones in the event of war," by which was meant northern Hamyong Pukto province. (See AD No 2164, 18 Sep 44). This did not include control of the area. The four northern provinces of Korea were not placed under Kwantung Army jurisdiction until 30 May 45, and the Seventeenth Area Army not until 9 August 1945.

MONOGRAPH NO. 154-B
MAP NO. 1

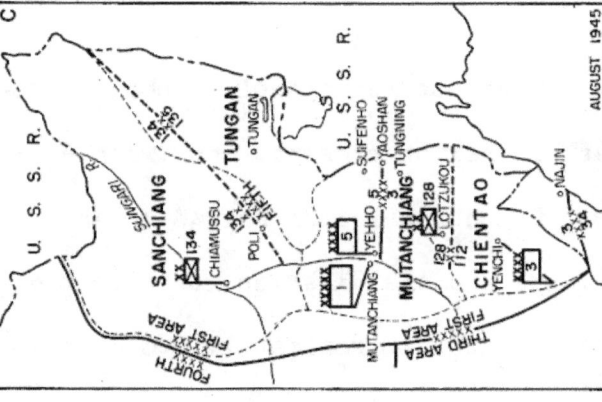

Boundaries of Second, Third, Fifth and Twentieth Armies and 10th Division.

OCTOBER 1943

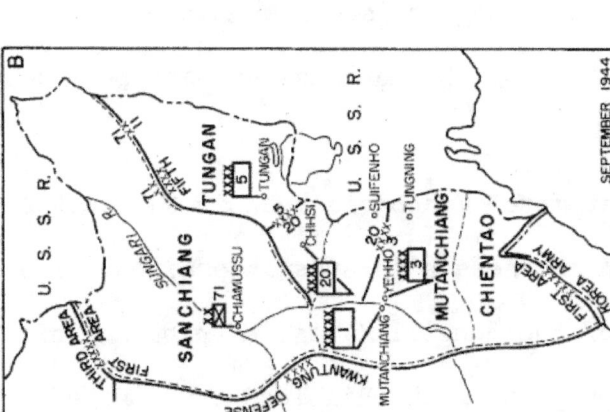

Boundaries of Third, Fifth, and Twentieth Armies. After Twentieth Army Headquarters was transferred in late September 1944, the boundary line between Fifth Army and Third Army was established roughly along the line dividing Tungan from Mutanchiang Province.

SEPTEMBER 1944

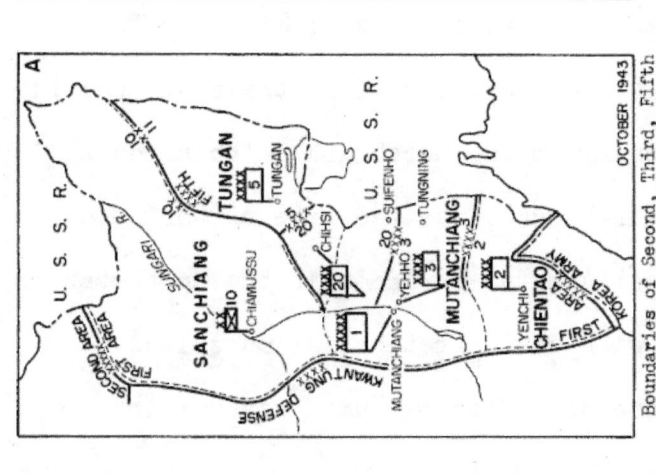

Boundaries of Third and Fifth Armies In February 1945 First Area Army began to assume control of portions of northern Korea and extended Third Army's area southward. Simultaneously, Third Army relinquished to Fifth Army responsibility for the border of Mutanchiang Province almost to Yaoshan. On 25 April Third Army Headquarters moved to Yenchi, and Fifth Army moved to Yehho.

AUGUST 1945

ARMY BOUNDARY CHANGES
EASTERN MANCHURIA

----- PROVINCE BORDER

(MAP C; UNTIL THE WAR STARTED, THE 128TH DIVISION WAS UNDER THE CONTROL OF THIRD ARMY, AND THE 134TH DIVISION UNDER FIFTH ARMY.)

SCALE 1:7,000,000

0   100   200   300
     MILES

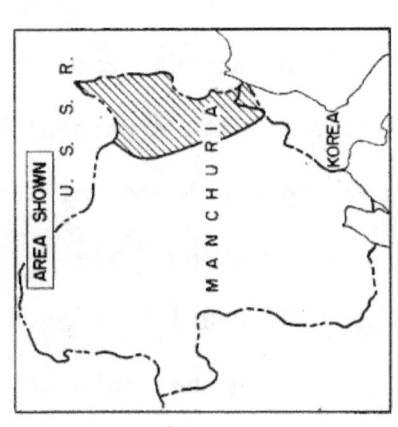

called "essentials of operations." Among other things this involved a study of natural and man-made features, including mountains, forests, rivers, roads, railroads and fortifications, which would have a direct influence on operations.

In climate and geography, the various regions of Manchuria present many contrasts, and the eastern region presents many within itself. The highlands of eastern Manchuria form a rugged upland barrier between the central lowlands and the Siberian maritime province. They attain their greatest width--approximately 220 miles--in the center. Most of these highlands consist of mountains, high, steep, and rugged in the center; along the margins they are penetrated by broad valleys.

Many of the main river systems of Manchuria head in the eastern highlands. The central section of these highlands is drained largely to the west by the headwaters of the Sungari River, a tributary of the Amur River. In the northern part of the highlands, drainage is mostly northward via the Mutan, Muleng, and Ussuri Rivers. The Amur approaching from the west and the Ussuri from the south provide Manchuria with a natural boundary in the northeast. (Khabarovsk, near the confluence of the Amur-Ussuri, was the site of the headquarters of the Soviet Far East Army.) Lowlands in the northeastern tip of Manchuria are covered with vast stretches of marshland. Drainage in the south is by the east-flowing Tumen River which empties into the Sea of Japan.

All rivers are deeply frozen during the winter. During summer, the high water and flood season occurs, although during the spring, floods follow any pronounced thaw of winter snows. During March-April and July-August wheeled vehicles will mire almost everywhere off the established roads. From November-December to March-April trafficability in most of the area is aided by deep soil freezing. Precipitation is greater in this area than in any other region of Manchuria; snow seldom exceeds 2 feet, however, even in the northern mountain valleys.

Japan had begun constructing fortifications of various kinds along the eastern border about 1935, the first positions being constructed near Suifenho where the double-tracked Eastern Chinese Railroad crosses into the maritime province of eastern Siberia.[23] These fortifications may be classified into three grades, first, barbed wire entanglements for minor defense positions, second, resistance nests consisting of concrete pillboxes, and third, strong points which consisted of a series of resistance nests. (Sketch No 1 contains a diagram of a strong point east of Tungning.)

The defense positions around Suifenho were gradually enlarged

---

23. This is the line which provides the Trans-Siberian Railroad with a short cut through Manchuria to Vladivostok. It enters Manchuria in the west at Manchouli. In 1935 when Manchukuo purchased this line from the USSR, the Japanese tore up the rails between Suifenho and the border. The Soviets, on the other hand, left the tracks on their side of the border in place.

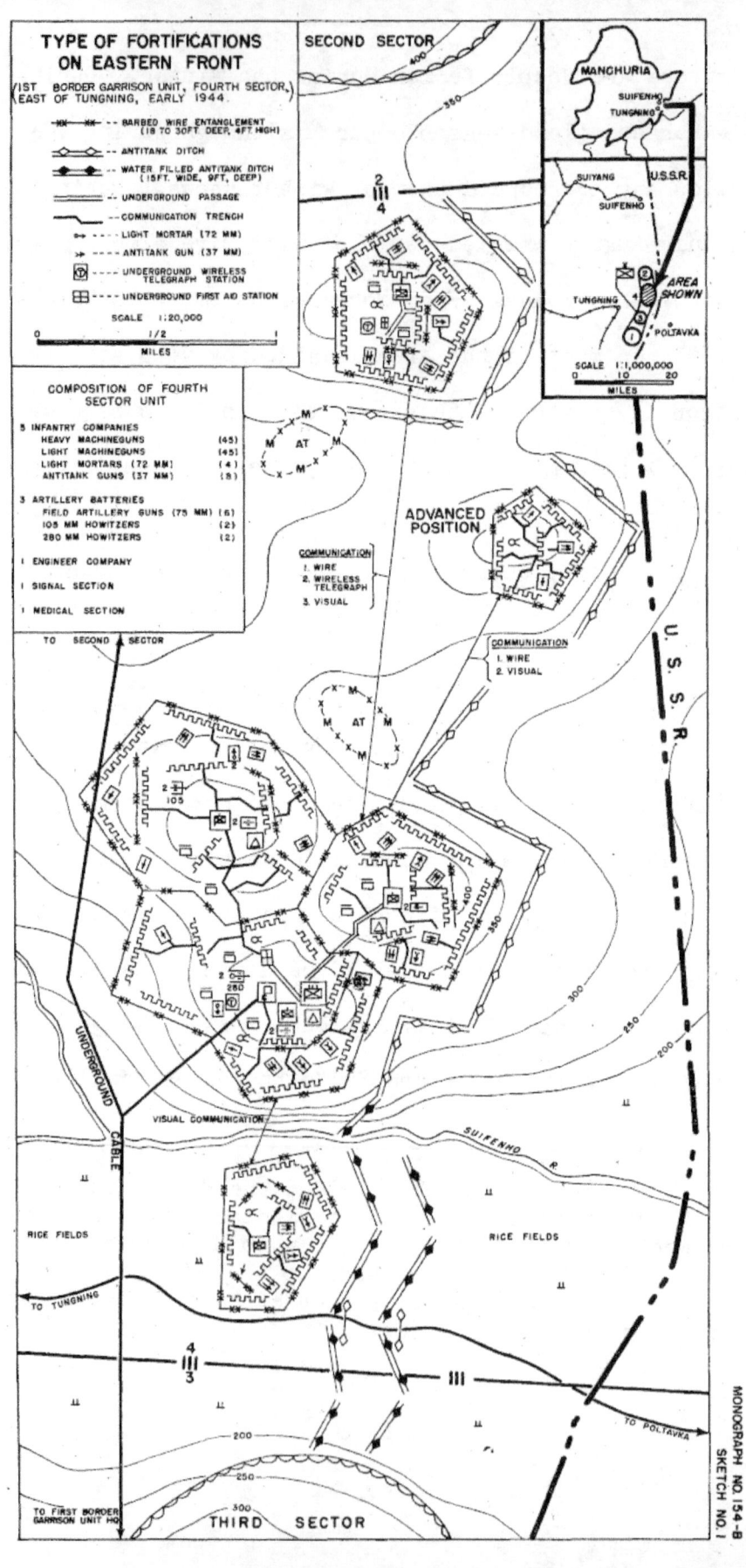

into resistance nests and strong points and these were extended northward about 15 miles and southward about 40 miles, although defense positions and resistance nests continued for about another 10 miles. Ultimately the defensive structure in this area stretched a distance of approximately 65 miles. Later, when Soviet counter-construction in this area partly offset these fortifications, the Japanese began building a new series of intermittent fortifications farther north. Fortifications of all types were constructed from the heights east of Pamientung to the area south of Tungan City for approximately 100 miles, with strong points at Panchiehho and Miaoling. Unlike the fortifications near Suifenho, these new positions were somewhat to the rear of the border. By 1944, therefore, there were two major fortified areas on the eastern front. Between them was a forested mountain area approximately 45 miles long, unsuitable for large-scale military operations, but suitable for border incursions. (Sketch No 2 shows the location of defense positions, resistance nests, and strong points.)

Between the southern point (Tungning) of these fortifications and the northern point (Tungan) ran a single track railroad more or less parallel to the border and approximately 35 miles to its rear. It was within the area bracketed by this railroad and the border that the fortifications described above were constructed. At distances ranging from 30 to 60 miles to the rear of the track ran another single track line from Korea north to Chiamussu. These

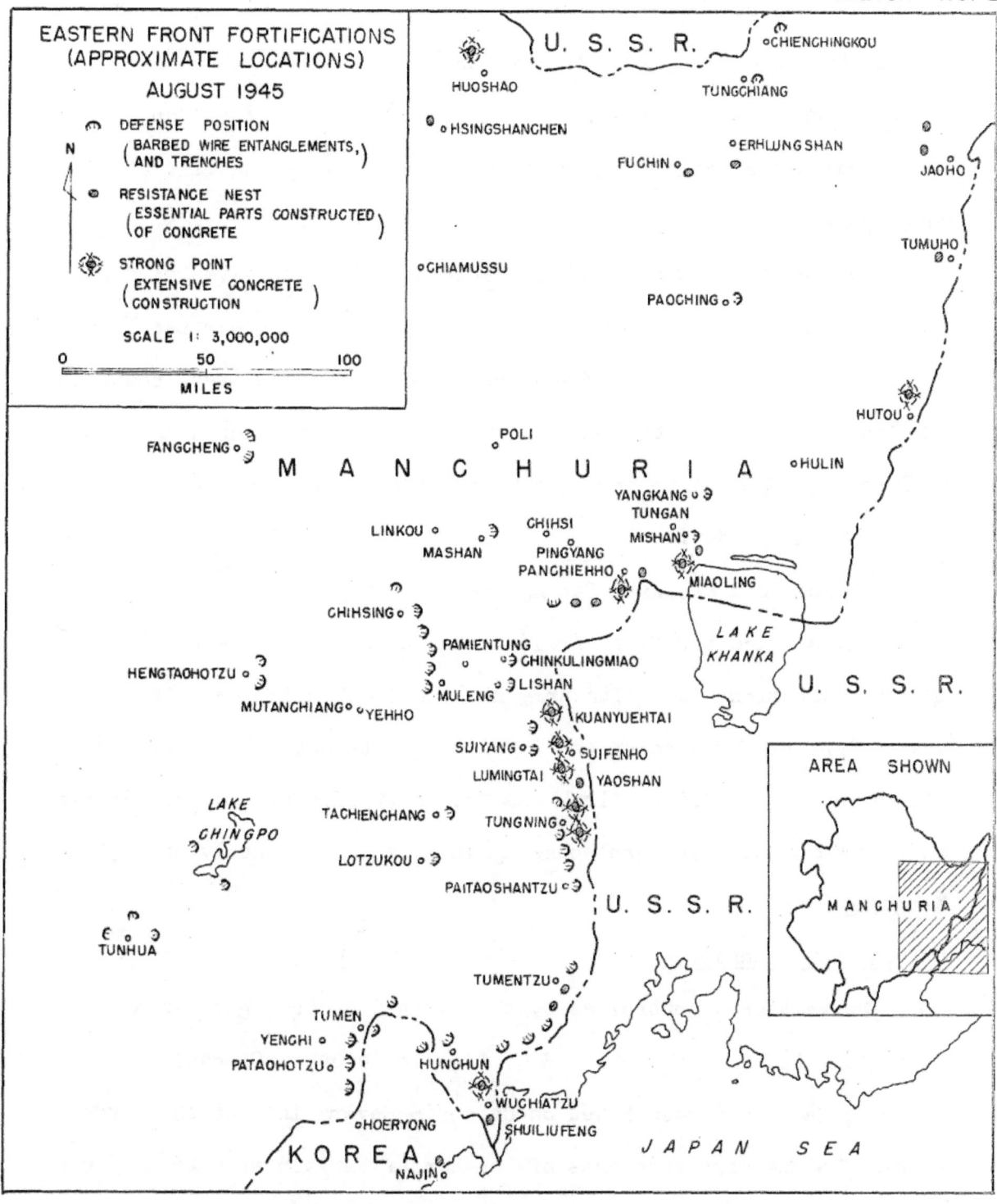

parallel single track lines were connected in two places--from Mutanchiang to Hsiachengtzu, by the Harbin-Suifenho Railway, and from Linkou to Chihsi by a line constructed by the Japanese for military purposes. In addition, a single track line from Tungning looped southward, connecting with the Tumen-Mutanchiang line at Wangching.

There were no paved roads in eastern Manchuria. Even dirt roads were few and the most important of these ran more or less parallel to the two north-south railroad lines, and to the east-west connecting lines. Two major tactical roads extended from Mutanchiang, one to Tungning eastward to the border, the other northeastward to Hulin, also near the border.

Manning this eastward-facing front in July 1945 were the First Area Army's Third and Fifth Armies, the latter on the left. On its extreme left flank the Fifth Army had the 134th Division. The extreme right of the area of the Third Army extended into Korea (see below), and on its right flank was the Thirty-fourth Army (organized on 17 June 1945) which was entirely in Korea and directly under the Kwantung Army.

Operational Planning

The vast area controlled by the First Area Army gave it a front facing the USSR approximately 800 miles in length. Operational planning had never been based on defending every inch of the border, however, since vast stretches of the border terrain were totally unsuited for military operations.[24] As one of the "essentials of operations," therefore, the First Area Army had early adopted a concept of defending only key sectors. It was as a result of this concept that the strongly fortified positions in the Suifenho and the Pamientung-Tungan sectors had been developed.

Naturally, this concept left gaps in the front. But the natural obstacles in the gap areas were sufficiently formidable to deter an enemy from undertaking major military operations in those sectors. Besides the natural boundary formed in northeast Manchuria by the Amur and Ussuri Rivers, the vast expanse of swamps and marshlands beginning at the Amur and extending almost as far south as Tungan accounted for almost one-third of the border. Along the Ussuri River border, however, the swamp land begins considerably to the rear of the border, making an incursion of the border at Hutou very likely.

---

24. The force necessary to hold every inch of such an extensive front would be prohibitive. By Japanese tactical principles of defense, one division was to be deployed for every 6 miles of front. At this rate, the number of divisions that would be required to defend the eastern border alone would be 133, almost half the total number of divisions that Japan was able to mobilize during the entire war. Furthermore, the largest force every envisaged for use in all of Manchuria never exceeded fifty divisions, and the largest ever planned for use on the eastern front never exceeded twenty. This number was planned for the Hachi-go plan, the most ambitious of the many Japanese plans for Manchuria. It called for the deployment of twenty divisions on the eastern front and fifteen each on the northern and eastern front. However, this plan was offensive in concept, the objective being the capture of the territory east of Lake Baikal. This plan was drawn up in 1938 for implementation in 1943. It was never used.

In view of this, strong points with emplaced guns of very large caliber had been constructed in the vicinity of Hutou.[25]

Between the Tungan area and the Pamientung area stretched the fortifications described above. South of these latter-day fortifications was an area of impenetrably dense forest reaching south to the northern extension of the Suifenho fortifications, the earliest and stoutest. South of the Suifenho fortifications and extending into the mountains of Korea stretches another heavily forested region. Aside from the key defense sectors, outpost positions or resistance nests had been constructed at various points along the border, especially at points where the Soviets had created incidents at one time or another. (See Sketch No 3, Terrain Analysis)

Another "essential of operations" that appeared in almost every First Area Army plan was the differentiation between the operational roles of "main forces" and "elements." Elements normally manned the front line strong points; main forces were generally concentrated in areas where decisive battles were expected to take place. This differentiation was made also by armies and divisions in their planning. The principal use of elements by both armies and divisions was to station them in the long-established border fortifications in their

---

25. The map of Manchuria prepared by the Army Map Service, scale 1/2,000,000, 1950, shows Hulin at the border. The Japanese renamed this city Hutou, and built another city about 30 miles to the southwest and called it Hulin.

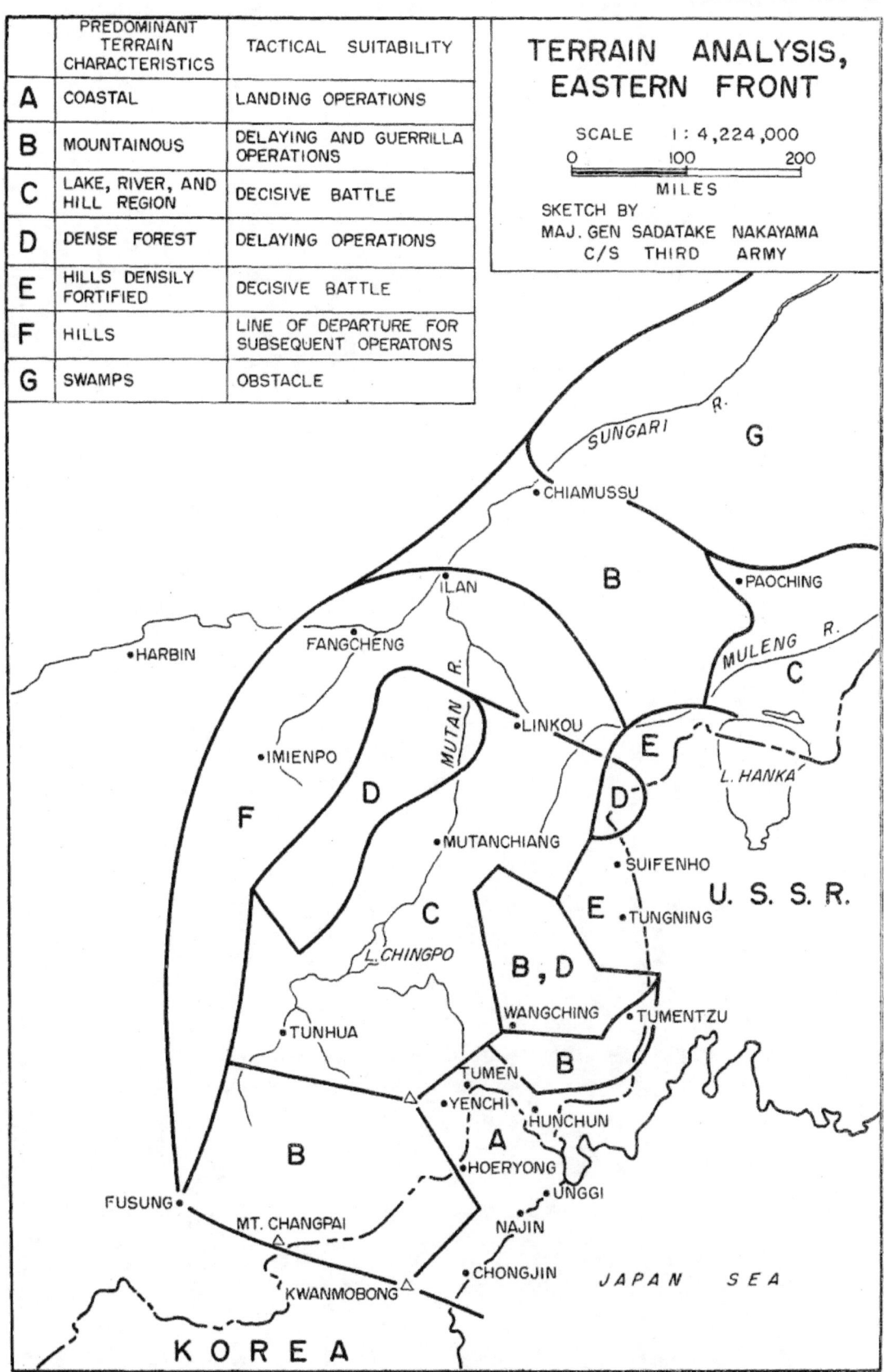

respective sectors. These elements in turn supplied personnel for the many lookout posts that dotted the border zone. In all operational plans drawn up after September 1944, the elements deployed in these fortifications constituted the first, but not the major, line of defense. Although comparatively small in numbers, their fortifications gave them advantages not enjoyed by the main force.

Operational Plans

In drawing up operational plans the First Area Army generally followed a broad outline prepared by the Kwantung Army. Whenever it learned that higher headquarters was discussing a change in operational plans it would initiate a draft of plans along similar lines, not waiting for the formal outline to arrive. In this way it kept pace with higher Headquarters. When in mid 1944, for example, Kwantung Army realized that offensive operations were no longer possible and began formulating a plan for holding operations, the First Area Army followed the same course, so that by the time the Kwantung Army plan was approved on 18 September 1944 and a copy furnished to subordinate commands, the First Area Army had already drawn up an outline of a holding plan for the eastern front.

All First Area Army plans drawn up during this period called for elements to defend the border area utilizing the fortifications there. As to the positions to be held by the main force, the plans differed somewhat. In a plan drafted during September 1944, main forces were to hold the Pamientung-Suiyang-Tungning and the Lishuchen-Linkou sectors. In a plan drawn up towards the end of 1944 and distributed to subordinate commands during February 1945, the Hoeryong-Tumen-Hunchun sector was added as a main force position in Third Army's sector on the right. In this plan provision was made, in the event of an enemy advance, for the area army to gradually shift its line of resistance rearward; with Tumen as the anchor of the line, it was to swing first to a line through Lake Chingpo to Fangcheng, then to a line connecting with Tunhua. (See Sketch No 4, Major Defense Lines of First Area Army.) This was done in conformance with Kwantung Army's plan of putting up final resistance in Manchuria in the area which, with Hsinking as its vortex, extended eastward to Tumen and southward to Dairen.

Upon closer examination of this plan, First Area Army Headquarters found that the central sector of Pamientung-Suiyang-Tungning was too long to be defended with available forces. It decided, therefore, to move the main defense line about 35 miles to the rear to a line connecting Chihsing (south of Linkou), the mountain ridges west of Pamientung, Muleng, Tachienchang, and Lotzukou. This would reduce the 82-mile length of the central front sector to about 52 miles. No change was to be made in the southern front sector.

During April 1945 Kwantung Army notified the First Area Army that it was recommending to Imperial General Headquarters the abandonment of the holding plan and the adoption of the delaying

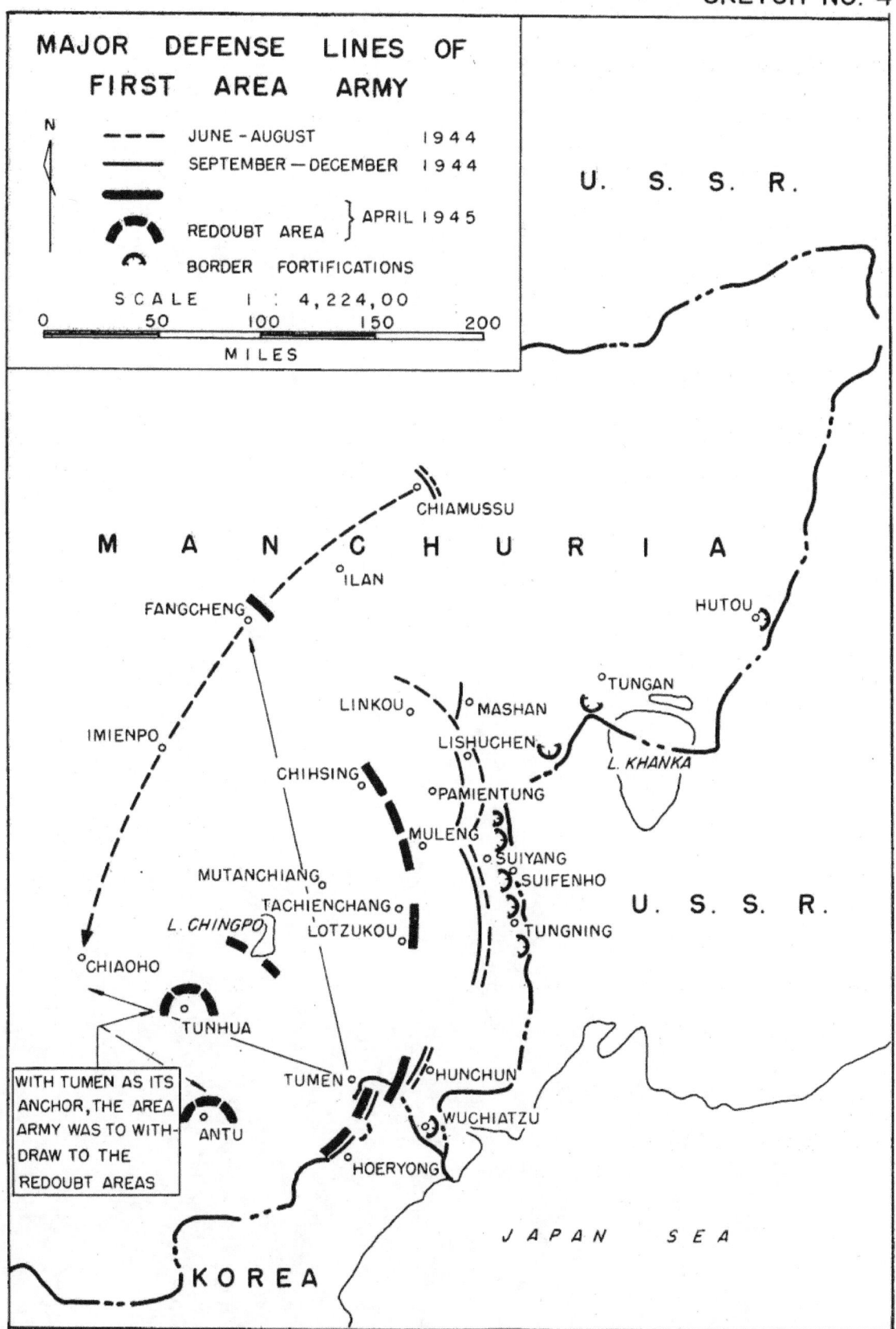

plan shelved in September 1944. Immediately upon receipt of this information First Area Army Headquarters began to draw up a delaying operational plan, and alerted its subordinate commands accordingly. After Imperial General Headquarters approval was received, Kwantung Army changed the mission of the First Area Army to one of conducting delaying operations in eastern Manchuria.

The delaying plan, though somewhat similar to the holding plan since both were defensive in nature, differed in several respects. Many of the steps taken since the adoption of the holding plan were equally valid for the delaying plan. The disposition of troops was to remain the same. Elements would still man border fortifications, and main forces would still take up positions to the rear. The important differences were that no last ditch stand was to be made in position, and provision was made for withdrawal to new positions. In this lay the principal difference between the two plans. For the First Area Army this meant that two operational bases would have to be prepared in the redoubt, one at Tunhua and the other at Antu.

The missions assigned to various units in this plan stipulated that elements of each unit were to utilize the fortifications in the first line of defense and to destroy the enemy at the border. The missions assigned to the main force of the Third Army were to take up positions in the Hoeryong, Tumen, and Hunchun sectors, and to destroy the enemy. The main body of the 128th Division was to take up positions in the sector of Lotzukou and Tachienchang between the Third and Fifth Armies to cover the inner flank of both armies. The main force of the Fifth Army was to occupy positions in the sectors west of Muleng west of Pamientung, and south of Linkou.

The mission assigned to the 134th Division, deployed on the left flank of the Area Army, was to delay the enemy who was expected to launch an invasion along the Sungari River, then offer resistance successively in the vicinities of Chiamussu and Fangcheng, finally withdrawing to the Chiaoho area via Imienpo, at the same time covering the left flank of the Area Army. In the rear areas, the 122d Division was to take up positions on both banks of Lake Chingpo to cover the retreat of the Area Army during the final stages of operations. The 139th Division was to construct positions for the Area Army's final stand in the vicinity of Tunhua.

Other changes adopted during the transition from a holding plan to a delaying plan were: the northern half of Hamyong Pukto in north Korea, including the units stationed there (79th Division, 101st Mixed Regiment, and the Najin Fortress Garrison Unit) were to be placed under the command of Third Army;[26] the front of the Third Army was to be most strongly fortified to become the right flank pivoting point of the Area Army; no limited offensives were to be

---

26. These units passed to Kwantung Army control on 10 June 1945. No exact information can be obtained regarding the manner in which north Korea gradually came under Kwantung Army jurisdiction and control, because available documents do not mention specific areas. According to the "best judgments" of consultants, only the northern part of Hamyong Pukto province was placed under Kwantung Army juris-

undertaken in the area of the Third Army because they would be unremunerative and would detract from the strength needed in subsequent operations elsewhere; units and operations in the Sanchiang area were to be placed under the direct control of the Area Army during wartime, but for peacetime preparations the units (principally the 134th Division) and area would remain under the control of Fifth Army; the 1st Mobile Brigade was not given a separate sector but was to be disposed in the area around Langchi (southeast of Lotzukou), where the terrain allows the widest scope of action, and was to be attached to Third Army; and the 128th Division and 132d Independent Mixed Brigade upon the opening of hostilities were to be grouped under the commander of the 128th Division (Lt Gen Yoshishige Mizuhara) and assigned directly to the Area Army, but until then were to remain as separate commands under the Third Army.

These modifying instructions were furnished to each Army during

---

diction on 18 Sep 44. Orders issued on 30 May refer to the Kwantung Army's mission in "northern Korea" and to the Seventeenth Area Army's mission in "central and southern Korea." The term "northern Korea" is believed to mean the four northern provinces of Korea. On this date the "Outline of the Plan for Operations against the USSR in Manchuria and Korea" was issued, and although this document is not available, it is believed to have specifically mentioned the four northern provinces. (Pertinent documents are Army Department Orders Nos 1130, 1131, and Army Directive No 2164, all dated 18 Sep 44, Army Department Orders No 1245, 6 Feb 45, Army Department Orders Nos 1338, 1339, 1340, all dated 30 May 45.) Orders No 1374, 9 August placed the entire Seventeenth Area Army under the Kwantung Army. The editor assumes that the Kwantung Army received limited jurisdiction over all forces in Korea on 18 Sep 44, the limitation being on matters relating to preparations against the USSR.

April, and later in the month First Area Army Headquarters conducted "table-top" maneuvers to determine the effectiveness of the new plan and the missions assigned to units. These exercises were attended by staff officers from the Third and Fifth Armies and from the Area Army itself. Controversy aroused regarding the right and left flanks of the Area Army left several questions open for further examination.

Meanwhile, First Area Army Headquarters was confronted with other problems connected with the transition from a holding to a delaying plan. Enormous stockpiles of war supplies in the border areas had to be removed to the rear, requiring additional transportation. Road improvement projects under way had to be re-evaluated, and those considered unessential for defensive operations abandoned, for example the road from Muleng to Tungning, and from Tungning to Shihtou (south of Ningan). A communications net had to be established at Tunhua to which the Area Army was to fall back. In addition, the training of troops was hampered by the lack of competent instructors as well as by the indecision to change the operational plan, and the fear that an abrupt change to defensive training might disclose operational plans.[27]

---

27. Another problem created dealt with the settlement of border disputes. Following the Wuchiatzu incident, Kwantung Army drew up a "Guide for the Defense of the Manchurian-Soviet-Mongolian Border." (See pages 82-87, Monograph 138.)

CHAPTER III

Composition of Major Units

General Structure

On 26 September 1944, when General Seiichi Kita[28] assumed command, the First Area Army consisted principally of six divisions, one cavalry brigade, and seven border garrison units. The divisions were, in Third Army, the 12th, 111th, and 112th; in Fifth Army, the 11th and 25th. The 71st Division was under the direct command of the Area Army. All of these divisions except the 112th were first-class divisions and were destined shortly to be transferred from Manchuria. The border garrison units (the 1st, 2d, 3d, 4th, 9th, 11th, and 12th) were destined to be used as the nucleus of some of the new divisions that would be organized to replace the first-class divisions. (Chart No 1 shows the organization of the First Area Army in September 1944.)

At the beginning of August 1945, the month of the Soviet invasion, the First Area Army consisted of ten divisions, plus several independent units: one mobile brigade, one mixed brigade, one mixed regiment, and two garrison units of regimental size. This constituted

---

28. General Kita had commanded the Twelfth Army in North China. From there served bridfly on the Army General Staff in Tokyo. He assumed command of the First Area Army on 26 Sep 44. In August 1945 he was taken captive by the Soviets. During 1951 word was received in Japan from a repatriated POW that General Kita had died in captivity.

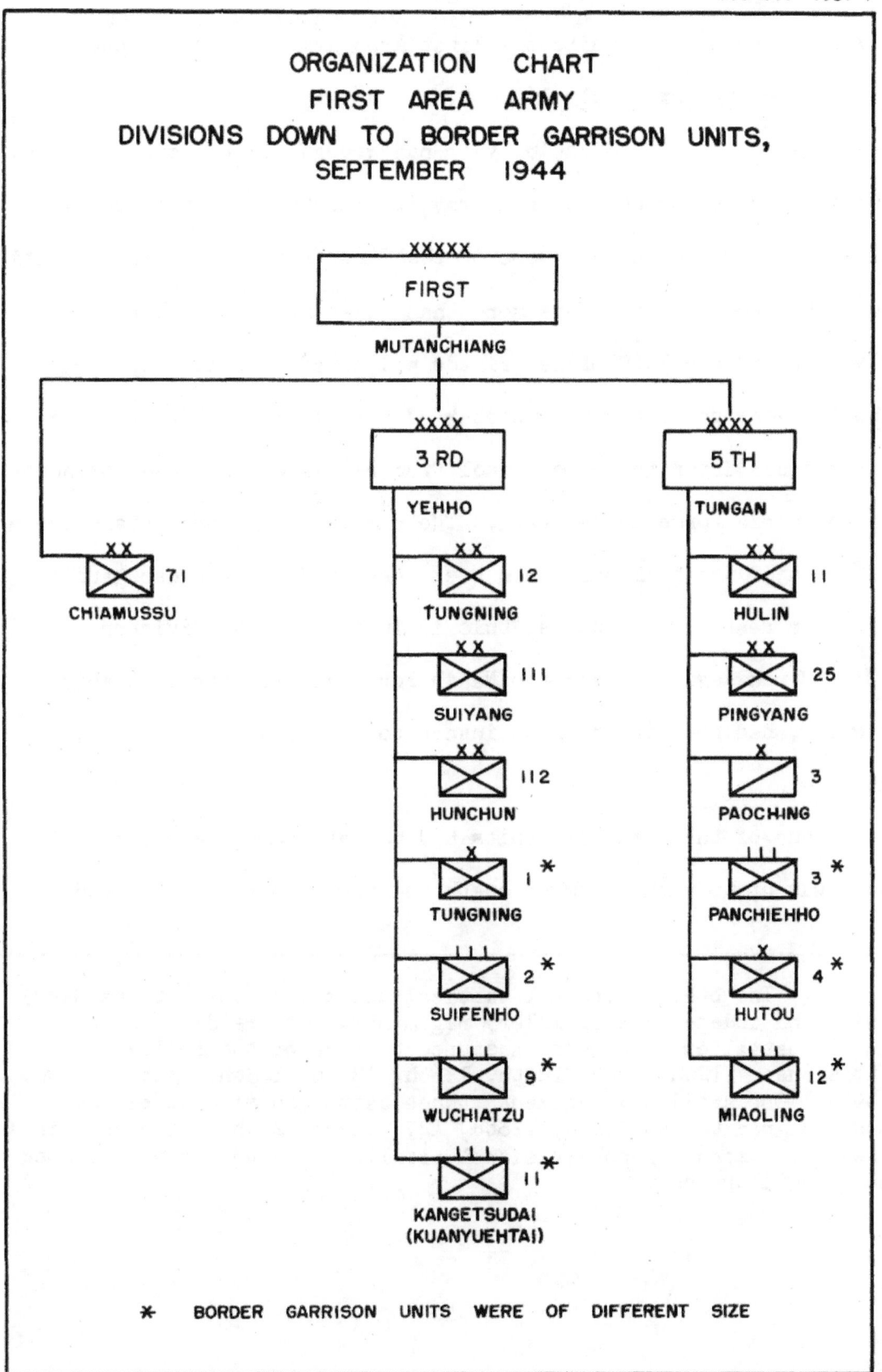

almost half of the tactical strength of the Kwantung Army. With auxiliary and supply units the First Area Army had a personnel strength of approximately 160,000.[29]

Although the intervening year had wrought little change in the numerical strength of the Area Army it brought about vast changes in qualitative strength. None of the First Area Army's major tactical units had been in existence more than seven months, except the 112th Division and the 1st Mobile Brigade which had come into existence about a year prior to the outbreak of hostilities. Six of the divisions had drawn their personnel from recruited Japanese residents in Manchuria formerly deferred. The remainder of the divisions and other major tactical units had been organized from border garrison units or rear echelon units; this included the 79th Division, the 101st Mixed Regiment, and the Najin Fortress Garrison Unit which, however, had been transferred intact to the Area Army on 10 June 1945.

None of the Area Army units had had any combat experience. None was up to authorized strength and none was fully equipped.

---

29. The other principal tactical units were assault (raiding) units and independent artillery regiments. One raiding unit (infantry battalion size) were assigned to each of the following divisions: 112th, 122d, 124th, 126th, 127th, 128th, 134th, 135th, 139th. One artillery regiment (three battalion size, 36 pieces) was assigned to the 124th, 126th, 127th, and 128th Divisions, since these divisions had no divisional artillery and were not stationed near artillery units.

Although there were ten divisions compared with six during the preceding year, the number of garrison units had dropped from seven to two. And all of the new divisions, except the 79th (and the 132d Independent Mixed Brigade) were from 25% to 50% understrength. The 128th Division, for example, with an authorized strength of 23,000 had only 12,634. Almost none of the commanders had been with their units a year.

At the time of the Soviet invasion, therefore, the First Area Army was a relatively new command. Aside from its newness, it had had scarcely any time for welding the various units under its command into an effective fighting machine. The Area Army's attention had been engaged by other activities, such as arranging for the transfer of its long-established elite units to Pacific fighting areas, organizing and training new units, and constructing new fortifications. In almost every respect the First Area Army was below standards.

The Headquarters of the First Area Army was located in Mutanchiang City. Its major subordinate commands were the Third Army with headquarters at Yenchi, and the Fifth Army with headquarters in Yehho.[30] Under the Area Army's direct command were the 122d,

---

30. Until April 1945, when the Kwantung Army decided that at the outset of hostilities Tungan Province would be abandoned, Fifth Army Headquarters was located in Tungan City. At this time the boundary between Third and Fifth Armies was moved southward about 35 miles.

134th, and 139th Divisions.

Of the three divisions under the Area Army's direct command, only the 134th had been formed from tactical units, possibly explaining its assignment to the front. Its source of personnel were the 78th Independent Mixed Brigade, the Fuchin Garrison Unit, and the 14th Border Garrison Unit. The division was organized during July-August 1945 and was stationed in the Chiamussu area.[31] Its commander was Lieutenant General Jin Izeki. Although directly under the First Area Army, the 134th Division was attached to the Fifth Army for operational preparations until the outbreak of hostilities.

Both the 122d and 139th Division were deployed in the rear areas. The 122d was detailed to construct covering positions in near Lake Chingpo, and the 139th to construct redoubt defenses in the Tunhua area. The 122d Division, organized during February 1945, was formed from recruits while the 139th Division, which was not formed until July-August 1945, drew its personnel from the 77th, 79th, and 80th Guard Units. Personnel in units directly under the Area Army totaled 55,000.

---

31. Until July 1944, Sanchiang Province was garrisoned by the 10th Division. It was replaced by the 71st Division which garrisoned the area until its transfer in February 1945. Pending the assignment of another division to the area, it was garrisoned by the Fuchin Garrison Unit and other smaller elements.

Third Army (See Map No 2.)

The Third Army, since 22 November 1944 commanded by Lieutenant General Keisaku Murakami, had four divisions--the 79th, 112th, 127th, and 128th--and the 1st Mobile Brigade, the 132d Independent Mixed Brigade, the 101st Mixed Regiment, and the Najin Fortress Garrison Unit (regimental size). Personnel in units assigned to Third Army totaled 50,000.

The 79th Division was one of the units acquired by Third Army from the Seventeenth Area Army (Korea) on 10 June 1945. It had been organized at Nanam, Korea, from the 19th Depot Division on 10 March 1945. It was transferred to Tumen, across the Korea-Manchuria border, at the end of July. Its commander was Lieutenant General Teisho Ota.

The 112th Division had been organized in August 1944 from newly-recruited personnel, and its main body stationed near Hunchun with a plan to withdraw to Michiangtun. The division was commanded by Lieutenant General Jikizo Nakamura.

The 127th and 128th Divisions were two of the eight divisions organized during January-February 1945 from newly-recruited personnel and cadres from various border garrison units to give the Kwantung Army the semblance of strength. The 127th, commanded by Lieutenant General Ryutaro Koga, was stationed near Pataohotzu, not far from the Korea border, and the 128th, commanded by Lieutenant General Yoshishige Mizuhara, at Lotzukou.[32]

---

32. The 128th Division replaced the 120th Division in March 1945, which in turn had replaced the 12th Division in December 1944.

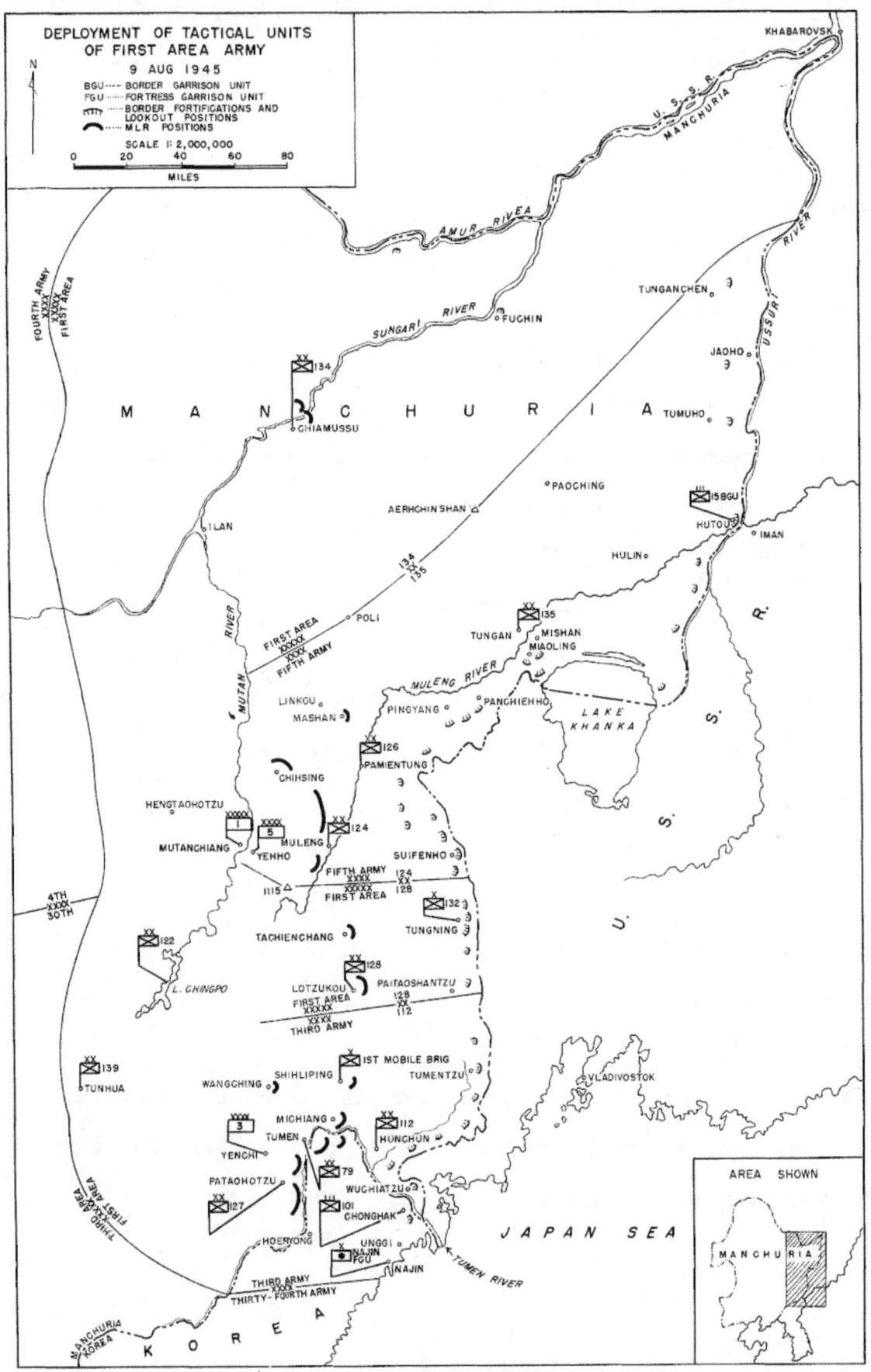

The 1st Mobile Brigade had completed its organization toward the end of August 1944. It consisted of picked troops and was to be assigned special missions. For this reason its training was supervised directly by Kwantung Army Headquarters. In June 1945 it was transferred from Kirin to the Shihliping area and placed under Third Army.

The 132d Independent Mixed Brigade, consisting mainly of four infantry and one raiding battalions plus three artillery companies, had been organized on 10 July 1945 from elements of the 1st, 2d, and 11th Border Garrison Units. It was stationed at Tungning with the mission of defending the border in that area.

The 101st Mixed Regiment and the Najin Fortress Garrison Unit, like the 79th Division, were acquired from the Seventeenth Area Army on 10 June 1945. The 101st Mixed Regiment was stationed near Chonghak, and the Najin Garrison Unit at Najin, both in Korea.

Fifth Army (See Map No 2.)

The Fifth Army's principal units were the 124th, 126th, and 135th Divisions and the 15th Border Garrison Unit (regimental size). It was commanded by Lieutenant General Noritsune Shimizu who had assumed command on 17 June 1944. Personnel in units assigned to Fifth Army totaled 55,000

The 124th and 126th Divisions were also organized from Japanese residents in January-February 1945 to give the Kwantung Army the semblance of a powerful force. The 124th Division, although initially assigned to Third Army, was transferred to Fifth Army shortly after it was organized; the division was commanded by Lieutenant General Masatake Shiina, and its main body was stationed near Muleng. The 126th, whose main body was near Pamientung, was commanded by Lieutenant General Kazuhiko Nomizo.[33]

The 135th Division had been organized during July-August 1945 from the 77th Independent Mixed Brigade, 3d and 4th Border Garrison Units, and the 46th Guard Unit. It was commanded by Lieutenant General Yoichi Hitomi, and its main body stationed near Tungan.[34]

The 15th Border Garrison Unit had been organized during July 1945 from elements of the 4th Border Garrison Unit. It consisted principally of one infantry battalion and two artillery companies, and garrisoned the Hutou border fortifications. Among its weapons were several emplaced guns of large caliber, including one 410-mm howitzer. Its mission was to sever the trans-Siberian railway near Iman which was within its range, and to place interdictory fire on enemy positions to the rear of Iman to prevent the massing of Soviet force there. (Chart No 2/ shows the organization of the First Area Army in August 1945.)

---

33. The 124th Division while in the Third Army's sector had replaced the 111th Division in March 1945. The 111th, in turn, had replaced the 8th Division in July 1944. The 126th Division replaced the 25th Division in March 1945.
34. The 135th Division replaced the 11th Division which was transferred in March-April 1945. Until the 135th Division was organized the area was garrisoned by the 77th Independent Mixed Brigade.

MONOGRAPH NO. 154-B
CHART NO. 2

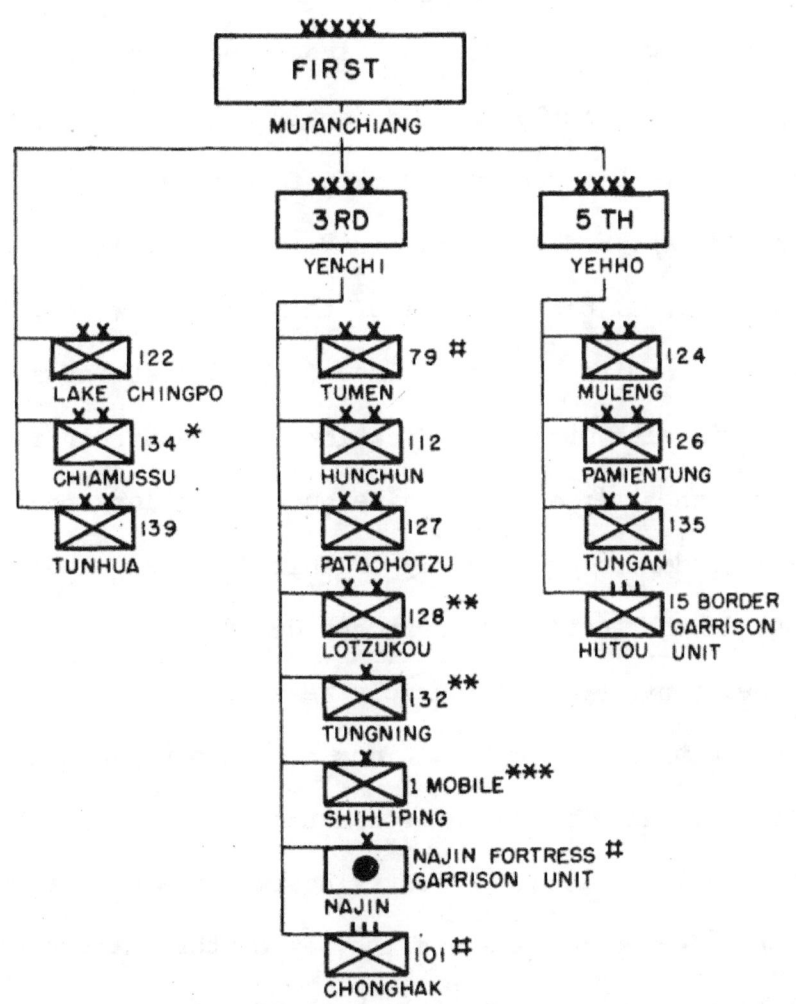

ORGANIZATION CHART
FIRST AREA ARMY
DIVISIONS DOWN TO SEPARATE REGIMENTS
8 AUGUST 1945

* Under control of Fifth Army for operational preparations until outbreak of hostilities.

** Transferred to direct command of First Area Army at outbreak of hostilities, at which time the 132d Independent Mixed Brigade was assigned to the 128th Division.

*** Assigned to Third Army in June 1945.

Assigned to Third Army when northern Hamyong Pukto was included in the operational area of Kwantung Army.

CHAPTER IV

Status of Preparations[35]

Fortifications

In addition to attempting to keep in readiness the old fortifications in the border zones, the First Area Army was busy during this period pushing to completion new fortifications, particularly in the positions to be used by the main forces, and those in cities and towns, in the redoubt area, in North Korea, and in the Area Army's operational bases. None of this work, however, was in satisfactory condition at the time of the Soviet invasion.

To begin with, the fortifications in the border zones had gradually been stripped of machine guns, artillery pieces, and other weapons in order to equip newly-organized forces. Stocks of ammunition kept in the fortified areas had dwindled. As a result these border positions were considerably weakened.

Construction of fortifications in the newly-designated positions to be used by main forces in accordance with the operational plan was begun in March 1945. In carrying out this work emphasis was placed on underground defenses in view of the enemy's superior capability for artillery and air bombardment. Although this work

---

35. More detailed information on the status of preparations in each unit is provided in subsequent chapters.

was pushed, it was hindered by the shortage of mason's tools and dynamite, and required more time than was expected. By the time the Soviet Union entered the war, although almost all caves for emplacing large guns had been completed in each position, other important installations such as communication trenches, field positions, and, what was particularly important, tank obstacles, were in imperfect condition.

As regards the fortification of Manchurian cities and towns which were scattered in an area of extensive depth and would constitute the strongpoints for sustained warfare, and also as regards the construction of positions in the Tunhua and Antu sectors which would constitute the redoubt for the Area Army, no work had been begun by the close of July because of the shortage of manpower and materials. The only thing completed by this time was the reconnaissance of the intended locations for positions.

Fortification of the North Korea sector which had only recently come under Kwantung Army jurisdiction was somewhat behind schedule. The Area Army Commander conducted an inspection of this sector shortly after he was given control of this area, and as a result of his encouragement and that of the Third Army Commander the work gradually took on a definite shape.

To accelerate the construction of positions by the 122d Division in the sector bordering on both banks of Lake Chingpo, the 6th Unit (about three infantry battalions and one motor transport company) of the Manchurian National Army located in the vicinity of Mutanchiang was placed under the 122d Division.

Revisions in Logistical Planning

To bring the logistical plan in line with the new operational plan, First Area Army had to consider relocating its supply installations, including its depots and dumps and those of the Third and Fifth Armies. In view of previous plans for offensive operations, most of these had been established in forward areas. But with the adoption of the plan for delaying operations, a plan was worked out to move them rearward. This applied not only to the depots and dumps as units but also to the supplies stored therein. Accordingly, a withdrawal schedule was drawn up, but before it could be fully met for any item of supply, hostilities commenced.

Kwantung Army Headquarters had hoped that the enemy could be delayed for about three months, but from a logistical viewpoint--especially as regards ammunition and fuel--it was realized that one month was all that could be expected before the defenders would have to withdraw to the redoubt astride the Manchurian-Korean border.

From the First Area Army's viewpoint it was necessary to develop two supply bases in the redoubt area, one in the Tunhua vicinity, the other at Antu. Within the Tunhua area, supplies were to be dispersed in three sectors: the sector south of Lake Chingpo, the vicinity of the airfield at Shahoyen, and the Tunhua sector itself. Items most needed were arms, ammunition, and medical supplies, and although the movement of all supplies was to begin simultaneously, priority was assigned to these items.

Supply installations under the Area Army's direct control (hospitals, construction units, and depots for transport, ammunition, food, clothing, medical and veterinary supplies) began to move to the Tunhua area during April.. By the time hostilities opened the percentage of principal types of supplies move to the Tunhua installations was roughly as follows:

Arms and ammunition	50%
Medical supplies	50%
Veterinary supplies	30%
Food and clothing	10-20%

The problem of provisioning Antu with food and fodder was investigated jointly with Manchukuoan Government authorities, from whom much of these provisions had to be purchased. In addition to looking into the matter of stockpiling provisions, investigations considered moving civilian-owned weapons repair shops in Tunhua, Chilin, and Yenchi to the Antu base. Before any visible results could be achieved in provisioning this base, however, the Soviet invasion began.

Third and Fifth Armies were to move their depots beginning in April also. The depots concerned maintained stocks of food, fodder, clothing, fuel, arms, and ammunition, and also medical and veterinary supplies. Third Army depots in the vicinity of Hunchun and Tungning were to withdraw to the vicinity of the Army's new headquarters at Yenchi. Fifth Army depots in the vicinity of Suiyang, Tungan, and Chihsi were to withdraw to the area around Mutanchiang and Tunhua. In view of the supply support that would be needed while the Area Army was withdrawing, however, branch depots of some classes of supply were to be established at Shitou and at Imienpo.

No breakdown of the types of supplies actually moved by the armies is available. Generally speaking, however, the volume moved back by Fifth Army by 9 August was between 70 and 80 per cent, and by Third Army approximately 50 per cent.

Meanwhile, during April medical agencies of the area army and both armies began a rapid evacuation of patients to rear areas. By the close of July no patients remained in forward area hospitals.

Communications   (See Sketch No 5)

From the decision to put up only nominal resistance in Sanchiang, the northernmost of the eastern front provinces, stemmed the requirement that the Headquarters of the First Area Army and of the Third and Fifth Armies move south where a more determined defense was to be made. The plan called for First Area Army Headquarters to move to Tunhua, for Third Army Headquarters to move to Yenchi, and for Fifth Army Headquarters to move to Yehho. These moves could not be made, however, until the communications network was adjusted so as to permit communications between higher and lower headquarters.

The main communications link between Kwantung Army Headquarters in Hsinking and First Area Army Headquarters at Mutanchiang was principally an underground cable via Harbin and, secondarily, overhead wires via Chilin, Tunhua, Yenchi, Tumen, and Tungchingcheng. By moving to Tunhua, First Area Army Headquarters could maintain contact with Hsinking by this secondary link, which consisted of

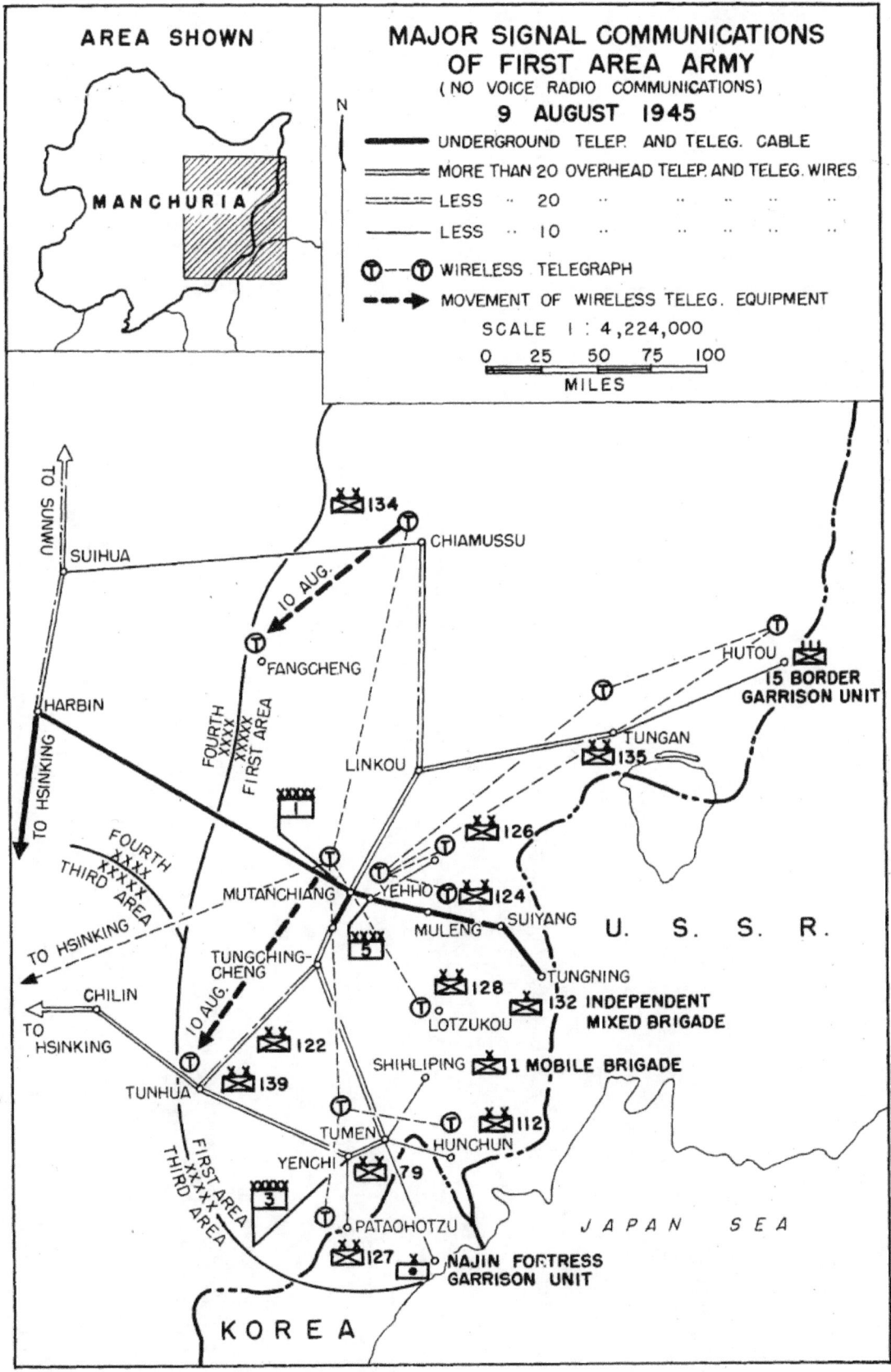

more than twenty overhead wires and which for great distances followed the railroad tracks.

First Area Army Headquarters had no voice radios. While at Mutanchiang, it maintained forward communication with Fifth Army Headquarters by means of overhead wires strung to Tungan via Linkou, and with Third Army Headquarters at Yehho (just across the river) by several adequate methods. It also had direct wires to the 134th Division at Chiamussu. Contact with the 128th Division at Lotzukou was by wireless telegraph. A signal regiment for servicing communications installations was attached to the Area Army and stationed near Mutanchiang.

Before First Area Army could move its headquarters to Tunhua, it had to transfer the center of the communication network from Mutanchiang to Tunhua. Between Tunhua and Mutanchiang, direct lines connected Tungchingcheng with Mutanchiang, but no wires connected Tunhua with Tungchingcheng. To close this gap, therefore, and provide direct lines from Tunhua all the way to Mutanchiang, sixteen wires were laid between Tunhua and Tungchingcheng. This was the principal signal installation needed to permit the Area Army Headquarters to communicate with Fifth Army Headquarters. This work was completed in early August. As for direct communication with Third Army Headquarters, the secondary overhead link from Hsinking to Mutanchiang ran through Tunhua and Yenchi and would be ample.

Communications with the 134th Division in Chiamussu and the 128th Division in Lotzukou would have to be the same from Tunhua as it had been from Mutanchiang, wire to Chiamussu and wireless telegraph to Lotzukou.

However, since the 134th Division was to withdraw to Fangcheng during operations, communications from Tunhua to Fangcheng would also have to be by wireless telegraph. First Area Army Headquarters had almost no confidence in its wireless contacts with these two places, a condition created partly by the fact that wireless equipment in those areas was operated by inexperienced personnel.

Since Fifth Army Headquarters was to move to Yehho, forward communications would be as good as they were while Third Army Headquarters was there: wireless to the outpost at Hutou where the 15th Border Garrison Unit was stationed, wire to the 135th Division at Tungan, and wireless to the 124th Division at Muleng and 126th Division west of Pamientung. To improve communications with the latter division, however, signal units began to lay wire to Pamientung; this was the second major wire installation preparatory to the moves.

Forward communication for the Third Army Headquarters from its new base at Yenchi were adequate for contacting the 112th Division in Hunchun and the 79th Division in Tumen. However, for the 1st Mobile Brigade at Shihliping and for the 127th Division at Pataohotzu wires had to be laid, the third and fourth installations required preparatory to the move.

By mid-April changes in the communications network to permit the Third Army Headquarters to move were completed, and on the 25th it vacated Yehho and moved to Yenchi. Soon afterwards, Fifth Army

Headquarters moved into Yehho.

Although it was urgent that the Area Army Headquarters move to its new base in Tunhua, it had to remain at Mutanchiang until the communication network centering around Tunhua could be completed. It did not move until 10 August. Earlier, however, it established an advance command post at Tunhua.

Training

From the time of the receipt of the operational plan until the beginning of hostilities, training was conducted concurrently with the construction of fortifications. After the issuance of the revised Combat Manual of the Kwantung Army in June, training was patterned after the principles laid down in the manual, emphasizing particularly actions against armored units, raiding tactics, and antiaircraft defenses. In addition, lessons learned from the battles of the Pacific war were incorporated into training schedules and applied in training exercises; these lessons pertained to the construction of fortifications as well as to tactics. At the same time, the First Area Army introduced several specialized subjects into the training programs for units scheduled to be transferred to other areas.

Border Garrisoning

During the period of the Soviet build-up in Siberia which began after the end of the war with Germany, Soviet forces along the Manchurian border began to show an increasingly challenging attitude.

On about 20 July 1945 Soviet troops crossed the border at Chiungshan, south of Panchiehho. For almost one week more than 300 of them were engaged in constructing fortifications inside the border at distances ranging from 100 to 300 meters and with a frontage of approximately 500 meters. This bold action not only displayed a flagrant disregard for Japanese troops in the area but also showed the hostile intent of the Soviets.

Farther north along the border, at Kanhsiatun, 40 kilometers south of Hutou, Soviet troops tresspassed the border at several points on 5 August. Within view of our thirty-man observation team, about twenty Soviet officers approached the Ussuri River border in motor vehicles, observing the Manchurian terrain through binoculars. About 100 Soviet infantrymen then crossed the river and commenced firing at our observation team from a distance of 500 or 600 meters. Our team restrained themselves and did not return the fire. As night fell, the Soviets showed little intention of retreating, and lay prone on the grass.

Fifth Army Headquarters dispatched one of its staff officers, Colonel Akiji Kashiwada, to the area to observe the situation for awhile. On the following day, however, information was received indicating that no Soviet troops were observed in the area; apparently, they had withdrawn during the night. Consequently, the Fifth Army staff officer was recalled.

During these provocative incidents our border troops, in compliance with Kwantung Army regulations, refrained from any positive actions. Nevertheless, throughout the incidents our troops remained vigilant. This alone was apparently sufficient to prevent a recurrence or at least to limit the scope of the incidents.

Changes in Strength and Materiel

The organization of new forces in February 1945 and the mass mobilization of all available manpower in July of the same year had practically exhausted all sources of personnel. During this period an almost complete turnover had taken place, both as regards units and personnel. Elite units had been transferred and in their place came newly-formed units; with these elite units went most of the experienced personnel, and these were replaced largely by recruits.

With the transfer of troops from Manchuria went also large quantities of weapons and ammunition. By the summer of 1945, supplies of arms and materiels in the First Area Army had become so scanty that guns necessary to equip newly-organized artillery units had to be obtained by dismantling gun emplacements at border fortifications. Since even this expediency provided an insufficient number of guns, the weapons of artillery units in some cases were supplemented by mortars, some of which had to be manufactured locally. In such cases, though the units may have had enough weapons, the types of weapons varied.

To remedy the shortage of swords and bayonets, various expediencies were taken, such as forging them out of the springs of scrapped motor vehicles. Even with the adoption of such expediencies, however, about one-third of communication zone personnel were left without bayonets.

Combat Effectiveness

Aside from the fact that almost half of the tactical units of the First Area Army (134th, 135th, 139th Divisions, 15th Border Garrison Unit, and the 132d Independent Mixed Brigade) did not begin to be organized until just one month prior to the outbreak of hostilities, each existing division was under strength. Furthermore, the recruits brought into the new units had had no prior military training, and the ability and morale of officers left much to be desired. A great deal of effort was yet needed to organize the new units and to whip the existing divisions into efficient fighting units.

In addition to the shortage of artillery weapons, there were virtually no antitank guns, and almost all infantryguns were obsolete models. The number of heavy and light machine guns and grenade dischargers was less than half of the amounts authorized. Ammunition amounted to slightly more than 100 rounds per rifle and 500 to 600 rounds per field artillery piece. Automobile fuel available for the entire Area Army amounted to 6,950 kiloliter, light oil to 764 kiloliter.

Provisions in the First Area Army were ample. Based on the number of days one standard division could be sustained there were enough staple rations to feed one division for 8,200 days, enough supplementary rations for 4,800 days, enough Manchurian rations (kaoliang, millet, wheat flour) for 5,300 days,[36] and enough forage for 8,000 horses for 9,000 days.

On the basis of the First Area Army's quality of troops, organization, equipment, and training, its combat effectiveness was estimated to be equal to that of 2.75 first-rate divisions. The estimated combat effectiveness of units was:

Unit	Per cent of Combat Effectiveness
79th Division	55
112th Division	35
122d Division	35
124th Division	35
126th Division	20
127th Division	20
128th Division	20
134th Division	15
135th Division	15
139th Division	15
132d Indep Mixed Brigade	10

The effectiveness of operational preparations was hindered by the fact that while considerable progress had been made on underground fortifications in the three months prior to August, scarcely

---

36. These three figures show an abundance of provisions in the First Area Army, an abundance prevalent throughout Manchuria, the "storehouse of the Japanese Army." They can roughly be equated, respectively, as 1,281, 750, and 828 US Army theater days of supply. However, approximately 300,000 Japanese residents also had to be fed from these stores.

any above-ground installations, such as positions for heavy weapons, communication trenches, and obstacles, had been completed. Perhaps the greatest hindrance was that the construction of roadblocks had to be delayed in order to keep the main roads open to traffic as long as possible. This accounted partly for the failure, when operations began, to delay enemy armored columns. Our preparedness to meet the enemy was further hindered by the fact that when main forces withdrew to construct new positions for the main line of defense, they left approximately one-third of their principal firearms in barracks areas to be used in training recruits. Furthermore, because of the lack of storage space near the new positions, large quantities of ammunition stocks were also left in the barracks areas by each unit. Hence, when hostilities began these supplies were between the forward elements and the main forces at the new positions, but were immediately available to neither.

CHAPTER V

First Area Army Operations on Eastern Front

Opening of Hostilities

A little after midnight of 8-9 August 1945 (it had been raining heavily during the night) a report from the Fifth Army stated that its positions in the Hutou area were under attack by Soviet artillery. This was followed by another report from Third Army stating that its positions in the Wuchiatzu area were being shelled by enemy artillery. The Area Army immediately relayed these reports to Kwantung Army Headquarters and summoned personnel of its own headquarters to their offices. It had not as yet definitely ascertained that an all-out invasion had begun.

As more and more reports came in, however, some of them stating that hostile planes were making sorties deep into Manchuria, First Area Army Headquarters concluded that the enemy was attacking in earnest along the entire border and that the invasion had begun. Wasting no time, Headquarters telephoned Operational Order No 1 to the Third and Fifth Armies, the 122d and 139th Divisions, the 134th and 128th Divisions, and also to smaller units under its direct command.

Operational Order No 1 placed into effect the plan for delaying operations, and called upon all units to resist the enemy invasion. It formally placed the 128th and 134th Divisions under the Area Army's direct command, and the 132d Independent Mixed Brigade directly under the 128th Division.

From reports that continued to come into the Headquarters, First Area Army learned of the developing situation. Along the Third Army front the enemy crossed the border at four points: Shuiliufeng Peak and Wuchiatzu in the 127th Division's sector, and at Hunchun and Tumentzu in the 112th Division's sector. The enemy forces that penetrated the border at the base of Shuiliufeng Peak (430 meters) crossed the Kyonghung Bridge and marched into North Korea. Those that penetrated the border at Tumentzu (6 miles inside the border) were advancing toward the Tuhuangtzu-Chintsang area; these towns are respectively 30 and 40 miles from the border. Other troops gradually pushed toward Tumen by way of Hunchun. To meet the enemy advance, each division of the Third Army took up its respective positions.

In the 128th Division sector the enemy surged in towards Tungning (9 miles inside the border) but was checked by the 132d Independent Mixed Brigade's Tungning Detachment consisting of two infantry battalions, two field artillery batteries, two heavy artillery batteries (280-mm howitzer), and two engineer platoons. The Brigade's main force, meanwhile, began withdrawing to Tachiengchang. Another enemy attack farther south, at Paitaoshantzu, was met by a company of the 128th Division.

In the Fifth Army's area, the enemy broke through the border at six points: Suifenho and Kuanyuehtai in the 124th Division's sector, Jumonji Pass near the boundary of the 124th and 126th Divisions, Chingkulingmiao and Panchiehho in the 126th Division's sector, and near Hutou in the 135th Division's sector. The most powerful and speediest thrust in the Fifth Army's area was that at Suifenho, where armored columns threatened the Suifenho-Mutanchiang-Harbin railroad and highway, the most important east-west arteries in eastern Manchuria. All divisions of Fifth Army took up previously designated positions to meet the enemy. On the afternoon of the 9th, however, one major disposition change was made when the Fifth Army Commander reinforced the 124th Division front with approximately two infantry battalions from the 135th Division.

In the northern sector, the 134th Division confronted enemy elements pushing along the Sungari River, but was compelled to begin withdrawing from Chiamussu towards Fangcheng.

Border defense units all along the eastern front of Manchuria heroically resisted the enemy's opening onslaught. Each continued to report its situation until communications were severed.

One addition was made to the strength of the First Area Army on the 9th, when the Kwantung Army assigned the 2d Noncommissioned Officer Candidate Unit stationed at Shihtou. Notwithstanding the title of this unit, at this time it consisted only of reserve officer candidates. The unit was organized into two infantry battalions, and one battalion of heavy weapons. Each battalion had approximately 1,000 personnel.

Operations - 10 August

On 10 August, the main force of Third Army continued to check the enemy advance in the Tumen area. In the 128th Division sector north of Third Army the situation was unknown because communications were temporarily out.

In the Fifth Army area the enemy by the evening of the 10th advanced as far as the Hsiachengtzu-Pamientung-Chihsi line, approximately twenty-five miles inside the border. The situation in the sector occupied by the 124th Division along the Suifenho-Mutanchiang road was becoming critical. In view of the enemy's major armored thrust in this sector and the threat it posed to the important east-west arteries, the Fifth Army commander during the evening of the 10th ordered the 126th and 135th Divisions to withdraw their main forces to Yehho, and to leave only small elements in forward areas. The withdrawal began immediately but was hindered by enemy action.

The Army commander reported these withdrawals to General Seiichi Kita, the Area Army Commander, and asked for any reinforcements that could be spared. The only divisions not then engaging the enemy were the 122d and 139th Divisions, but neither of these divisions could be spared: the 122d was rushing to completion the construction of positions in the Lake Chingpo area, and the 139th was at Tunhua, too far away to be brought up in time to be effective.

The only other unit not engaged was the 2d Noncommissioned

Officer Candidate Unit, assigned to the Area Army on the preceding day. Since this unit was the only reservior of reserve officers available to the Kwantung Army in the event of a protracted war, the Area Army Commander hesitated to commit the whole unit for initial operations. The unexpectedly swift advance of the enemy reported by the Fifth Army Commander, however, became such a threat that General Kita decided to assign part of it to Fifth Army. Accordingly, he issued orders assigning one infantry battalion (about 1,000 men), commanded by Major Araki, to Fifth Army. General Kita also visited Fifth Army Headquarters to encourage its commander, Lieutenant General Noritsune Shimizu.

Following General Kita's return to his headquarters at Mutanchiang, he prepared for the scheduled move of First Area Army Headquarters to Tunhua. Leaving some of his staff officers and enlisted personnel at Mutanchiang, he departed for Tunhua, via Lake Chingpo, on the evening of the 10th.

Information from the 134th Division in the north sector of the Area Army's front was meager on the 10th. A report from the Chiamussu signal station, however, confirmed earlier reports that the division was withdrawing to Fangcheng.

Operations - 11 to 14 August

From 11 to 14 August events moved rapidly. Reports to First Area Army Headquarters often were sketchy, and the situation was sometimes obscure. The cause of this is traceable to both the sending and receiving ends. On the one hand, enemy action cut communications with some units; on the other hand, the newly-installed communications center at the new headquarters in Hunhua was not what it should have been.

Enemy pressure continued to be applied in three sectors of the Third Army front. In north Korea the Najin Fortress Garrison Unit and the 101st Mixed Regiment were forced to retreat gradually towards Musan. The large enemy armored column which had crossed the border south of Tungning, in the 128th Division sector, headed for the Third Army boundary and Chientao Province. On the evening of the 13th it reached Mt Laohei (800 meters). Here the enemy tank force supported by infantry divided into two units. The unit going north of the mountain began a fierce attack against 128th Division positions near Lotzukou early the following morning. Colonel Matsuyoshi, commander of the 128th Division's right sector regiment (284th), and his men fought desperately to stem the enemy attack, but by evening it became impossible to hold the positions and the entire division fell back to its second line of defense in the neighborhood of Huapitientzu. From this second defense line the 128th Division fought against a superior enemy from 16 August until hostilities ceased.

While the attack on Lotzukou was taking place on the morning of the 14th, the main body of the 132d Independent Mixed Brigade, which at 1400, 9 August had been ordered to withdraw, arrived at Tachienchang. There it took charge of the 283th Regiment (less one battalion) of the 128th Division stationed there. This combined unit, called the Tachienchang Detachment, took up defense positions in this sector. On the 16th it engaged some hostile tanks sweeping southward from Muleng and routed them.

The other enemy column, proceeding south of Mt Laohei, continued in the direction of Chientao Province in the Third Army sector. In the vicinity of Shihliping the 1st Mobile Brigade attacked the column, repulsing it and inflicting heavy losses. The Third Army's main force, meanwhile, continued to prevent a breakthrough of the Area Army's right flank, the 79th Division holding its positions near Tumen and the 112th Division delaying the enemy in the sector west of Hunchun.

On the Fifth Army front the main body of the enemy armored force, consisting of no less than two divisions, advanced along the Suifenho-Mutanchiang road reaching Muleng on the evening of the 11th. At dawn on the following day it laid down a heavy artillery barrage upon our positions on a plateau west of Muleng. The enemy followed through with an attack that finally broke through the 124th Division's positions, and by the evening the enemy was in front of Motaoshih.

In the vicinity of Motaoshih the Fifth Army Commander on the 11th had deployed the infantry battalion of the 2d Noncommissioned Officers Candidate Unit, commanded by Major Araki, and reinforced it with the Intendance Reserve Officer Candidate Unit. This combined unit, beginning on the 12th, carried out repeated desperate attacks against an enemy tank unit and succeeded in repulsing it.

North of the breakthrough on the 124th Division's defense line, the enemy severely attacked our artillery position near Hsiaotushan on the 13th. A majority of the officers and men, including Colonel Matsumura, commander of the 20th Heavy Field Artillery Regiment, and Colonel Koketsu of the Mutanchiang Heavy Artillery Regiment, died heroically manning their guns. In the evening the position fell into the enemy's hands.

On the evening of the 13th the enemy broke through the Motaoshih position and continued to attack Fifth Army's new position stretching from Yingchitun to an upland south of Hualin via Ssutaoling and 371 Meter Hill. At this time the rear of the Army's operational zone was the Mutanchiang River. General Kita, the Area Army Commander, planned to follow the operational plan and withdraw Fifth Army from its positions east of the River at the appropriate time, its main force to a sector south of Lake Chingpo and an element to Hengtaohotzu. On the evening of the 14th, while he was studying this problem at the headquarters in Tunhua, a telephone report was received by Staff Officer Hiroshi Matsumoto from Staff Officer Akiji Kashiwada of the Fifth Army. The telephone had been inoperative until this time, and Staff Officer Kashiwada summed up the situation since the 12th. He informed Colonel Matsumoto of the enemy breakthrough of the 124th Division's position at Muleng on the 12th, of the enemy attack on the Army's main position near Yehho on the 13th, adding that "today, (the 14th) the enemy overran the 126th Division's main position in the vicinity of Aiho and nearly annihilated the division's artillery." Colonel Kashiwada ended his report by stating that "the commander of the Army and all personnel are now ready to die in the area east of the Mutanchiang River; the fate of the Fifth Army will be decided tonight or tomorrow."

After receiving this report, Colonel Matsumoto asked Colonel Kashiwada to hold the phone, and reported the Fifth Army's situation to General Kita. After some minutes, Colonel Matsumoto resumed the telephone conversation, and transmitted the following instructions from the Area Army Commander:

> Soviet forces have broken through the Manchurian border at several places. The Kwantung Army plans a protracted war, using the mountainous zone around Mt Changpaishan and the Manchuria-Korea border zone as the last redoubt.
>
> The First Area Army plans a long resistance, using the area around Tunhua as the last redoubt.
>
> The Fifth Army will secure positions east of the Mutanchiang River as long as possible, and when the position becomes untenable will gather as many troops as possible and retire to the vicinity of Tunhua or Hengtaohotzu.

These instructions took into account the possibility that enemy pressure might prevent the Fifth Army from withdrawing to Tunhua, and left to the Army Commander's discretion the decision to withdraw, the place to withdraw to, and the timing of the withdrawal.[37]

In the meantime, Area Army Headquarters ordered the 122d Division to haul ammunition, fuel, and other materiel stored in the Hsinglung and Shihtou sectors for the use of units directly assigned to the Area Army, to the rear areas. It also directed the 122d and 139th Divisions to take up their defense positions in the Lake Chingpo and Tunhua areas respectively, the 122d to facilitate the withdrawal of the main force of the Fifth Army, and the 139th to hold the enemy.

The 122d Division, using all available motor transport facilities, did its utmost to carry supplies to the rear, all the time fending off enemy harassing attacks. An element of its engineer unit destroyed two bridges, one at Ningan, and the other across the Mutanchiang River, west of Tungchingcheng.

At the time that one infantry battalion of the 2d Noncommissioned Officer Candidate Unit was assigned to Fifth Army, the remainder of the Unit was assigned to the 122d Division. Commanded by Colonel Komatsu, this unit consisted of one infantry battalion and one battalion of heavy weapons and infantry guns; each battalion had approximately 1,000 reserve officer candidates who although well

---

37. Normally, the Chief of Staff (Major General Ryozo Sakurai) would transmit these instructions. However, since he could not conveniently use the telephone, (he was hard of hearing) he permitted Colonel Matsumoto to transmit them.

trained were not fully equipped. On about 13 August, this unit was detached from the 122d Division and ordered to reinforce the Manchurian troops (three infantry battalions - about 3,000 men) defending the western shore of Lake Chingpo. Just before this "Komatsu unit" reached its assigned position, it encountered an enemy tank force racing down the left bank of the Mutanchiang River. The Manchurian troops fell into confusion and dispersed beyond control.

Estimate of Losses

Japanese losses in the First Area Army are not fully known. There are several reasons for this. The battlefield was extremely wide; we were unable to control the movements of subordinate units; the clearance of battlefields was impossible; no well-prepared reports were preserved for the completion of available records; the Soviets destroyed our army organization immediately after the cessation of hostilities; small-scale battles raged for over a month here and there throughout Manchuria because the ceasefire order could not be relayed to outlying units, and many soldiers deserted their units or otherwise could not be accounted for.

Although exact figures are not available, it is estimated that our losses (dead, wounded, or missing) in men were 15,000 in the Third Army, 20,000 in the Fifth Army, and 5,000 in units directly under the Area Army--for a total of 40,000. Soviet losses were estimated as 10,000 men killed or wounded, and 600 tanks destroyed.

Situation at the End of Hostilities

At the time of the cessation of hostilities the main force of the Third Army was still holding the line of Hoeryong, Tumen, and the heights west of Hunchun, respectively about 50, 40, and 20 miles inside the border. The 128th Division was in the vicinity of Huapitientzu, about 60 miles inside the border. The main force of the Fifth Army, after abandoning its positions near Yehho, was concentrated in the neighborhood of Hengtaohotzu, while the 124th Division was in the vicinity of Tungchingcheng; both these towns are about 100 miles inside the border. The 134th Division was concentrated near Fangcheng. The main body of the 122d Division was holding its positions at Lake Chingpo, and the 139th Division was at Tunhua.

The most hopelessly disorganized of the Area Army forces were the 1st Mobile Brigade and the 112th Division of the Third Army, the 128th Division, all the divisions under the Fifth Army, and in addition those units attached to the divisions mentioned above. Accurate estimates of the combat effectiveness of each unit at the end of the war are not available, but according to rough estimates the Third Army retained about two-thirds of its pre-hostilities combat effectiveness, the 128th Division and the Fifth Army each about one-half, and the 134th Division about two-thirds.[38] The

---

38. Cf combat effectiveness prior to hostilities, page 56.

122d and 139th Divisions retained their original combat effectiveness.

Cease Fire Measures

On 15 August the commander and all personnel of the Area Army Headquarters heard the broadcast of the Imperial Rescript announcing the end of hostilities. They were so stunned that they stood speechless, weeping bitterly at the thought that their negligence of duty as subjects of the Emperor had caused defeat, for which they justly deserved death.

Some members of the staff insisted that the Area Army should continue military operations if the Commander in Chief of the Kwantung Army decided to disregard the Imperial Rescript and fight. On receiving the Kwantung Army cease-fire order, however, the Area Army made every effort to transmit the order to all units under its command, even using planes to drop copies of it.

On the 18th General Sakurai, the Area Army Chief of Staff, went to Kwantung Army Headquarters at Hsinking. After being informed of the Imperial Will, the intention of the Commander in Chief of the Kwantung Army, and the substance of the cease-fire memorandum exchanged between General Hata, Kwantung Army Chief of Staff, and the Soviet Supreme Commander, General Sakurai returned to Tunhua.

At the same time that the Commander of the First Area Army issued the cease-fire order, he issued instructions to burn the colors, important documents, and maps. Despondency filled the soldiers of the Area Army. Lieutenant General Jikizo Nakamura, commander of the 112th Division, and his chief of staff, Colonel Kameji Yasuki, committed suicide. Colonel Watanabe, commander of the Tungning Heavy Artillery Regiment, as well as officers and men of the regiment, blasted themselves to death. Lieutenant Colonel Mitsunori Wakamatsu, Commander of the 3d Mobile Regiment, also killed himself. Many others deserted and after leaving their units acted as they pleased.

The delivery of the cease-fire order to some of the small frontline units was delayed because of the lack of communication or liaison. While the Soviets made repeated protests, small-scale resistance continued at various places even after 20 August. The bulk of the Tungning Detachment died defending its border position, while one of its elements, holding a position south of Sanchakou, offered determined resistance until about 27 August.

Communications with the 134th Division were out since about 11 August because of the breakdown of the division's wireless. On 19 August one of the division's staff officers, Colonel Saito, arrived in Tunhua by airplane and was given a copy of the cease-fire order to take back to Fangcheng.

Negotiations with the Soviet Army and Disarmament

The First Area Army Headquarters prepared for negotiations with the Soviet forces by establishing a liaison agency at Tunhua. The Third and Fifth Armies and each frontline group negotiated and made arrangements for disarmament with the commanders of the respective

Soviet forces confronting them.

On 17 August the commander of the Soviet tank battalion which had raced down the west coast of the Mutanchiang River a few days earlier met Colonel Komatsu, whose 2d Noncommissioned Officer Candidate Unit was then occupying established positions near Lake Chingpo. Asking the colonel not to offer any resistance, the Soviet commander hurriedly led his battalion away towards Kirin without demanding disarmament.

On the 18th the commander of the Soviet division which had entered Tunhua met with General Sakurai, Chief of Staff of the Area Army, to give instructions on disarmament and other matters. The substance of the Soviet commander's instructions was:

> The troops around Tunhua will be disarmed by 1200 hours on the 19th and be bivouacked near the Tunhua airfield.
>
> Officers will be permitted to wear swords. The guards of the headquarters will be authorized to carry rifles and bayonets to maintain peace and order.
>
> Military supplies stored in each depot will be delivered in accordance with instructions to be given by the Soviet officers in charge.
>
> The Area Army shall be permitted to communicate by telephone with the Third and Fifth Armies for several more days.

After that, Soviet units came into Tunhua in a continuous stream from the directions of Mutanchiang and Yenchi, and then proceeded towards Kirin and Hsinking. This coming and going meant so many changes in negotiators that it became extremely difficult for us to execute agreements or to maintain peace and order.

By 19 August the Soviets began moving Japanese forces to concentration points. For the 139th Division and other units under the direct command of the Area Army in the Tunhua area, the concentration point was Shahoyen Airfield, about 16 kilometers north of Tunhua. All lieutenants and enlisted personnel were formed into labor battalions of 1,000 each and marched to Shahoyen where they were bivouacked. During late August and September these battalions were marched to unknown destinations, presumably in Soviet territory. Officers of the grade of captain and higher were temporarily assembled in barracks of the Shahoyen airfield. In mid-October they were marched to the concentration center at Mutanchiang where the main forces of other First Area Army commands were being assembled. During early November the officer units assembled at Mutanchiang as well as the troop labor battalions formed there were transported in a steady stream by train to Soviet territory.

Meanwhile, on 21 August, approximately half of the generals and staff officers of the First Area Army, accompanied by some orderlies, were flown to the Dokhodskoi airfield (about 23 miles northeast of Suifenho) to receive cease-fire orders. They were brought back to Tunhua on the 22d, but on the following day were again sent to Soviet territory by air, this time for interrogation and internment, presumably to Pokrovka (about 20 miles northwest of Voroshilov), where the Soviet Far East Army's advance command post was located.

Civil Affairs

Kwantung Army Headquarters early recognized that in the event of a war with the Soviets it would be responsible for the safety of Japanese residents in Manchuria, including Army dependents, immigrant farmers, and businessmen. During the late spring of 1945, when the build-up of Soviet troop strength in Siberia was being accelerated, it took several steps to assure the safety of Japanese residents.

First Area Army Headquarters, with more than 300,000 Japanese residents in its zone of responsibility, was no less keenly aware of the restrictions on freedom of operational movement that the presence of large numbers of civilians would impose. During the spring it discussed the problem of evacuating non-combatants (to either the Japanese mainland or the interior of Manchuria) with Manchukuoan administrative authorities and with the president of the Manchuria Agriculture Development Company, the latter being responsible for the farmers brought to Manchuria from Japan for agricultural reclamation projects.

The program of evacuating non-combatants had several disadvantages. It would place an additional drain on transportation facilities already taxed by the withdrawal of military supplies to rear areas. The evacuation of Japanese residents from zones in front of military positions would reveal a defensive attitude and perhaps encourage the Soviets to encroach the border. Moreover, it was felt that the evacuation of only the dependents of Army personnel would have an adverse effect upon other Japanese residents.

Speaking for the immigrant farmers, President Saito of the Manchuria Agriculture Development Company, stated that these cultivation groups had no intention of retreating and that they were determined to remain behind and defend their own land in the event of an enemy invasion. Nevertheless, plans for prior evacuation of Japanese residents were drawn up.

Enforcement of the plan, however, was slow. When the enemy invaded Manchuria, his advance was rapid. Japanese residents showed no signs of remaining on their land and began to abandon everything and to rush to the rear areas in search of safety zones. Extreme confusion prevailed.

Since the railroads could be expected to be bombed before long and possibly rendered inoperative, it was imperative that they be used, while still in operation, for only the most urgent purposes. The withdrawal of war supplies to the rear areas was urgent in order to prevent seizure by the enemy and to make possible a prolonged resistance. Nevertheless, the evacuation of Japanese residents could not be disregarded. Consequently the transport of war supplies was suspended and the evacuation of non-combatants was given priority. As many freight trains as possible were placed in operation to evacuate civilians.

Even with this measure, train space was insufficient for transporting all Japanese residents. Those who missed trains began evacuating on foot towards the west and south. Facing hostile enemy plane attacks, being plundered by enemy ground units and hostile Manchurians and Koreans, and suffering from hunger, these people were in wretched condition.

Those who managed to board trains eventually got to Harbin or Hsinking. Assembly areas for other Japanese evacuees were Kirin for those in that vicinity, Chiaoho and Tunhua for those in the Fifth Army's area, Tungchingcheng for those from the areas of the 122d and 128th Divisions, and Tunhua for Japanese residents fleeing from Chiamussu and Mutanchiang; those in the Third Army area assembled in the vicinity of Yenchi.

Those who assembled in the vicinity of Tunhua were accommodated in official houses, hangars, schools, temples, and whatever other places were suitable. During September, however, at the direction of the Soviet Army, they began to move to Kirin or Hsinking. The behavior of the officers and men of the Soviet Army was quite brutal and inhuman at that time. Babies died one after another owing to malnutrition and other diseases.

Relations with agencies of the Manchukuoan government were relatively smooth during this period. The direction of these agencies within the First Area Army's zone of responsibility was in the hands of the army commander in whose area they were located. These agencies cooperated fully with the Army in the maintenance of peace and in preparing for the defense of cities. This applied particularly to the Japanese officials of these organs. After the war's end, they were busily engaged in carrying out negotiations with the Soviet Army, with Manchurians, and with Koreans for the relief of refugees.

On the other hand, relations with the Manchukuoan National Army and with Manchukuoan police deteriorated rapidly. The Manchukuoan troops stationed in the vicinity of Paoching, Mishan, and Poli under the command of the Fifth Army had been engaged in the construction of positions, but upon the outbreak of war they rose in revolt, dispersed, and became bandits. However, those stationed in the vicinity of Mutanchiang and helping the 122d Division construct positions, continued their work in earnest until hostilities were suspended. The efficiency of the work of this group was superior to that of the Japanese Army. Upon the termination of the war, however, they too rose in revolt and became uncontrollable. The Manchukuoan police likewise turned on the Japanese. After the Soviet invasion began, they abruptly changed their attitude, began to despise and resist Japanese, and in general obstructed the activities of Japanese residents.

Most Manchurian and Korean civilians assumed an indifferent attitude toward the Japanese when the invasion began. When the Soviet Army marched into their towns however, they welcomed it by displaying red flags at their houses, and were generally hostile to the Japanese. However, there were not a few Manchurians who secretly entertained goodwill towards the Japanese people.

Most White Russians, fearing Soviet retribution, assumed an indifferent attitude towards the Japanese. There were some, however, who remained friendly and afforded us conveniences of various kinds.

Mohograph No 154-C

CHAPTER VI

The Third Army[39]

Composition of Third Army

The Japanese Third Army which in August 1945 under the command of Lieutenant General Kiesaku Murakami was to bear the brunt (together with Fifth Army) of the Soviet invasion of Manchuria was organized on 13 January 1938, with Headquarters at Mutanchiang. During the entire period of its existence, Third Army was deployed along the vital eastern front of Manchuria, undergoing in the meantime several boundary changes. It moved its headquarters across the river to Yehho when the First Area Army Headquarters was organized on 4 July 1942 as its parent organization. General Murakami assumed command on 22 November 1944.

At the beginning of January 1945 the principal tactical units of Third Army, and their stations, were

111th Division	Suiyang
112th Division	Hunchun
120th Division	Tungning
1st Border Garrison Unit	Sanchakou
2d Border Garrison Unit	Suifenho
9th Border Garrison Unit	Wuchiatzu
11th Border Garrison Unit	Kuanyuehtai
12th Hv Arty Bn (150-mm guns)	Pamientung
13th Hv Arty Bn (150-mm guns)	Pamientung

---

39. The information in this chapter was furnished by Lieutenant Colonel Naotomo Hosokawa, Third Army operations officer.

```
        Mutanchiang Hv Arty Regt (240-mm how)    Hsiachengtzu
        3d Hv Arty Regt (240-mm how)             Hsiachengtzu
        Tungning Hv Arty Regt (240-mm how)       Tungning
        2d Hv Arty Regt (240-mm how)             Acheng
        2d Ind Hv Arty Btry (240-mm how)         Acheng
```

The area of responsibility of the Third Army in the right sector of the First Area Army (the Fifth Army held the left sector) covered the southeastern border provinces of Mutanchiang and Chientao. Its northern boundary ran approximately 10 miles north of Pamientung. Its southern boundary, until September 1944, followed the line of the Manchuria-Korea border but subsequently, because of the gradual manner in which Kwantung Army jurisdiction over north Korea was granted, followed no determinable line.[40]

Except for the 112th Division and the 9th Border Garrison Unit, all of the principal units of Third Army were deployed in the Army's northern sector. The 112th Division and 9th Border Garrison Unit were stationed in the south between Hunchun and Wuchiatzu. The gap between these two forces was manned by small units (from squad to company size) at key defense points along the border. (The 2d Heavy Artillery Regiment and the 2d Independent Heavy Artillery Battery, although assigned to Third Army, were undergoing training at the heavy artillery training center near Acheng in January 1945.)

In February when the southern extension of Third Army's juris-

---

40. See footnote 26, Monograph 154-B.

diction (over the northern part of Hamyong Pukto Province in north Korea) took on added importance, Third Army relinquished the northern segment of its border sector to Fifth Army. Fifth Army's border garrisoning responsibilities were extended correspondingly southward to a point north of Yaoshan, and in conjunction therewith was given control of the units in its new sector—the 111th Division and the 2d and 11th Border Garrison Units.[41] This reduced to two the number of divisions and the number of border garrison units remaining with Third Army.

To replenish Third Army's strength Kwantung Army late in February directed Third Army to organize the 124th, 127th, and 128th Divisions. Although these divisions were built around a nucleus of disbanded units, they consisted principally of recruits, and, therefore, did little to improve the Army's fighting effectiveness. Furthermore, the 124th Division, the first to be organized, was transferred to Fifth Army during March.

Preliminary Operational Planning

At about this time, Third Army Headquarters was informally advised that the delaying plan which the Kwantung Army had shelved at the time of the adoption of the holding plan in September 1944 was being reconsidered in view of adverse developments in the war situation. On the basis of this informal advice, Third Army Headquarters drafted a tentative delaying plan with the following pro-

---

41. The 111th Division remained with Fifth Army only about one month and was then transferred to Korea.

visions:

> Each border garrison unit will firmly hold existing border positions.
>
> The 111th Division will secure the sector north of Suiyang and maintain contact with the right flank of the Fifth Army; heavy guns now in the Acheng and Hsiachengtzu area will be redeployed to the Suiyang area.
>
> An element of the 120th Division will secure the vicinity of Mt Laohei, while the main force of the division will secure positions in the vicinity of Chengtzukou. If isolated by enemy action, the division will hamper the enemy's advance.
>
> The 112th Division will operate independently in the Hunchun sector.

Although the assignment of the 111th and 120th Divisions to Third Army was shortly to be terminated, this tentative plan formed the basis for constructing new defense positions and establishing appropriate line of communications facilities.

The Hsinking Conference

Late in March, when the troop exodus from Manchuria was at its peak, Kwantung Army Headquarters summoned key staff officers of subordinate commands to a conference in Hsinking. The Third Army sent its chief of staff and its operations and logistics chiefs.

The conference was to have a material effect on Third Army's composition and disposition of forces. Kwantung Army Headquarters outlined its new operational plan calling for delaying instead of holding operations, then being prepared for submission to Imperial General Headquarters. To Third Army representatives it issued instructions to the following effect:

> Third Army Headquarters will move from Yehho to Yenchi.
> Third Army's strength will be augmented in the near future by the addition of the 79th Division and other units in Korea presently under Seventeenth Area Army.
> Kwantung Army's limited jurisdiction in north Korea will be extended to the four northern provinces.
> A new Army headquarters will be organized to command the four northern provinces on Third Army's flank, except the northern part of Hamgyong Pukto Province.
> Certain units in Third Army will be transferred; others will be re-deployed.
> Third Army will prepare its own delaying operational plan.

Upon the return of Third Army representatives to Yehho, the effects of the conference began to be felt. Towards the end of March the 120th Division was transferred to south Korea. At the same time, large quantities of guns and ammunition were shipped to the homeland, and in addition all Third Army's 150-mm gun units were transferred to Japan. Of the heavy artillery units the 3d Regiment and the Tungning Regiment (less one battery, which was scheduled for transfer to Fifth Army) were transferred to the Tumen area, arriving there late in April;[42] the Mutanchiang Heavy Artillery Regiment was ordered to move to positions in north Korea, but pending completion

---

42. These two regiments were attached to the 79th Division on 9 August.

of its new positions remained near Hsiachengtzu.⁴³ The 2d Heavy Artillery Regiment and the 2d Independent Heavy Artillery Battery were recalled from Acheng and attached to the 127th Division near Pataohotzu. On 25 April Third Army Headquarters moved to Yenchi, close to the Korea border.

The Final Operational Plan   (See Sketch No 1.)

On the basis of Kwantung Army's instructions relative to the delaying operational plan, Third Army Headquarters mapped out its own plan, integrating portions of its own draft plan previously prepared. The plan contained the following provisions:

> The main force of the Army will be disposed in the sectors on both sides of the Hunchun-Tumen road and will destroy the enemy invading these sectors, and will also secure communications between Manchuria and Korea.
>
> Small elements will be disposed along the border to maintain watch against, and to obstruct, possible enemy action.
>
> The main body will take strong positions along a line running north and south from Hunchun to Unmurei, and from Tumen to Kyodaiho. From this line it will destroy the invading enemy.
>
> With the outbreak of the war the 128th Division and the 132d Independent Mixed Brigade will be placed

---

43. On 18 June, while still at Hsiachengtzu, the Mutanchiang Heavy Artillery Regiment was attached to the Thirty-fourth Army Headquarters (transferred from the China Expeditionary Army to Kwantung Army on 17 June 1945, with station in north Korea.) This regiment did not start to move to its new positions, however, until the war started. On 13 August, while en route, it was annihilated west of Muleng.

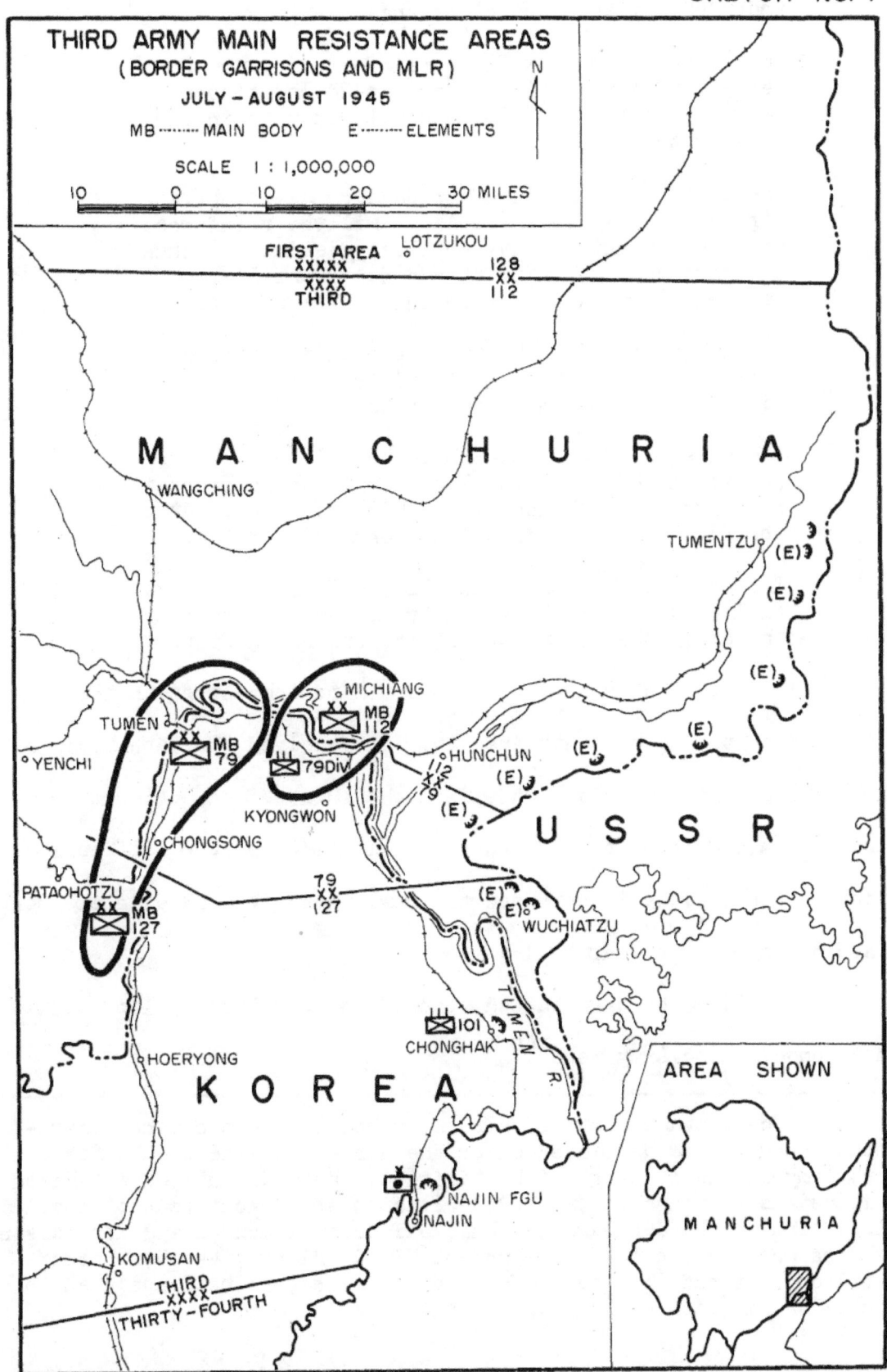

under the direct control of the Area Army.

The 127th Division will be reinforced by the 2d Heavy Artillery Regiment and the 2d Independent Heavy Artillery Battery, and will operate in the Pataohotzu sector.

The 79th Division (less its Cavalry Regiment, assigned directly to Third Army) will be reinforced with the Tungning Heavy Artillery Regiment (minus one battery), and with the 3d Heavy Artillery Regiment, and will operate in the Tumen sector.

The 101st Mixed Regiment and the 112th Division will operate in their assigned sectors, respectively near Chonghak, and Hunchun.

The mission of the 1st Mobile Brigade will be to operate in the sectors along the Tumentzu-Wangching road and the Laoheishan-Wangching road in order to obstruct the enemy invasion along these roads.

The main body of the Najin Fortress Garrison Unit will hold out in the vicinity of Kantoho and deny the enemy the use of Unggi Port and Najin Port.

On 10 June a major augmentation of Third Army strength took place. From the Seventeenth Area Army it received the 79th Division, the Najin Fortress Garrison Unit, and the 101st Mixed Regiment in north Korea, and from the Kwantung Army it received the 1st Mobile Brigade. On 30 July it obtained the newly organized 132d Independent Mixed Brigade. (See Map No 1.)

By the time the war started, therefore, the principal tactical units under Third Army were:[44]

---

44. The 128th was under Third Army only for operational preparations and was to be placed under the direct command of the First Area Army at the outbreak of hostilities, the 132d Independent Mixed Brigade was assigned to the 128th Division at the outbreak of hostilities. The 1st Border Garrison Unit had been disbanded and its personnel assigned to the 132d Independent Mixed Brigade; the 9th Border Garrison Unit had also been disbanded and its personnel assigned to the 127th Division.

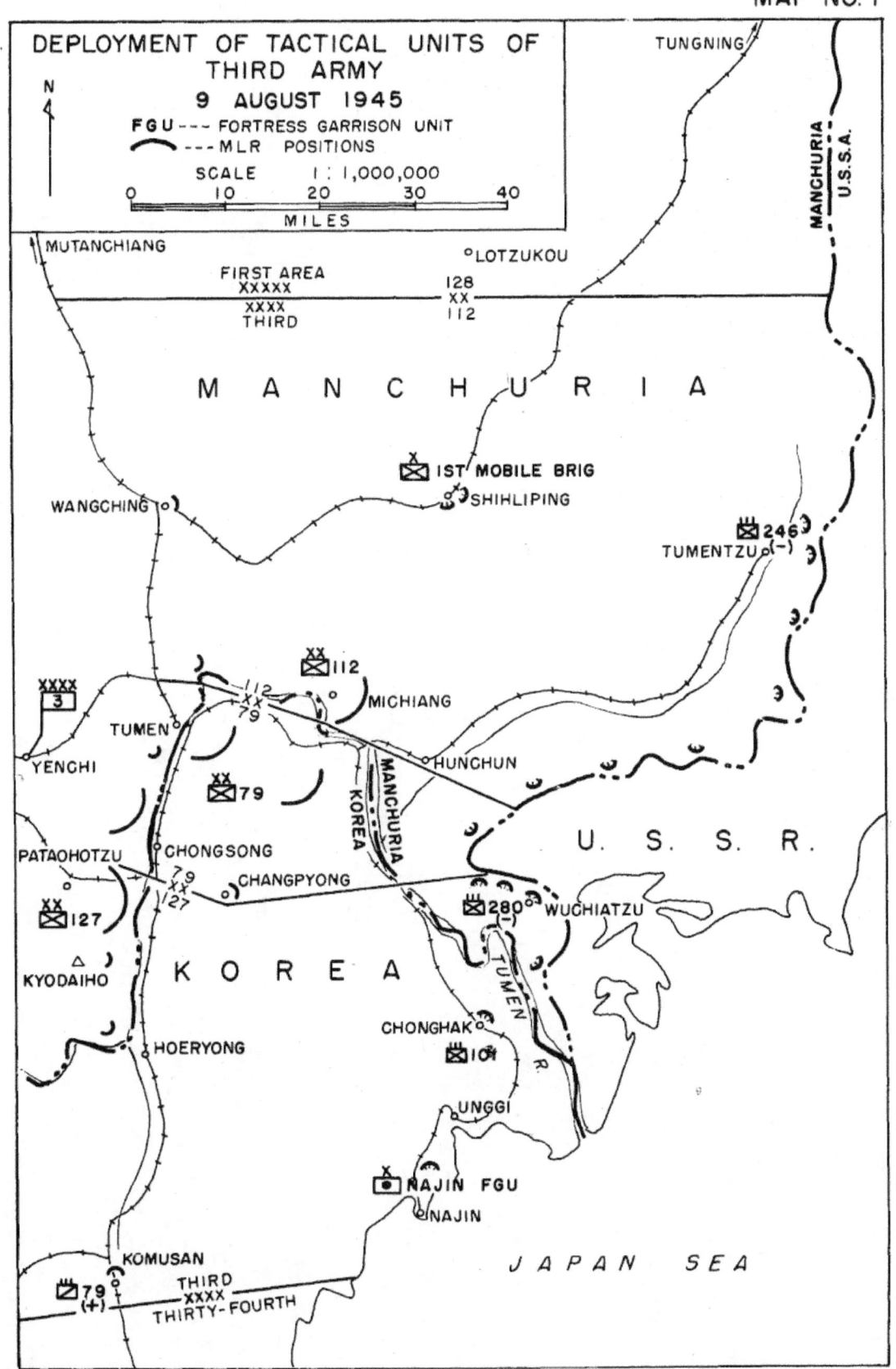

Unit	Commander	Station
79th Division	Lt Gen Teisho Ota	Tumen
112th Division	Lt Gen Jikizo Nakamura	Hunchun
127th Division	Lt Gen Ryutaro Koga	Pataohotzu
128th Division	Lt Gen Yoshishige Mizuhara	Lotzukou
1st Mobile Brig	Col Hideaki Kinoshita	Shihliping
132d Ind Mixed Brig	Maj Gen Goichi Onitake	Tungning
101st Mixed Regt	Col Shizuo Yamanouchi	Chonghak
Najin Fortress Garrison Unit	Lt Gen Kei Seya	Najin

All of these units were of recent origin. On the Third Army's right was the Thirty-fourth Army (with two divisions present and one independent mixed brigade on the way), and on its left was the Fifth Army (with three divisions and one border garrison unit).

In addition, the Third Army had the following separate artillery units, all with weapons of 240-mm:

Unit	Assignment
3d Hv Arty Regt	79th Division
Tungning Hv Arty Regt	79th Division
2d Hv Arty Regt	127th Division
2d Ind Hv Arty Btry	127th Division

Main forces of Third Army units were deployed in rear positions where new fortifications were being constructed. Elements manned border fortifications as follows. The strong points north and south of Tungning were manned by the 132d Independent Mixed Brigade. One company of the 128th Division held positions north of Paitaoshantzu, and one company south. The resistance nests at the border east of Tumentzu were manned by one regiment of the 1st Mobile Brigade. At lookout posts and defense positions south of Tumentzu and in front of Hunchun were two companies of the 112th Division. In the Wuchiatzu-Shuiliufeng sector one regiment (less one battalion) of the 127th Division was in the border zone, and in the Najin coastal area the entire Najin Fortress Garrison Unit consisting of five infantry companies and an artillery regiment was in position. (See Map No 2, Monograph 154-B.)

Construction and Improvement of Defense Installations

The adoption of the delaying plan at the Hsinking conference meant that Third Army's main body would have to be redeployed to the rear, along a new defense line. This in turn meant the construction of new defense positions.

Shortly after the Hsinking conference the Army commander inspected the new defense zones, and ordered each unit to initiate new fortification work as promptly as they could move to the new areas. He also conferred unofficially with commanders of units scheduled to come under his command, and discussed with them the same matter.

In carrying out this work, emphasis was placed on the construction of positions for artillery and other heavy weapons. These were principally caves dug into earth or into natural rocks to offset the anticipated superiority of the enemy in aircraft, artillery, and tanks. This type of heavy construction was hampered, however, because of the shortage of rockdrills and explosives.

To facilitate the construction of defense installations in north Korea, Third Army was given command of the Nanam Divisional District Unit late in April. Early the following month, Headquarters dispatched the staff officer in charge of operations to Nanam to outline the construction work needed in north Korea.

In July First Area Army directed Third Army to prepare defense installations in the vicinity of Antu and Musan where a second line of resistance was to be established. Although these areas were reconnoitered shortly thereafter, not much work had been done by the time hostilities broke out.

Logistical Plan

In April 1945 a new logistical plan was drawn up in accordance with the new operational plan. It called for (1) the evacuation of munitions and materiel accumulated in front line areas and their redistribution based on the new plan, (2) adjustments in the command structure of the supply depots in the Tungning, Hunchun, Chaoyangchuan, and Yenchi sectors, and (3) modifications in the disposition and missions of other zone of communication units.

As a result, new dumps were established at Tachienchang, Huapitientzu, Lotzukou, and Shihliping, principally in support of the 128th Division; these dumps were to be re-supplied by depots in the Tungning sector. Other dumps were established at Chaoyangchuan, Pataohotzu, and Mingyuehkou under the main depots in the Hunchun sector. In addition, stocks of munitions were accumulated at Langchi in the vicinity of which the 1st Mobile Brigade was to conduct operations. (See Sketch No 2 and No 3 for the disposition of depots prior to and after the delaying plan was announced.)

Like tactical units, zone of communication units were transferred

MONOGRAPH NO. 154-C
SKETCH NO. 2

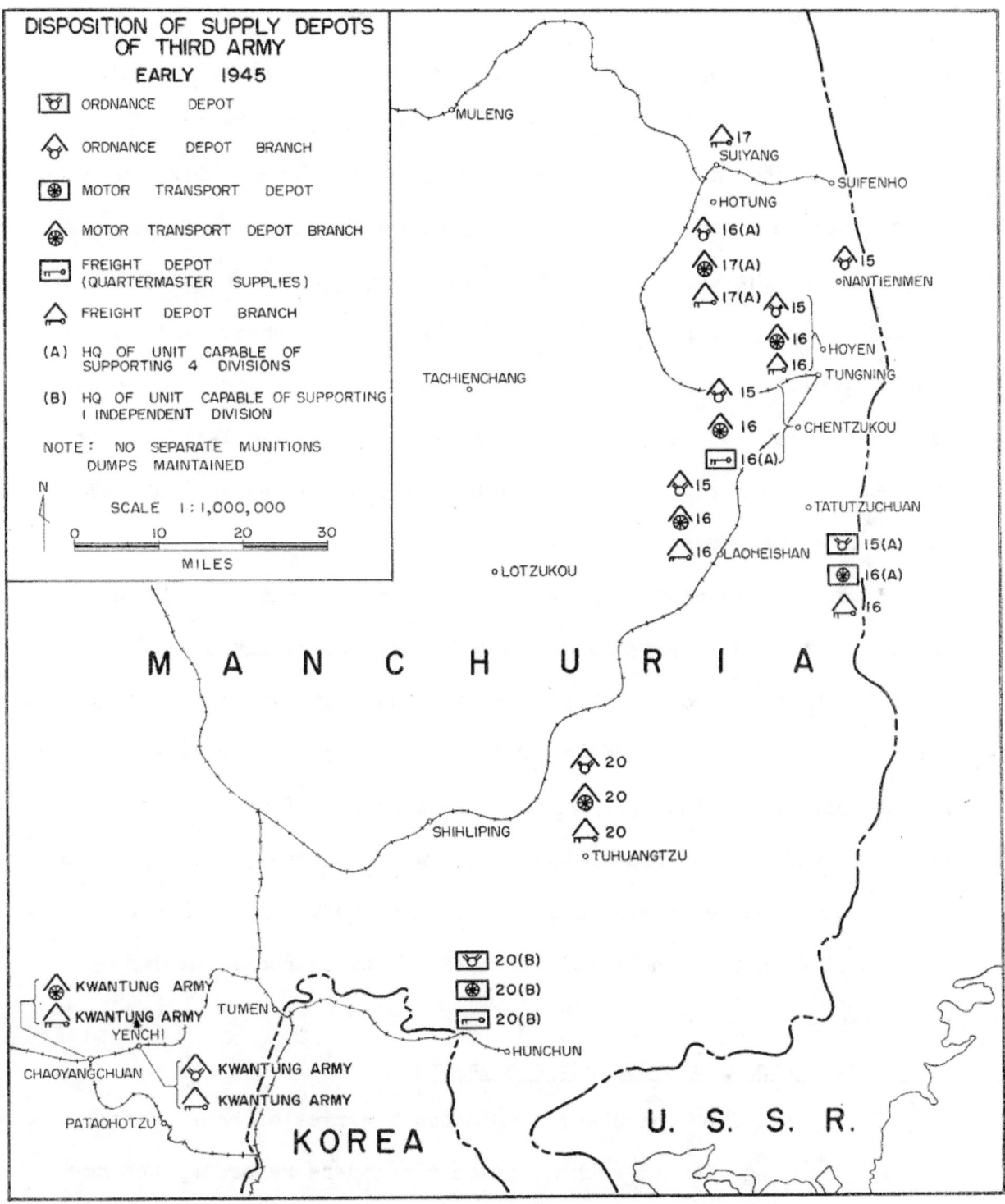

one after another to areas outside of Third Army. Moreover, the large-scale transfer of war supplies to the homeland resulted in acute shortages, especially in motor fuel, and in railway and truck facilities. These shortages were aggravated by a shortage in laborers.

Hampered by these limitations, Third Army had great difficulty establishing new supply dumps. A goal of October was set for the completion of the stockpiling of materials but by the onset of the war only about 50 per cent of the goal had been reached. All tools and equipment in depot machine shops used for making simple weapons such as bayonets and antitank mines were to be removed last. By the outbreak of the war they had not been moved, and almost all of them were deliberately destroyed.

Of all the materiel shortages, those that it was feared would particularly hinder operations were weapons, especially artillery and other heavy weapons, automobile fuel, helmets, and winter clothing. Strenuous efforts were made to compensate for these shortages by local procurement or manufacture. Except for a number of mortars and bayonets, however, no great quantity of weapons were produced. Automotive fuel requirements were barely met by producing an alcohol substitute at each area and also by converting to charcoal-burning engines.

Status of Training and Other Preparations

In May and June Third Army conducted a series of conferences at Nanam, Tumen, and Yenchi with division commanders regarding the new operational plan, with particular emphasis on the Army Commander's view as regards fortifications and training requirements.

During this period training was based on the Kwantung Army Combat Guide. This was a set of rules, issued about June, corresponding to those in the Japan Army manuals but supplemented by experiences gained in the Pacific fighting and by the special training needs of Manchuria. (See Appendix No 5, Monograph No 138.)

Most of the troops in the Third Army at this time were recruits, and their skill in arms was minimal. Basic training was given, but group training could not be carried out effectively since some of the units were in the process of being organized.

New construction lagged behind schedule. Emplacements for artillery pieces and heavy weapons had barely been begun, while the construction of auxiliary structures, such as underground storage dumps and living quarters, had scarcely gone beyond the planning stages. At the beginning of hostilities, therefore, practically no arms, ammunition, or explosives were underground in the new positions.

In some types of weapons, units were almost up to the level of tables of equipment; in others they were seriously short. For example, the authorized and actual weapons of the 127th Division, one of the last to be organized, were:

Weapon	Authorized	Actual
Heavy grenade-launchers (mortar-type)	108	48
Light machineguns	108	81
Heavy machineguns	24	18
Infantry battalion guns (37-mm)	6	6
Infantry regiment guns (75-mm)	4	6
Artillery (75-mm guns and 105-mm how)	36	32

As close as can be determined, the actual strengths of major tactical commands of Third Army just prior to the beginning of hostilities were: (Standard organization of Japanese infantry division may be found in Chart No 3, Monograph No 154-F.)

79th Division	15,633
127th Division	13,130
112th Division	16,218
132d Independent Mixed Brigade	5,545
128th Division	12,634

CHAPTER VII

Third Army Operations

Situation at the Start of the War

Shortly after 0000, 9 August, Lieutenant Colonel Fujimoto, Third Army's chief of intelligence, on night duty in Headquarters Third Army in Yenchi, received a report from a unit in the Wuchiatzu area stating that it was being shelled by the Soviet Army. (The 280th Regiment, less one battalion, of the 127th Division was guarding this area.) He immediately went to the quarters of Lieutenant Colonel Naotomo Hosokawa, operations chief, and told him of the report. Both staff officers then proceeded to the quarters of Major General Hanjiro Iketani, chief of staff, and after informing him of the matter, together returned to Army Headquarters where they took measures to summon all personnel to the office.

Normal procedure required that higher headquarters be given first a report of the incident and second an account of the action taken or planned. Colonel Hosokawa, upon arriving at the Headquarters, promptly telephoned the details of the incident to the First Area Army Headquarters in Mutanchiang, giving the message to the chief of operations, Lieutenant Colonel Hideo Shibo. He then told Colonel Shibo that Third Army intended to order its units to stop all construction work and to assume their battle positions. According to a prearranged plan, this meant that the 79th Division would take up positions near

Tumen, the 112th Division near Hunchun, and the 127th Division near Pataohotzu; border units were not, of course, engaged in any major construction, and since they were under attack were presumably holding their positions and awaiting further orders.

After concluding his report to First Area Army, Colonel Hosokawa notified all Third Army divisions by phone to occupy predesignated positions according to the Army's plan, and to repel the enemy invasion. Shortly thereafter the Commander of the Third Army arrived at his office, and at about 0530 Third Army issued its Operational Order No 1. The salient points of this Order were immediately transmitted by telephone; the complete text was telegraphed later.

Details of the incident were explained personally to the Thirtieth Army commander, chief of staff, and other staff officers. These officers had come to Yenchi the day before to attend a ceremony marking the completion of Headquarters Thirtieth Army's organization, which had been carried out under the supervision of Third Army Headquarters. Immediately after daybreak these officers departed from the Yenchi airdrome bound for their headquarters in Meihokou.

Consolidation of various items of information received from frontline areas revealed that Soviet forces were attacking in force. By 0500 Soviet troops had penetrated the border in the vicinity of Paitaoshantzu where elements of the 128th Division were stationed, and near Tumentzu in the sector manned by one regiment of the 1st Mobile Brigade. Farther south enemy troops, after making a circuit around Shuiliufeng Mountain, at 0200 crossed the Kyonghung Bridge spanning the Tumen River and forced our 9th Casualty Clearing Unit to evacuate towards Hoeryong. Communications with the 280th Regiment in the Wuchiatzu area had been interrupted since receipt of the first report of hostilities and the situation thereafter in that sector was never clear.

By the evening of the 9th no further word had been received from the Pataoshantzu area. On the Tumentzu front the enemy was making a frontal attack against our positions. In front of Hunchun where two companies of the 112th Division were manning border defenses, he was advancing slowly. The enemy force that marched across the Tumen River bridge near Kyonghung was moving towards either Hoeryong or Unggi, it was not clear which. However, on the probability that he was headed for the coast, it was estimated that he was going in the direction of Unggi to take that port. On the evening of the 9th, the 79th Reconnaissance Regiment,[45] which had just arrived in the vicinity of Komusan, was ordered to reconnoiter the movements of the Soviet force in the Kyonghung and Agochi areas on the theory that if headed for the port of Unggi the Soviet force would have to pass near those towns.

---

45. Normal strength of a reconnaissance regiment was 689. It consisted of a headquarters (144 personnel), two mobile infantry companies (168 each), two reconnaissance armored car companies (52 each), and one motor transport company (105).

On the night of the 9th, Third Army Headquarters dispatched three raiding parties with the mission of blowing up railroads in Soviet territory.[46] Each raiding party, whose members were well trained and well briefed for their mission, consisted of from five to ten men and one radio set. Also during the night, hostile planes flew to Yenchi and dropped bombs but did not cause serious damage.

Situation from 10 to 13 August

In view of the enemy's air raid on Yenchi, Army Headquarters decided on the 10th to establish an alternate command post at the Army Officers Club of Yenchi. Beginning at noon all key sections began transferring personnel to the Club. Meanwhile, the 112th Division Headquarters, which had been in Hunchun, moved to Michiang.

Reports from the front indicated that the Soviet Army had broken through the vicinity of Laoheishan. In the Tumentzu sector our troops were withdrawing. Late in the day, Hunchun, about ten miles inside the border, fell into the enemy's hands. Along the coast of northern Korea, Chongjin was subjected to enemy naval bombardment and air attack.

On the 11th, Army Headquarters intercepted London and New Delhi broadcasts announcing Japan's unconditional surrender but dismissed the report as false propaganda, and continued hostilities.

---

46. Presumably the trans-Sibierian stem from Razdolnoye to Posyet Bay.

The main body of the infantry regiment of the 1st Mobile Brigade on the Tumentzu front reported that it was beginning to retreat to Shihliping. In the Hunchun sector the enemy infantry division supported by a tank brigade that had entered the city the preceding day began advancing toward 112th Division positions near Michiang. An artillery unit of the 112th Division engaged several hostile tanks leading the advance, and destroyed them. This action raised the morale of our men.

In the Unggi area, elements of the Soviet infantry division and tank brigade that had crossed the Kyonghung Bridge on the 9th, reached Unggiryong, pushing back elements of the 101st Mixed Regiment and heading for the commercial port of Unggi. From reports received from the area, Army Headquarters estimated that a sizable enemy mechanized unit was passing through this coastal valley.

Between 1000 and 1100 hours of the 11th, a Soviet amphibious battalion began an assault landing at Najin, the naval base directly south of Unggi.[47] The Najin Fortress Garrison Unit offered slight resistance to the attackers and then began to retreat south along the coast towards Chongjin, another commercial port. The situation in that area was not clear thereafter.

---

47. On 13 August a Soviet force (about division size) carried out an assault landing at the commercial port of Chongjin in the Thirty-fourth Army's area. These were the only two amphibious assaults or landings carried out by Soviet forces.

reports to Army Headquarters dwindled. The Army Commander dispatched Colonel Hosokawa, his operations chief, to the 112th Division's sector to survey the situation in front of Michiang. The 112th Division Commander, Lieutenant General Jikizo Nakamura, asked Colonel Hosokawa how much resistance the division should offer at the battle line, then in front of Michiang, adding that if the division offered stubborn resistance at that line it would be in a weaker position to offer organized resistance later at the Tumen line. Colonel Hosokawa, considering the over-all trend of the Army's situation and the conditions prevailing in the division's area, replied that the division should offer the utmost resistance at its present battle line.

On the 13th, Army Headquarters received a report that the enemy tank unit with "about 300 tanks"[48] that had penetrated to the rear of Hunchun was turning north towards the mountainous area. Also on the 13th, in the evening, the commander of the 3d Regiment of the 1st Mobile Brigade, Lieutenant Colonel Wakamatsu, returning from Kirin stopped briefly at Army Headquarters before proceeding to Wangching, where the main body of his regiment was then located.

Situation from 14 to 16 August

Army Headquarters estimated that enemy pressure on Tumen would be relatively small compared with the powerful hostile effort being

---

48. This number appears to be an exaggeration, since only one enemy tank brigade (about 140 tanks) was in the area.

made in the Chongjin area. A hasty study was made of a plan to send the main force of the 127th Division plus an element of the 79th Division to the Najin area to intercept the enemy. However, in view of the fact that no definite estimate of the enemy strength in that area had been made and considering reports that hostile tanks were converging on the Wangching area from both the north and east this plan was cancelled. Instead, Army Headquarters took measures to cope with the threat to Wangching, located some twenty-five miles northeast of Army Headquarters at Yenchi: it directed the 79th Division Commander to send one artillery battery to reinforce his infantry company in the Chiulungping area about half-way to Wangching; it asked First Area Army Headquarters to furnish reconnaissance planes to reconnoiter the movements of the enemy advancing along the defile from Paitaoshantzu, Laoheishan, to Wangching, and also of the enemy force in the Najin area,[49] (only the Paitaoshantzu area was actually reconnoitered); and it directed zone of communication units to improvise antitank mines for use against enemy tanks threatening the area.

---

49. Third Army had no tactical air support, and only rarely had the use of a reconnaissance plane. Kwantung Army had only 360 tactical planes (225 fighters, 40 bombers, 45 reconnaissance planes, and 20 assault aircraft) and about 640 training planes. For the entire First Area Army on the eastern front only two planes (reconnaissance) were provided, but no assault aircraft. A direct support air unit with ten training planes was organized at Tunhua (First Area Army Headquarters) on 12 August, but it was never used. During hostilities the 2d Air Army devoted its main efforts to attacking the enemy invading from Outer Mongolia.

Beginning on the morning of 15 August, enemy air activity against Army Headquarters became very intense. Meanwhile, the Army Commander and several staff officers departed via Pataohotzu to inspect the defenses in the Hoeryong area, towards which the 101st Regiment was retreating from the Chonghak sector.

At noon, while at Headquarters of the 127th Division in Pataohotzu, General Murakami and staff officers accompanying him heard the Emperor's broadcast concerning the termination of the war. Opinion was divided as to the truth of the broadcast and, after a brief discussion it was decided to continue military operations according to existing instructions until a formal cessation order was received.

A formal order directing that all active resistance be stopped but that self-defense measures should be taken when necessary arrived that night from First Area Army Headquarters. Simultaneously, a report was received from the 1st Mobile Brigade stating that its positions in the Wangching area, about 25 miles northeast of Army Headquarters at Yenchi, were under attack by a sizable Soviet tank force. Hastily, a counterattack force consisting of about two infantry battalions of the 127th Division was formed and directed to proceed to Wangching along the Yenchi-Chiulungping road to meet the enemy tanks.

On 16 August the enemy tanks broke out of Wangching in two columns, both converging on Yenchi, one via Chiulungping, the other via Tumen. As a result of this breakout, there was great confusion in the area between Wangching and Hunchun as fighting raged for the positions of the 112th Divisions. The vanguard of hostile tanks proceeding south on the Wangching-Chiulungping-Yenchi road made its appearance in the Chiulungping sector where one infantry company of the 79th Division was awaiting the arrival of a supporting artillery battery. The counterattack force of the 127th Division ordered to this sector, meanwhile, had started out in trucks provided by the 113th Independent Motor Transport Battalion bound initially for Yenchi; it arrived at Yenchi about noon but because of the end of hostilities did not continue to Chiulungping.

In the afternoon a report was received that enemy tanks from Wangching had arrived in the vicinity of Tumen. This brought the double threat to Army Headquarters to within 15 miles, and also posed an immediate threat to the 79th Division's rear. To cope with it Army Headquarters, utilizing locally available troops, organized one force to cover the road approaches to Yenchi from Chiulungping, another to cover the road approaches from Tumen, and a third (composed of Army Headquarters guards) to protect Yenchi itself; meanwhile, the 79th Division Headquarters organized its own headquarters guards into a special force for the defense of Tumen. By the time fighting stopped one enemy armored column had reached Chiulungping and the other was on the outskirts of Tumen.

Summary of Movements and Disposition
of Zone of Communication Units

The 113th Independent Motor Transport Battalion had been stationed in Yenchi since the beginning of its organization late in April as Third Army's temporary transport battalion. At the beginning of August, when its organization was completed, it was transferred to the Chaoyangchuan and Yenchi sectors where it took charge of the new supply accumulation operations and of maintaining daily supply to those sectors. It was this unit that on the night of 15 August was given the special mission of rushing elements of the 127th Division to Yenchi.

The 52d Independent Transport (packhorse) Battalion, with headquarters at Tatutzuchuan and one platoon (about fifty men) each at Shihliping, Tumen, Chaoyangchuan, and Yenchi, was in charge of supply and transportation operations in these sectors. At the outbreak of the war each platoon was placed under the operational control of the local tactical unit.

The 69th Independent Transport Company was stationed in Laoheishan and was charged principally with transporting timber from Suwonshan to Laoheishan for use in constructing under ground pass ways of supply depots. With the outbreak of the war it worked with the 128th Division.

The 77th and 79th Zone of Communications Duty Companies, stationed respectively at Chengtzukou and Laoheishan, were in charge of guarding the supply depot in their respective areas.

The 46th Field Road Construction Unit, its main body at Tungning and an element in Yenchi, was responsible for constructing and repairing roads in their respective areas. An element of this unit was formed into close-quarter combat squads on 16 August and sent out to locate and destroy hostile tanks invading from the direction of Wangching-Chiulungping.

The 84th Land Duty Company, stationed near Tuhuangtzu, guarded the branch supply depots there; one element of this company was assigned to guard the new dumps in Mingyuehkou. The 95th Land Duty Company at Laoheishan guarded the supply depot located in that vicinity, and also helped in loading timber. The 32d Construction Duty Company was responsible for constructing barracks and reconstructing warehouses for the supply depots in the Yenchi and Chaoyangchuan areas.

The 13th Zone of Communication Medical Unit Headquarters, stationed in Mutanchiang, administered hospitalization in that area. The 97th Zone of Communications Hospital had been divided in the spring of 1945, half going under the command of the Haicheng Army Hospital in southern Manchuria, and the other half under the Ningan Army Hospital which was directly under the First Area Army.

The 9th Casualty Clearing Unit stationed in the vicinity of Agochi in northern Korea, although a medical unit, was given the duty of transporting supplies daily for the regiment (less one battalion) of the 127th Division that was guarding the border near Wuchiatzu. At the outbreak of the war this unit was attached to the Wuchiatzu unit.

Of the Army hospitals near Tungning, the 1st had been moved in May 1945 to Lungching, and after the outbreak of war was sent to Yenchi. The 2d remained in its station at Langtungkou at the outbreak of war in support of the 132d Independent Mixed Brigade. The 3d, stationed in the Chengtzukou area, at the outbreak of the war furnished hospitalization service to the 128th Division. The Laoheishan Army Hospital established a dispensary at Changchiatien; after the war started both the hospital and dispensary serviced the 128th Division. The Hunchun Army hospital was annexed to the Yenchi Army Hospital. The Tumentzu Army Hospital supported the 112th Division.

The 15th Veterinary Quarantine Station at Shentung was preparing to move to either Mingyuehkou or Lungching when the war broke out. It remained at Shentung, however, in support of the 128th Division.

The Cessation of Hostilities

Shortly after midnight of 16-17 August a second order relating to ending hostilities was received from First Area Army. This directed that all hostilities be stopped. At daybreak General Murakami sent his intelligence chief, Lt Col Fujimoto, to Chiulungping to notify the Soviet tank battalion commander there of the end of hostilities. At the same time he directed all divisions under his command to stop all fighting.

At about 1600 hours the Soviet tank battalion commander arrived at the Army Officers Club in Yenchi and conferred with Major General Hanjiro Iketani, the Army Chief of Staff. On the following day General Iketani went to Wangching to conduct armistice negotiations. There, General Chushchakov, commander of the Soviet 25th Army and senior Soviet commander in the area, issued disarmament instructions to the following effect:

> By noon of 19 August the Army must be completely disarmed; arms will be piled in the Hunchun, Tumen, and Yenchi areas. Officers will be permitted to carry swords.
>
> Officers holding positions higher than that of regimental commander will assemble in the Army Headquarters at Yenchi.

Pursuant to the Soviet commander's directions, Army Headquarters at about 2300 hours sent one officer to the 79th Division and another to the 112th Division to transmit Soviet disarmament instructions.

On 19 August General Kita, the First Area Army Commander arrived in Yenchi from Tunhua to see the Soviet 25th Army Commander. But since a meeting could not be arranged, he paid his respects to General Murakami and then returned to Tunhua.

For the next few days disarmament procedures were gradually carried out. On the 20th the building which housed Third Army Headquarters was turned over to the Soviet Army. On the 21st all officers (except generals) and men in Yenchi were interned in the barracks in the compound formerly occupied by the 281st Infantry Regiment (127th Division). On the next day, all noncommissioned officers and men (except orderlies) were separated from officers and organized into labor battalions; at a later date they were removed from Yenchi, presumably to the USSR.

On the 24th, with fighting still raging in areas with which there was no communication, the Soviet Commander requested that liaison officers be sent to those areas. Accordingly Third Army Headquarters sent its logistical chief, Lieutenant Colonel Kono, to Kachidoki-yama, south of Sanchakou in the Tungning area, to deliver cease fire orders to Japanese forces there. It sent Colonel Hosokawa, operations chief, on a similar mission to the 1st Mobile Brigade still holding out north of Wangching.

Officers were detained in Yenchi until 3 November when about 50 per cent departed Yenchi for internment in camps at Rada in Tambov Oblast, southeast of Moscow. About two weeks later the rest of the officers followed.

Civil Affairs

After the end of hostilities about 16,000 of the 32,000 Japanese in Chientao Province began to assemble in Yenchi city. Of the 16,000, about 11,000 were commercial residents (mostly employees of municipal offices, or of the Manchurian Railroad Company), and about 5,000 were personnel connected with the Army (dependents of military personnel and of civilian personnel, and female civilian employees attached to the Army. Male civilian employees of the Army were regarded as prisoners of war by the Soviets and were interned).

Providing shelter for the 16,000 Japanese in Yenchi developed into a major problem. On the evening of 17 August, in view of the threatening attitude of the natives, especially of the Koreans, all personnel connected with the Army were moved to the Army camp in Yenchi. Commercial residents remained in official residences or in company houses except that the overflow was housed in the Army camp.

With refugees from the border districts continuing to pour into Yenchi, the problem of sheltering all Japanese was aggravated. On the 18th the problem was discussed at Army Headquarters with Vice Provincial Governor Nishio of Chientao Province and Provincial Councillor Hattori. Since it was the responsibility of the Province to care for all Japanese not directly connected with the Army, they decided to house the overflow of commercial residents in the Japanese primary schools and in the local prison. Even with this expediency, however, some of the commercial residents had to remain in the Army camp. On 20 August military dependents were moved to a separate area of the Army camp and occupied the barracks formerly used by the 281st Infantry Regiment; on the 21st, as noted above, officers, male civilian employees of the Army, and local troops, were interned in the same compound but in spearate buildings.

Because of the general decline of nutritional standards and the abrupt change in living conditions the sick rate rose sharply among both the commercial residents and military-attached personnel. Particularly prevalent were acute cases of pneumonia and diphtheria; most children under five years of age were suffering from one of these diseases. Among the dependents of the military personnel and civilian employees, whose sanitary facilities were comparatively good, deaths among their children numbered 500 or thereabouts. Japanese commercial residents who became ill could not receive satisfactory medical treatment because of the lack of medicinal supplies and equipment, and those that consulted native physicians were charged exorbitant fees. Many died of unidentified diseases.

Beginning late in September, shortages of food, winter clothing, fuel, and other necessities of life began to be felt. At about this time, Soviet officers visited the army barracks and made a list of dependents, including name, age, permanent address, and relatives. Soon afterwards, military-attached personnel were moved to the German church in Yenchi. In the middle of October some dependents were again moved, this time to the Kempeitai buildings or to the municipal office buildings. About ten medical officers and three intendant (supply and finance) officers were given permission to accompany the Army dependents and civilian employees in their new quarters.

Early in October the plight of the commercial residents worsened, and the number who became day laborers or street peddlers gradually increased. Among the young girls those who cropped their hair or dressed like men increased in number. A dance hall was opened in the city through arrangement with the Soviet Army, and several women worked there ostensibly as dancers. These women often visited the dependents of Army personnel in efforts to persuade the young girls to become "dancers."

By mid-October the lives of even the dependents reached bottom. To make ends meet some parted with their last valuable possessions, including such items as clothing. Some began to look for odd jobs; some took to rolling cigarettes. All were faced with the serious problem of earning a living.

As for the natives, at first both Manchurians and Koreans showed bitter resentment and antipathy towards the Japanese. The Manchurians, however, later showed a gradual softening of their attitude towards us. The Koreans, on the other hand, continued to bear malice, particularly the members of the Korea Youth League who under the influence of the Russians oppressed the Japanese. Meanwhile, between the Manchurians and Koreans there developed increasing signs of animosity.

Monograph No 154-D

CHAPTER VIII

The 79th Division[50]

Origin of the 79th Division

To trace the origin of the 79th Infantry Division, one must go back to the 19th Infantry Division of Japan's Korea Army. On 22 November 1944 Imperial General Headquarters directed the 19th Division, stationed in Nanam, to prepare for movement to a southern theater of operations; in December the division left the continent for the Philippines. To replace it, the 19th Depot (Training) Division was organized in Korea shortly thereafter with personnel furnished largely by the 2d Divisional District.[51] In February 1945 the Korea Army was reorganized into the Seventeenth Area Army (responsible for operational preparations) and the Korea Administrative District Army (responsible for maintaining peace and order). The 19th Depot Division, as a training unit, was assigned to the latter.

On 10 March 1945, on orders from Imperial General Headquarters, the 19th Depot Division was reorganized into the 79th Division at

---

50. No monograph on 112th Division operations has been prepared. As the left flank of the 79th Division, however, its role was closely related to that of the 79th, and a considerable amount of data on the 112th Division is contained in this section, which was prepared by Colonel Takaharu Shinabe, former chief of staff, 79th Division.

51. The 2d Divisional District was a geographical area centering around Sendai, Japan, responsible for furnishing personnel to the 19th Division (and also to the 2d Division).

110

full T/O strength. About 35 per cent of its personnel were regulars, about 50 per cent reservists, and the remaining 15 per cent Korean recruits. Like its predecessor, the 79th Division was stationed at Nanam near the east coast of north Korea. During the five months of its existence before hostilities began it was given missions primarily of organizing other units and constructing fortifications.

On 20 April the 79th Division was directed to organize the Nanam Divisional District Unit and, in addition, to furnish approximately 500 personnel to the Taegu Divisional District Unit.[52] The Nanam Unit trained recruits for the 79th Division, and in this respect took over some of the functions formerly performed by the 19th Depot Division. The mission of organizing the Nanam Divisional District Unit was the forerunner of similar missions that were to be assigned to the 79th Division.

Third Army Commander Announces New Plan

On 1 May 1945 Lieutenant General Keisaku Murakami, Third Army Commander, accompanied by several of his staff officers, arrived at the hot springs resort of Chuuronbo, about 8 kilometers south of Nanam. There he called together the commanders and chief of

---

52. There were three other such units in Korea: the Kwangju, the Seoul, and the Pyongyang Divisional District Units. Each of these units, consisting of 10,000 personnel, was given the missions of maintaining peace and order and of training recruits for tactical units.

staff of the 79th Division, the Nanam Divisional District Unit (then being organized), and the Najin Fortress Garrison Unit, as well as the commander of the 101st Mixed Regiment.

Since at this time none of these units was under the command of Third Army, General Murakami conducted the conference informally and unofficially. He outlined the delaying operational plan newly adopted by the Kwantung Army and in conjunction therewith announced that each of the units represented at the conference was scheduled to come under Third Army's control. He explained the details of Third Army's operational plan and outlined what he regarded as the essentials of the defensive disposition of units in Hamyong Pukto Province. In this connection he advised the 79th Division that at a subsequent date it was to move farther north and take up positions immediately south of the Korea-Manchuria border where it would be called upon to begin extensive fortification construction for Third Army and also to assist the Nanam Divisional District Unit in its fortification work. Although this was merely advance information of future action, for all practical purposes these units came under the jurisdiction of Third Army at this time. Instructions took the form of requests rather than orders. Meanwhile, the 79th Division would continue to receive orders from the Seventeenth Area Army.

Instructions were not long in coming. In late May, Third Army sent an urgent request for an engineer construction unit to assist the 127th Division in its fortification work near Pataohotzu for about one month. The 79th Division quickly organized a unit of about 200 men selected from its infantry regiments and dispatched it to Tumen.

On 18 May the 79th Division was directed by Seventeenth Area Army to organize the 20th Independent Mountain Artillery Regiment. At this time it was still organizing the Nanam Divisional District Unit, and assigned the work of organizing the new artillery unit to the 79th Mountain Artillery Regiment. The formation of these units was carried out promptly. Each unit was fully equipped, and the condition of equipment was generally good.

Early in April, meanwhile, all units under the division had moved to training areas for one month's training. They returned in mid-May. In June, all units again went to the camping site for an additional three week's training. But orders received by Headquarters caused it to suspend this training and to direct the return all troops to their regular stations to prepare for the movement north. Elements and units of the 79th Division at this time were:

    289th Infantry Regiment
    290th Infantry Regiment
    291st Infantry Regiment
    79th Mountain Artillery Regiment
      (two battalions of 75-mm guns)
    79th (horse) Cavalry Regiment
    79th Engineer Regiment
    79th Transport Regiment
    Division Signal Unit
    Division Ordnance Duty Unit
    Gas Control Unit
    Veterinary Depot (Hospital)

All these elements were stationed in Nanam except the 290th Infantry Regiment and the 79th Engineer Regiment which were in Hoeryong, and the 79th Transport Regiment which was in Kyongsong, 4 kilometers south of Nanam. (The Transport Regiment was moved to Nanam after the organization of the Nanam Divisional District Unit was completed.)

Organization of Division into Engineer Sector Units

As explained by General Murakami, the area in which the 79th Division was to undertake fortification construction projects was divided into four sectors. The size of the projects made it clear that almost the entire division would have to be used in this work.

As a first step the division late in May formed a Fortification Headquarters. Headed by the chief of staff, it consisted of the commanders of the Engineer Regiment and the 1st Mountain Artillery Battalion, members of each special staff section of division headquarters, and other officers. The Fortification Headquarters was responsible for directing the entire fortification work of the division, and for collecting and distributing equipment, materials, as well as for supplying weapons, ammunition, and provisions to each position. It established itself in Tumen, which subsequently was to become the site of the division's headquarters.

Next to be formed was an engineer construction unit for each of the four sectors. Upon being formed, these units immediately dispatched necessary officers to the scene where the unit was to work, with instructions to make full preparations, and also to assume the duties of the former engineer unit there. At about this time the division was given advance notice that it would be required to furnish a detachment of troops for the Komusan area, on the Army's extreme right. (The composition and location of these sector units and the Komusan Detachment are shown in Chart No 1.)

As part of the project, the construction of a number of artillery positions was allotted to each sector. This work was to be directed by the commander of the 79th Mountain Artillery Regiment whose headquarters was at Tonggwan. To handle signal communications, the division signal unit was to be stationed in Tumen near division headquarters, and was to maintain wireless telegraph contact with Sector A, C, and D, and telephone contact with Sector B. To handle transportation the main body of the Transport Regiment was also to be stationed in Tumen; its commander was to exercise general control over transportation between Fortification Headquarters and the supply base of each sector. To each sector was attached an ordnance duty unit principally to repair equipment.

While making preparations for the move, the 79th Division received orders assigning it officially to Third Army effective at 0000, 10 June.

Before the move began, Third Army formally ordered the division

Monograph No 154-D
Chart No 1

Construction Sector Units
79th Division

Sector	Components	Comdr	Area of Responsibility	Headquarters	Supply Base
A	291st Regt (-3d Bn) 6th Btry, 79th Mt Arty Regt Main Body, 2d Engr Co One-third, 2d Trans Co 2 Squads, Div Sig Unit Gas Control Unit	C.O. 291st Regt	Unmurei, Getsumeisan, and Hunyung areas	Kyongwon	Kyongwon
B	289th Regt 1st Mt Arty Bn (-2d Btry) Main Body, 1st Engr Co	C.O. 289th Regt	High ground south of Namyang and south-west of Tumen	Namyang	Tumen and Pungni
C	1st Bn, 290th Regt 2d Btry, 79th Mt Arty Regt	C.O. 290th Regt	Changpyong area	Chongsong	Tonggwan
D	290th Regt (-1st Bn) 2d Bn (-4th and 6th Btries), 79th Mt Arty Regt One-half, Ammo train, Arty Regt Main Body, 3d Engr Co One-third, 3d Transport Co	C.O. 290th Regt	Samdongdong area and high ground near Hujipyong	Chongsong	Tonggwan
Komusan Det	79th Cavalry Regt 3d Bn, 291st Regt 4th Btry, 79th Mt Arty Regt One Platoon (60 men), 79th Engr Regt	C.O. 79th Regt	Komusan area	Komusan	Komusan

116

to send a detachment of troops to Komusan. Although the Komusan area was a considerable distance from the new positions of the division, the Komusan Detachment was to remain under divisional control; at the outbreak of hostilities, however, it was to be attached directly to Third Army.

Movement to the sectors by the main body of each unit began in late June, and was carried out under the code name of Maneuver No 11. According to plan, the Komusan Detachment began the move at the same time as the rest of the division; at the appropriate time, it left the convoy and proceeded to Komusan. Part of the division headquarters and some personnel of each divisional unit remained at Nanam to help organize and supply the newly activated 137th Division and other smaller units. In addition, a small number of personnel of the 290th Regiment and the 79th Engineer Regiment remained at Hoeryong.

In moving to the construction area, the normal amount of ammunition was taken, except that the transport regiment took only half its normal load. Arrangements were made to store a two-month supply of provisions at each supply base and at each engineer sector unit. All men wore summer uniforms; winter uniforms were stored in Hoeryong. All units reached their respective sectors in early July. (See Map No 1.)

Upon arriving at its new area in north Korea, the division occupied positions already begun by the 127th Division, and resumed the construction work in those positions. Once the move was com-

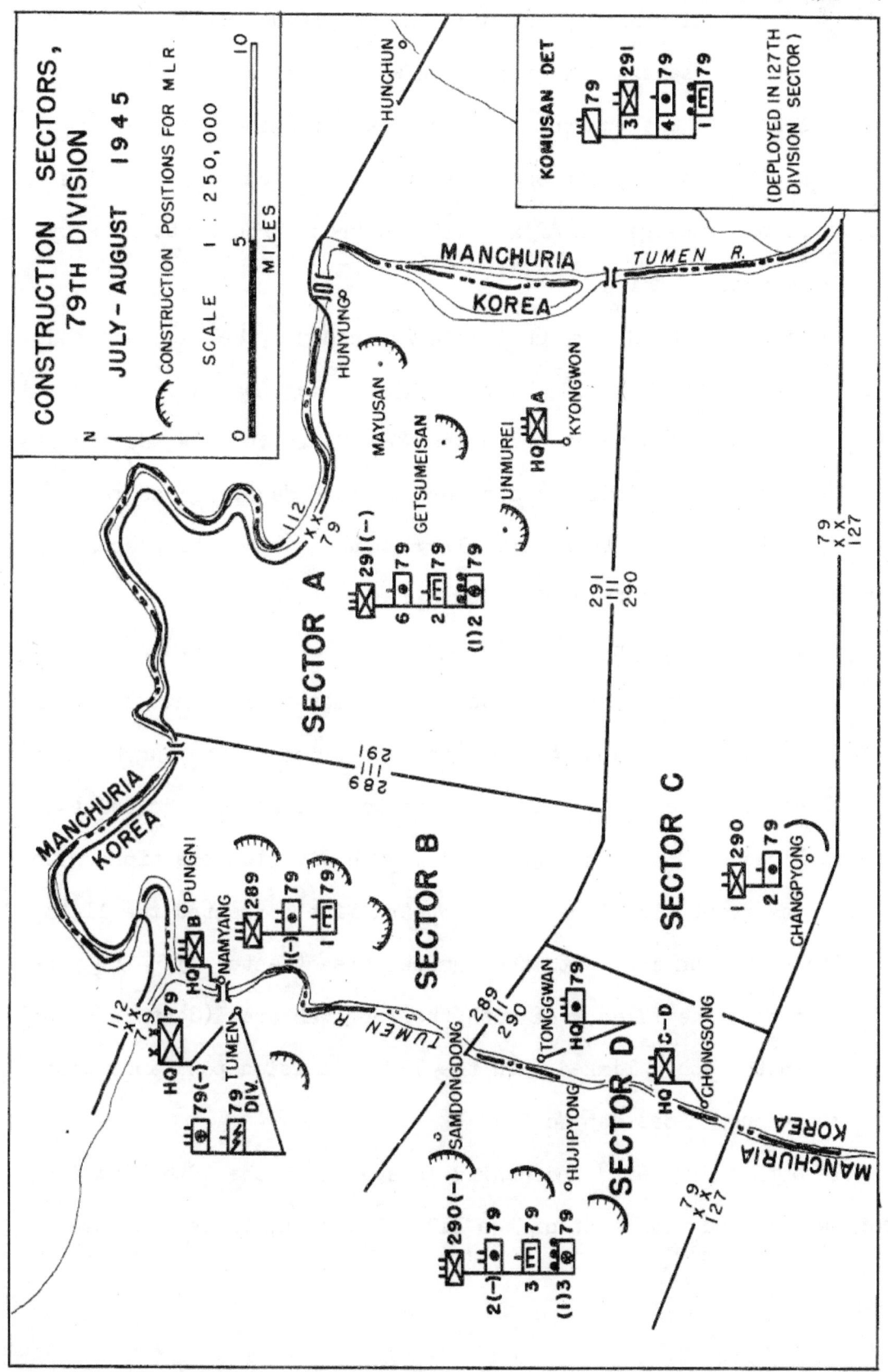

pleted, no radical changes were made in the planned disposition of troops, although several minor changes were made as a result of reconnaissance. Furthermore, a priority was assigned to the construction of antitank positions, based on Third Army's plan which emphasized the frustration of assault and breakthrough attempts by hostile mechanized units.

In mid-July Third Army unofficially informed the division that at a later date the Tungning Heavy Artillery Regiment and the 3d Heavy Artillery Regiment, then in the 79th Division area but directly under Third Army, would be assigned to it. Negotiations were begun immediately with these artillery units in order to prepare them for close cooperation with the division.

Operational Preparations

During July Third Army announced that its operational plan called for disposing its main strength on both sides of the Hunchun-Tumen line, astride the Korea-Manchuria border, and designated two defense lines within this area linking 79th Division positions with those of adjacent divisions. The forward line connected the 112th Division's Hunchun area with the Unmurei area (Sector A). The rear line connected the Tumen area with the Tonggwan area (Sectors B and D), and in the south linked with the 127th Division positions west of Sambongdong. (See Map No 2.)

In both the forward and rear defenses where the 79th Division front was linked with that of the 112th Division, there was some imbalance in each line. In the forward line, the positions of the 112th Division were relatively strong, manned as they were by almost the entire division and supportable by elements in the 79th Division sector. On the other hand, the positions of the 79th Division sector were held by less than a regiment whose lines were overextended and on whose right flank was approximately an 8-mile gap resulting from the adoption of the principle of defending key points only; this portion of the forward defense line was therefore extremely vulnerable.[53]

In the rear defense area the reverse was true. The 79th Division positions formed a strong divisional defense line, being held by the main body of the division, while the neighboring positions of the 112th Division, held by only small elements, were vulnerable. Hence neither the forward defense line nor the rear defense line designated by Third Army was satisfactory as the Third Army's main

---

53. The adoption of this principle was made necessary because of inadequate strength for such a wide front. According to Japanese Army tactical principles, in an ideal defense situation the normal width of a front for a division was 5 to 8 miles. By these standards the 79th Division, assigned a front which was between 15 and 20 miles wide, did not have an ideal defense situation. Adjustments were therefore necessary. Although the division did not abandon the principle of a continuous line of defense, it was necessary in view of the limited strength at the division's disposal for deployment along such a wide front, to adapt its capabilities to the requirements of its mission. Like many other divisions in Manchuria, therefore, the 79th Division adopted the principle of selecting, fortifying, and defending key points, devoting maximum attention to the skillful use of terrain.

MONOGRAPH NO. 154-D
MAP NO. 2

PROGRESS OF OPERATIONS, 79TH DIVISION
(SHOWING PART OF 112TH DIVISION'S SECTOR)
AUGUST 1945
SCALE 1:125,000

FOR 112TH DIVISION, MATCHING OF POSITIONS WITH DIVISIONAL ELEMENTS CANNOT BE VERIFIED

AREA SHOWN

UNITS AT MAYUSAN POSITION

KOMUSAN DET

(DEPLOYED IN 127TH DIVISION SECTOR)

INFANTRY REGIMENTAL GUN UNIT
COMBAT ENGINEER UNIT

line of resistance. Nevertheless, the rear defense line was satisfactory as a divisional main line of resistance, and actually was part of the First Area Army's main line of defense.⁵⁴

In view of the fact that Third Army designated two defense lines, the 79th Division Headquarters decided to establish two subordinate command posts, one near each of the junctures with the neighboring 112th Division, and to construct positions for these posts. The construction unit assigned to work on the command post positions at Unmurei in Sector A consisted of the Divisional Signal Unit, Gas Control Unit, and one-third of the 2d Engineer Company; it was led by the commander of the Division Signal Unit. That for Sector D, near Samyanggok, consisted of the 3d Engineer Company (minus ferrying personnel), and was commanded by the engineer company commander. Construction of these command post positions was started in late July. To provide the timber for these positions, the division formed a timber unit from the main body of the Ammunition Train of the 79th Mountain Artillery Regiment, to be led by the commander of the 2d Mountain Artillery Battalion. The timber was to be gathered from the forests in the Samsangsan maneuver area (east of Hoeryong). The division also assigned one transport company to haul the timber from Samsangsan to the Hoeryong railway station.

---

54. This would seem to indicate that the deployment of the main strength of the 112th Division along the forward defense line thwarted the design of the First Area Army of offering the main resistance along the rear defense line.

Another unit was diverted at this time when the main body of the 79th Engineer Regiment, then scattered among the various sectors, was withdrawn and dispatched to Musan to direct and assist the fortification work being done there by indigenous coolies under direct control of the Army.

Training, and Changes in Organization

With almost the entire division diverted to some type of fortification construction work, training was minimal. The division therefore decided to inaugurate a special training program in defensive combat techniques, emphasizing antitank defense, hand grenade throwing, and sniping. A training unit was formed at Hoeryong with a cadre of about twenty officers and men selected from various divisional units. About 3,000 trainees (70 per cent from infantry units, 30 per cent from other branches) were to be given this specialized training, which was to be conducted from mid-July through mid-October, with a total of 250 men being accommodated each week. Each Sector was authorized to send a certain number of selected troops to the training center for the one-week course. This training program began on schedule.

Meanwhile, during July, two changes took place in the organization of the 79th Division. About the middle of the month, a rocket-launcher unit (of about 600 troops) was attached to the 290th Infantry Regiment. The unit was not equipped with its main arms, however. Late in the month, the division was required to transfer about 1,000 of its personnel to the 139th Division for the formation of a raiding battalion. Toward the end of the month, 79th Division Headquarters moved from Nanam to Tumen; its offices were set up in the primary school there.

Status of Preparations

In number of personnel and level of equipment, the 79th Division was perhaps the best in Third Army. The division had the advantage over other divisions in the matter of unity since most of its officers and men were recruited from the three prefectures of Miyagi, Fukushima, and Niigata, representing the old recruiting districts of the 19th Division. Its personnel, moreover, were generally superior in quality to those of other divisions. Particularly, the quality of its officers was considered equal to that of officers of the old 19th Division. In view of the fact that much of its personnel had come from the 19th Depot Division in November 1944, it was considered one of the oldest divisions remaining in Manchuria. In addition, the division was fully equipped. Each of these factors contributed to raising the morale of the division and to making its fighting capacity excellent. The division's medical unit and its field hospital, however, were as yet unorganized.

By the end of July, the construction of new field positions, such as trenches, was nearing completion. The construction of new permanent defense fortifications (cement structures, etc.) however, lagged behind because of delays in the delivery of materials, particularly cement. The completion rate of the latter fortifications was below the 10 per cent mark, only one or two pillboxes having been completed in each sector.

Opening of Hostilities

With the completion of the organization of the 137th Division, the commander of the 79th Division, Lieutenant General Teisho Ota, accompanied by his chief of staff and special staff section chiefs went to Nanam on 6 August for talks with the commander of the new division and his staff. On the following day, they left Nanam for Hoeryong to inspect the newly formed training center. On 8 August, they inspected the progress of fortification work in the Changpyong Sector C and passed the night there.

At midnight the sound of distant bombing or shelling was heard. In the early morning hours of 9 August, General Ota received a telephone report from Division Headquarters in Tumen that Soviet forces at midnight had crossed the Kyonghung bridge into Korean territory. He immediately cancelled scheduled inspection tours of Sectors A and B, and hurried to Tumen. There he ordered all Sector Units to remain in their present positions and to take emergency defensive measures.

Later in the morning 79th Division Headquarters at Tumen received its first operational order from the Third Army Headquarters at Yenchi. Confirming earlier reports that the Soviets had launched the invasion and were rushing into Korea and Manchurian territories, the Army's order stated that its immediate intention was to strengthen its positions and halt the enemy invasion. The order also announced that:

> The Komusan Detachment will be attached directly to the Army.
>
> The main force of the 79th Cavalry Regiment (at Komusan) will scout the enemy situation in the Najin area.
>
> The main body of the Tungning Heavy Artillery Regiment and all of the 3d Heavy Artillery Regiment will be assigned to the 79th Division.
>
> The main force of the Engineer Regiment previously dispatched to direct and assist fortification work of the Army in the vicinity of Musan will be returned to the 79th Division.
>
> The 79th Division will dispatch to front areas a security force, an observation party, and other small units for reconnoitering purposes. It will also dispatch liaison officers to establish contact with the 101st Mixed Regiment and with the Komusan Detachment.

Later in the day, the division issued its own orders to the following effect:

> The commander of the 291st Infantry Regiment (Sector A) will be assigned the duties of blowing up vehicular and railway bridges over the Tumen River at Kyongwon and Hunyung.
>
> All units of the division remaining in Nanam and Hoeryong will immediately take up defensive positions.
>
> The Timber Unit in Samsangsan will be recalled and assigned a defensive mission.
>
> The Gas Control Unit and the Division Signal Unit helping in the preparation of fortifications for the division command post in Sector A will rejoin their organization.

Each sector engineer unit will become a sector defense unit and be ready to go into defensive action at any time, and meanwhile will complete such emergency fortifications as are necessary.

The Engineer Construction Unit in Sector C will be organized for tactical employment as the Changpyong Detachment and will be directly attached to Division Headquarters.

Progress of Operations

Although the enemy was reported to be attacking at various points along the eastern front during the first few days, he was not active in front of the 79th Division positions.[55] On 11 August, however, he advanced toward Hunchun in the 112th Division's sector on the left and toward Wuchiatzu and Najin in the 127th Division's sector on the right flank, thereby threatening both flanks. On that day the front line subordinate command post at Unmurei was ordered to move back a short distance to Getsumeisan.

Until the 15th no engagements were fought in the 79th Division sector. The division during this period was preoccupied with preparations to meet the enemy; meanwhile, it kept informed of the developing enemy situation, particularly in the 112th Division area on the left and the 127th Divisions area on the right.

---

55. The positions of the 79th Division were well shielded by natural barriers, particularly the Tumen River which looped in an inverted U that inclosed most of the division's area and protected it from the enemy infantry and tank units that routed the 112th Division on the 79th Division's left flank.

On the 12th, after several unsuccessful attempts by the 291st Regiment to blow up the vehicular bridge east of Kyongwon and the railroad and vehicular bridges north of Hunyung, the Engineer Regiment Commander was ordered to try; late in the day the mission was successfully completed. This action contributed largely to denying the enemy egress into the 79th Division's sector until 15 August.

Also on the 12th, the division chief of staff went to Third Army Headquarters for information on the general situation. On the 13th he returned and proceeded to Sector A to observe the enemy situation and to inspect defensive structures there. On the same day most of the engineer units previously dispatched to Musan, Kyodaiho, and Unmurei, the Timber Unit, the training center unit, and personnel still in Nanam and Hoeryong rejoined their respective units.

Forward elements of the 112th Division under pressure from the enemy withdrew on the 13th to their main positions (the Army's forward defense line) in front of Michiang. The attacking enemy force, meanwhile advanced to the vicinity of the river bank on the north side of the bridge near Hunyung.

On the same day, reports were received that the Wuchiatzu regiment of the 127th Division was engaging the enemy in a fierce battle. In the Unggi area where the 101st Mixed Regiment was being attacked by an enemy force of approximately regimental strength, the progress of the battle was unknown because of loss of contact with the liaison officer sent to the regiment.

On the 14th the enemy captured the Hunchun airfield; Soviet planes promptly began to use the airfield. Meanwhile, west of Hunchun an enemy infantry force supported by tanks began concentrating. Although all this action was taking place across the Tumen river, it directly threatened our positions. By the close of 14 August the 79th Division had not received any enemy attacks. However, two were forming, one against our front near Hunyung, the other against our left rear flank near Tumen. Both attacks were threatening from the 112th Division's sector, and both were impeded by the natural barrier of the Tumen River.

On 15 August an enemy force of approximately battalion strength supported by about ten tanks attacked positions of the 112th Division in the vicinity of Unggidong on the opposite bank from Hunyung. Artillery units of the 79th Division on the south side of the river opened fire and threw the enemy back. Another element of the enemy fired on a security unit guarding the south side of the river in the vicinity of the destroyed bridges at Hunyung. Shortly thereafter the Soviet force, after repairing the vehicular bridge, crossed the river and entered the 79th Division sector. This first and only serious penetration of the division's area was aimed at our Mayusan positions. (See Map No 2.)

Meanwhile, in the Tumen area there was considerable bustle and commotion on 15 August. In the morning the 79th Division, in response to a Third Army order of the preceding day, sent one mountain artillery battery north to Chiulungping to support an infantry company guarding the approaches to Yenchi.

At about 1300 hours on 15 August several hostile planes bombed Tumen, site of division headquarters. The planes directed their main effort on the railroad station, causing the explosion of a large number of artillery shells on military freight cars parked in the station. The explosions continued sporadically for more than three hours showering the town with shell fragments. The confusion resulting from the explosions was relatively minor, most of the inhabitants having already evacuated to the suburbs. The arrival and departure of evacuation trains, however, plunged the entire neighborhood into wild confusion. Coincidentally, at the Army supply depot about 3 kilometers north of Tumen, a gasoline tank exploded, gushing columns of black smoke into the air that could be seen for miles.

During the day the division chief of staff received a message from the branch manager of the Manchurian Telegraph and Telephone Company making reference to an "important broadcast." He gave the message to the division commander and recommended that the news be kept from subordinates.

With the bombing of Tumen, with artillery shell fragments showering the city, with the explosion of a gas tank within 3 kilometers, and with reports of tanks approaching Tumen, 79th Division decided to open a command post across the Tumen River in Namyang. Late in the afternoon it established a command post in the primary school there. The tactical reason for this move was that it placed the Tumen River between the division command post and the advancing enemy tanks, then threatening Wangching and capable of attacking the 79th Division from the rear.

To protect the division's rear several other steps were taken. Orders to blow up the vehicular bridge which crosses the Haerhpatung River (a narrow river between Tumen and Yenchi) about 2 miles north of Tumen were promptly carried out. A company of the Nanam Divisional District Unit (equipped with eight machineguns) charged with the air defense of the Tumen River railway-vehicular bridge connecting Tumen to Namyang was placed under the 79th Division's command. (Farther to the front, and apart from the action developing near Tumen, a platoon of the 280th Regiment at Wuchiatzu, having become separated from its parent organization on this day, was placed under the command of the 291st Infantry Regiment.)

The Attack on the Mayusan Positions

On 16 August division headquarters received a report that the Soviet force which had crossed the River near Hunyung on the preceding day was beginning to attack. About two battalions of enemy infantry with an estimated twenty to thirty tanks and supported by artillery fire from across the river were striking towards the Mayusan positions west of Hunyung. These positions were the most northeasterly in the 79th Division's forward defense line.

General Ota took several steps to meet this threat to Mayusan.

He ordered the main body of the 2d Engineer Company,[56] then in Tumen en route to its Sector A positions, to proceed immediately toward Hunyung by train with the mission of demolishing strategic points along the road and railroad between Tumen and Hunyung, and also of seeking and attacking enemy armored units. This unit succeeded in blowing up at least one strategic point—the small railway bridge at Hwangpa, thus denying the enemy the use of this railway in his advance westward. The company commander, reporting the demolishment of the bridge by one of his advance platoons, stated that the main part of his company was then near Onsong; he was thereupon given responsibility for controlling railway transportation in that vicinity.

In connection with the Mayusan threat, General Ota also ordered the commander of the 289th Regiment to deloy the main body of his antitank gun unit in the vicinity of Pungni and to continue to direct the main defense effort in that sector. He also ordered his chief of ordnance to prepare improvised antitank mines and packaged explosives, his intendance chief to transport by rail to Tumen about eight car-loads of rice, wheat, red beans, then standing in the Onsong freight yards, and other provisions in various localities east of Tumen, and his medical department personnel to establish a dispensary at Tumen. Meanwhile, a liaison officer dispatched to 112th Division Headquarters at Michiang reported that division to be under attack in all its sectors.

---

56. An engineer company's normal strength is 254.

Details of the action fought in the Mayusan positions are not known. What is known is that the engagement began on the morning of 16 August and lasted one day; that the Soviet attacking force consisted of two columns each with one infantry battalion and one tank company; that the Japanese force consisted of approximately one battalion (Headquarters of the 1st Battalion of the 291st Regiment, the 4th Infantry Company, one company of regimental guns, one company of engineers, and two platoons of the division signal unit); that on the 15th (when the Soviet river crossing began) one platoon of infantry from the Getsumeisan area was sent to the Mayusan area; that on the 16th the Soviet forces captured the outworks of the Mayusan defenses; that on the morning of the 17th one platoon of the 5th Company of the 291st Regiment was sent to the Mayusan position where it encountered the right column of the Soviet force which after capturing the outworks had continued westward to flank our positions, and that this platoon was annihilated. The Soviet penetration did not reach the main defense positions of the Mayusan sector by the time hostilities stopped, although it had begun to by pass some of them. The 79th Division losses, all in this Mayusan sector, totaled about 140 officers and men killed or wounded; Soviet losses were estimated at about fifty.

The Enemy Crossing near Tumen

On the evening of the 16th, Division Headquarters received a report that an enemy armored force from Wangching was headed south along three roads and threatened not only division headquarters but also Third Army Headquarters at Yenchi. (See Map No 2.) General Ota immediately ordered the assembling in Namyang of the 2d Battalion of the 289th Regiment, one-half of the 3d Mountain Artillery Company, and one platoon of the engineer unit in Sector B. He then ordered these units to deploy along the Tumen-Yenchi road across the Tumen River to check a breakthrough by enemy armored forces into the rear of the division. At the same time division headquarters organized one platoon of its guards into a close-quarter combat unit, for use in Tumen. Until this time, although hostilities had technically ended, fighting had continued. Late that evening, however, General Ota, on instructions from Third Army, ordered each infantry regiment to commit its colors to fire, and gave orders to refrain from active operations.

Early on the morning of 17 August an enemy mechanized division rushed down along the Wangching-Tumen road. The vehicular bridge 2 miles north of Tumen having been blown up earlier by our engineers, the enemy column of infantry, tanks, and self-propelled guns halted on the road. At about 0900 hours, however, an infantry unit forded the river and launched an attack against us under the covering fire of the self-propelled guns.

Meanwhile the force assembled by General Ota at Namyang had been ready since about 0400 but, in view orders from the Army to cease active operations, was not employed. However, one platoon of the engineer regiment was dispatched under the escort of a platoon of headquarters guards to blow up a railway bridge about 6 miles northwest of Tumen.

Cease-fire Order

Shortly after 0700 hours on 17 August, Third Army orders were received directing that all operations be stopped. Division Headquarters transmitted it to each Sector, and also sent instructions to prepare to assemble troops. The assembly areas designated were: for Sector A, Kyongwon; for Sector B, Namyang, and for Sectors C and D, Chongsong. The Mountain Artillery Regiment Headquarters and the main body of the Regimental Ammunition Train were to assemble in Tonggwan, the Engineer Regiment in Sugupo, the main body of the Transport Regiment in Samyanggok, west of Tumen, and the Tungning and 3d Heavy Artillery Regiments in their respective positions. The units stationed in Tumen (headquarters guards, the Gas Control Unit, a part of the Ordnance Duty Unit, the Dispensary, and the Veterinary Hospital) were ordered to return to Namyang; meanwhile, the 2d Battalion of the 289th Regiment was ordered reinforce the defense of the vehicular-railroad bridge connecting Tumen and Namyang, the only one (other than the Onsong vehicular bridge) which had not been destroyed.[57]

---

57. Battle reports sent in during the actions lacked exactness. The condition of these combat units after operations is not known in detail because the troops were interned in Hunchun following the cease-fire order and acted independently of the division headquarters.

Hostilities were brought to a halt with little confusion. The two enemy thrusts into the 79th Division positions had not gotten very far. In the Mayusan sector the enemy was in front of the inner defenses. In the Tumen area, where the enemy's advance was slow, he was on the outskirts of the city, but all Japanese units had been withdrawn to Namyang or to the area west of Tumen and the opposing forces were never joined in battle. Hence the cease-fire order was issued not only before the Soviet forces reached the main defenses, but also before they reached the main body of the 79th Division. Except for the losses in the Mayusan outworks, the 79th Division's fighting capacity remained unimpaired.

Negotiations with the Soviet Army

Shortly after noon on the 17th, the 79th Division chief of staff together with the senior staff officer and officer-interpreters went to Tumen where they conferred with the Soviet division commander. An agreement to the following effect was reached:

> Japanese and Soviet divisions will immediately stop hostilities.
>
> The Soviet force in Tumen will not cross the Tumen River into Namyang.
>
> The 79th Division Headquarters and units directly attached thereto will be assembled in the Tumen camps during the day for disarmament.
>
> Other divisional units will be assembled in front of the Tumen railway station on 18 and 19 August to be disarmed.

All the Japanese officers who took part in the negotiations were detained by the Soviets, except the senior staff officer who was ordered to deliver the agreement to the 79th Division commander.

The Soviet commander's orders were carried out immediately. Division Headquarters and units attached thereto were disarmed upon their arrival in Tumen on the evening of the 17th. The Veterinary Depot commandant and one noncommissioned officer committed suicide. On the same evening almost all of the officers and men of the Tungning Heavy Artillery Regiment, including the commander, gathered around their artillery pieces and blew themselves up at their positions, one battery north of Tumen, two batteries south of Namyang. (One of the regiment's four batteries had been left at Tungning.)

In view of the possibility that the message transmitted to divisional units requiring them to assemble in Tumen might not have reached them, Division Headquarters on 18 August dispatched officers to deliver the cease-fire order as well as the Soviet commander's instructions. One officer was sent to each of the following places: along the Namyang-Chongsong Railway line, along the Tumen-Onsong-Changpyong road, along the Tumen-Onsong-Kyongwon road, and along the Tumen-Samyanggok-Chongsong road, including the Tumen River's left bank.

Meanwhile, a number of soldiers committed suicide. The commander of the 79th Engineer Regiment and several headquarters officers blew themselves up at Sugupo (presumably by hand grenades). The main body of the 3d Engineer Company, the commander included, blew itself up at the site of the division alternate command post west of Samyanggok.

In many units, soldiers of Korean nationality were released from service. The remaining troops of each unit arrived at Tumen on 18 and 19 August and were disarmed. In all units there was a large number of desertions because orders were either not fully understood or were utterly ignored. Many of the deserters were later interned at the Komusan Internment Camp, which had been organized principally for the internment of personnel of the Divisional Districts Units.

Captain Senda, commander of the 1st Battalion of the 291st Infantry Regiment, and about 150 of his men who survived the engagement at the Mayusan outworks were interned in Hunchun by order of the local Soviet force commander.

On 20 August officers and warrant officers of the division were transported by train to Yenchi. Officers and men suffering from self-inflicted wounds were sent to Tunhua by train. All able bodied men accompanied by some officers were marched to Yenchi on 21 and 22 August; upon arrival there, officers and men were interned separately.

Other Third Army units began to arrive at Yenchi for internment in succession, including the 101st Mixed Regiment, and elements of the 1st Mobile Brigade and of the Nanam Divisional District Unit. They remained there until the end of September.

In early October evacuation to Soviet territory began. The first group of officers, numbering some 2,000, were sent, via Hsinking, to Lada on the outskirts of Tambov City in European Russia. A second group, with about an equal number of officers, was transferred to the same destination via Hunchun, Kraskino, and Khabarovsk.[58]

Men were organized into labor battalions of approximately 1,000 each, with several officers as leaders. In organizing these labor units, the Soviets destroyed the original organization of units so that each unit was formed from a mixture of various branches of the services. The battalions were then marched to different places in succession.

Japanese Residents in the 79th Division Area

At the opening of hostilities in Manchuria, the greater part of Japanese civilian residents in the division's operational zone voluntarily moved to the Hoeryong and Nanam areas. The remainder moved either to the Tumen or Yenchi areas or to nearby villages, particularly to positions of the 3d Heavy Artillery Regiment in Samyanggok. On about 16 or 17 August, none but men in the prime of life were to be found in Tumen, Namyang, Onsong, Hunyung, Kyongwon, and neighboring positions.

Dependents of officers of the division had remained in Nanam and

---

58. In July 1946 about 7,500 officers, warrant officers, and civilians interned at the Lada Camp moved in four groups to the Yerabuga (No 97) Camp in Tatar Republic, where they joined about 2,000 other officers and civilians. The internees were put into Camps A or B. Of them, some 6,500 were repatriated to Japan between October and November 1947, about 1,000 in May 1948 (after first being moved to Kazan), and about 1,600 in July of the same year; about 300 were moved in July to Khabarovsk for internment at sub-Camp No 14 of the 16th District.

Hoeryong when the division moved to north Korea in June-July. On 14 August most of the dependents in Hoeryong were returned to the homeland arriving there toward the end of the month; those that remained committed suicide at Sugupo with the Engineer Regiment Commander. Dependents in Nanam, including those of officers of the Nanam Divisional District, moved to Hyesanjin. They were detained by Soviet troops at Paegam, and interned at Hamhung at the end of the war. Although they were to have been sent home in successive groups after May 1947, many died of illness during the intervening period.[59]

---

59. There were no cultivating parties in the division's operational area, most of which was in Korean territory; such groups were used only in Manchuria.

Monograph No 154-E

CHAPTER IX

The 127th Division[60]

Organization and Source of Personnel

The 127th Infantry Division was organized beginning in February 1945 at Hunchun under the supervision of Third Army. It was one of the eight divisions organized in Manchuria in early 1945 to give the Kwantung Army some semblance of strength after it had been seriously weakened by repeated withdrawals.

The first two regiments organized by the division was formed principally from the disbanded 9th Border Garrison Unit which had been stationed in the Hunchun area, plus some personnel from the 112th Division. They later acquired a considerable number of recruits.

On 26 February, while the division was still in the process of being organized, it was assigned to the Third Army. By the end of March the two initial regiments—the 280th and 281st—were ready. Early in May an additional regiment, the 282d, was formed from two independent battalions that had been stationed at Fuchin, plus some personnel from the two regiments formed earlier.

In mid-May, when the organization of the Division was completed, the three regimental commanders went to Tokyo where they were received

---

60. The information in this sector was prepared by Major Masao Sakai, staff officer of the 127th Division.

by the Emperor at the Imperial Palace and presented with the regimental colors.

The division's strength was reinforced in June by the assignment of the 2d Heavy Artillery Regiment and the 2d Independent Heavy Artillery Battery, (both 240-mm howitzer). During the July mass-mobilization in Manchuria when many new units were being formed, the division's organic strength was filled out by the assignment of the 37th Artillery Regiment and one Raiding Battalion. Arms and equipment for the division were acquired gradually, and by late June the authorized levels had been reached.

Meanwhile, division headquarters, originally at Hunchun, had been transferred to Tumen. During June-July, when the 79th Division moved to north Korea and took up some of the positions being prepared by the 127th Division, division headquarters moved to Lungching. It remained there only a short while, and was then moved to Pataohotzu, where it remained.

Deployment of 127th Division

The area of responsibility initially assigned to the 127th Division consisted of the entire Third Army area south of the Tumen-Hunchun line. After the 79th Division moved to Tumen in July, and its southern boundary established along the Chongsong-Changpyong line, the 127th Division maintained control of the area south of that line, and hence held the Third Army's extreme right flank. This area was partly in Manchuria and partly in Korea. Between the

Korea and Soviet border a part of Manchuria stretches to south of Lake Hasan (site of a major border incident in 1938). From there the Korea border is contiguous to the Soviet border and follows the line of the Tumen River to the Sea of Japan. South from the mouth of the Tumen to slightly north of Chongjin the 127th Division's boundary was the north Korea coast, along which, as it turned out, the Soviets were to make two amphibious assaults.

The 127th Division's front extended from north of Wuchiatzu to north of Chongjin, a distance of about 40 miles. The main body of the division, including the 281st and 282d Regiments plus one battalion of the 280th Regiment, were deployed inland west of the Tumen River. Along the border were deployed the 280th Regiment (less one battalion) near Wuchiatzu, the 101st Mixed Regiment near Chonghak, and the Najin Fortress Garrison Unit at the naval base at Najin; along the 127th Division's (also Third Army's) boundary with the 34th Army, the 79th Division's Komusan Detachment was deployed. (See Map No 1.)

Both the 101st Mixed Regiment and the Najin Fortress Garrison Unit were under Third Army's direct control. At the outbreak of hostilities the 127th Division was to be given control of the 101st Mixed Regiment, and Third Army was to assume direct control of the Komusan Detachment and retain control of the Najin Fortress Garrison

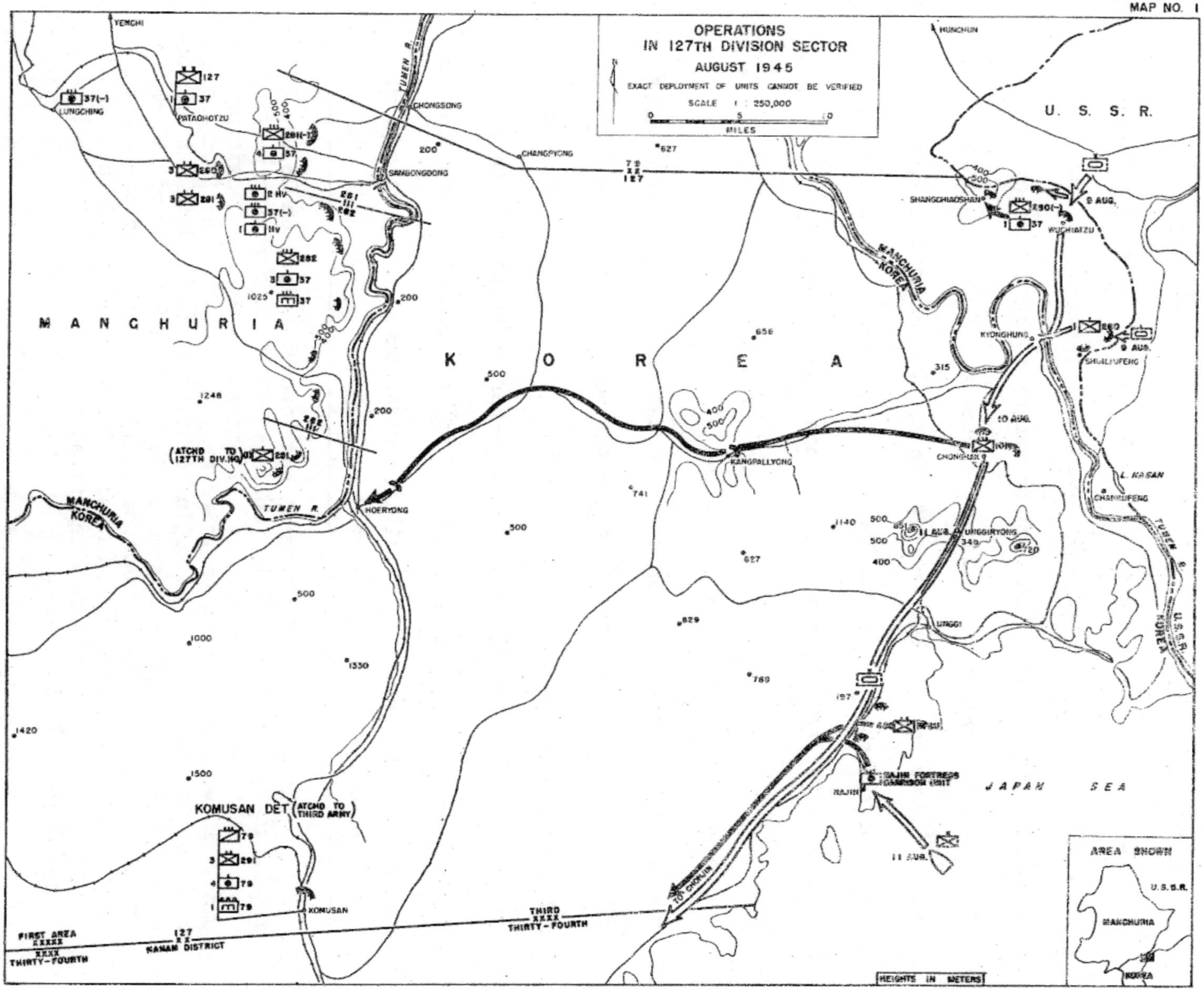
OPERATIONS
IN 127TH DIVISION SECTOR
AUGUST 1945
EXACT DEPLOYMENT OF UNITS CANNOT BE VERIFIED
SCALE 1 : 250,000
MILES
U. S. S. R.
M A N C H U R I A
K O R E A
J A P A N S E A
MANCHURIA
KOREA
TUMEN R.
YENCHI
LUNGCHING
PATAOHOTZU
CHONGSONG
SAMBONGDONG
CHANGPYONG
HUNCHUN
SHANGCHIAOSHAN
WUCHIATZU
KYONGHUNG
SHUILIUFENG
CHONGHAK
KANGPALLYONG
HOERYONG
L. KASAN
UNGGI
NAJIN
NAJIN FORTRESS GARRISON UNIT
KOMUSAN
KOMUSAN DET (ATCHD TO THIRD ARMY)
(ATCHD TO 127TH DIV.HQ)
8 AUG.
9 AUG.
10 AUG.
11 AUG.
TO CHONJIN
FIRST AREA
THIRTY-FOURTH
127
KANAM DISTRICT
THIRD
HEIGHTS IN METERS
AREA SHOWN
U.S.S.R.
MANCHURIA
KOREA

Unit.[61]

Operational Preparations

Since the time it was organized the 127th Division was engaged principally in the construction of fortifications. All personnel of the division remained in bivouac during most of this period, and each unit was assigned specific construction missions. Initially this work was carried out in north Korea, but after the 79th Division moved there the 127th Division concentrated on the fortifications in the sector west of the Tumen River, from Sambongdong to Hoeryong.

Concurrent with the construction mission, which was pushed resolutely, the division conducted education and training programs with the objective of strengthening the solidarity of the command. Emphasis was placed on defensive combat training. All men were trained to become proficient in close-quarter combat and to discipline their minds for this type of fighting. Even units stationed along the border, whose positions were camouflaged, were given

---

61. The 101st Mixed Regiment had been organized on 28 Sep 1942, at Chonghak, north Korea. It consisted of three infantry battalions, one mountain artillery battalion (75-mm guns), and one engineer company. It was transferred to Third Army on 10 June 1945 from the Seventeenth Area Army. The Najin Fortress Garrison Unit was an old-established unit. It consisted of four batteries (two of 150-mm howitzers, two of 280-mm howitzers, all emplaced), and the 460th Specially Established Guard Battalion of five infantry companies. For the Komusan Detachment's organization see Chart No 1, Monograph No 154-D, page 116.

appropriate training; in order to conceal training activities from the Soviets particular advantage was taken of foggy weather.

Meanwhile, in view of the shortage of arms, the Ordnance Duty Unit and Veterinary Depot were ordered to improvise weapons for close-quarter fighting. These included metal-tipped bamboo spears (about 6 feet in length), and hurling-type explosives for use against tanks; the latter were to be made from air bombs, a supply of which was stored at the Air Supply Depot in Hoeryong.

In carrying out its border garrisoning duties, the division maintained close liaison with the Nanam Divisional District Unit and the 101st Mixed Regiment, as well as with the 112th Division up until the time the 127th Division moved south. The policy of exchanging information was strictly observed, and the rapidity with which the exchanges were carried out left nothing to be desired. Along the border, efforts were made to avoid any action that might provoke the Russians, in compliance with border garrison regulations of the Kwantung Army.

Status of Preparations Prior to the Outbreak of Hostilities

Immediately prior to the Soviet entry into the war, the principal weapons (other than individual weapons) in the hands of the divisional units were as follows:

```
Each Infantry Regiment
    Grenade launchers                48
    Light machineguns                81
    Heavy machineguns                18
```

          Infantry battalion guns
            (37-mm guns and 75-mm how)   6
          Antitank guns (37-mm)   6

      37th Artillery Regiment
          Field artillery (75-mm guns)   18
          Mountain artillery   10
          105-mm Howitzers   4

Ammunition was stored mainly in forward positions, particularly in Wuchiatzu. It was planned to store enough ammunition for 1.5 engagements (one engagement is considered to last three months) in the divisional area, and to keep sufficient ammunition for .5 engagements in division reserve. The withdrawal of supplies to rear areas after the adoption of Kwantung Army's delaying plan of operations had proceeded slowly, and a major part of the division's ammunition supplies remained in forward positions when the war broke out. Food and fodder sufficient for one month were stored in the rear areas. Although the division was relatively well supplied it did have shortages of automotive fuel and signal batteries, shortages which prevailed throughout Manchuria.

Construction work of the division consisted principally of positions in caves where arms larger than heavy machineguns could be installed. Approximately one-third of this type of construction work was completed. The construction of fortifications in general was unsatisfactory. The work was hampered by lack of equipment and supplies. These difficulties could not be overcome even though the various facilities of local coal mines were available.

During June and July, training in field tactical exercises was given to commanders directly under division control as well as to battalion commanders and company commanders. All training was conducted in the respective areas of units. By the end of July all training exercises planned by the division for officers had been completed. Officers of the lower ranks did not react spiritedly to this training and it was felt that they had not gained confidence. The training of troops was not thorough in view of the fact that much time had to be devoted to organizing units and to constructing fortifications.

Situation at the Outbreak of Hostilities

At midnight of 8-9 August the barracks in Wuchiatzu were subjected to concentrated fire by Soviet heavy artillery. Although the 280th Regiment (less one battalion) there got through a message reporting the enemy shelling, its wireless apparatus was destroyed shortly thereafter. The enemy initial shelling was followed by limited attacks on our positions at Wuchiatzu and Shuiliufeng.

The Soviet Army, it was later determined, had massed a force of one infantry division and two tank brigades in front of the Wuchiatzu positions; one of the tank brigades was in position between Wuchiatzu and Shuiliufeng. Although the attack was launched from the Wuchiat'zu area, the infantry division plus one of the tank brigades turned north immediately upon entering Manchuria and headed for the 112th Division sector. The other tank brigade crossed the border near Shuiliufeng, turned south, by-passing our sector, and then crossed the Kyonghung Bridge to join, as it later turned out, the Soviet force making the amphibious assault landing at Najin and Chongjin. Thus the 127th Division did not receive a major attack.

Meanwhile, after Third Army received word of the invasion it placed the main elements of the 280th Regiment (less one battalion) in the border areas under its direct command. (The division nevertheless continued to supply these elements with ammunition and provisions). After the Soviet attack, this regiment withdrew to Shangchiaoshan, northwest of Wuchiatzu, and made that its base of operations. The attacks ceased on the 11th; thereafter elements in the Shangchiaoshan positions, although subjected to occasional shelling, did not participate in any engagements.

The Army also changed the status of the 101st Mixed Regiment at Chonghak, attaching it to the 127th Division. This regiment fell back gradually and took up positions near Kangpallyong and Hoeryong. By the time hostilities ended, the enemy had not attacked the area held by the division's main body.

On 11 August a Soviet amphibious force of about battalion size made an assault landing at Najin. Details of this action are not known except that the landings occurred between 1000 and 1100 hours and that the defending force fell back towards the south.

Situation After the War

Almost all of the KIA casualties sustained by the Division were borne by the 280th Regiment (less one battalion) guarding the border. It counted about thirty killed and about 100 missing. Other divisional units, principally the 281st and 282d Regiments, sustained approximately 500 missing, mainly as a result of the fact that they sent guerrilla troops far ahead of the front line.

The cease-fire order could not be promptly disseminated nor properly carried out because of the hordes of Japanese refugees who kept surging into the division's operational area from such places as Hunchun, Tumen, Unggi, and Najin. Supplies that had been accumulated near Pataohotzu in the division area, including medical supplies, clothing, and food, were distributed among the various units; some supplies were also given to Koreans residing in the locality.

Weapons were collected on 19 August and, after the number was ascertained, were turned over to a Soviet cavalry lieutenant (company commander) who arrived at Pataohotzu for negotiations. On the 20th, officers and men of the division were interned in barracks.

Monograph No 154-F

CHAPTER X

The Fifth Army[62]

Organization

Ever since the "special maneuvers" held by the Kwantung Army in 1941 the Fifth Army, in northeastern Manchuria, had maintained a powerful force. After the unfavorable turn of the war in the Pacific and in China, Kwantung Army units were transferred one after another to reinforce these active operational areas. These transfers sapped the strength of Fifth Army along with other armies in Manchuria.

By the end of March 1944 Fifth Army consisted of three main tactical units, all in the eastern part of Tungan Province: the 11th Division deployed in the Hulin sector, the 24th Division in the Tungan sector, and the 3d Cavalry Brigade in the Paoching sector. (See Map No 1.) In addition it had numerous zone of communication units and the following auxiliary units:

```
Artillery Command (1)
Heavy Field Artillery Regiments (3)
Artillery Intelligence Regiment (fire-control) (1)
Engineer Command (1)
Independent Engineer Regiment (1)
Transport Headquarters (1)
```

In the summer of 1944, when the Allied counteroffensive in the Pacific was well on its way towards the Philippines there began a series of transfers from Manchuria that was to continue for more

---

62. The information in this chapter was furnished by Colonel Akiji Kashiwada, operations officer of Fifth Army Headquarters.

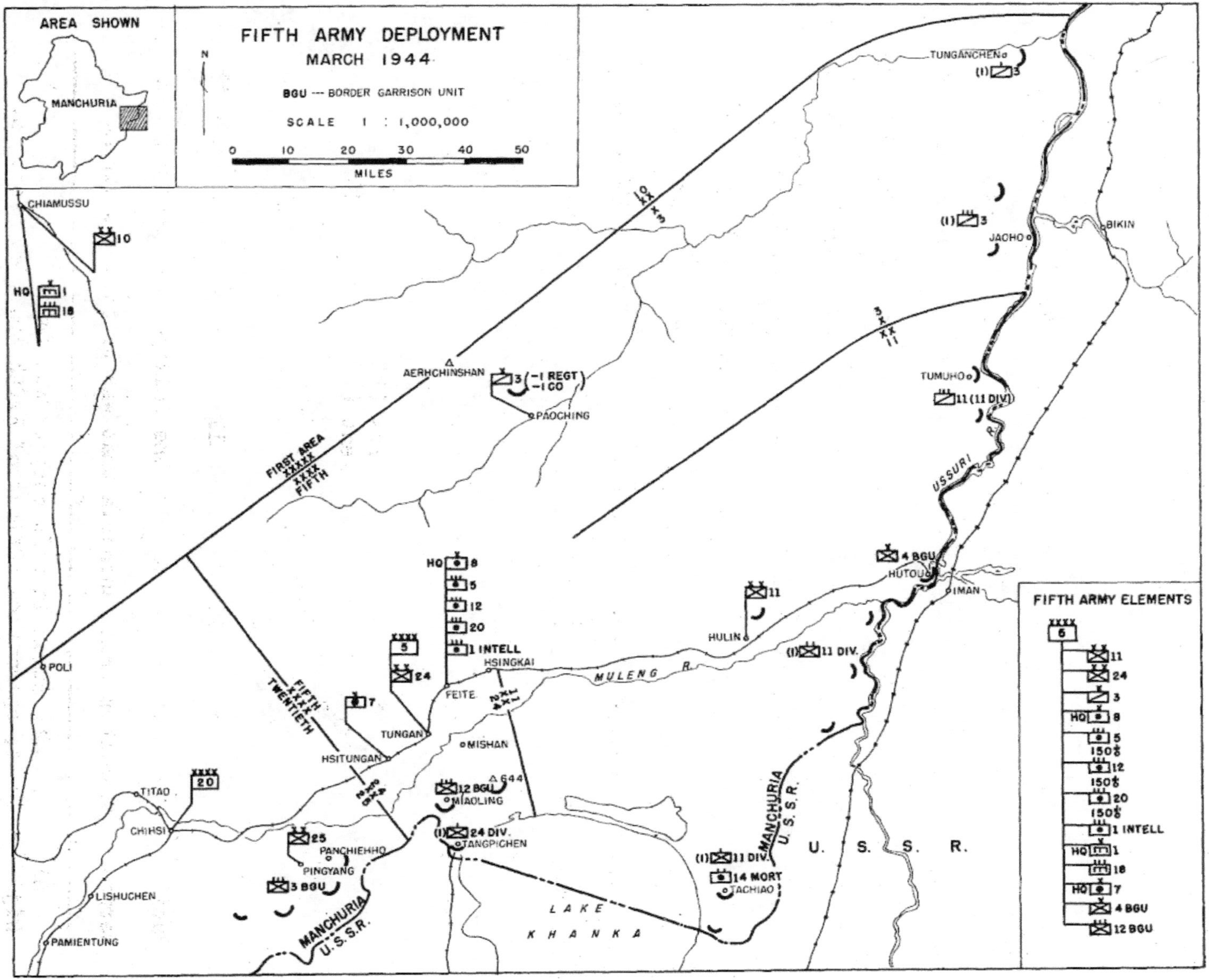

MONOGRAPH NO. 154-F
MAP NO. 1

FIFTH ARMY DEPLOYMENT
MARCH 1944

BGU --- BORDER GARRISON UNIT

SCALE 1 : 1,000,000

MILES 0 10 20 30 40 50

AREA SHOWN — MANCHURIA

FIFTH ARMY ELEMENTS

than a year. The first major unit to go was the 24th Division which was sent to Formosa about the middle of July. At about the same time the 12th Heavy Field Artillery Regiment (150-mm howitzers) was transferred to the 14th Army in the Philippines. Several zone of communications units were also transferred. At the beginning of September the land survey company of the 1st Artillery Intelligence Regiment was transferred to the Thirty-second Army in Okinawa.[63]

Until September 1944 there were three armies in Eastern Manchuria-- the Third, Fifth, and Twentieth. Toward the end of September, Twentieth Army Headquarters was transferred to the Sixth Area Army for the "Ichigo" operations in the China area. (See pages 52-3, Monograph No 138.) Twentieth Army itself was disbanded and its units assigned to neighboring commands in Manchuria. The Fifth Army got the 25th Division, deployed in the Pingyang sector, two border garrison units, one heavy field artillery regiment (150-mm howitzers) and several zone of communications units.

---

63. An Artillery Intelligence Regiment, with a total of about 667 personnel had a headquarters (258), one Ground Survey Company (93), one Plotting Company (225), and a Sound Locating Company (91). The Ground Survey Company, by triangulation of landmarks in both the enemy and firendly positions surveyed the general field of artillery fire. The Plotting Company plotted the exact positions of enemy weapons in relation to friendly weapons. The Sound Locating Company determined the range of enemy guns by sound devices. Each artillery battalion and regiment had equipment and personnel to perform similar functions (except sounding), but on a smaller scale. An artillery intelligence regiment was usually assigned to an Army, and was deployed in the area where it was most needed.

Since only the Third and Fifth Armies were left in eastern Manchuria (from the four in 1943), the eastern front was divided between these two armies, the Fifth Army getting control of the two northern provinces, Sanchiang and Tungan, and Third Army getting control of the southern provinces of Mutanchiang and Chientao. (See Map No 1, Monograph 154-B) Actually, the Sanchiang Province--northernmost on the eastern front--was the responsibility of a separate division, which was to remain under Fifth Army jurisdiction only until the opening of hostilities at which time it was to revert to the control of First Area Army. On the Fifth Army's right flank a similar situation existed, with a division holding a sector of the front between the Fifth and Third Armies, assigned to the Third Army until the opening of hostilities.

In February 1945, Fifth Army was ordered to activate the 126th Division, the 77th Independent Mixed Brigade, and the 31st Independent Antitank Battalion. The Army organized the 126th Division mainly with surplus personnel of the 25th Division, then being reorganized for transfer to the homeland, and began organizing the 77th Independent Mixed Brigade with men of the 3d Cavalry Brigade. The latter brigade was inactivated.

Towards the end of February another boundary change was made when Third Army's area was extended southward into northern Korea, and it relinquished the northern sector of its front--to a point north of Yaoshan--to Fifth Army. Thus, Fifth Army was given the additional duty defending eastern Mutanchiang Province. With this added responsibility it was given command of the 124th Division in the Suiyang area, the 2d Border Garrison Unit near Suifenho, and the 11th Border Garrison Unit near Kuanyuehtai. The addition of the 124th Division gave Fifth Army four divisions, two seasoned and two in the process of being organized. But this harvest was soon to be consumed by further transfers.

During March 1945 transfers from Fifth Army reached a peak. About the middle of the month the 25th Division, acquired six months earlier upon the disbandment of the Twentieth Army, was transferred to the Sixteenth Area Army in the homeland, while the 14th Mortar Battalion was transferred to the Thirty-sixth Army, also in the homeland. At the end of the month the 11th Division was transferred to Fifteenth Area Army in Japan, the 8th Artillery Command and the 11th Independent Heavy Artillery Battalion (150-mm gun) to the Twelfth Area Army, the 10th Heavy Field Artillery Regiment (150-mm howitzer), the 1st Artillery Intelligence Regiment, the 7th Signal Regiment, and the 7th Field Transport Headquarters to Sixteenth Area Army. Since the 25th and 11th were the only seasoned divisions in Fifth Army, (the two other divisions--the 124th and 126th--were then in the process of being organized) their transfer had a paralyzing effect on the strength, organization, and combat effectiveness of Fifth Army. Toward the end of April, furthermore, additional units (principally zone of communication units) were transferred to the Twelfth, Sixteenth, and Seventeenth Area Armies.

As a result of all these organizational changes the Fifth Army late in April 1945 consisted of the following units (in addition to zone of communication units):

        124th Division
        126th Division
        77th Independent Mixed Brigade
        2d Border Garrison Unit
        11th Border Garrison Unit
        15th Border Garrison Unit (provisionally organized)
        9th Raiding Unit (provisionally organized)
        31st Independent Antitank Battalion
        20th Heavy Field Artillery Regiment (150-mm how)
        5th Independent Heavy Artillery Battalion (300-mm how)
        8th Independent Heavy Artillery Battalion (300-mm how)
        1st Independent Heavy Artillery Battery (150-mm gun)
        13th Mortar Battalion
        1st Engineer Command
        18th Independent Engineer Regiment (bridge-building)
        3d Field Fortification Unit
        46th Signal Regiment

After the peak withdrawals of March no major transfers were made. In mid-June, however, several non-tactical units were transferred to the Seventeenth Area Army in Korea. These were the 70th Independent Motor Transport Battalion, the 72d and 74th Independent Transport Companies, the 19th Construction Duty Company, and the 71st Zone of Communications Hospital.

In early July, in accordance with War Office Order No 105 (Imperial General Headquarters), the 135th Division and 15th Border Garrison Unit were formally activated. On the 30th, when their organization was completed, they were assigned to Fifth Army. Personnel for these two units were obtained from the recently organized 77th Independent Mixed Brigade and the 3d and 4th Border Garrison Units which were inactivated the same day.[64] On 30 May, meanwhile, an Order of Battle had been issued to Fifth Army signifying that it was in a war status. (See Chart No 1.)

Operational Preparations

From the time of Kwantung Army's "special maneuvers" in 1941, the Fifth Army had maintained the operational plan calling for offensive operations on the eastern front. This plan remained in effect until at least the spring of 1944. After the spring the Army's fighting effectiveness was drastically reduced by the transfer of numerous units to active operational areas. Fifth Army, foreseeing the need for revising its plan, and acting independently of higher headquarters, originated a plan for holding operations, and used it for its map maneuvers held in June. This revised plan required border garrison units to hold key defense positions along the border to facilitate a counterattack by two divisions of the Army, the objective being to destroy in Manchurian territory the superior Soviet force which was expected to surge in from the eastern half of Tungan province.

Kwantung Army, meanwhile, itself beset with transfers from all

---

64. The 3d Border Garrison Unit had been stationed at Panchiehho, and the 4th at Hutou. The Fifth Army's 2d and 11th Border Garrison Units were formed into the 132d Independent Mixed Brigade which was assigned directly to the First Area Army, and later attached to the 128th Division.

(Monograph 154-F)
Chart No 1

Order of Battle of the Fifth Army
(Issued on 30 May 45)

Fifth Army Commander: Lt Gen Noritsune Shimizu

Fifth Army Headquarters
124th Division
126th Division
135th Division*
15th Border Garrison Unit*
9th Raiding Unit*
31st Independent Antitank Battalion
20th Heavy Field Artillery Regiment (150-mm howitzers)
5th and 8th Independent Heavy Artillery Battalions (300-mm howitzers)
1st Independent Heavy Artillery Battery (150-mm guns)
13th Mortar Battalion
1st Engineer Command
18th Independent Engineer Regiment (heavy bridge building)
3d Field Fortification Unit
46th Signal Regiment
Zone of communications units under direct command of the Fifth Army
    46th and 80th Zone of communications Duty Companies
    64th Independent Transport Battalion (horse drawn)
    70th and 71st Independent Transport Companies
    45th Field Road Construction Unit
    64th and 92d Land Duty Companies
    19th Zone-of-communications Medical Unit
    47th Casualty Clearing Platoon
    2d and 3d Mutanchiang Army Hospitals
    Hulin, Hutou, and Paoching Army Hospitals
    Pingyangchen, Chining and Muleng Army Hospitals
    Suiyang and Pamientung Army Hospitals
    20th Veterinary Quarantine Station (Second Class)
    17th Field Ordnance Depot (First Class)
        (minus a mobile repair section)
    17th Field Motor Transport Depot (First Class)
        (minus a mobile repair section)
    17th Field Freight Depot (First Class)
        (minus a mobile clothing repair section)
628th and 629th Special Guard Companies*
630th and 641st Special Guard Companies*

   * Added 30 July 1945. These units, though not formally organized until July 1945, were mentioned in April planning outlines.

parts of Manchuria to the active operational areas, had developed a similar plan for all of Manchuria, and during its October map maneuvers simulated the conduct of an all-out protracted war of resistance (holding operations). As a result of these maneuvers, Kwantung Army unofficially chose as the Fifth Army's main line of resistance (MLR) the line connecting Linkou, Pamientung, and Hsiachengtzu, and instructed Fifth Army to begin studies along these lines. The line chosen, however, was only a starting point. Further study of it, together with reconnaissance of actual positions, were to lead Fifth Army to change the line repeatedly.

Kwantung Army got Imperial General Headquarters approval for the concept of its holding plan on 30 September 1944. But it was not until January 1945 that it drew up a draft of the plan, and not until February that it showed the plan to First Area Army. On the basis of this plan, which First Area Army showed to Fifth Army, as well as the First Area Army's plan resulting therefrom, Fifth Army made various studies, and finally drew up its own outline of the plan. The gist of it was:

> Elements of each main force will check and destroy the advancing enemy by taking advantage of border positions and the terrain. The main bodies will smash the enemy by quickly massing troops at the main defensive positions to be established on the eastern side of Pamientung, the eastern and northern side of Lishuchen, and Mashan (about 20 kilometers east of Linkou.)

This outline thus contained the initial revision of the Army's

main line of resistance. The principal change was that the center
of the line was projected forward to Mashan and Lishuchen, a step
Fifth Army was compelled to make when Third Army designated the
border positions along the Tungning-Suifenho line as its main line
of resistance. The forward projection of Fifth Army's MLR was
unsatisfactory because it was too extensive a line to be defended
by three divisions and, furthermore, from the viewpoint of terrain
was unsuitable for prolonged resistance. Nevertheless the terrain
and positions along the line were reconnoitered, and the preparation
of fortifications was begun.

About the beginning of April 1945, however, First Area Army
Headquarters revealed that it had been informed by Kwantung Army
that a plan for delaying operations had been submitted to Imperial
General Headquarters for approval, to supersede the holding plan.
In transmitting this information First Area Army redesignated Fifth
Army's MLR as the line running from the southwestern sector of
Muleng north through the mountainous region west of Pamientung, to
the area south of Linkou. This was the second revision, but it was
based on a delaying plan rather than a holding plan. It differed
from the preceding plan primarily in that the southern end of the
line at Hsiachengtzu was extended to Muleng. Even this second revision, however, was subjected to further study and revision.

Subsequent studies by Third Army, meanwhile, had led it to discard the Tungning-Suifenho line and to select a line connecting the west of Hunchun with Lotzukou and Tachienchang as the MLR for itself and the 128th Division. Tachienchang, being about 40 kilometers south of Muleng, Fifth Army thereupon redesignated its MLR as the line extending from west of Muleng, through the western side of Pamientung to Chihsing, thereby eliminating the Mashan-Lishuchen bulge. (See Sketch No 1.) This third revision corrected the unsatisfactory feature of the second revision, and was made in order to contract the frontage and to utilize favorable terrain for operations against mechanized units. Following this change, Fifth Army immediately reconnoitered the area designated, and made plans to organize positions there. Meanwhile, it unofficially notified each division under its command of the plan, instructing commanders to reconnoiter their respective areas and to formulate a detailed plan of operations on the basis of this line and also to make preparations for the construction of positions.

The constant study of Fifth Army's plan resulted in several changes over the outline prepared in February for holding operations. In late April Fifth Army prepared an outline on the basis of the new delaying plan, to the following effect:

> Elements of the Army will crush the fighting power of the invading enemy, utilizing established border positions and terrain features. The Army's main body, formed around three divisions, will quickly dispose itself in depth along the MLR extending from west of Muleng, through west of Pamientung, to the area between Chihsing and Linkou, with the object of resisting and destroying the enemy. To accomplish this, bold and desparate raiding opera-

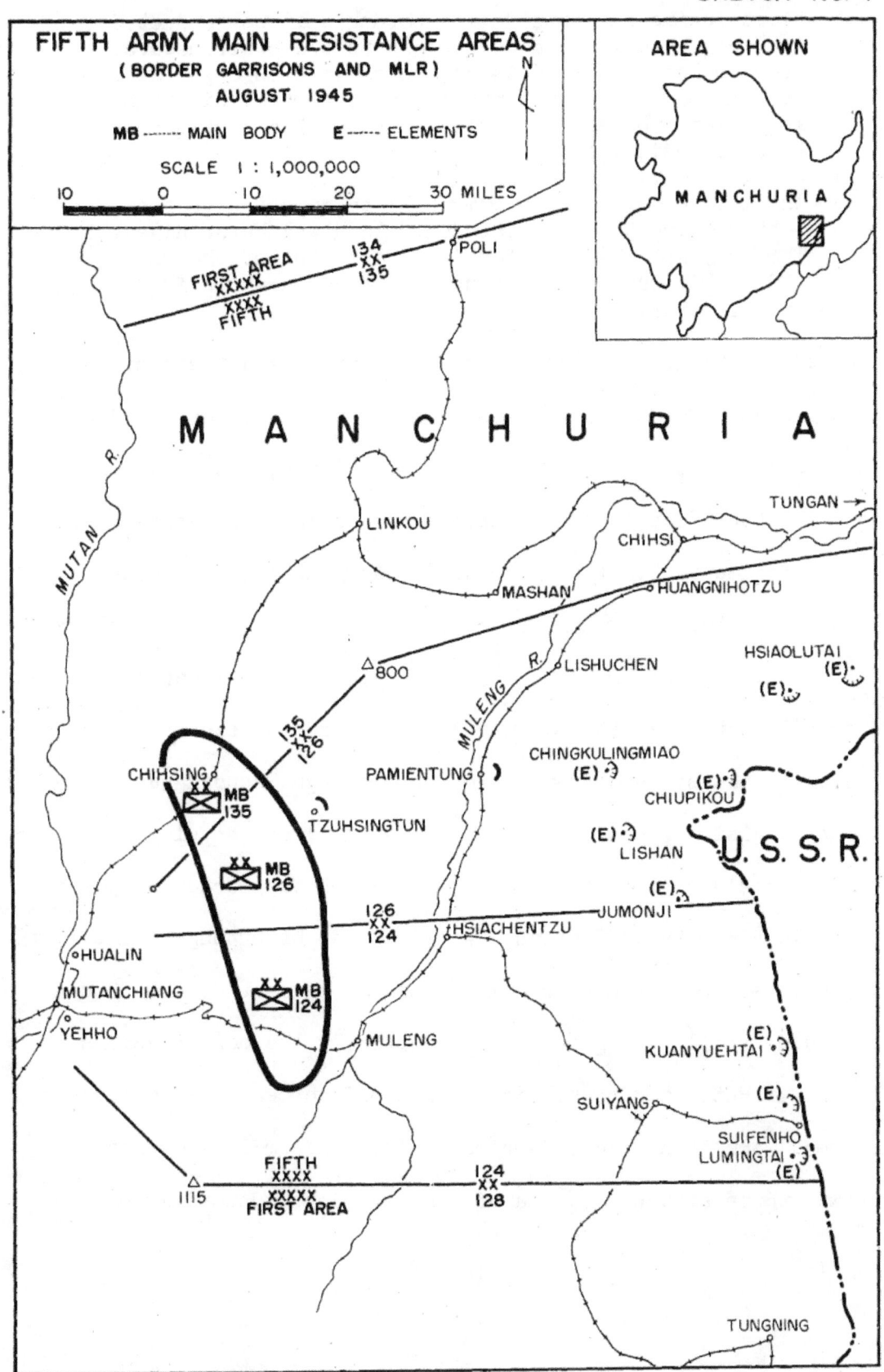

MONOGRAPH NO. 154-F
SKETCH NO. 1

tions inside and outside the border will be conducted actively by utilizing dense forests and other natural terrain features. Resistance organized in depth will be carried out against the enemy to destroy his fighting power, thereby accomplishing the objective of protracted resistance.

The main effort of the Army will be directed to the sector along the road between Muleng and Mutanchiang. The Army will heavily fortify the sector of the MLR and will insure that adequate supplies are provided in that area.

Based on this plan, the deployment of units and their missions were announced. To defend the sector along the east-west road between Muleng and Mutanchiang: the 124th Division, the 31st Independent Antitank Battalion, the main force of the 20th Heavy Field Artillery Regiment, the 1st Independent Heavy Artillery Battery, one battery of the 1st Tungning Heavy Artillery Regiment, the 13th Mortar Battalion, and two provisional independent engineer battalions (temporarily activated at Chiamussu); to defend the sector along the northeast-southwest road from Pamientung through Tzuhsingtun to Yehho: the 126th Division (less one infantry regiment) and an element of the 20th Heavy Field Artillery Regiment; to defend the sector south of Linkou (the vicinity of Chushan, Chihsing, and Hsientung): the 135th Division (less one infantry regiment) and an element of the 20th Heavy Field Artillery Regiment; to hold firmly the border defense positions at Hutou and to harass and cut off the enemy's rear in the Iman area: the 15th Border Garrison Unit; to form an Army reserve which was to be attached to one of the divisions, depending on the situation: one infantry regiment of the 126th Division and one of the 135th Division.

Units were deployed according to their missions. Main bodies moved to the rear (MLR) areas and immediately began the construction of fortifications.

By mid-June Kwantung Army Headquarters completed its draft of the delaying operational plan and summoned all Army commanders to Hsinking to show it to them. Although the Fifth Army Commander, Lieutenant General Noritsune Shimizu, attended, the Fifth Army did not find it necessary to change the plan it had previously mapped out.

Fortifications

Up until mid-1944 fortifications in Fifth Army's area had been constructed principally at strategic points along the border. In August or September 1944, upon learning that Kwantung Army was drafting plans for holding operations, Fifth Army came to the conclusion that it would be difficult to follow such a plan with its dwindling strength and the quality of its personnel. Specifically, the Army felt that it was impossible either to resist a powerful Soviet Army at the border in positions widely distributed over an extensive frontier, or to defeat it in detail at established strong points in the border areas. For these reasons, a proposal was put forward to call a halt to all border fortification work that was to be carried out that year but, because no definite instructions were received from higher headquarters, the work was continued according to schedule. (See Chart No 2.)

Following the designation of the Fifth Army main line of resistance at the beginning of April 1945 it was decided to prepare defense positions for about three divisions, the positions to extend from the sector west of Muleng to the area south of Linkou through the western side of Pamientung. Reconnaissance of the area and other preparations by Fifth Army were completed so as to launch actual fortification work as soon as the thawing season set in. The Army showed the final draft of construction plans to its divisions and other subordinate units, and issued appropriate instructions.

Priority for this 1945 construction work was to be given, the Army announced, to underground installations in view of experiences gained in Pacific operations. Such installations as dug-outs and gun shelters were to be constructed deep in the ground so that they could be safe from heavy field guns and light bombs. In selecting defense positions, particular attention was to be given to fully utilizing terrain features to cope with attacks by enemy mechanized units. Concurrent with this work, the Army announcement continued, a training program would be carried out, the training to be conducted at the scene of the fortifications.

At the beginning of May each division reconnoitered its respective area, prepared construction materials, and set to work under the personal direction of commanders. As for fortifications materials,

(Monograph No 154-F)
Chart No 2

New Fortification Construction in 1944

Sector	Fortifications	Defense Strength	Unit Responsible for Work	Remarks
Mishan	Field fortifications	One infantry battalion	25th Division	Performed by one infantry battalion in March
Hutou Position	Ferro-concrete gun shelter and other types	One 410-mm howitzer section	Hutou Border Garrison Unit	Carried out from spring to autumn, the purpose being to cut off communications in the Iman Area
Jaoho Position (about 8 km west of Jaoho)	Strong point	About two infantry battalions and one artillery battalion	Kwantung Army Fortifications Department	Carried out from spring to autumn, the purpose being to check the enemy's advance from the Jaoho Area
Paoching Sector	Field fortifications	About two infantry battalions	Temporary fortifications unit	To check the enemy's advance from the Jaoho Area
Yangkang	Field fortifications	About three infantry battalions	11th Division	In cooperation with the positions near Fengmishan, to check the enemy's advance from the Hulin area.

Remarks: Besides those mentioned in this table, works were carried out to reinforce existing positions.

161

lumber was no problem, but cement was never supplied in the sufficient quantity.

To some extent fortification construction had to be carried out at the expense of training. Despite the Army's advocacy that training should be conducted at the site of the construction work, each unit began training recruits in their barracks areas. Consequently, considerable quantities of weapons were retained in barracks areas; relatively few weapons were taken to the construction sites. Early in July, the Army commander inspected the fortifications, and pointed out that weapons should be brought to the construction positions. Although some units promptly complied, others were not able to move their weapons. When the war broke out, about one-third of the light and heavy machineguns and about an equal percentage of the artillery guns of each unit were still at the barracks areas forward of the MLR.

By the beginning of August 1945 the slow rate of completion of construction became evident. Of the fire trenches and communications trenches for infantry troops, only about 80 per cent had been completed; of the antitank ditches and other tank obstacles about 50 per cent had been completed. Pillboxes with portholes and fire trenches were only half completed. Large caliber guns could not be mounted because of the shortage of artillery tractors. Each division spent so much time on underground work that, when the war broke out, hardly any surface wire entanglements had been erected. Excavation work for antitank ditches in the vicinity of the road running from Muleng to Mutanchiang had to be postponed because of congested traffic. Immediately after the outbreak of hostilities, enemy mechanized units had little trouble breaking through this road and invading this area.

Those units that left their ammunition stores in barracks areas had to rely, at the outbreak of hostilities, upon whatever supplies of arms and ammunition the Army could furnish from its supply depots at Taimakou, Ssutaoling, and Hsientung, just behind the MLR.

Logistical Planning

During 1944, while Fifth Army was still thinking in terms of offensive operations, it moved some of its supply installations forward and enlarged them. It moved the main field ordnance depot and the field motor transport depot to Hsitungan, and the main field freight depot (general supplies) to Tungan. Furthermore, it opened sub-depots or branch depots near the regular stations of subordinate commands, for example at Mishan, Feite, Hulin, Hutou, and Paoching. Thus these huge supply dumps and their branches, although established conveniently for offensive operations, were not well placed for delaying operations, since they were located at points vulnerable to attack by the Soviet Army.

In September 1944 when the Twentieth Army Headquarters was transferred to the China area, Fifth Army acquired its field ordnance depot, field motor transport depot, and field freight depot, all at Chining. These too were in forward areas.

The changes in operational plans between September 1944 and June 1945 had just as much effect on the location of supply bases as it did no fortification construction. When, late in 1944 Fifth Army was notified that Kwantung Army was preparing a holding plan, it found that all of its supply dumps were forward of the designated MLR. It immediately began a series of conferences with First Area Army Headquarters with a view to pulling supply bases back of the main line.

According to the holding plan Fifth Army's MLR was the Muleng-Pamientung-Linkou line. Fifth Army decided therefore to move a part of war materials stored in forward supply dumps to rear sector dumps to be established at the following places: Taimakou (about 10 kilometers west of Muleng), the left bank of the Muleng River at a point about 8 kilometers west of Pamientung, Hsientung (about 40 kilometers south of Linkou), and also to a base just north of Yehho. For this purpose it set about constructing bomb-proof, tunneled shelters near the western side of Pamientung, Hsientung, and Yehho about the beginning of March 1945. (Shelters had earlier been constructed at Taimakou by Third Army). Later, when the MLR was revised, construction of the shelters west of Pamientung was stopped because they proved to be forward of it. The main effort was then directed to the shelters in the Hsientung and Yehho sectors.

With the decision to move supplies to the rear, and having ordered the construction of rear dumps the Army towards the end of

February began evacuating by train large quantities of weapons, ammunition, and provisions stored east of Linkou, leaving the rest behind for daily supply of forward units. The evacuation program was to be completed by the summer of 1945 but, because of the inefficient operation of railways, the amount evacuated monthly did not exceed 60 or 70 per cent of that scheduled.

Meanwhile, to prevent the enemy from gaining knowledge of the change in operational plans, Fifth Army in early 1945 decided not to stop construction work on several projects in forward positions begun in 1944 and employing a large number of coolies. The largest of these projects, all in the vicinity of Hsingkai (Khanka) and susceptible of observation by the enemy, were: a semi-underground field ordnance depot about 4 kilometers west of that village, and two semi-underground branch field motor transport depots, one about 4 kilometers north of it and the other about 5 kilometers to its east. These installations were pushed to completion as a ruse, and were never used.

When Kwantung Army's planning shifted from holding to delaying operations about March 1945, plans for the withdrawal of supplies were again revised, and Fifth Army designated the vicinities of Mutanchiang and Yehho as its main supply bases for depots. It also added one more dump; besides those at Tamaikou and Hsientung, it directed that one be established at Ssutaoling (about 8 kilometers east of Yehho) as a rear storage base for munitions. Accordingly, supplies in the Hulin, Tungan, Chining, and Suiyang areas were hastily moved back to these depots and dumps after April. The quantities evacuated by the time hostilities began did not meet more than 70 or 80 per cent of the schedule. (See Sketch No 2.)

Of the amounts accumulated behind the MLR, about 30 or 40 per cent were in dumps at Ssutaoling, Taimakou, and Hsientung; the remainder was in the Mutanchiang depot. The levels of ammunition were so small, however, that there were only 100 rounds for each rifle and 500 or 600 shells for each field gun; the quantity of fuel in stock was so low that the Army had only a ten-day supply. Nevertheless, when the war broke out, the Army was able to furnish what supplies it had accumulated without much difficulty.

At the outbreak of hostilities, the Army ordered the rearward movement of considerable quantities of substitute explosives made from powder extracted from large caliber shells stored in the branch ordnance depot at Chining. The transportation of this material to Yehho by truck began on 9 August, but none of its reached there because of interception by enemy mechanized units near Pamientung.

Communication

During 1944, roads in Fifth Army's operational area were considered to be adequate. Some repair work, however, was undertaken during the year. The vehicular road between Tungan and Poli, for example, important for troop movements, operations, and the transportation of supplies to the Tungan sector, had fallen into disre-

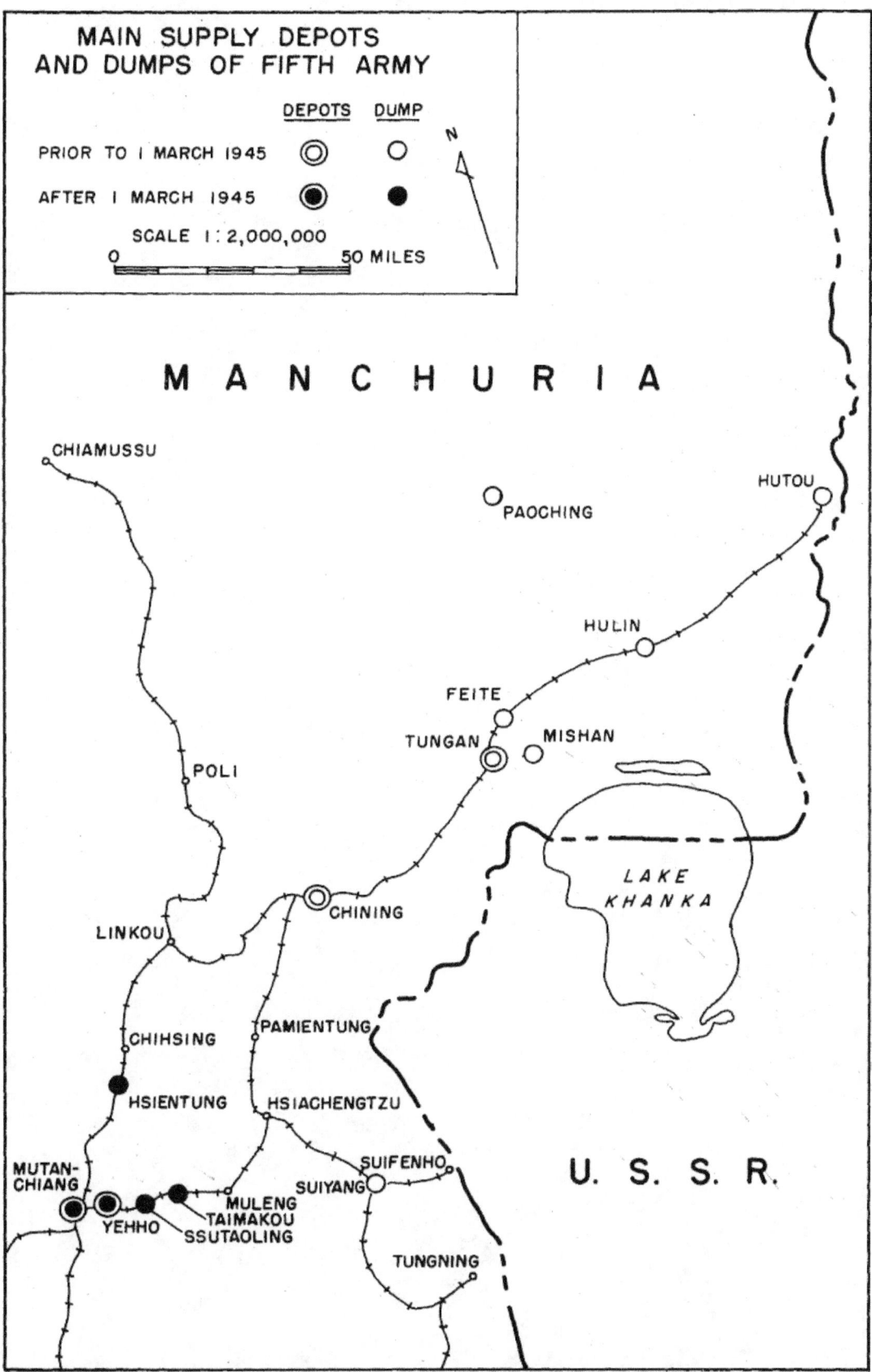

pair. During the year the Army repaired some sections of this road and undertook new construction in other sections. In addition, new arteries were needed. In particular, a path connecting Hulin and Tumuho (about 40 kilometers north of Hutou) through the southern side of the Wanta Mountain Range was required for the transportation of supplies by packhorse. By the time war broke out only about 50 per cent of the work planned for Hulin-Tumuho path had been completed. Both of these roads were needed in conjunction with the old (offensive) operational plan.

After the delaying operational plan was informally announced, the importance of communications within the main line of resistance was stressed. About the middle of April, work was begun to improve the road connecting Linkou, Chushan, Hsientung, and Yehho, which near Chushan was impassable for vehicles. This road paralleled the Tumen-Chiamussu Railway. The 45th Field Road Construction Unit began work to enlarge the Chushan section of the road but did not complete the work in time. Consequently, when the war started motor transport units in the Tungan area after retreating to Poli along the Tungan-Poli road, had to continue the journey to Yehho by train.

Road construction within the MLR positions of each unit was generally the responsibility of the unit. Most of the interior network within each position was in usable shape by the time the war started. (See Sketch No 3.)

Telephone and telegraph lines had earlier been established from

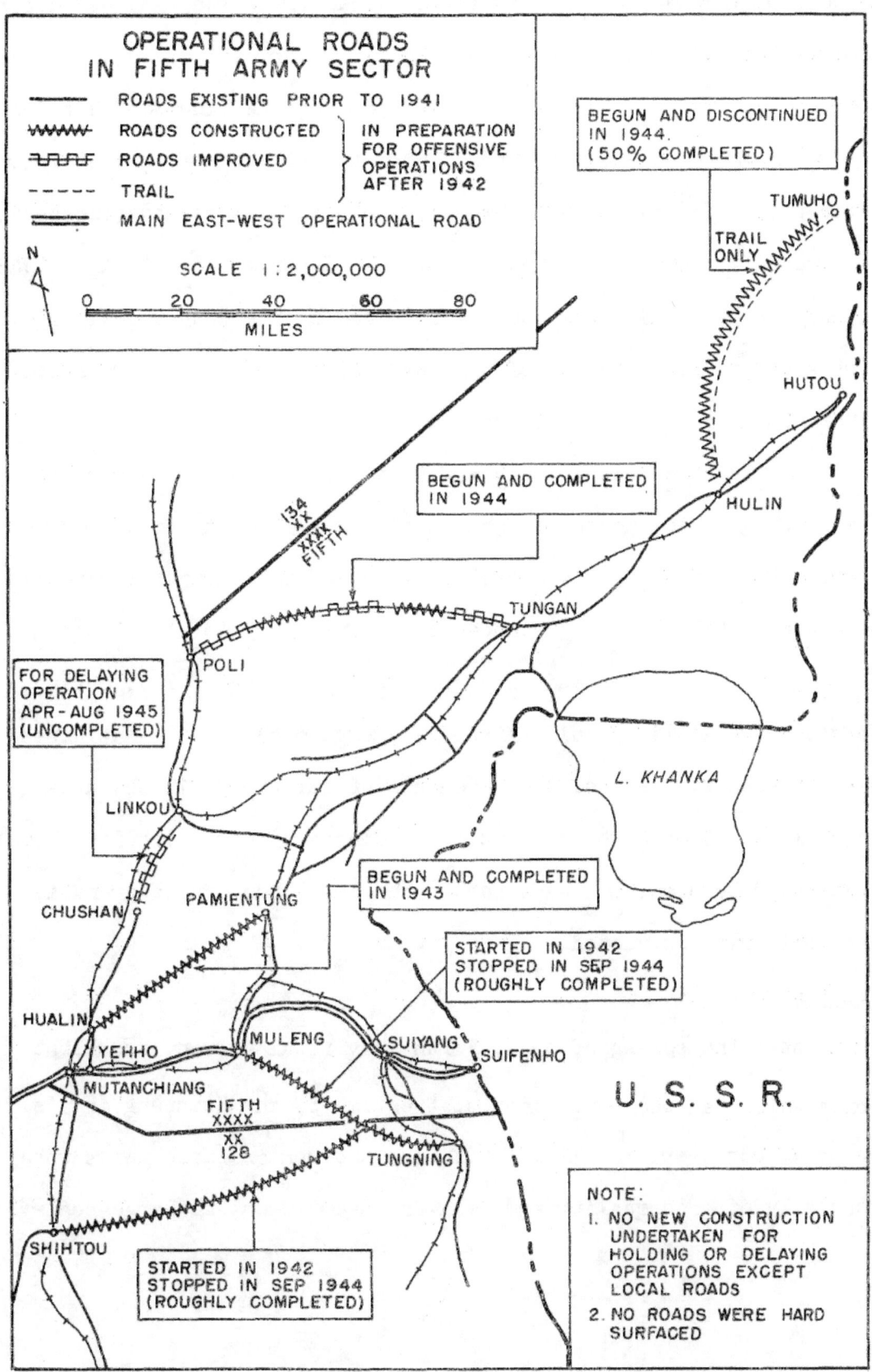

MONOGRAPH NO. 154.-F
SKETCH NO. 3

Yehho to Muleng and to Linkou, and consequently Fifth Army had direct lines to the 124th and 135th Division. However, it had no lines to the center division—the 126th—in Pamientung. A line was therefore needed along the operational road connecting Yehho-Hualin-Tzuhsingtun-Pamientung. To install these wires preparations were made and necessary meterials were assembled during the winter months of early 1945 so that the work might be started in March by the 46th Signal Regiment after it completed the first phase of its training. Overhead wires were strung along this road during June and July.

Another line became necessary at the outbreak of the war when the 124th Division moved its headquarters from Muleng to the dense forest area about 15 kilometers northwest of that city. A service wire was hastily laid a distance of approximately 10 kilometers, tapping in on the overhead line along the main road. Yet, during operations this line could not be used even once because the wires were severed by the frequent movements of our troops in the area. Actually, neither wire nor wireless (telegraph) communication to this unit could be used, and as a result the direction of its operations was seriously obstructed.

Training

Until the spring of 1944, Fifth Army retained many excellent units which had been organized at the time of the Kwantung Army's "special maneuvers" of 1941. Officers and men of these units were generally of good quality and well-trained. When the large-scale transfers from Manchuria began in the spring of 1944, Fifth Army began to lose a large number of these experienced units with competent officers and men. Replacements, when available, were of poor quality. As a result of the transfer and poor replacements there was a marked decline in the combat effectiveness of each unit. Following the transfer of the 24th, 25th, and 11th Divisions in rapid succession, the strength of each Army unit was reduced below its T/O authorization. (See Chart No 3.) In addition, the sharp decline in the quality of men--the replacements were generally old and untrained--reduced the combat effectiveness of each unit, a weakness aggravated by the shortage of equipment. As a result combat effectiveness in the spring of 1945 was only-half or one-third of the 1941 level.

Fifth Army took steps to remedy this situation, stressing the vigorous leadership of commanders. Troops were made keenly aware of the necessity to be ready for the battles ahead. To give them confidence in victory in spite of inferiority in equipment, Fifth Army instituted rigorous training programs and stirred up fighting spirit. In accordance with the Kwantung Army's Combat Guide, each man was trained to kill ten enemy, to attack enemy mechanized units boldly from close quarters, to disperse fully during enemy bombing and shelling, and to operate under cover of darkness. However, even after some of these units had achieved some degree of unity and

(Monograph No 154-F)
Chart No 3

Actual Strengths of Infantry Divisions
June - August 1945

| 124th Div | 14,442 | 126th Div | 16,613 |
| 134th Div | 14,056 | 135th Div | 14,228 |

Standard Organization of Japanese Army Infantry Divisions
(up to Early part of Pacific War)

```
Inf Div ─┬─ Inf Group ──┬─ HQ (300)
(approx) │  (16,638)    │
(25,500) │              ├─ Inf Regt (5,546) ──┬─ HQ (90)
         │              │                     ├─ Inf Bns (three) (4,572)
         │              │                     ├─ Inf Regt Gun Co (156)
         │              │                     ├─ AT Gun Bn (370)
         │              │                     └─ Sig Co (142)
         │              ├─ Inf Regt
         │              └─ Inf Regt
         │
         ├─ Cav Regt (1,048) ──┬─ HQ
         │         or          ├─ Cav Cos (three)
         │                     └─ Machinegun Co
         │
         ├─ Recon Regt (689) ──┬─ HQ
         │                     ├─ Inf Cos (two)
         │                     ├─ Recon Car Cos (two)
         │                     └─ Track Co
         │
         ├─ Fld Arty Regt (3,254) ──┬─ HQ
         │          or              ├─ 75mm Gun Bns (three)
         │                          ├─ 150mm How Bn
         │                          └─ AM Train
         │
         ├─ Fld Mt Arty Regt (3,793) ──┬─ HQ
         │                             ├─ 75mm Mt Gun Bns (two)
         │                             ├─ 105mm How Bn
         │                             └─ AM Train
         │
         ├─ Engr Regt (898) ──┬─ HQ
         │                    ├─ Cos (three)
         │                    └─ Repair Plat
         │
         ├─ Trans Regt (1,813) ──┬─ HQ
         │                       ├─ Horse Bn
         │                       └─ Track Bn
         │
         ├─ Signal Unit (239)
         │
         └─ Medical Unit (1,109) ──┬─ HQ
                                   └─ Cos (four)
```

skill through intense training, transfers of troops continued and impaired what progress had been made. Thus, the combat effectiveness of all units remained in a highly regrettable state.

As regards the types of training given at construction sites, every spare moment was devoted to training in defensive warfare. Defense installations at the scene of fortifications were used for such training.

Throughout this period the Army strictly adhered to the principle of giving top priority to constructing fortifications, and the Army as a whole devoted too much of its efforts to construction work, particularly after April, often at the sacrifice of military training. Yet the Army tried to train its men in the field according to its slogan "Train While Fighting." When mass mobilization was enforced throughout Manchuria at the end of July and large numbers of untrained reserves were sent to the 135th Division and other units, the Army became especially busy with fortification work on the one hand and military training on the other. Such being the cease, when the war began the lack of training of new personnel seriously hampered the operations of the 135th Division and other units.

Intelligence

Fifth Army observation units outposted in the border area extending from Jaoho southward to Lake Hanka, favored by their location near the USSR's Ussuri Railway, periodically provided useful information to the Kwantung Army General Headquarters. These units succeeded in detecting the eastward transportation of Soviet forces from western Europe after February 1945. They smelled out even such details as the classification and number of troops and the types and amounts of equipment. Their reports provided very important data for determining Soviet plans. (See also Monograph 154-I.)

Also active in Manchuria, however, were pro-Soviet spies, especially after the spring of 1945. These spies seemed equally interested in the status of Japanese forces and in the domestic situation in Manchuria. Mainly Koreans and Manchurians, they infiltrated principally from the sector west of Lake Hanka, between Panchiehho and Mishan, and secondarily from the sector between Hutou and Jaoho. Some spies were equipped with large, stationary radios, and operated from bases in such places as Panchiehho, Chining, Poli, and Chiamussu. Although the military police searched these places, they failed to make a substantial number of arrests. Some spies also had portable radios; one such group was arrested near Motaoshih in June 1945.

After April 1945 the activity of the Russians became more positive, and the number of spies carrying radio sets increased. Their method seemed to be to hide in Manchuria for a long period and gather intelligence systematically, and then return to Soviet territory. Furthermore, in the border zone some spies made use of shooting rocket signals at night to send messages. Steps were taken several times to arrest them, but no results were achieved. Counter-espionage was generally ineffective.

Border Garrisoning

During the summer of 1944, Fifth Army was given responsibility for garrisoning that part of the border extending from the vicinity of Tungancheng (about 60 kilometers north of Jaoho) south through Jaoho, Hutou, and Tachiao and westward to Miaoling (about 15 kilometers south of Tungan). Numerous border units garrisoned this extensive frontier. The 12th Border Garrison Unit was at Miaoling, the 4th Border Garrison Unit at Hutou, an infantry company, reinforced, of the 24th Division at Tangpichen (the northwestern extremity of Lake Khanka), about one infantry battalion, one cavalry regiment, and one mortar battalion of the 11th Division from the region extending from the northern sector of Lake Khanka north through Hutou to Tumuho (about 40 kilometers north of Hutou), and one cavalry regiment of the 3d Cavalry Brigade at Jaoho. In addition, some of the observation units (each with one officer and twenty to thirty men) were given the secondary mission of garrisoning the border. (See Map No 1.) Each of the units engaged in border garrison duty exercised patience and prudence, and endeavored to prevent disturbances along the border in accordance with Kwantung Army instructions.

Soviet forces, presumably taking advantage of the unfavorable progress of Japanese operations in the Pacific and of the favorable progress of their war against Germany, created a series of outrageous shooting incidents at Hutou. From Soviet territory across the Ussuri River shots were fired once a day on 5, 6, and 10 December 1944, and twice on the 9th. In February 1945 they extended an insulated wire across the frozen Ussuri River into Manchurian territory and brazenly connected in with our telephone wire in the sector north of Jaoho. With the advent of the spring of 1945, they became bolder and bolder. They began dispatching spies more actively and constructing fortifications openly on the border; for our part, meanwhile, every means was taken to maintain calmness in Manchurian territory.

Towards the end of July, when transportation via the Ussuri Railway increased in tempo, the Soviets became so defiant as to cross the border and construct fortifications in front of Panchiehho. On 5 August about 100 Soviet infantrymen crossed the Ussuri River which separates Manchuria from Siberia and set foot on Manchurian territory, approaching within 500 or 600 meters of our outpost near Kanhsiatun, about 40 kilometers south of Hutou.[65]

Thus, as tenseness increased, the Soviets assumed a very imperious and insulting attitude towards us, going so far as to carry out openly and in broad daylight border movements which formerly they had conducted secretly at night.

In view of such unlawful and contemptuous acts of the Soviets and of such facts as the unilateral abrogation of the Japanese-

---

65. The Kanhsiatun incident is described in greater detail under "Border Garrisoning" in Monograph 154-B.

Soviet Neutrality Pact in April,[66] and also in view of Germany's surrender and the unfavorable situation in the Pacific, it was considered highly probable that Soviet invasion of the territory of Manchuria was imminent. Kwantung Army Headquarters estimated that the Soviet invasion would begin after August or September.

During the months of rising tension, Fifth Army placed emphasis on the following measures:

> Rapid completion of fortification construction on the main line of resistance.
>
> Accumulation of arms, ammunition, and materiel, in the fortified areas.
>
> Redisposition of Army units to cope with the imminent commencement of hostilities.
>
> **Transfer of Army Headquarters from Tungan to Yehho. (carried out 25 April)**
>
> Maneuvers for higher headquarters in accordance with the new operational plan.
>
> Role of various Manchurian Government agencies in the event of an outbreak of hostilities, particularly as regards the evacuation of Japanese residents.

The new units that composed Fifth Army by August 1945 deployed garrisons in the border areas in substantially the same positions as the old units. These consisted principally of divisional elements, except in the Hutou sector. On the 124th Division front one infantry

---

66. This pact had one more year to run, but might be denounced one year before its expiration by either party. Langer, Encyclopedia of World History, P 1143.

175

battalion of the 277th Regiment was deployed in the Pamientung sector from Jumonji Pass to Chingkulingmiao, and one battalion of the 278th in the Pingyang sector from Hsiaolutai to Shangchihtun via Panchiehho. On the 135th Division front one infantry battalion of the 369th Regiment was deployed at Miaoling, one company of the 368th at Tachiao, one platoon of the 368th south of Hutou, and one battalion (less one company) of the 369th in the Jaoho sector, including Paoching in the rear. The principal force at Hutou was the 15th Border Garrison Unit (assigned to the 135th Division on 9 August), which consisted of one infantry battalion (four infantry companies, one infantry artillery battery, and one antitank battery) one artillery unit (about two batteries), and one engineer unit (about one company). (See Map No 2.)

Status of Supplies and Equipment

The equipment of each unit of the Army was excellent and sufficient until about the summer of 1944 when the transfers to the Pacific and China areas began. Because many of the transferred units took along most of the reserve supplies and enough ammunition for two major engagements (about a six months supply) the stocks in the Army supply depots decreased sharply compared with the levels maintained during the Kwantung Army "sepcial maneuvers" of 1941.

Units departing Manchuria for active operational areas naturally had to be well equipped, and when possible, newly equipped. The surplus weapons and materials left behind by these units were given

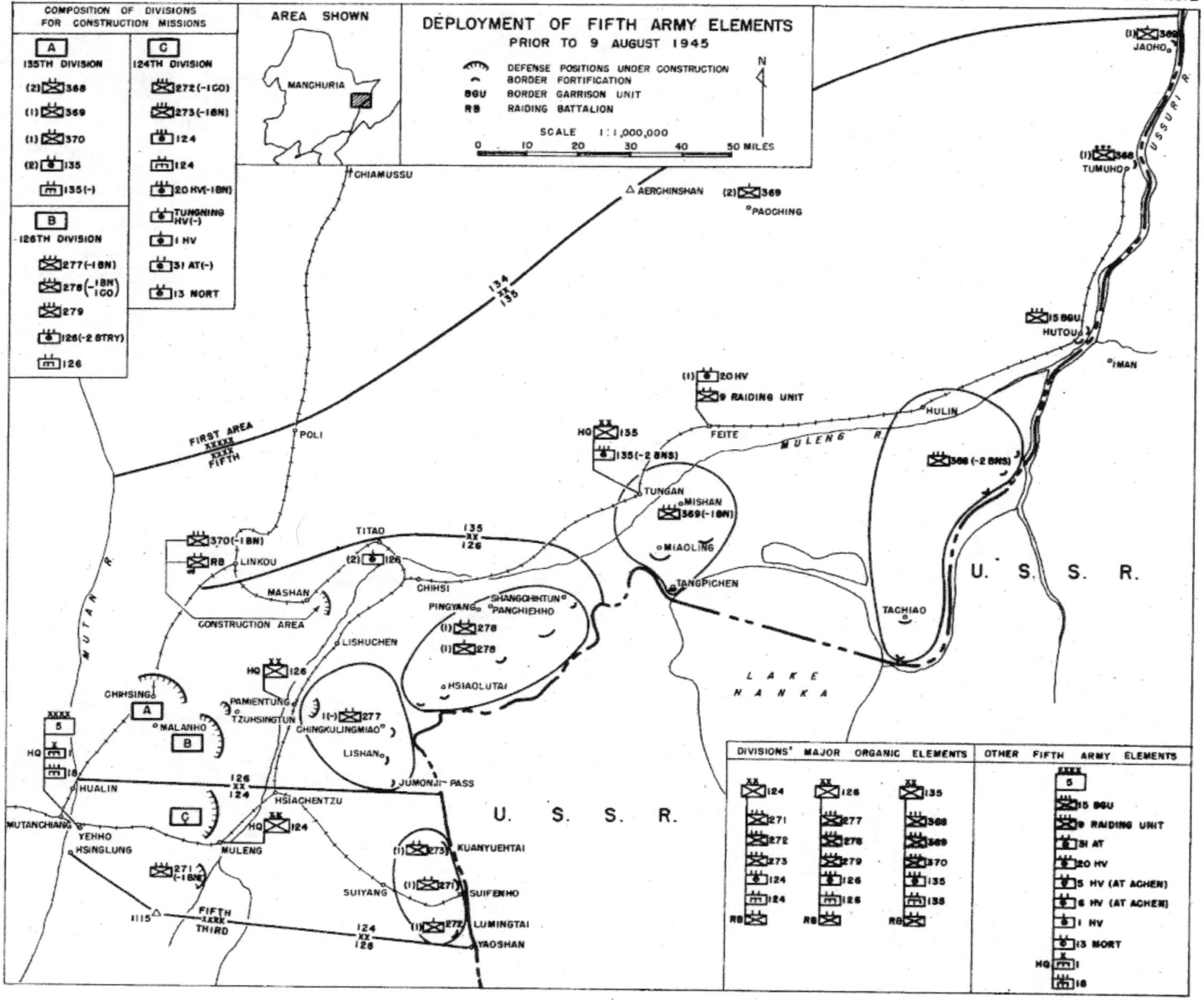
DEPLOYMENT OF FIFTH ARMY ELEMENTS
PRIOR TO 9 AUGUST 1945
DEFENSE POSITIONS UNDER CONSTRUCTION
BORDER FORTIFICATION
BGU BORDER GARRISON UNIT
RB RAIDING BATTALION
SCALE 1:1,000,000
0 10 20 30 40 50 MILES
N
AREA SHOWN
MANCHURIA
COMPOSITION OF DIVISIONS FOR CONSTRUCTION MISSIONS
A
135TH DIVISION
(2) 368
(1) 369
(1) 370
(2) 135
135(-)
B
126TH DIVISION
277(-1BN)
278(-1BN 1CO)
279
126(-2 BTRY)
126
C
124TH DIVISION
272(-1CO)
273(-1BN)
124
124
20 HV(-1BN)
TUNGNING HV(-)
1 HV
31 AT(-)
13 MORT
DIVISIONS' MAJOR ORGANIC ELEMENTS
124
271
272
273
124
124
RB
126
277
278
279
126
126
RB
135
368
369
370
135
135
RB
OTHER FIFTH ARMY ELEMENTS
5
15 BGU
9 RAIDING UNIT
31 AT
20 HV
5 HV (AT ACHEN)
6 HV (AT ACHEN)
1 HV
13 MORT
HQ 1
18
U. S. S. R.
U. S. S. R.
LAKE HANKA
USSURI R.
MULENG R.
MUTAN R.
CHIAMUSSU
AERCHINSHAN
PAOCHING
(2) 369
JAOHO
(1) 369
TUMUHO
(1) 368
15 BGU
HUTOU
IMAN
HULIN
368 (-2 BNS)
(1) 20 HV
9 RAIDING UNIT
FEITE
HQ 135
135(-2 BNS)
TUNGAN
MISHAN
369(-1BN)
MIAOLING
TANGPICHEN
TACHIAO
POLI
FIRST AREA
FIFTH
134 XX 135
135 XX 126
TITAO
(2) 126
370(-1BN)
RB
LINKOU
MASHAN
CHIHSI
CONSTRUCTION AREA
PINGYANG
SHANGCHIHTUN
PANCHIEHHO
(1) 278
(1) 278
LISHUCHEN
HQ 126
HSIAOLUTAI
CHIHSING
A
MALANHO
B
PAMIENTUNG
TZUHSINGTUN
1(-) 277
CHINGKULINGMIAO
LISHAN
JUMONJI- PASS
5
HQ 1
18
HUALIN
126 XX 124
HSIACHENTZU
C
HQ 124
MUTANCHIANG
YEHHO
HSINGLUNG
MULENG
271 (-1BN)
(1) 273
KUANYUEHTAI
(1) 271
SUIFENHO
SUIYANG
(1) 272
LUMINGTAI
YAOSHAN
1115
FIFTH
THIRD
124 XX 126

to newly organized units. Some of the new units, even after being organized, were sorely in need of certain items. The infantry units of the 126th Division, for example, was equipped with only half of the authorized number of heavy machineguns, light machineguns, grenade dischargers, and other weapons; its artillery unit was only two-thirds equipped.

In the autumn of 1944 Fifth Army had received a verbal message from Kwantung Army Headquarters to the effect that Manchuria could no longer depend on the homeland for explosive powder, but would have to produce it locally. In this same message Fifth Army was assured an allocation of more than 10 tons from the Kwantung Army. However, until the spring of 1945 none of this allocation was received. In these circumstances the Army made efforts to prepare several tons of antitank explosives from powder charges of ammunition for large caliber guns.[67]

By the spring of 1945 stocks of some weapons were so low that improvisation had to be made. The ordnance depot and the motor transport depot forged swords, bayonets, and other weapons from such materials as the springs of motor cars in order to equip zone of communication units and also for the 135th Division.[68]

---

67. Ammunition for guns of large caliber, such as 240-mm and 300-mm, useless in China and the Pacific, had been stored by Fifth Army since the Kwantung Army "special maneuvers" of 1941.
68. Although the 135th Division was not formally activated until July 1945, its scheduled activation was announced several months earlier.

After April 1945 considerable quantities of ammunition were transferred to the China area and the homeland, resulting in further shortages in Manchuria. The artillery regiment of the 124th Division, the nucleus of the Army, was only two-thirds equipped despite the fact that it supplemented its meager equipment of Model 38 field guns with Model 90 field guns, and Model 41 mountain guns (all 75-mm).[69]

The artillery units of the 135th Division, the last division to be organized, was the most poorly equipped unit in the Army. Organized at the end of July, it was only two-thirds equipped with cavalry guns (75-mm), trench mortars, and other weapons. The inferiority of equipment in this division, coupled with the low quality of men and their inadequate training, greatly reduced its fighting effectiveness.

Except for the supply of food, there was a shortage of almost all items of supply in Manchuria, a shortage which Fifth Army felt equally with other commands. The shortage of ammunition, explosives, and automotive fuel was particularly acute in Fifth Army, and led to the belief that it was quite impossible for the Army to fight an extended war of resistance.

---

69. The nomenclature of the Model 38 gun was derived from the fact that the prototype was wrought in the 38th year of the Meiji Era (1905). The name of the Model 41 mountain gun was similarly derived. This was not a hard and fast method of nomencloture, however. The Model 90's name was derived from the 25<u>90</u>th year of the Japanese Imperial Era (1930). The Model 38 had a range of 11,600 meters; the Model 90, with a longer tube, had a range of 14,400 meters, and the probability of hits was better than the Model 38.

Status of Preparations Immediately Prior to the War

Considering the newness of its units the incomplete status of training of new personnel, the unfinished fortifications, and the serious shortages of equipment, Fifth Army Headquarters believed that if the Army were to fight in earnest, its fighting power would be exhausted in less than ten days.

Compared with the combat effectiveness of the Kwantung Army's well-trained divisions of 1941, such as the 12th, the combat effectiveness of the new divisions was extremely poor. Rating the 12th Division as 100 per cent effective, the 124th Division was 35 per cent effective, the 126th Division 20 per cent, and the 135th Division only 15 per cent.

Because of construction work underway in the MLR positions, the main body of each division at the beginning of August was away from its barracks area, and was encamped at construction sites. Although the recently organized 135th Division was similarly deployed, it had a large number of recruits in barracks areas undergoing training. When the invasion began, each division headquarters was forward of its main body, with only the border elements between itself and the enemy.

Moreover, for four days in early August the Army conducted conferences, training, and field exercises at Yehho with agencies of both the Japanese and Manchurian Governments to finalize plans regarding evacuation of Japanese residents and cultivating groups, the handling of railroad transportation and signal communications, and other related matters.

These exercises were followed by war games for division commanders and chiefs of staff, scheduled to last for about five days beginning on 7 August. On the evening of 8-9 August, therefore, when the Soviet Army marched into Manchuria, each division commander, each chief of staff, and the commander of the 15th Border Garrison Unit were staying at Yehho. Army Headquarters was caught off guard by the invasion; it had believed that the Soviet Union would soon step into the war, but not until September.

CHAPTER XI

Fifth Army Operations

Opening of Hostilities   (See Map No 3.)

At about 0100 hours on 9 August, Fifth Army Headquarters at Yehho received a continuous flood of urgent telephone messages from units garrisoning the border areas, and from observation parties. All reported on the sudden change in the situation. The information obtained by putting these reports together was that hostile planes, after crossing the border, were flying over Manchuria at will, and that the border garrison at Suifenho and Kuanyuehtai, and the 15th Border Garrison Unit at Hutou were being shelled by artillery. These units had not taken up the challenge, however, in view of the fact that orders to maintain peace along the border had not been revoked.

At 0300 the Army Commander summoned to headquarters every commander and staff officer staying at the Yehho Officers Club in connection with war games, and issued orders to the following effect:

> Since the night of 8-9 August hostile forces have been shelling our border garrison units all along the line. An element of their infantry seems to have broken through the border. Enemy planes, penetrating deeply, have flown at will over Manchurian territory.
>
> The plan of the Army for meeting the situation is that border elements will delay the advance of the attacking enemy by taking advantage of terrain and established border positions, while the main force will destroy the enemy's fighting power by putting up stubborn resistance in depth in our main defen-

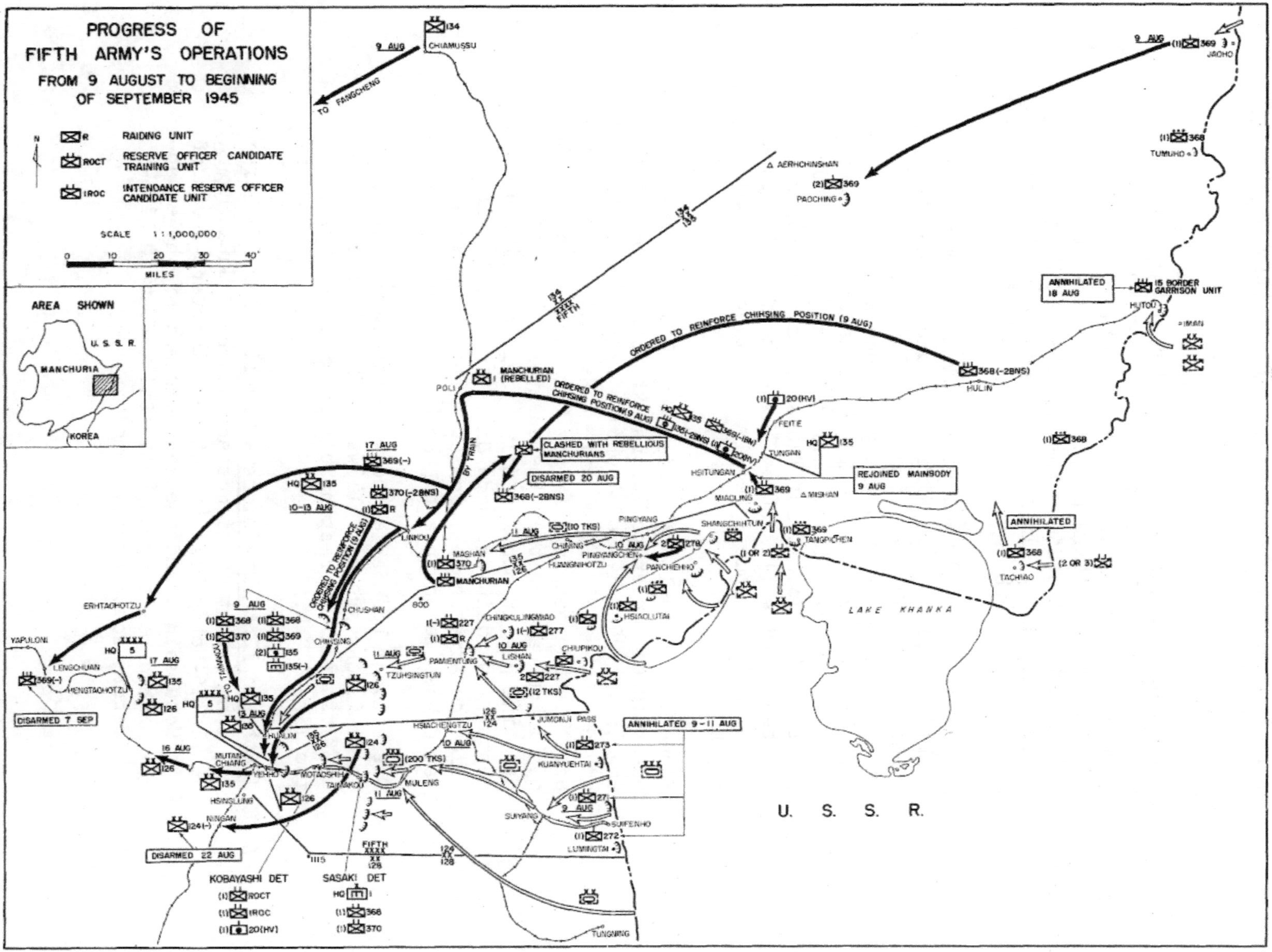

MONOGRAPH NO. 154-F
MAP NO. 3

PROGRESS OF FIFTH ARMY'S OPERATIONS FROM 9 AUGUST TO BEGINNING OF SEPTEMBER 1945

sive positions extending from the western side of Muleng through the west side of Pamientung to the area south of Linkou.

Elements of the 124th Division will occupy the established border positions at Lumingtai, Suifenho, and Kuanyuehtai in an effort to stem the hostile advance, while the division's main force will immediately take up MLR positions west of Muleng and will destroy the enemy's fighting power by opposing him in our defensive positions disposed in depth.

Elements of the 126th Division will occupy established positions extending from Jumonji Pass to Shangchihtun (through Lishan and Panchiehho) in an effort to delay the enemy advance and to facilitate the movement of the 135th Division toward Linkou. The main force will hold established positions in the vicinity of Tzuhsingtun, west of Pamientung, and will destroy the enemy fighting power by resisting in our defensive positions disposed in depth.

Elements of the 135th Division will occupy the established border positions extending from Miaoling to the vicinity of Jaoho to delay the hostile advance; the main force will take positions in the established positions in the Chihsing sector (south of Linkou) and destroy the enemy fighting power by opposing him in our defensive positions disposed in depth. In addition, some divisional units will hold the advance position at Mashan to prevent a rapid hostile advance to the Linkou Area.

Operational boundaries between the zone assigned to divisions are as follows. (The division listed first will be responsible for the defense of the line.)

128th and 124th Divisions - The line linking Hsinglung (about 10 kilometers south of Mutanchiang), 1,115-Meter Hill (about 40 kilometers south of Motaoshih), and the southern end of the established position at Lumingtai (about 10 kilometers south of Suifenho)

> **124th and 126th Divisions** - The line linking Hualin, Hsiachengtzu and Jumonji Pass.
>
> **126th and 135th Divisions** - The line linking Malanho, 800-Meter Hill, Huangnihotzu, and Manjenchuankou.
>
> **135th and 134th Divisions** - The line linking Poli and Aerhchinshan.
>
> The 15th Border Garrison Unit will defend existing border positions firmly and will cut off the enemy line of communications in the Iman sector to facilitate the Army's operations.
>
> Annex (Showing Attachment of Units)
>
> 124th Division
>   31st Independent Antitank Battalion (minus one battery)
>   20th Heavy Field Artillery Regiment (minus two batteries)
>   1st Independent Heavy Artillery Battery (150-mm cannons)
>   One battalion (minus one battery) of the Tungning Heavy Artillery Regiment
>   Mutanchiang Heavy Artillery Regiment
>   13th Mortar Battalion
>   Two provisionally organized independent engineer battalions
>
> 126th Division
>   One battery of the 31st Independent Antitank Battalion
>   One battery of the 20th Heavy Field Artillery Regiment
>
> 135th Division
>   One battery of the 20th Field Heavy Artillery Regiment
>
> 15th Border Garrison Unit
>   Hutou Army Hospital

Each division and unit commander, having received these Army orders at Yehho, called his respective headquarters by phone and gave his staff instructions regarding the measures to be taken to carry out the orders. The commanders of the 124th and 126th Divisions then left Yehho by motor car for their headquarters at Muleng and

Pamientung, respectively. The commander of the 135th Division, Lieutenant General Yoichi Hitomi, expected to return to his headquarters in Tungan by plane early in the morning but, in view of the enemy's air activity, started back by rail (gasoline engine railway car), accompanied by the commander of the 15th Border Garrison Unit, Colonel Takeshi Nishiwaki. General Hitomi arrived at Tungan at 1800, but Colonel Nishiwaki was unable to join his command at the front.

As soon as the border garrisons were placed under fire by the enemy they took up defense positions and awaited orders. Since the beginning of the invasion, owing to the interruption of telephone communications, no information had been available concerning the fate of the border garrisons and observation units, except those in the Suifenho sector, the Pamientung front, the Shangchihtun area, and those near Miaoling, Tachiao, Hutou, and Jaoho. Of the unreported elements it was believed that either their positions had been overrun or that they had been annihilated during the period from dawn to midday of the 9th, except those disposed in the dense forest zone in front of Pamientung, and the 15th Border Garrison Unit in Hutou, which held out considerably longer.

Operations of Border Garrisons on the 124th Division Front

In the Suifenho sector, the main force of the superior enemy instead of dashing against our established positions, at dawn of the 9th penetrated through border gaps between Lumingtai and Suifenho, and between Suifenho and Kuanyuehtai. Toward the evening of that day the enemy entering the latter gap pressed on northeast of Suiyang, and began attacking the Suifenho garrison from the rear. Troops who remained in that area were encircled by the enemy and after offering desperate resistance on the 9th and the 10th were almost entirely annihilated; only a few succeeded in retreating to join our main force.

Meanwhile, early in the morning of the 9th, the commander of the 124th Division ordered Colonel Takehiko Asu, commander of the 271st Infantry Regiment, which normally was stationed in Suiyang but which at this time was in Muleng for fortification work, to return to Suiyang to direct the withdrawal of the arms and ammunition in the Suiyang barracks to Muleng using the units still in the Suiyang sector. Colonel Asu reached the Suiyang barracks at about noon. With a convoy of troops and munitions, he left on the night of the 9th and was back in Muleng the following day. At the Muleng River, however, the trucks loaded with guns of the division artillery could not cross the river because the bridge had been hastily blasted by retreating troops on the preceding day to prevent the enemy from dashing into the town. Though an attempt was made to get the trucks across the river near a dam in the lower reaches, the attempt was thwarted by the enemy. Thus, to our great regret several guns, including new Model 90 type field guns (75-mm), the treasures of the division artillery, did not reach the MLR positions. Most of the troops escaped, however. The enemy, meanwhile, hotly pursued this force and by the evening of the 10th advanced to the line of the Muleng River in the vicinity of Hsiachengtzu.

Operations of Border Garrisons on the 126th Division Front

In the Pamientung sector, our garrison unit in Chiupikou (about 20 men including the leader) was annihilated in a fight against a superior enemy force which attacked at dawn on the 9th. The garrison units of the 277th Regiment occupying positions at Jumonji Pass (one platoon of 3d Company), and to the rear at Lishan (2d Company), and at Chingkulingmiao (1st Company less one platoon) were attacked around 1000 hours on the 10th by five or six enemy battalions having a great number of guns, and though these garrisons held their positions firmly, by the evening of that day the greater part of their positions had been captured; some elements, however, retreated to Pamientung under cover of night. The enemy mechanized unit with more than ten tanks that had appeared in Jumonji Pass area (presumably from the Kuanyuehtai area) advanced toward Pamientung where it attacked on the evening of the 10th. At dawn of the 11th the garrison in the Pamientung sector (about two companies of the 1st Battalion, 277th Regiment plus an element of a raiding battalion) was again attacked by the same tank unit, this time supported by infantry. Pamientung and its vicinity were occupied by the enemy by noon on that day.

In the Pingyang sector, most of our frontline border garrisons at Panchiehho and Hsiaolutai were annihilated by surprise attacks of powerful enemy forces at dawn on the 9th. Near the Panchiehho positions a division-sized enemy force pressed on north of the positions in the evening of the 9th. The commander of the garrison unit (2d Battalion of 278th Regiment) decided to withdraw from the area at midnight. The garrison retreated to rearline defenses near Pingyangchen by noon of the following day, but an element of the enemy force had already broken through other positions, near Hsiaolutai, and was pressing on Pingyangchen. (See Map No 2) A bitter battle was waged near Pingyangchen beginning at noon of the 10th and continuing until the evening. During this action most of our combatants were either killed or wounded and only part of the force (about 200 out of 850) managed to pull out of the line and retreat during the night.

Operations of Border Garrisons on the 135th Division Front

In the Miaoling and Mishan sector, a border observation unit detailed to the forward line by the main garrison in Miaoling was attacked by the enemy at dawn of the 9th and was annihilated in its position. Meanwhile, an element of the enemy force appeared in front of the area occupied by the main force of the Miaoling garrison (approximately one infantry battalion of 369th Regiment) around noon, but it did not immediately attack. Our garrison, under orders from the 135th Division to withdraw to Chihsing, began to move towards Tungan around 1900 hours on the 9th before contacting any enemy. It seemed that the enemy who had penetrated into the Miaoling and Mishan areas was at first only one or two battalions strong and was gradually reinforced up to division strength, but he did not invade Tungan on the 9th or 10th.

In the sector south of Hutou, the observation parties and the several border garrisons (most of them consisting of from twenty to thirty men each) were disposed along the Ussiri River (border line). Communication with these garrisons was completely cut off at dawn on the 9th, perhaps because they had been either annihilated by a surprise attack or completely encircled. The Tachiao (60 kilometers south of Hulin) garrison (consisting of one reinforced infantry company of the 368th Regiment) which had been under attack since noon on the 9th by two or three enemy battalions broke off communications with us during the evening and was concluded to have fought to the last man.

North of Jaoho the enemy crossed the Ussuri River early on the morning of the 9th and later gradually pressed on Jaoho. Our garrison (one company of the 369th Regiment) counterattacked, but after being overcome by the superiority of the enemy, an element of the garrison escaped toward Paoching under cover of night.

On the evening of 9 August, in compliance with Army orders issued at 0300 at Yehho, the 135th Division Commander directed major elements of the division to pull back to Chihsing. The 368th Regiment (less one battalion) departed on foot from the vicinity of Hulin, led by the regimental commander, Colonel Iizuka. Troops of the regiment pushed their way through the Wanta Mountain Range north of Tungan, beating off Manchurian rebels on the way. When they arrived in the area northeast of Linkou a week later, they were informed of the cease-fire. Around 20 August they were disarmed in this vicinity.

The Army order of 9 August had directed that the main body of the division be redeployed to Chihsing, where four of the divisions nine infantry battalions were already in position. The units stationed in Tungan, Feite, and Hsitungan and their neighborhoods (principally elements of the 369th Regiment) were informed by railroad officials that an element of the enemy force had penetrated into a sector located between Tungan and Chining and that they could not withdraw along the railroad. Therefore, they left Tungan for Poli on the night of the 9th along the Tungan-Poli road under cover of darkness. At Poli they entrained for Yehho. Foot troops took longer to assemble at Poli and entrained on 17 August, but being informed of the enemy's advance to Linkou while aboard the train, they detrained and proceeded westward north of Linkou, and then turned south. After crossing the railroad bridge (specially constructed for transporting timber) spanning the Mutanchiang River near Erhtaohotzu, they finally arrived at Lengchuan, east of Yapuloni, by way of a point north of Hengtaohotzu. There, most of them were disarmed between the end of August and early September. The rest of them escaped to as far away placed as the Tunhua and Kirin Areas, and some units were disarmed in those places at the end of August or the beginning of September. However, no detailed information on the fate of these troops in known.

During the afternoon of the 9th, the Army Commander tried to get a message to the 135th Division Commander (General Hitomi was then en route to Tungan) directing him to sent two battalions already in the fortified Chihsing area immediately to Taimakou to reinforce the 124th Division sector where the enemy appeared to be making his main effort. Unable to reach General Hitomi, the Army Commander intervened directly and ordered the two battalions to go to the aid of the 124th Division. These battalions (one of the 368th and one of the 370th Regiments) arrived at Taimakou at about noon of the 10th, and were formed into the Sasaki Detachment, but because of the enemy's unexpectedly rapid advance were shortly ordered to the rear to-defend the Yehho perimeter, where they arrived during the night of the 11th.

Operations of the 15th Border Garrison Unit

In the vicinity of Hutou, on the front occupied by the 15th Border Garrison Unit, there had been border crossings by enemy planes since midnight of 8-9 August, and subsequent thereto artillery shelling from the Iman sector across the river. Each of our units there immediately stood to arms in prearranged positions. The Hutou Army Hospital promptly moved into the position and prepared to collect the sick and wounded. The enemy in this area, estimated to be about two infantry divisions in strength, seemed to have crossed the Ussuri River at several points on a wide front south of Hutou. By noon he had advanced to the area of the airfield southwest of Hutou, and gradually pressed on behind our positions. During the early stages of the fight, about 200 noncombatants (consisting of the dependents of army personnel, Japanese residents, and a cultivating party in Hutou and its vicinity) arrived in these positions and threw in their lot with the garrison. The enemy's shelling continued all day on the 9th but no attack was mounted by the enemy infantry units. Meanwhile, the garrison's 410-mm howitzer and 100-mm cannons laid interdictory fire on the enemy's railroad near Iman, and also harassed the enemy's rear.

On the evening of the 9th, the Army Commander, Lieutenant General Noritsune Shimizu, telegraphed the following pathetic farewell message to the 15th Border Garrison Unit through the 135th Division Headquarters in Tungan: "In view of the present war situation and the position of the garrison, all of you under the leadership of the commander[70] are requested to fight to the last breath and meet your fate, when it comes, as courageously as flowers on eastern front, so that you may become the pillar of our State."

Thereafter, the garrison though greatly outnumbered, hurled violent counterattacks against the enemy's two divisions, repeating contests for the seizure of positions day and night.

---

70. This refers to the acting commander, Captain Masao Oki, commander of the artillery unit. The commander had been unable to return to Hutou after attending the war games at Yehho.

On the 17th and 18th the enemy's attack seemed to have reached its height in relentlessness and ferocity. Men of the garrison held out in the underground casemates, beating off fierce attacks by the enemy who repeatedly tried to capture the entrance of the casemates. Heavy casualties were suffered by both sides in this action. Finally, as the last resort, the enemy seemed to have used oil and smoke [gas?] in an attempt to annihilate the men of the garrison in the tunnel. The garrison under the courageous leadership of the commander fought with its forlorn force to the last man against the overwhelming enemy, and appears to have shared the fate of its positions, which were overrun by the enemy around 18 August.

CHAPTER XII

Operations in the MLR

Operations of the 124th Division Near Muleng (See Map No 4.)

The enemy from the Suifenho area closed in on Hsiachengtzu on the evening of the 10th, and penetrated into the city of Muleng on the evening of the 11th. There he paused to prepare for an attack on the 124th Division's main positions on the hills west of the city.

The 124th Division commander, Lieutenant General Masatake Shiina, after being informed of the Soviet's entry into the war early on the morning of the 9th at Yehho, had hastily returned at Muleng to give necessary orders to the border garrisons. At the same time that he directed the 271st Regimental commander in Muleng to return to Suiyang and supervise the evacuation of munitions to Muleng, as mentioned above, he also directed him to assign the units withdrawn from the Suiyang area to positions in the main line of resistance and to order the units remaining in the area to stand by for action. The latter units, however, were unprepared for operations. The emplacement work for artillery, especially for large calibre guns, was so incomplete that the troops had time only to assemble around the guns and pile ammunition nearby, before being overwhelmed.

Meanwhile, the Mutanchiang Heavy Artillery Regiment (stationed in Hsiachengtzu and equipped with 240-mm howitzers) which had been scheduled prior to the outbreak of war to be transferred to Hamhung,

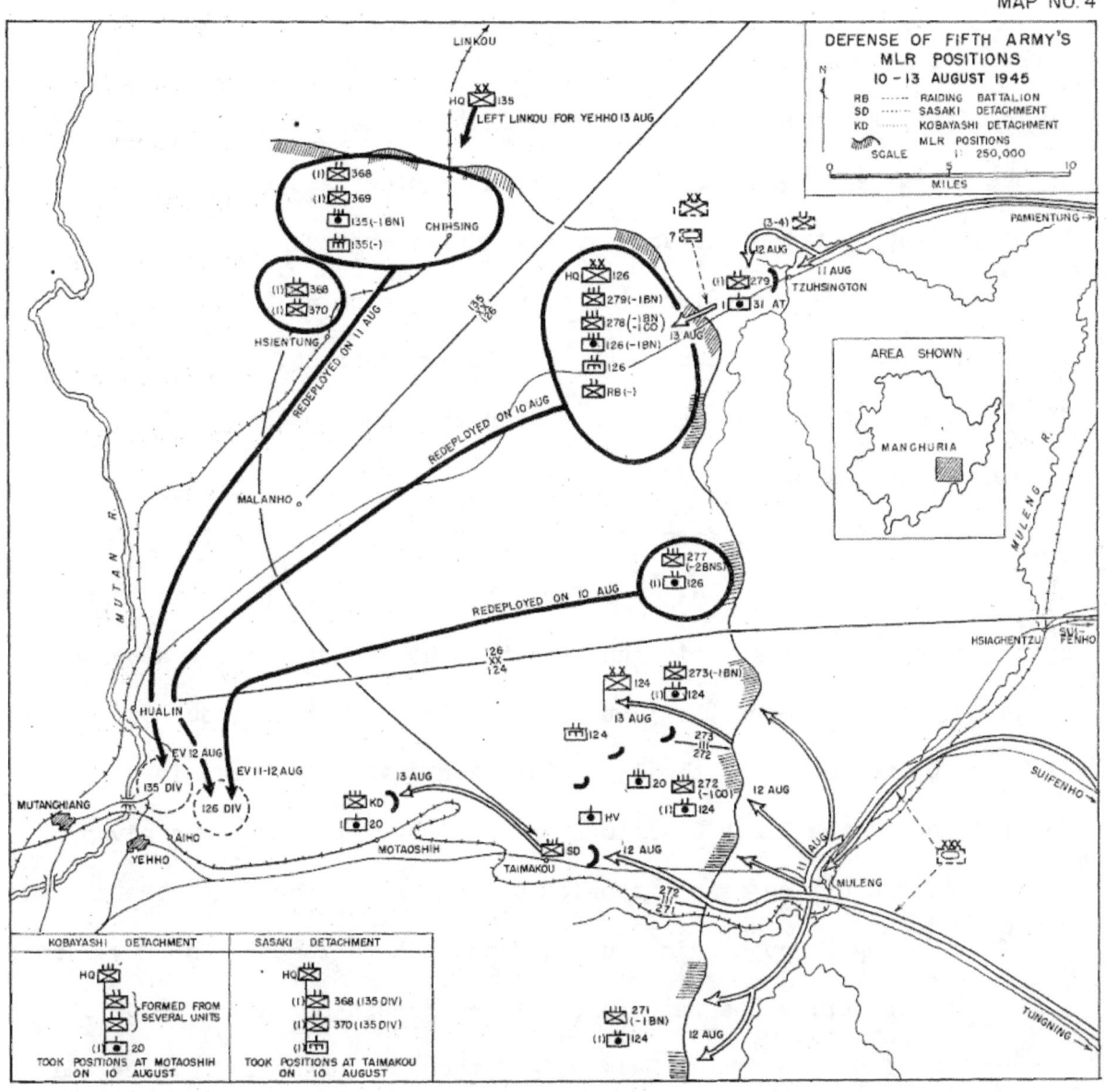

in northern Korea, according to plans of the First Area Army, was still in Fifth Army's area, though not assigned to it. The commander of the regiment, Colonel Koketsu, himself had received a transfer order and was awaiting his successor. After hostilities started, First Area Army assigned this regiment to Fifth Army. However, only two of its howitzers could be brought to the Muleng MLR positions due to the shortage of tractors; the regiment's other six howitzers had to be destroyed at the barracks area at Hsiachengtzu.

Despite these irregularities in the situation of the 124th Division and the Mutanchiang Heavy Artillery Regiment, the preparations for operations in the MLR had been arranged somehow by the evening of the 11th.

Judging from all information, the Army commander concluded that the enemy was making his major effort along the Suifenho-Hsiachengtzu-Muleng road. It was at this juncture that he decided on the afternoon of the 9th to reinforce the 124th Division's front with about two infantry battalions from the 135th Division. At that time, in the disposition of the 124th Division, only slight importance was given to the defense of the rear extension of this road, the part stretching from Muleng through Taimakou and Motaoshih to Yehho. The division's plans were to deploy its main force in the forest north and south of the sector of the road near Muleng, and then to engage in raiding and close-quarter fighting to the rear of the enemy. Hence, division headquarters had moved to forest about 20 kilometers northwest of

Muleng, a considerable distance off the main road.

The Army Commander, however, decided that the road itself should be defended. He therefore directed Colonel Sasaki, commander of the 1st Engineer Command, to form the Sasaki Detachment with the two battalions then on their way from the 135th Division as a nucleus, and to deploy it along the portion of the road east of Taimakou in order to interdict the advance of the enemy's mechanized units. He also directed Staff Officer Kashiwada to convey this change in plan to the two infantry battalions detached from the 135th Division, which arrived at Taimakou around noon of the 10th. Moreover, the Army commander told Colonel Kashiwada to visit the 124th Division headquarters to convey the Army commander's instructions requiring the main effort of the division to be directed to the sector along the Muleng-Yehho road and the division commander to take command of the Sasaki Detachment. Upon receiving these orders General Shiina moved his headquarters to Mt Milinshan (Mitsurinyama), 15 kilometers northeast of Taimakou, on the 11th.

The enemy in the Muleng area was estimated, on the evening of the 11th, to consist of not less than two divisions composed chiefly of mechanized units, whose strength was being further reinforced from the Suifenho-Kuanyuehtai gap. At dawn of the 12th enemy elements, after fiercely shelling our positions north and south of the road, mounted attacks with twenty or thirty tanks against our positions on the hills west of Muleng and in the sector north of the town. Our guns of large and medium caliber immediately returned the fire, causing the enemy to stampede down the hill. The enemy, however, persistently mounted attacks and succeeded in breaking through our infantry outpost line near the Muleng road. One powerful column advancing along the Muleng-Taimakou road drove a breach through the MLR with tanks. By midday an element of the enemy tank unit had closed in on the division's rear positions, 4 kilometers northeast of Taimakou. Thus most of the division's main positions near Muleng were trampled upon by the enemy in half a day.[71]

Having deployed the Sasaki Detachment east of Taimakou, and foreseeing that the enemy's main body would dash along the Muleng-Yehho road, the Army Commander decided to deploy some troops east of Motaoshih also. He ordered Colonel Kobayashi, commander of the 3d Field Fortification Unit, to take command of a 1000-man battalion (formed from the Reserve Officer Candidate Training Unit at Shihtou which had been transferred from the First Area Army to the Army, and the Intendance Reserve Officer Candidates Unit (about 600 men) of the Kwantung Army), supported by one battery of the 20th Heavy Field Artillery Regiment (150-mm howitzers) and to occupy a sector along the road approaching Motaoshih from the east. The Kobayashi

---

71. From the Fifth Army's viewpoint, the moment enemy tanks breached the Army MLR, the line collapsed. The 124th Division, on the other hand, viewing its own sector separately, felt that the resistance it was able to offer till the 14th did not denote collapse. (See Monograph No 154-G.)

Detachment occupied positions around Motaoshih on the evening of the 10th and stood by for action. In this way the Army commander established two stop gaps along the enemy's route of advance, one at Taimakou, the other at Motaoshih.

Meanwhile, the enemy armored units from Tungning rushed along the Muleng road and, after by-passing the division's main force, broke through the rear positions of elements of the 124th Division east of Taimakou on the evening of the 11th. Though the major portion of this enemy force seemed to have withdrawn that night, it attacked again early the following morning. After easily breaking through the positions of the Sasaki Detachment (most of which had withdrawn) east of Taimakou, it appeared in front of Motaoshih by the afternoon of the 12th and clashed with the Kobayashi Detachment there. The Kobayashi Detachment offered violent resistance and pinned the enemy down for awhile. (See below)

In the sector west of Muleng, meanwhile, despite the enemy tank breakthrough, the 124th Division's main force still occupied the forest zone extending north and south of the road. Launching a fierce counterattack against enemy infantry elements which were following the tanks along the road, the division harassed them by artillery shelling and close-quarter fighting. The enemy, while pushing his advance armored units far in advance, returned fierce infantry and artillery attacks against our positions on both sides of the Muleng breach, especially against our artillery positions on

Mt Hsiaotushan, north of the road, where the remaining guns of the 20th Heavy Field Artillery Regiment, the Mutanchiang Heavy Artillery Regiment, the 1st Independent Heavy Artillery Battery, and the division's artillery were interdicting the enemy's westward drive. In attacking the Hsiaotushan sector the enemy infantrymen adopted extremely cautious tactics. They attacked only after devastating artillery shelling and if the attack proved ineffective they repeated the same procedure. Eventually, our positions in this sector were thoroughly demolished and even the configuration of the mountain was changed and all vegetation thereon was blasted away by the shells. By the evening of the 13th our positions around Mt Hsiaotushan had been overwhelmed by the enemy, and the commanders of both artillery regiments (Colonel Matsumura of the 20th Heavy Field Artillery Regiment, and Colonel Koketsu of the Mutanchiang Heavy Artillery Regiment) were killed in action. Guns were destroyed, and almost all the men and officers shared the fate of their guns. The units of the 124th Division that survived this engagement occupied the forests north and south of the road and tried to interfere with the enemy's rear under cover of night or by ambushing passing units. However, deprived of all heavy guns and running out of ammunition and other materiel, the survivors of the division's main force were compelled to withdraw. Crossing the road at a point between Taimakou and Motaoshih on 18 August, they retreated to the sector south of the Muleng-Yehho, and then withdrew farther to the Ningan area, where on 22 August they were disarmed.

Operations of the 126th Division Near Tzuhsingtun

Aware that the enemy's main force was opposing the 124th Division in the Muleng area, the Army Commander on the night of the 10th ordered both the 126th and the 135th Divisions to withdraw their main forces to Yehho, and to leave some elements behind in the MLR positions. Thereupon the 126th Division left behind the 2d Battalion of the 279th Infantry Regiment and the 1st Company of the 31st Independent Antitank Battalion at Tzuhsingtun to check the enemy advancing from the direction of Pamientung in order to gain time to permit the orderly withdrawal of the main bodies of the 126th and 135th Divisions to Yehho.

The units left at Tzuhsingtun were attacked by an enemy mechanized force about the noon of the 11th and, due to weakness of our antitank guns, the enemy successively passed through our hill positions in overwhelming force. About noon of the 12th approximately three or four enemy infantry battalions, under the protection of powerful gunfire, detoured and attacked our rear from the north in an attempt to wipe out our positions completely. Lieutenant Yamagishi, acting battalion commander, repeatedly reorganized his positions and fought bravely but by dawn of the 13th the battalion had lost all its positions. The enemy then left an element in this position to keep the remaining Japanese troops under surveillance, while he led his main force on towards Hsientung. The battalion commander assembled his surviving troops and withdrew to Yehho on the evening of the 16th.

By this time, however, the main force of Fifth Army had already evacuated Yehho and was withdrawing toward Hengtaohotzu. On the 20th, the survivors of the Tzuhsingtun battle reached Tungchingcheng, where they were disarmed.

Operations of the 135th Division South of Linkou

Upon first perceiving that the enemy advancing toward Linkou was moving slowly General Shimizu, the Army Commander, had transferred about two infantry battalions from the 135th Division to the 124th Division area to organize the Sasaki Detachment. On the night of the 10th, when it became clear that the Linkou sector was not in danger but that Yehho, upon which the enemy's main force was converging, was threatened, he further ordered the 135th Division to withdraw its main body to the vicinity of Yehho and to leave some elements at positions in the neighborhood of Chihsing. This was similar to the order given the 126th Division Commander.

At that time the 135th Division Commander, Lieutenant General Yoichi Hitomi,[72] was at Linkou, directing the railway movement to Yehho of the units that had assembled at Poli from the Tungan area, units which the day before he had directed to redeploy to Chihsing. On the 13th General Hitomi entrained with small elements of the 370th Regiment (stationed in Linkou) and one battalion of the 20th

---

72. General Hitomi had planned to go to Yehho immediately. However, suffering from dysentery, he remained in Linkou until the morning of the 13th, when he departed by train.

Heavy Field Artillery Regiment (which had evacuated Feite). The train was bound for Yehho via Mutanchiang. At Hualin however, the train was intercepted by an enemy tank unit which earlier had engaged the 126th Division at Pamientung and later at Tzuhsingtun. A battle ensued in the Hualin area throughout that day. Escape routes were closed since both the Mutanchiang River railway bridge and the vehicular bridge southwest of Hualin had been burned by units under the direct control of the First Area Army when they were evacuating Mutanchiang. The train was immobilized, and those units which did not disperse were annihilated. General Hitomi with some of the troops walked along the right bank of the Mutanchiang River and arrived at Yehho on the 14th where he assumed the command of the divisional units that had managed to concentrate there.

CHAPTER XIII

Fifth Army Operations Near Yehho

Preparations for the Defense of Yehho (See Map No 5)

Judging from all available reports, the Army concluded that its base of operation in the vicinity of Yehho was in danger of imminent capture. It had anticipated that the enemy's entire mechanized force would make a dash along the Muleng-Yehho road, but the defenses of the area along the road had been weak. It was for this reason that the Army Commander on the night of the 10th ordered the 126th Division and 135th Division to transfer their main forces to the vicinity of Yehho. In accordance with these orders, the 126th Division concentrated its force near Yehho during the period from the evening of the 11th to the evening of the 12th and the 135th Division did the same from the evening of the 12th to that of the 13th.

From its Yehho command post, the Army issued orders to the following effect:

Fifth Army Order
1200 hours 11 August at Yehho

> The enemy confronting the Army appears to be directing his main force to the vicinity of Muleng, and the 124th Division is now engaged in a fierce interception operation against him.
>
> The Army plans to occupy positions in the vicinity of Yehho and to crush the fighting strength of the enemy in the sector east of Mutanchiang.

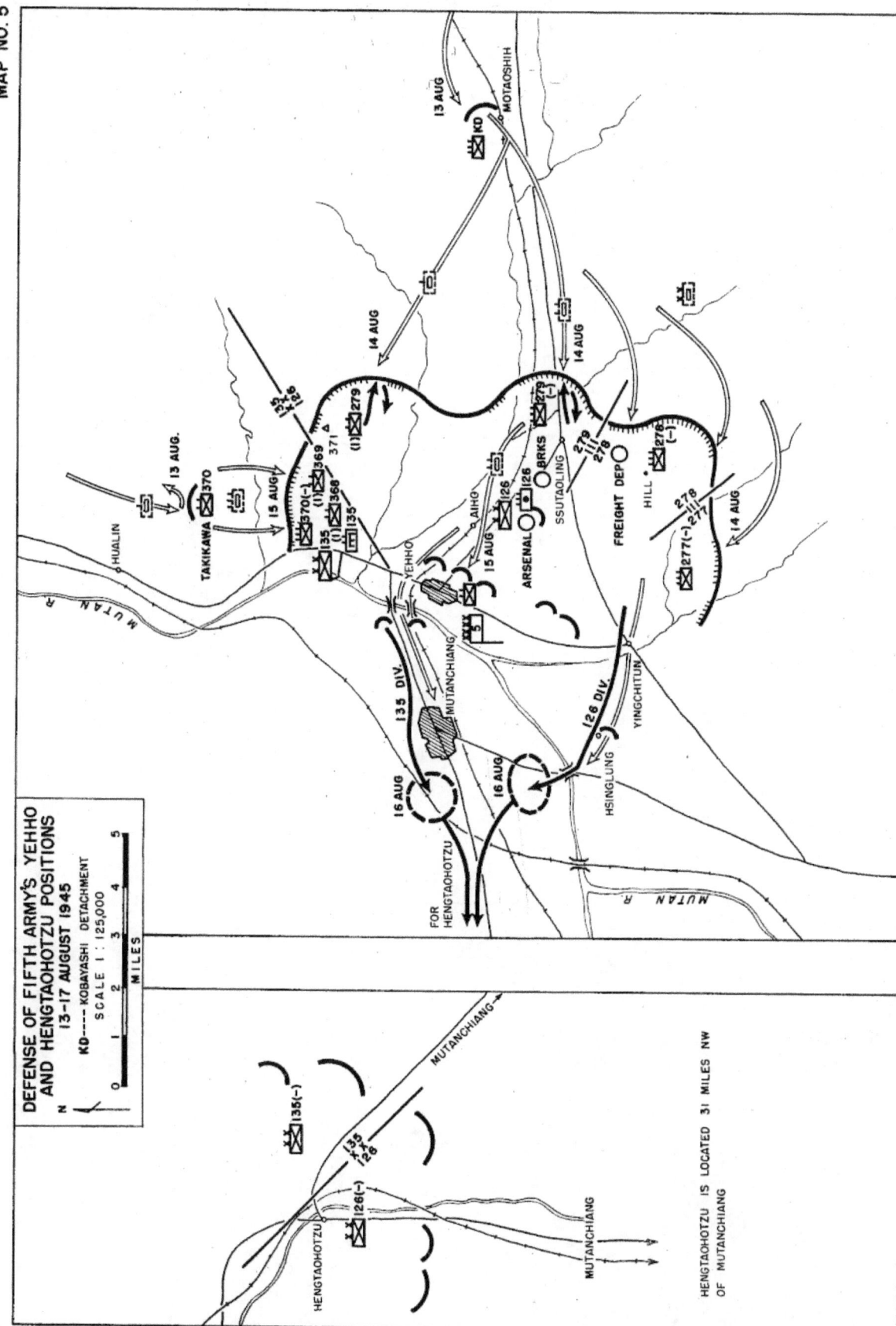

The 126th Division will occupy the positions along the line extending from the vicinity of Yingchitun to the 371 Meter Hill, by way of the hill where the freight depot is located and Ssutaoling, and will shatter the combat strength of the enemy. The following units will be attached:

    One field heavy artillery battery
    The raiding battalion of the 135th Division
    The 2d and 3d Companies of the 18th Independent Engineer Regiment
    Four light armored cars

The 135th Division in concert with the 126th Division will occupy the positions extending over the area from the west of the 371 Meter Hill (not including the hill) to the hills south of Hualin, and will break the enemy's fighting power.

The line connecting the northwestern extremity of Yehho with the 371 Meter Hill (not including the hill) will be fixed as the operational boundary line between the 126th Division and the 135th Division.

The Kobayashi Detachment at Motaoshih will continue holding its present position firmly and will check the enemy mechanized force making a dash along the Muleng-Yehho Road.

The Shihtou Reserve Officer Candidate Training Unit (except the portion attached to the Kobayashi Detachment) will establish second line positions at Yehho and on the hill south thereof for the Army.

    The effect of this order was to establish a defense perimeter around Yehho, to the rear of the MLR. Accordingly, elements of the 126th Division began digging in on the night of the 11th; its main force commenced construction of positions on the evening of the 12th, and the 135th Division on the same evening. The construction of "standing-position" fire trenches and some communication trenches was generally completed by the evening of the 13th but not to the extent of forming a chain of connected positions. Defense works such as barbed wire entanglement, and antitank ditches were entirely lacking. Obstacles of a temporary nature were made by piling up packages from the freight depot on principal roads as a mere token of resistance. A large number of 15 kilogram bombs from the Wenchun airfield (about 15 kilometers south of Mutanchiang) were used as substitute for antitank mines.

The 126th Division was able to concentrate the main body of its artillery, with more than twenty guns, in the vicinity of Yehho, while the 135th Division was able to assemble there only about ten guns, and the Army artillery unit only one field heavy artillery battery (attached to the 126th Division). This was an extremely poor showing against an enemy mechanized force.

Operations of the Kobayashi Detachment Near Motaoshih

The Kobayashi Detachment on the 11th occupied a position in the sector along the main road approaching Motaoshih from the east. On the evening of the 12th, it was engaged by an enemy unit equipped with twenty to thirty tanks which after penetrating the Muleng sector had advanced westward. The rapidly advancing mechanized unit came suddenly under the gunfire of the Kobayashi Detachment, especially its attached artillery (one battery of the 150-mm howitzer unit), and when two or three leading tanks were either destroyed or rendered unserviceable, the enemy unit hastily fell back and subse-

quently became more cautious. At night the detachment launched a
daring close-quarter attack on the camping area of the Soviet mechanized unit and struck terror into the enemy's heart. The detachment
had no antitank defenses other than one heavy field artillery battery
and some explosives. When the battle was resumed on the morning of
the 13th, the detachment suffered many casualties (including Colonel
Kobayashi and several key officers) despite the brave fighting of
all officers and men. By noon of that day the vicinity of Motaoshih
at last was penetrated by the enemy. Thereafter, remnants of the
detachment remained in the area and harassed the enemy rear while
others either withdrew to the vicinity of Yehho and joined the main
force of the Army or fell back to the Tungchingcheng and Ningan areas
where they were disarmed late in August. Thus, this detachment in
its last days became disorganized and it became impossible to coordinate
its fighting strength.

Operations of the 126th Division Near Ssutaoling

An element of the enemy mechanized unit appeared in front of
the 126th Division's Ssutaoling positions on the evening of the 13th
and conducted a reconnaissance of Japanese positions. About fifty or
sixty enemy guns were deployed east of Ssutaoling, near the main road,
on the morning of the 14th preparing to assault the Ssutaoling Heights
and Hill 371 simultaneously. Beginning at about 1100 hours the enemy
tanks directed their main firepower on our division artillery positions arrayed south and north of the old tank unit barracks. At

about 1300 hours the enemy began to place neutralization fire on our artillery while placing concentrated fire on the Ssutaoling Heights. At about the same time, seven enemy tanks came rushing into the southeastern salient of the 371 Meter Hill and, in spite of the brave fighting of the defending soldiers, the enemy captured the hill at about 1500 hours, and thus the Japanese lost this advantageous observation point. The enemy shelling of the Ssutaoling Heights, meanwhile, continued for four hours with the result that our positions were thoroughly destroyed. At about 1500 hours in the midst of this shelling, about thirty enemy tanks, supported by infantry, rushed the Ssutaoling Heights. The defending soldiers allowed the tanks to pass through and then fired at the infantrymen following. The enemy foot troops fled in great confusion. Following this the enemy tank reserves in the rear rained gunfire on our defending infantrymen and engineers, who staged a vigorous close-quarters counterattack. Finally, however, most of the Ssutaoling positions were captured by the enemy. The division conducted night attacks on Ssutaoling and the 371 Meter Hill to recapture them, but unfortunately these were not successful.

Operation near Aiho

The enemy concentrated his gunfire on our artillery along the main road near Aiho continuously for eight hours beginning about 0800 hours on the 15th. When our division artillery and light armored cars were almost completely annihilated, about thirty enemy tanks smashed into our positions south of the main road. Our defending troops, including even the division transport soldiers, organized close-quarter combat teams and attacked the enemy tanks, causing the enemy to retreat and assemble in the locality of Ssutaoling on the evening of the 15th.

Operations of the 135th Division South of Hualin

The enemy tanks that appeared in near Hualin after advancing from the Pamientung and Tzuhsingtun areas attacked and destroyed the train carrying the commander of the 135th Division and elements of a battalion of his 370th Regiment. On the morning of the 13th about ten enemy tanks attempted to capture a height south of Hualin held by the Takikawa Infantry Battalion of the 135th Division. But when the fire of our division artillery, located on a height north of Yehho, hit and disabled two or three leading tanks the main force turned back in great haste and fled toward the north slope of the height. The tanks attempted to break through our positions with the same tactics several times on the 13th, but our defending men held their positions firmly, repulsing the attack each time.

On the morning of the 14th the enemy resumed the attack, this time with infantrymen following the tanks. The Takikawa Battalion (370th Regiment) tried to check the tanks by close-quarter attacks but, due to inferiority of its antitank firepower, it was unable to do so. Consequently, on the evening of the 14th, the sector along the Yehho-Hualin Road was breached by the enemy. This battalion hid in positions on both sides of the road and launched several close-quarter attacks, but these was not enough to reverse the unfavorable situation.

The enemy mechanized units which overrode our positions on the heights south of Hualin on the 14th then directed their artillery firepower to the second line positions of the 135th Division on the heights north of Yehho on the morning of the 15th in an effort to annihilate the division artillery and to destroy our infantry positions. Although the enemy captured some of the second line positions during the afternoon, his attack was not so bold as that carried out in front of the 124th Division, and consequently most of the main positions of the division remained in our hands.

CHAPTER XIV

The Withdrawal to Hengtaohotzu

Withdrawal Orders from the First Area Army

In a hurry to evacuate its personnel, the Mutanchiang office of the Manchuria Telegraph and Telephone had destroyed its telephone communication facilities between Mutanchiang and Tunhua too hastily. As a result the only communication available between the Army Headquarters at Yehho and First Area Army Headquarters at Tunhua was by wireless telegraph. The Army undertook the repair of the telephone line in the Mutanchiang Telegraph and Telephone Office, and the line was reopened to service on the night of the 14th. At midnight a telephone call came from Chief of Staff Sakurai of the First Area Army Headquarters at Tunhua. He talked to Staff Officer Kashiwada, who reported on the situation on the Yehho front and on other matters.

The First Area Army was anxious to know about the advance of the enemy confronting the Army and the number of days the Army could hold its positions in the vicinity of Yehho. Saying, "I am a bit hard of hearing, so Staff Officer Colonel Matsumoto will take over," Chief of Staff Sakurai gave his place to the staff officer. Colonel Kashiwada then reported the Fifth Army situation, stating that "the enemy in front of the Fifth Army broke through the center of the position of the 124th Division at Muleng. He has been attacking the main position of our Army in front of Yehho since the 13th and overran the main position of the 126th Division today, the 14th. The 126th Division's artillery has been annihilated. All personnel of the Army from the Army commander downward are ready to die a glorious death today or tomorrow in the area east of Mutanchiang River" (The rearmost boundary of the operational zone of the Army was Mutanchiang River). Hearing this, Staff Officer Matsumoto seemed to be alarmed at the rapid development of the situation. "Wait a moment," he said and after holding the line for a while returned to the telephone and transmitted the following instructions of the First Area Army:

> The invading Soviet Army has broken through the Manchurian border at various points. The Kwantung Army plans to organize a structure for protracted war of resistance with the Manchurian-Korean border zone running along Mount Paektu (Changpaishan) as the final defense line. The Fifth Army will try to hold the positions east of Mutanchiang River as long as possible and then retreat to the locality of Tunhua or Hengtaohotzu. (Compare this text with that on page 67.)

After completing the telephone conversation, Staff Officer Kashiwada repeated these instructions to the Army commander and was going to draft the orders for withdrawal of the Army to the vicinity of Tunhua, when the Army commander said, "Wait a moment on the drafting of the orders," and then he sank in meditation.

Finally, however, he decided to withdraw the Army, selecting Hengtaohotzu in preference to Tunhua because of the distance to the latter and the tactical situation. The plan called for the rear units to withdraw immediately after sunset of the 15th, with front line units to follow at midnight.

The gist of the Army orders concerning the withdrawal of the first line groups issued at 1200 hours, 15 August, was as follows:

> Under cover of night the Army plans today to cross the Mutanchiang River to withdraw to the vicinity of Hengtaohotzu, where it will map out its further course.
>
> At 2400 hours tonight the 126th Division will withdraw toward the west side of the Mutanchiang City by way of the Hsinglung Bridge. The road on the southside of Yehho village will be used by the 126th Division.
>
> The 135th Division will withdraw from its positions at the same time and cross the bridge on the west side of Yehho by way of the road on the north side of Yehho, and will withdraw first toward the northwestern side of the Mutanchiang City.
>
> To cover the Army's withdrawal the Shihtou Reserve Officers' Candidate Unit will secure its present position (the line from the eastern end of Yehho to the southern heights), and after the main force of the Army is completely across the river, will withdraw toward the west side of the Mutanchiang City.
>
> All units will send a liaison officer to the former office building of the First Area Army Headquarters at about 0800 on the 16th to receive further orders.

The Army took necessary steps for evacuation of the rear units, particularly the sick and wounded, under successive orders issued beginning about noon on the 15th, and opened the rear area for the first line unit to retreat after midnight. Under the Army's direction, all the rear units started moving right after sunset toward Hengtaohotzu by way of the bridge on the west side of Yehho and the Hsinglung bridge.

The withdrawal of the rear units of the Army was carried out without any great confusion. It caused no hindrance to the retreat of the first line groups at 2400 hours. The retreat of the first line groups beginning about midnight was also orderly, in spite of the confusion during daytime. No division orders could reach the units engaged in desperate fighting during daytime, such as the central sector unit of the 126th Division (278th Infantry Regiment) and Takikawa Battalion at the first line position of the 135th Division, however, and these units had to be left alone till daytime on the 16th. However, when they found themselves isolated from other Army elements, they either retreated in groups or dispersed in all directions with utter lack of control. At night numerous illuminating signal shells were shot up in the vicinity of Yehho and the enemy was believed to have perceived that the Japanese units were being withdrawn, but no pursuing enemy unit was witnessed even up to daybreak of the following day. The main body of the 135th Division crossed the Yehho bridge by daybreak of the 16th and the 126th Division crossed Hsinglung Bridge by 0900 hours on the same day and assembled as previously arranged. Thereupon, the Army ordered the 126th Division and 135th Division to proceed toward Hengtaohotzu by the Mutanchiang-Hengtaohotzu Road. The Army directed some of its units to occupy rear guard positions on heights west of Mutanchiang, while its main force kept on retreating toward Hengtaohotzu day and night under the bombing of enemy planes. The motor transport units had concentrated at Hengtaohotzu by the evening of the 16th and the main force of the two front line divisions by the evening of the 17th. (See Map No 5.)

Occupation of Hengtaohotzu Positions and Disarmament

The Army gradually reorganized the units that assembled at Hengtaohotzu and decided to occupy existing positions (those which the Area Army had previously ordered the 12th Independent Engineer Regiment to construct) in the hilly zone about 6 kilometers east of Hengtaohotzu and to check the enemy advance for as long as possible. Orders were given on the morning of the 17th to the 126th Division to occupy the positions south of the main road (not including the road) and the 135th Division to occupy those north of the road, and to crush the fighting power of the enemy. These groups set about the task of occupying these positions on the evening of the 17th.

The important broadcast by the Emperor at noon on 15 August had been monitored by several of the signal personnel of the Army Headquarters staff. However, Staff Officer Maeda, in charge of communication, had forbidden them to spread the news because of the fierce battle then raging in the vicinity of Yehho and also because he suspected that the broadcast might be an enemy strategem, originating in either Vladivostok or Khabarovsk.

Since the commencement of withdrawal of the Army, communications with Area Army Headquarters at Tunhua had been totally disrupted. On the morning of the 17th a member of the Manchurian Telegraph and

and Telephone Company's Harbin office sent in a message by railway telephone concerning disarmament, adding that he had been asked by the First Area Army Headquarters to relay the message. The Army Commander and his staff suspected that it was another ruse of the enemy fifth column. They all agreed that prudence should be exercised in dealing with the matter and decided to dispatch Staff Officer Maeda to Area Army Headquarters at Tunhua by railway gasoline engine car to ascertain the truth. Colonel Maeda proceeded to the railway station. There, while preparing to depart, he received a railway telephone call from Staff Officer Tsumori of Area Army Headquarters concerning the cease-fire order. Thereupon, the Army at about 1400 hours called a meeting of representatives of each unit to announce the Army cease-fire orders. Soviet forces began entering Hengtaohotzu on the evening of the 17th and immediately started to disarm Japanese forces.

Losses Suffered by Both Sides

No thoroughgoing survey could be conducted of losses suffered by the Army since the opening of hostilities by Soviet Russia against Japan. One reason for this was that it was impossible from the outset to control our troop movements effectively because of inadequate facilities for transmitting orders and reports. This was aggravated by the suddenness of the initial attack of the enemy and by the peculiarities of the fighting in Manchukuo with its vast territory and its long meandering border line.

During the withdrawal from the east bank of the Mutanchiang River some troops went directly towards the Tunhua area or towards the Tungchingcheng and Ningan areas because the Mutanchiang River blocked their retreat; these were disarmed in those areas. Others kept on fighting in the area east of Mutanchiang River for more than a month after the truce due to the non-receipt of orders. Hence casualty counting was beyond control.

Estimates, however, put Army battle casualties at about 20,000, including those killed, wounded and missing, out of the total strength of some 60,000. Artillery pieces destroyed or abandoned on the battlefield include about sixty field guns (approximately twenty-four pieces per division, including mortars assigned to the Division Artillery), sixteen 150-mm howitzers, two 150-mm cannons, four 100-mm cannons, two 240-mm howitzers, two 300-mm howitzers, and eighteen mortars. Four light armored cars, 600 trucks and 6,000 horses were also destroyed or abandoned.[73] Estimated losses incurred by Soviet forces include some 7,000 or 8,000 casualties and more than 300 tanks destroyed or disabled.

Situation at the Time the War Ended

The lightning war waged by the Soviet Army made impossible from the start the efficient conduct of Army operations under single con-

---

73. This pertains to losses during the fighting only. Actually, of course, all equipment was lost.

trol. At the time the war ended, units under the direct or indirect control of the Army were in a chaotic condition, divided as they were by wedges driven by the enemy into this vast defensive area. Consequently, the number of personnel disarmed in Hengtaohotzu, including those of the Army Headquarters, reached no more than a half of the total strength. Part of the 124th Division was still fighting in the Muleng Sector. Besides this, quite a number of units, large and small, were unaware of the termination of hostilities and continued fighting east of Mutanchiang River. This made it necessary for officers on both sides to drive up to the battle areas several times and for pilots to drop handbills from their planes in order to make known the truce.

Some of the units located east of Tungan made their way on foot toward Yapuloni via Poli or Linkou and the sector north of Hengtaohotzu. Of these units some were disarmed in the vicinity of Linkou, still on their way to Yapuloni; some were disarmed in the vicinity of Yapuloni; others were disarmed upon reaching the vicinity of Tunhua or Kirin. Some of the units which had been fighting in the vicinity of Muleng and Yehho fled to Tunhua via the vicinity of Lake Chingpo while the others were disarmed in the vicinity of Ningan and Tungchingcheng. So disorganized was the Army at the time the war ended that units massed in Hengtaohotzu had practically no artillery pieces, nor even explosives for use against enemy armored units, rifles being the only arms they carried. Thus the fighting capacity of the Army was completely exhausted, and personnel reduced to almost a rabble.

Negotiations with the Soviet Army

On the evening of the 17th, the day the order regarding a cease-fire reached him, the Army Commander sent out from Hengtaohotzu his Chief of Staff, Major General Shigesada Kawagoe, Staff Officer Kashiwada, Colonel Masakichi Mochizuki (commander of the 135th Division's 370th Infantry Regiment and an expert in the Russian language) to the Commander of the Soviet First Army in Mutanchiang to conduct negotiations concerning a cease-fire and relevant matters. The negotiators reached the Soviet Army Headquarters early the following morning and opened talks with the Soviet Commander, who received them in a dignified attitude with the chief of his staff and others attending. Major Japanese requests were as follows: (1) That Japanese units be assembled under the Commander of the First Area Army in Tunhua after disarmament; (2) the men be supplied with sufficient food as they were exhausted, (3) officers be permitted to take such items as sabers, pistols, and binoculars, along with them; (4) Japanese troops be authorized to clear the battlefield; (5) the Army be permitted to dispatch officers and men to such units as were still without cease-fire orders; (6) Japanese residents be protected against Koreans and Manchurians, and be supplied with sufficient food as well; (7) plundering and raping by Soviet soldiers be prevented.

To this request, a Soviet reply was received to the following effect: Item 1, the assembling of Japanese troops to Tunhua, unacceptable. Item 2, Accepted. Item 3, 4, and 5, disapproved in accordance with the intent of the Soviet Far Eastern Army Commander. Item 6 and 7, efforts will be made to meet the wishes expressed.

Main Soviet demands were as follows: (1) the Japanese Army will immediately regroup its troops and establish discipline; (2) the Japanese Army will move from Hengtaohotzu to Mutanchiang in accordance with Soviet instructions; (3) the Japanese Army will not destroy munition stocks on hand from now on, and the destruction by fire of civilian buildings, or other installations, will be strictly prohibited; (4) the Supreme Commander of the Japanese Army will insure thorough transmission of orders and messages concerning the cease-fire to all units in order to avoid any possible clash with Soviet forces; (5) the Japanese Army will surrender all its documents, maps, etc. to the Soviet Army, instead of burning them; (6) the Japanese Army will prepare an itemized list of weapons, ammunition, provisions, and all other war supplies abandoned or concealed by it in the battle area or elsewhere, for prompt submission to the Soviet Army; (7) the Japanese Army will submit to the Soviet Army a detailed statement of its antitank mine fields; (8) the Commander of the Japanese Army will proceed to Mutanchiang with all general officers by the 18th.

The Russians ordered Staff Officer Kashiwada and all the other Japanese negotiators (except Chief of Staff Kawagoe) to return immediately to Hengtaohotzu to inform the Japanese Army Commander of the Soviet demand. They left Mutanchiang at about 1000 hours on the 18th, and arrived at Hengtaohotzu at 1500 hours. The Army Commander, upon receipt of the report of the Soviet demands, took necessary steps concerning the removal of his units to Mutanchiang and took care of other relevant matters. On the evening of the 18th, accompanied by division commanders and other general officers, he left Hengtaohotzu for Mutanchiang by car.

The Japanese troops in Hengtaohotzu were completely disarmed on the 18th, and took their departure on the morning of the 19th. The main road was being used just then by Soviet troops rushing toward the Harbin area, so the Japanese troops had to make their way to Mutanchiang mostly along a path alongside the main road deep with mud and in a drizzling rain. En route their watches and other valuables were plundered by Soviet soldiers. Upon arrival at Hailin and Laku toward the evening of the 20th, after a march without sleeping or resting, they were interned in the barracks (practically destroyed by fire) formerly occupied by Japanese air units.

Some of these internees were transferred to a camp in the city of Mutanchiang. Later, internees were organized into labor units consisting of about 500 men each, and towards the end of August were ordered to move into Soviet territory, one group after another, on foot via Suifenho. At about the same time, Fourth Army personnel from the Harbin area were also interned in the Mutanchiang area.

After they too were organized into labor units, they were marched to Soviet territory.

Meanwhile, skirmishes took place day and night in the former battle areas and in the Mutanchiang sector between Soviet garrisons and a number of Japanese units which had not received the cease-fire order. Mixed parties of Japanese and Soviet officers and men were formed and sent several times to transmit the orders to these units.

In Hailin and Laku, the principal buildings had been burned by Japanese forces, with the exception of hangars and warehouses. These unburned structures and new improvised barracks, roofed with galvanized iron sheets and barely affording shelter from the rain, constituted the facilities for housing internees. Food saved from the fire at the Mutanchiang Field Freight Depot was parceled out but the amount was below the prescribed allowance. Vegetables were out of stock and had to be bought from Manchurians or Koreans by each unit. Units of the Fifth Army, however, did not have sufficient funds to buy vegetables and were compelled to draw to some extent from Fourth Army stores. Most of them had no Manchurian notes in their possession because prior to their internment they had either run out of them or had burned them.

CHAPTER XV

Civil Affairs

Japanese Residents and Cultivating Parties

Beginning on the day the war broke out, Japanese residents within the operational area of the Fifth Army were successively evacuated to the west of Mutanchiang by freight cars as well as coaches. Almost all members of the cultivating parties were also evacuated by train, under the direction of the prefectural governor.

Japanese residents and members of the cultivating parties in remote districts were brought to local railway zones by truck and were then evacuated by train under the direction of Japanese officials of the local government. Many of those in the Tungan area who tried to withdraw to Poli or Linkou on foot seem to have succumbed on the way to atrocities committed by Manchurians or rebel units of the Manchukuoan Army garrisoned in Poli. Even those who could safely reach Poli or Linkou had to cross Mutanchiang River by a bridge near Erhtaohotzu west of Linkou to escape to Hengtaohotzu or Imienpo through a mountain path, because a battle was raging in the Yehho area. These people were estimated to number between 20,000 and 30,000, most of whom carried nothing but the clothes they wore in their hasty flight. Having neither money nor food with them, they took from the fields corn or other crops grown by Manchurian or Korean farmers and ate it uncooked. Many, however, were murdered brutally by members of vigilance organizations in Manchurian or Korean villages. Some lost their young children during the journey. The situation was tragic.

When hostilities started the Army began transferring dependents of military and civilian personnel to the area west of the Muleng-Chihsing MLR. The dependents who were in the area east of Tungan were gradually evacuated to Chiaoho (midway between Tunhua and Kirin), beginning the morning of 9 August. Army Adjutant Sekimoto and several others were ordered to take care of all the dependents of the Army. The bulk of these dependents was moved to Tunhua after the hostilities ended.

Manchukuoan Government Agencies

At the beginning of hostilities, Japanese officials of the Manchukuoan Government cooperated with the Japanese Army in the maintenance of internal peace and other matters, but Manchurians and Koreans in its employ generally took an unconcerned attitude toward hostilities and neglected their work. As the fighting progressed, Japanese officials began to be preoccupied with their preparations for evacuation, and the hostilities ended before they could achieve anything to meet the emergency. Only the Governor of Mutanchiang Province (Mr Kenzo Isoko) and the Superintendent of the Mutanchiang office of Manchurian Telegraph and Telephone Company (Mr Shinzo Saizu) reported daily at the Army Headquarters in Yehho and assiduously performed their duties until 14 August when they were permitted by the Army to leave the combat zone.

The Manchukuoan Army and Police

Prior to the outbreak of hostilities, elements of the Manchukuoan Army garrisoned in Paoching were engaged in the construction of positions at Mashan under the direction of the Japanese Army. When hostilities started, however, they rose in revolt, dispersed in all directions, obstructed the evacuation of Japanese residents and even committed acts of murder and rape. The 1st Division of the Manchukuoan Army stationed at Poli also rose in rebellion and its Commander and Japanese officers under him immediately left the units.[74] The Commander of the 11th Army District in Mishan, who withdrew to Poli with his Japanese advisors, continued to take his advisors along with him in the face of the rebellion started by the Manchukuo forces in Poli; he fled from Poli to Hengtaohotzu with them and was disarmed in its vicinity.

The Manchukuoan police unmistakably took a cooperative attitude toward the Japanese Army at the beginning of Pacific hostilities, but once they sensed that the Japanese Army was losing the war, they began to adopt an antagonistic and contemptuous attitude toward the Japanese everywhere. With the invasion of Manchuria by Soviet forces,

---

74. The Manchurian National Army consisted principally of eleven districts and two divisions. The divisions, unlike the districts, were mobile forces that could be moved to any section of the country. The districts, on the other hand, generally had fixed stations. The districts were each about brigade size.

they switched their allegiance to the Soviet Army, and obstructed the movements of Japanese residents and members of the cultivating parties, and in some cases even brutally murdered them.

Attitudes of Manchurians, Koreans, and White Russians

Manchurians and Koreans in general assumed an indifferent attitude toward the Army from the outset of the hostilities, probably because they anticipated Japan's defeat as a consequence of her adverse war situation in the Pacific. Once the Soviet forces moved in, however, they did all they could to welcome the Soviet Army with red flags hung out at every door, fully demonstrating their contempt for Japan. Cases of plunder, rape, and murder against evacuated members of the cultivating parties and Japanese residents occurred frequently.

Quite a number of White Russian youths living west of Mutanchiang were employed as Japanese fifth columnists as soon as hostilities started, while many of their families fled to the depths of the mountains for fear of an invasion by Soviet troops in their locality. The Soviet Army seems to have conducted a rigorous examination of White Russians after the end of the hostilities. Those who had been sympathetic with the Japanese Army were arrested. Many White Russians located in the vicinity of Hengtaohotzu were favorably disposed toward the Japanese Army even after the end of hostilities and afforded it facilities in various ways.

Monograph No 154-G

CHAPTER XVI

The 124th Division[75]

Organization

The 124th Division was organized in the Suiyang area by Third Army during February 1945. It was one of the divisions formed principally to compensate for the numerous transfers from Manchuria and to give the Kwantung Army the appearance of a powerful force. The cadre for the division consisted of approximately 1,000 personnel left behind by the 111th Division; recruits filled out the body of the division. Regiments of the division were organized in the following areas: the 271st near Suiyang, the 272d near Suinan, and the 273d near Suihsi. Division headquarters was at Suiyang, and the division was commanded by Lieutenant General Masatake Shiina.

On 26 February, when the formation of the division was almost completed, it was assigned to Third Army, which had organized it. During March, however, in conjunction with boundary adjustment between the Fifth and Third Armies, the 124th Division was transferred to Fifth Army. Its main body remained in the Suiyang area.

During May the 124th Division was directed to take over responsibility for garrisoning the border at the fortified positions near

---

75. The information in this chapter was furnished by Colonel Toyoharu Iwasaki, chief of staff of 124th Division.

Kuanyuehtai and Suifenho. These areas were then being garrisoned by the 11th and 2d Border Garrison Units respectively, which were scheduled for inactivation in order to provide personnel for new tactical units.

General Shiina sent approximately two battalions to the border. To Kuanyuehtai he sent a battalion of 273d Regiment; to Suifenho he dispatched a battalion of the 271st Regiment, and to Lumingtai, about 10 miles south of Suifenho, he sent one company of the 272d Regiment. Artillery and other units that had been attached to the border garrison units remained at their posts and were attached to the divisional elements. The relieved 2d and 11th Border Garrison Units were each about regimental size. The effect of the change therefore was to deploy a force of less than regimental size in an area which formerly was garrisoned by two regiments.

During June a major redeployment of the 124th Division took place. As a result of Kwantung Army's adoption of the delaying operational plan Fifth Army was assigned a new main line of resistance extending from Muleng to Chihsing. The main body of the division was therefore moved to the area west of Muleng and immediately began constructing positions for the new MLR. At the same time, division headquarters moved to Muleng. Meanwhile, small divisional elements remained in the Suiyang area.

During the early July mass mobilization in Manchuria many new units were formed. To the 124th Division was assigned one raiding battalion, stationed near Hsiachengtzu, and one artillery regiment, stationed near Suihsi. When war broke out on 9 August, the division was further augmented by the attachment of the following units:

>Mutanchiang Heavy Artillery Regiment (Hsiachengtzu)
>20th Heavy Field Artillery Regiment (less two batteries)
>31st Independent Antitank Battalion (less one battery)
>One battalion (less one battery) Tungning Heavy Artillery Regiment
>1st Independent Heavy Artillery Battery
>13th Mortar Battalion
>Two independent engineer battalions (provisionally organized)

Fortifications in the MLR

In accordance with the Army operational plan, the 124th Division was assigned the sector along the Suifenho-Mutanchiang road. In this sector ran the most important east-west artery in eastern Manchuria, the trans-Manchurian railway,[76] which until 1935 had been used as a short-cut by the Trans-Siberian Railway. In addition, one of the best gravel roads in eastern Manchuria extended from Suifenho to Mutanchiang. Hence the sector assigned to the 124th Division was considered the most important in the Army's defense plan.

Upon receipt of orders to deploy the main body of his division to the area west of Muleng, General Shiina dispatched officers and

---

76. This line has been variously called the North Manchurian Railway, the Harbin-Suifenho Line, the Chinese-Changchun Railway (meaningless), and the Manchouli-Suifenho Railway. The trans-Manchurian Railway, constructed by Russia, was bought by Manchukuo for ¥170,000,000 ($42,500,000) in 1935, when it was changed from broad gauge (5') to standard guage (4'8½"). In 1942 the section from Hsinking to Suiyang, via Harbin, was double-tracked.

men to conduct a reconnaissance of positions. The division was to construct a frontal position line in the MLR, approximately 27 kilometers in length, in the heavily forested area west of Muleng, and several rear positions. Regimental main bodies were assigned positions as follows: the 271st Regiment southwest of Muleng, the 272d Regiment west of Muleng, and the 273d Regiment northwest of Muleng.

By the outbreak of war, fortification work was in various stages of completion. Firing positions and communication trenches at key points in forward positions of the MLR were nearly ready. For flanking weapons, such as machineguns for cross-firing, protective covering against medium shells and bombs had been roughly completed. Double wire entanglements were completed at important points, and single wire at others. As for underground installations, fairly solid dugouts had been roughly completed. In addition satisfactory progress had been made in the construction of living shelters, medical facilities, and anti-gas shelters.

Communication trenches and barbed wire entanglements connecting key points in forward positions of the MLR had been started, as had also those connecting with the rear positions of the MLR; none of these, however, had reached a satisfactory stage when hostilities began.

Artillery emplacements had been almost completed for weapons of the division artillery (about twenty 75-mm guns), as well as for two 300-mm howitzers of an attached unit of the Tungning Heavy

Artillery Regiment, two 150-mm guns of the 1st Independent Heavy Artillery Battery, and about two batteries of 150-mm howitzers of the 20th Heavy Field Artillery Regiment. Emplacements for the 240-mm howitzers of the Mutanchiang Heavy Artillery Regiment had not been constructed since this regiment was not attached until the outbreak of war, at which time it was able to bring only two of its eight weapons to new positions west of Muleng, and had to destroy the others at Hsiachengtzu. Construction of the division command post and other second-line positions had not been started although reconnaissance had been completed.

Communications

Communication routes between the division's border positions and the Army Headquarters at Yehho were open at all times prior to the outbreak of hostilities, the main routes being the Suifenho-Mutanchiang Railway and the vehicular operational road parallelling the railroad. Within the MLR, communication with the 126th Division on the left was maintained with difficulty, mainly through a narrow mountain path. The situation was worse with regard to the 128th Division on the right to which no direct route existed within the MLR. Communication routes within each unit's position were in fair condition for use by both vehicles and horses.

Signal communication was mainly by wireless telegraph since the division had such an extensive area of responsibility. Telephone was used for short distances only. The division had no radios.

Training

After the division's organization was completed in early March, training programs were begun and were carried out in the face of many difficulties. By the end of three months, basic training had been completed, and group training was nearing completion. Late in June, when the division's main body moved to the Muleng area, training was continued and was conducted concurrently with the construction of positions. Training in defensive tactics progressed satisfactorily at the construction sites, and by the outbreak of war each unit had attained the level that would enable it to fight with confidence. All personnel of the division were particularly trained in close quarter fighting against tanks. The combat effectiveness of the division as a whole was about 35 per cent of the earlier well-trained divisions.

Intelligence and Border Garrisoning

The division had been receiving, without undue delay, information gathered directly by three sources: its border garrison units, lateral divisions, and Army Headquarters. During July and August the division received information from subordinate and lateral units indicating the gravity of the situation with regard to the USSR. This information was utterly inconsistent with the optimistic information received from higher commands. The division was at a loss for the truth, and consequently was often apt to take an optimistic view. It was most regrettable that it erred in its ultimate estimate as to the time of the outbreak of war.

About the middle of July, a Soviet deserter who had crossed the border in front of Kuanyuehtai Hill confessed to the Mutanchiang Special Intelligence Agency that the Japanese-Soviet war was imminent. A noncommissioned officer who before enlistment had been a middle-school teacher from Central Asia, he had crossed the border into Manchurian territory with the object of escaping from war. Another incident occurred about the same time and in the same Kuanyuehtai Hill positions. A member of one of our lookout posts on his way to a neighboring observation post for liaison purposes disappeared and seems to have been taken away by the Soviets. Elsewhere along the border, furthermore, on 3 or 4 August such incidents occurred as a border crossing by Soviet troops, illegal shooting at the border in the Hulin area, and Soviet aircraft flights across the border. These events served only to worsen the already tense situation.

Upon assuming responsibility for border garrisoning in May, the division elements dispatched to the frontier took up previously constructed positions that were strong and semi-permanent. With the increase in tension along the frontier, the division ordered them to intensify their watch, and at the same time to undertake strenuous training day and night in order to be prepared for operations.

Status of Preparations Immediately Prior to the Outbreak of War

When the division completed its organization in March, it had insufficient personnel and equipment. Although it continued to receive personnel, the quality of new arrivals, as well as of the earlier assigned personnel of all ranks was poor. This condition was aggravated by the fact that transfers of personnel continued even after organization was completed. This in turn had a deleterious effect upon the unity of the division and impeded training.

The supply of arms and materiels of war was grossly insufficient. Of particular concern was the shortage of antitank weapons.

Outbreak of Hostilities

On 5 August General Shiina left Muleng to attend a meeting of division commanders at Fifth Army Headquarters in Yehho. At that time the situation on the frontier was somewhat tense.

Following with division commanders' meeting (on 6 August) at Yehho, a second meeting of commanders and chiefs of staff of each division and commanders of separate units was held beginning on 7 August for the purpose of conducting table-top maneuvers. These maneuvers were to last five days. Commanders and chiefs of staff were billeted at the Yehho Officers' Club.

At about 0200 hours of 9 August, all chiefs of staff received an urgent message while at their quarters summoning them to the Army Headquarters office. After the chief of staffs had assembled, further orders were issued for division commanders to gather at the headquarters.

The Army chief of staff, Major General Shigesada Kawagoe, explained that the 15th Border Garrison Unit at Hutou had been attacked by the Soviet Army and was engaging the enemy, and added that there were indications of Soviet penetrations at other points along the border. He then instructed all division commanders to return to their posts immediately.

General Shiina and his party promptly departed by motor car for Muleng. Towards dawn, while at a spot several kilometers west of Muleng, they saw several Soviet aircraft flying over Muleng, and heard intermittent firing. The Division Headquarters at Muleng, they later learned, had already been subjected to attack by enemy aircraft.

The Division Commander and his party immediately proceeded to headquarters where they were briefed by the senior adjutant concerning developments since midnight. General Shiina ordered the division to occupy positions then under construction in the MLR, to intercept the advance of the Soviet Army at these positions, and to destroy it in the vicinity. He also took immediate measures to

> Have the garrison units at Suifenho and Kuanyuehtai Hill secure their positions and concentrate all their efforts on delaying the advance of the enemy.
>
> Send Colonel Asu, commander of the 271st Infantry Regiment, to the Suiyang area to take charge of

withdrawing personnel, weapons, ammunition, and other supplies of each unit at Suiyang to the Muleng sector, and to supervise the evacuation of Japanese residents.

Use service and supply personnel at the Muleng barracks to augment tactical troops, and strengthen positions.

Expedite the evacuation of hospital patients as well as Japanese residents in the vicinity of Muleng.

Summon representatives of the prefectural government offices, police units, railway and other public as well as municipal offices, to give them necessary instructions.

Make preparations for the demolition of bridges, barricading of roads, burning of barracks, government residences, prefectural offices and other important buildings.

Make preparations for receiving ammunition, equipment, and provisions, from the Mutanchiang depots.

Remove the division headquarters to a prearranged position at Mt Ikkoku.

At about 1400 hours, General Shiina and part of his staff departed Muleng for Mt Ikkoku. En route he inspected the positions of the Central Sector Unit west of Muleng. He found each unit calm, and with good morale. That night he bivouacked in the positions of the 1st Independent Heavy Artillery Battery. There he received a report that border units, although under fierce attack, were maintaining extremely high morale especially among officers. No new reports came in concerning the developments in the enemy attack.

The next morning General Shiina continued on foot towards the new command post. At about noon he reached the western foothills of Mt Ikkoku. He then climbed to the top of the mountain where the command post afforded a full view of the fronts of the Central and Left Sector Units (respectively the 272d and 273d Regiments) and hence of the major portion of the battlefield. However, Mt Ikkoku was too far to the left from the standpoint of the entire division, and also was too far from the anticipated route of the enemy tanks-- the Suifenho-Mutanchiang road. General Shiina therefore decided that on the following day he would transfer the command post to a more centralized location. Meanwhile, at about 1500 hours, Colonel Kashiwada, Fifth Army operations officer, arrived for a liaison visit.

Reports received on the 10th from the border positions indicated that the fury of the fighting was gradually being intensified by air and ground attacks of the enemy. At the MLR positions, however, no change was observed, except for frequent flights of enemy aircraft.

On 11 August the enemy continued to make gains at the three points of penetration along the border, but our garrison units fought stubbornly. A report was received that on the preceding day an enemy force (estimated at one armored division) had broken through the border and attacked Suiyang. The enemy force had formed two columns, one advancing along the Suifenho-Muleng road and the other along the Kuanyuehtai Hill-Hsiachengtzu road. Another powerful armored unit was reported to be advancing towards Muleng from the direction of

Tungning. (See Map No 1.) Meanwhile, on the morning of the 11th, MLR positions were attacked for the first time when the Central Sector Unit was engaged by a vanguard of enemy infantry.

Attack on the MLR

On the morning of the 12th, the enemy infantry unit attacking the Central Sector Unit was reinforced by tanks. The attack continued all day, and after nightfall it mounted in fury. At the same time the fronts of the Right and Left Sector Units were harassed by enemy artillery fire. Meanwhile communications were in an extremely bad condition and it was difficult to transmit orders.

At about 0900 hours on 13 August, a tragic report was brought to the command post by a mounted noncommissioned officer from the Central Sector Unit commander. It stated that:

> Because of the difficulty of holding our positions, the regiment will launch a counterattack with the regimental colors in the lead. This is perhaps the last report from our regiment to the division.

The division commander was astonished at the Central Sector Unit commander's desire to launch a suicide attack in full strength instead of continuing organized resistance, and was rather suspicious of the lack of tenacity on the part of the Central Sector Unit. Its front was most vital to the entire Army, and the engagement had only recently been initiated. General Shiina therefore ordered the Central Sector Unit commander to put up stubborn resistance by holding his positions. At the same time, to get a better view of the

MONOGRAPH NO. 154-G
MAP NO. 1

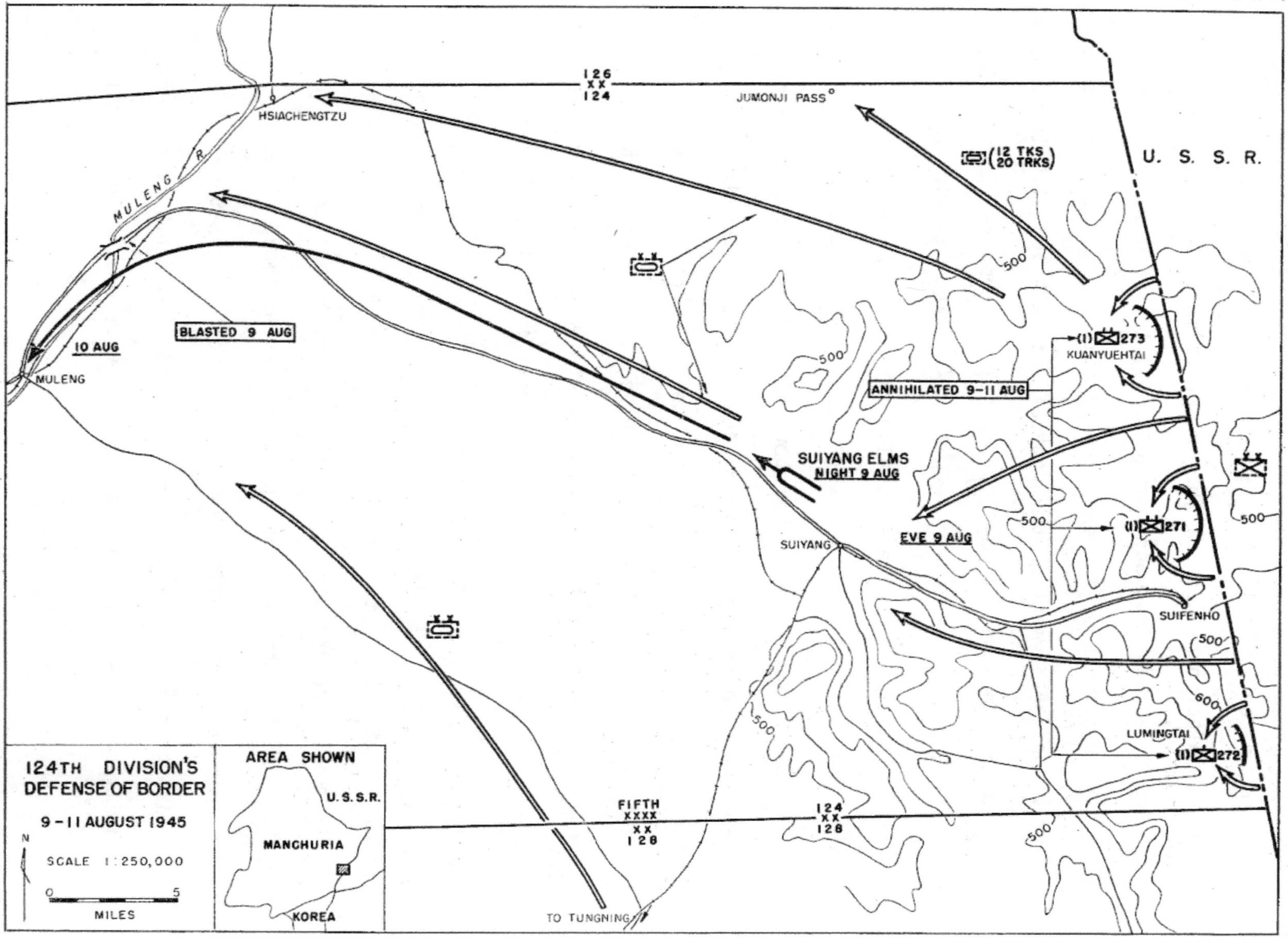
124TH DIVISION'S DEFENSE OF BORDER
9 - 11 AUGUST 1945
SCALE 1:250,000
0
5
MILES
N
AREA SHOWN
U. S. S. R.
MANCHURIA
KOREA
U. S. S. R.
126 XX 124
JUMONJI PASS
HSIACHENGTZU
(12 TKS 20 TRKS)
MULENG R.
MULENG
10 AUG
BLASTED 9 AUG
(I) 273
KUANYUEHTAI
ANNIHILATED 9-11 AUG
SUIYANG ELMS
NIGHT 9 AUG
EVE 9 AUG
SUIYANG
(I) 271
SUIFENHO
LUMINGTAI
(I) 272
FIFTH XXXX
XX 128
124 XX 128
TO TUNGNING
500
600

situation, he transferred the division command post to Mt Shozu (Shozusan), directly behind the Central Sector Unit.

In the afternoon, General Shiina met Colonel Koketsu, the artillery command, at the Shozusan command post, listened to his explanation of the condition of the enemy confronting them, and took direct command of the engagement on the Central and Left Sector Unit fronts.

Even from Shozusan it was not possible to observe minutely the enemy action in front of the Central Sector Unit. Nevertheless, General Shiina felt that the situation was not so serious as to warrant that unit's immediate abandonment of its positions, especially since the front of the Left Sector Unit (273d Regiment) was relatively quiet. To coordinate the situation better, the division commander sent a staff officer to the Central Sector Unit with delegated authority to withdraw the regiment if necessary to the east-west line running through Shozusan and paralleling the main road. At midnight this staff officer reported that the Central Sector Unit was still repulsing the attacks of a superior enemy, and that it would take advantage of the darkness to carry out a partial adjustment of its position.

Meanwhile, before dark, a powerful enemy tank force from the Tungning area had attempted to force its way westward along the Muleng-Taimakou sector of the main road. Most of the tanks, however, under fire by the artillery weapons concentrated north of the road—especially our 150-mm howitzer battalion—were destroyed, disabled, or retreated. Only a few succeeded in breaking through our lines and advancing westward. An officer returning at midnight from patrol duty reported that he had witnessed more than 110 tanks destroyed or disabled along the road from Muleng westward to Taimakou. His patrol brought back several maps and documents found on dead officers in tanks. Although the disabling of over 110 tanks was not confirmed, it is certain that we dealt a severe blow to the enemy in this action.

On the morning of 14 August the Left Sector Unit (273d Regiment), whose front up to this time had been relatively quiet, was attacked by an enemy force approximately one infantry division in strength. This action revealed that the enemy's plan to break through the front of our Central Sector Unit with his armored force was being balked by the stubborn resistance of our Central Sector Unit, particularly by the effective firing of the 150-mm howitzers of the 20th Heavy Field Artillery Regiment north of the road. It was as a result of the stubborn resistance in this sector, apparently, that the enemy reverted to an orthodox attack by directing an infantry division to neutralize the Left Sector Unit in its hill positions before renewing the attack in the center. In the afternoon, the engagement in the left sector mounted in fury.

Under continous enemy pressure the Central Sector Unit retreated at dawn to the line on the southern foothills of Shozusan. After daybreak the enemy tanks again tried to advance westward along the road, but seemed to have suffered considerable losses from our artillery fire.[77]

Details of the action on the front of the Right Sector Unit (271st Regiment) were not known because of poor communications. From all appearances, however, the enemy action on this front seemed very weak, and only the sound of intermittent artillery fire was heard from that direction.

With the retreat of the Central Sector Unit, the division commander again decided to move the command post, this time to Hill B. (See Map No 2.) He departed Shozusan at about 0900. The decision was a fortuitous one, for shortly thereafter the hill was subjected to a surprise attack from enemy rocket guns. So intense was the concentration that Shozusan instantly became a bald mountain. At about 1600 hours, General Shiina arrived at the side of Hill B.

With the retreat of the Central Sector Unit, the enemy tanks unleashed an intense attack upon our 150-mm howitzer positions north of the road that had stalled the tank advance. At about the same time all communications were disrupted with both subordinate

---

77. Japanese consultants assisting the editor in preparing this monograph feel that this is a highly overstated account of the 124th Division's battle in this sector. They point out that Fifth Army, which deployed the Sasaki and Kobayashi Detachments along the main road and was in a position to know tha situation, reported that, on the 11th, enemy tanks had broken through the Muleng positions causing the collapse of Fifth Army's critical sector on that day.

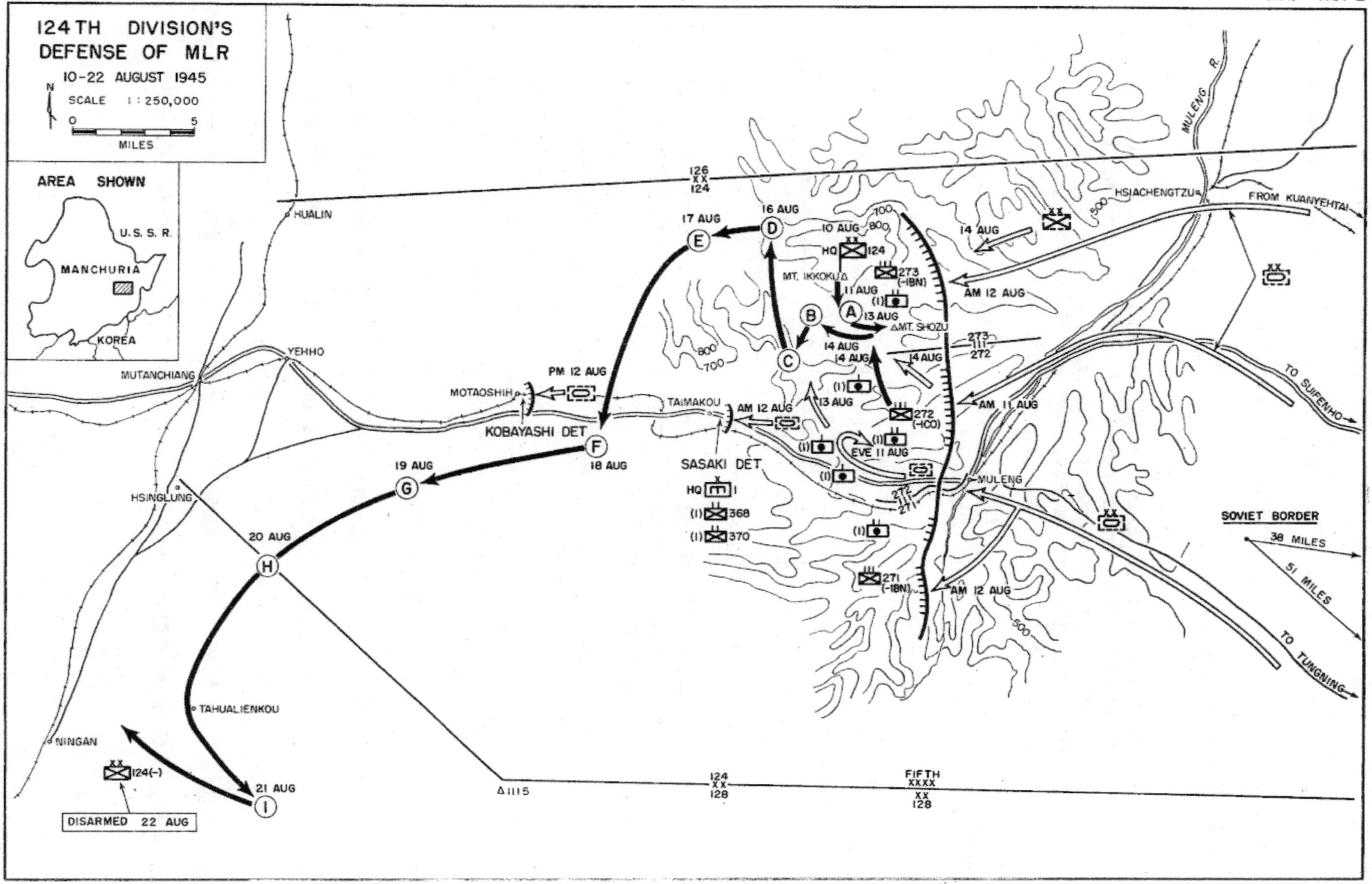

MONOGRAPH NO. 154-G
MAP NO. 2

124TH DIVISION'S
DEFENSE OF MLR
10–22 AUGUST 1945
SCALE 1:250,000

and higher commands. At this juncture the tide of battle seemed to turn against us, and the division commander issued instructions to the following effect:

> All personnel of the division, with firm determination to die in honor, shall repeatedly carry out raiding tactics under cover of darkness, and will smash the enemy's combat strength bit by bit. To this end all units will carry out tenacious attacks, according to the following procedures:
>
> The main target of attack will be the enemy located along the Mutanchiang road.
>
> Units north of the road will charge and break through the enemy line to the south; those south of the road will charge and break through to the north. Each will advance to the hilly zone of the opposite side. In the daytime they will endeavor to seek cover and conceal their movements and intentions as much as possible. During the ensuing night they will return and repeat the same action.
>
> In attacking, adjoining units will maintain close contact and exercise utmost care to avoid engagements among themselves.
>
> Movement towards the sector west of Taimakou will be prohibited.
>
> The raiding tactics stipulated in these instructions will be carried out beginning on the night of 15 August.

Along about sunset a liaison officer from Army Headquarters arrived at the division command post. The orders he brought, however, had been issued and sealed on or before the 12th, and since several days had elapsed, no new information or timely instructions were obtained from him. After dark the entire combat area became somewhat quiet, although rifle shots and artillery gunfire were heard intermittently, both far and near. At the division headquarters all personnel including the division commander, discarded unnecessary items of equipment and clothing. Lightly clad, they spent the night at ease.

With the morning of 15 August, rifle shots and the roaring of heavy guns were heard continuously and with renewed intensity all over the battlefield. We gradually became familiar with the sound of rocket launchers. Meanwhile Headquarters was busy making preparations for the first night raiding attack.

About 2000 hours the Signal Unit commander, who incidentally for some days had taken great pains to restore telegraph communication, heard over a wireless telegraph set what seemed like a Tokyo broadcast. Astonished at the report relating to an Imperial cease-fire order, he reported it promptly to the chief of staff in strictest secrecy.

The chief of staff, taking into consideration the effect such a report would have on the morale of troops, strictly prohibited the Signal Unit commander from divulging the information. At the same time he reported it to the division commander. Furthermore, with a view to confirming the broadcast he personally listened to a subsequent broadcast and confirmed that it was not Soviet propaganda.

After due consideration the division commander concluded that since the Imperial cease-fire order had, in truth, been issued there was no need to sacrifice the life of even one soldier. He therefore temporarily postponed the raid scheduled for that night and, after confirming the matter by telegraph on the following morning, took the following measures: he directed that the Imperial cease-fire order be conveyed to each unit; he directed the division to disengage the enemy and to withdraw to the sector south of Mutanchiang to await further orders; and he ordered each unit to leave the combat zone at an opportune moment and to act in accordance with the Imperial command.

At daybreak of the 16th we again confirmed the Imperial cease-fire order by telegraph. The measures directed by the division commander were promptly carried out and each unit under the division's command was ordered to assemble first in the vicinity of C, and then in the vicinity of D. (See Map No 2.)

During the 17th and 18th, divisional units began to assemble. Elements of the Central and Left Sector Units (272d and 273d Regiments), the division artillery, the majority of the engineer unit, and signal unit, and parts of others units withdrew together to the vicinity of E (See Map No 2); there they sought cover while awaiting further orders. After sunset the troops commenced the next leg of the withdrawal and, taking advantage of darkness, moved in several groups in order to break through the road to the south. After 0300 hours on the 18th, while enemy tanks, trucks, and foot troops were pushing westward in droves along the road, the spearhead of our withdrawal force broke through the road, followed successively by small elements which took advantage of the gap in the enemy's line of traffic. This procedure took considerable time. The rear echelon consisting principally of the division artillery was unable to break through the road that night. On the following evening this group, after waiting between the road and the railway tracks during the day, finally broke through after sunset.

On the night of the 18th the division bivouacked south of the road and waited for delayed elements to join. On the morning of the 19th, after being joined by the rear echelon, the division moved out. Troops march for three days through mountainous areas, avoiding all contact with the enemy, and on the night of the 21st bivouacked on a hill about 15 kilometers south of Tahualienkou.

According to natives in the vicinity, Ningan had already been occupied by Soviet forces. Tanks were seen almost every day in Tahualienkou. In view of the situation, the division commander decided that it was not advantageous to delay negotiations with the Soviets any longer, and therefore dispatched two scout officers and their teams on the night of the 21st with a message stating: "The 124th Division is ready to open peace negotiations with the Soviet Army."

At daybreak on the 22d, representatives of the Soviet Army came to our sentry post, and negotiations were opened. The division was ordered to descend the hill and to disarm on the afternoon of the 22d. Thus, disarmament of the 124th Division was effected at the foot of a hill northeast of Ningan.

That night the division bivouacked along the banks of the Mutanchiang River, east of Ningan. On the following morning division troops began a march to the village of the Kutami Cultivating Group, 7 kilometers south of Tungchingcheng. Internment camp life began on the 26th.

Those units which had been unable to accompany the main body of the division during the withdrawal, marched along the same general route about two or three days later. Some of them, instead of going to Ningan, withdrew farther south and were disarmed in various areas. In the meantime, the division commander on the morning of the 23d took his leave of the division and went to Mutanchiang with an adjutant, in compliance with an order of the Soviet Army.

Civil Affairs

Prior to the outbreak of hostilities a great number of resident Japanese women and children were evacuated to Hsinking or Harbin because of the tense border situation; some of these later returned to the homeland.

At the outbreak of hostilities, however, there was still a considerable number of Japanese residents in the division's area. Most of these withdrew from the border districts by train, and those who missed the train were evacuated by Army vehicles or on foot. Thus very few were subjected directly to the ravages of war.

Yet there were some tragic incidents. The last train carrying refugees from Tungning was unfortunately disabled by shelling from enemy tanks in the sector west of Hohsi. Some people aboard were killed; others were obliged to retreat through the hills. A large number of Japanese residents near Suifenho threw in their lot with the garrison stationed there, participated in the engagement of the garrison, and died a glorious death. One cultivating group centered around the area south of Suifenho sustained heavy losses because it delayed in seeking refuge.

Monograph No 154-H

CHAPTER XVII

The 126th Division[78]

Organization

The 126th Division was organized in the Linkou area by Fifth Army during February 1945. Like the 124th Division, it was one of the divisions formed at that time to restore Kwantung Army's waning strength, and to give it the appearance of a powerful force. The cadre for the division was obtained from the 12th Border Garrison Unit and some personnel left behind by the 25th Division after its transfer. The division was fleshed out in March with personnel from the 3d and 12th Border Garrison Units plus engineer remnants of the 11th Division, and in June with additional personnel from the 11th Border Garrison Unit.

Completion of the organization of the division took three and half months (until mid-June 45). Infantry regiments of the division were organized in the following areas; the 277th at Panchiehho, the 278th at Miaoling, the 279th at Kuanyuehtai. Other newly organized main units were 126th Field Artillery Regiment, 126th Engineer Unit (battalion size), 126th Transport Regiment, 126th Divisional Signal Unit, and one raiding battalion which was organized in July with personnel selected from the three infantry regiments of the division.

---

78. The information in this chapter was furnished by Colonel Masashi Tanaka, chief of staff of 126th Division.

Division headquarters was at Linkou, and the division was commanded by Lieutenant General Kazuhiko Nomizo.

During May the 126th Division was given responsibility for garrisoning the fortified positions along the border near Panchiehho and Lishan. (These areas had previously been garrisoned by the 3d Border Garrison Unit and 25th Division elements respectively; the former unit was scheduled for inactivation and the division for transfer.) General Nomizo sent approximately two infantry battalions to the border. To Pingyang sector he sent a battalion and a company of 278th Regiment, and to the Pamientung sector a battalion (minus one company) of 277th Regiment.

At the same time that the 124th Division moved to positions in the Army's new MLR, the main body of the 126th Division was redeployed to its sector of the MLR, located in the general area west of Pamientung, and began constructing positions.

At the outbreak of war on 9 August, the strength of the division was augmented by the assignment of one battery of the 20th Heavy Field Artillery Regiment, and one battery of the 31st Independent Antitank Battalion.

Intelligence and Estimate of the Soviets

Approximately 8,000 vehicles, including tanks and automobiles, as well as many artillery pieces, pontoons, and other equipment were among the war materiels observed on south-bound trains passing through the vicinity of Iman during the three months from April to

June 1945. Simultaneous with this stepped-up reinforcement of its Far East bases, the USSR intensified its spy activities. The spy channels consisted principally of the Panchiehho-Hataho route and the Lishuchen-Chining route. Employing many Koreans and Manchurians the Soviets endeavored to collect intelligence even in front of the 126th Division positions. (At the termination of the war, a lieutenant colonel of the Soviet Guard Unit stationed in the area revealed that these spies, amply provided with money, had been planted in Manchuria for at least three months.) Especially during June and July, it was quite certain that spy posts had been set up in the vicinity of Hataho and Chining to collect intelligence concerning the movements of our army. It was difficult, however, to arrest these enemy agents since they were shield by Koreans and Manchurians.

The boldness of the Soviet's provocation is indicated by their construction of over-the-border fortifications. For example, on about 20 July 1945 Soviet troops crossed the border in front of Chiungshan, southeast of Panchiehho and tresspassed to distances of 100 to 300 meters. They started constructing fortifications over 500 meters in length, and continued this work for about seven consecutive days, employing more than 300 men per day. Though the Soviet attitude was provocative, our border garrison unit, in conformity with instructions of Kwantung Army, took no positive action, and merely observed and reported the enemy's activities. A considerable volume of troop movements within the enemy positions on the

Soviet side of the border was also witnessed. On 6 August, furthermore, an estimated 100 enemy infantrymen crossed the border and attacked a Japanese observation unit at Kanhsiatun, 40 kilometers south of Hulin, in the 135th Division's area on our left.

During May or June a Fifth Army intelligence officer made the following estimate of the situation:

> There is a strong indication that the Soviet Army will attempt to invade Manchuria in concert with the US Army's landing on the homeland. The time of the invasion is estimated to be during or after September.

In late July the same source made the following estimate:

> In view of the recently intensified movements of the Soviet Army, it is probable that a Japanese-Soviet war will take place in the near future.

The 126th Division intelligence officer in late July estimated that:

> In the present circumstances, when Soviet movements on the frontier have become extremely active, a serious incident may occur. Such an incident might eventually lead to war.

On the basis of the foregoing estimates, the division commander stepped-up preparations. In July he inspected the border garrison units and issued instructions on the defense program of each, cautioning them particularly to prepare against a surprise attack by the enemy. He ordered that study and training be carried out based on these instructions. He also urged each unit deployed in the MLR to hasten the construction of fortified positions. Furthermore, he directed that training exercises be conducted at the fortifications near Tzuhsingtun for five days beginning on 1 August in order to train regimental and battalion commanders in tactics to cope with break-throughs by enemy mechanized units. In addition he directed that the organization of incomplete units be accelerated, and that personnel and weapons and ammunition be concentrated in fortified areas.

Operational Preparations for Border Defense

The 126th Division's border fronting the Soviets followed an irregular northeast-southwest line about 75 miles long that extended from east of Heilingshan to forward of Jumonji Pass. Along this border were two major defense lines, one shielding the Pingyang area, the other the Pamientung area. The Pingyang line ran northeast-southwest from Shangchihtun to west of Hsiaolutai, a distance of about 45 miles. The Pamientung line ran from Chingkulingmiao to Jumonji Pass, a distance of about 25 miles.

The Pingyang Line

The Pingyang line had six key defense sectors, each with long-established fortified positions. The northernmost was at Shangchihtun at which was deployed one platoon of about fifty men, with a squad of about fifteen men posted at a lookout point near Erhjenpan. The most important sector of the Pingyang line, both from the standpoint of the size of fortifications and the forces deployed there, was at Panchiehho; although these positions could accommodate two battalions, less than one was deployed in them. To the immediate right of the Panchiehho positions was a position for one company, at which only one platoon was deployed. Southwest of the Panchiehho position, at Nanshan, were fortifications to accommodate one battalion, but only one platoon was maintained there, with a lookout patrol positioned on a hilltop overlooking the border. At Hsiaolutai, the position closest to the border, fortifications capable of accommodating one battalion existed, but only one company was deployed there. At the right end of the Pingyang line, in positions to accommodate one battalion, one reinforced infantry company was deployed near the vital road leading to Pamientung. The unit defending this line consisted principally of the 2d Battalion of the 278th Regiment. (See Map No 1.)

The defense plan of the border garrison unit in the Pingyang area was roughly as follows:

> The enemy will be checked at the present defense line as long as possible. It the situation becomes unfavorable, border elements will retreat first to Pingyang and subsequently to the position of the division's main force, via Lishuchen.
>
> The Garrison Unit will contract its front to the line connecting Shangchihtun, Panchiehho, Nanshan, and Hsiaolutai, and will check the enemy as long as possible. Of the elements stationed at Erhjenpan and Shangchihtun, one platoon will be left at Shangchihtun and the rest will be assembled in the Panchiehho.
>
> Since Hsiaolutai is on the shortest route to the Pingyang area (from the border) the garrison unit there will defend that position to the last man.

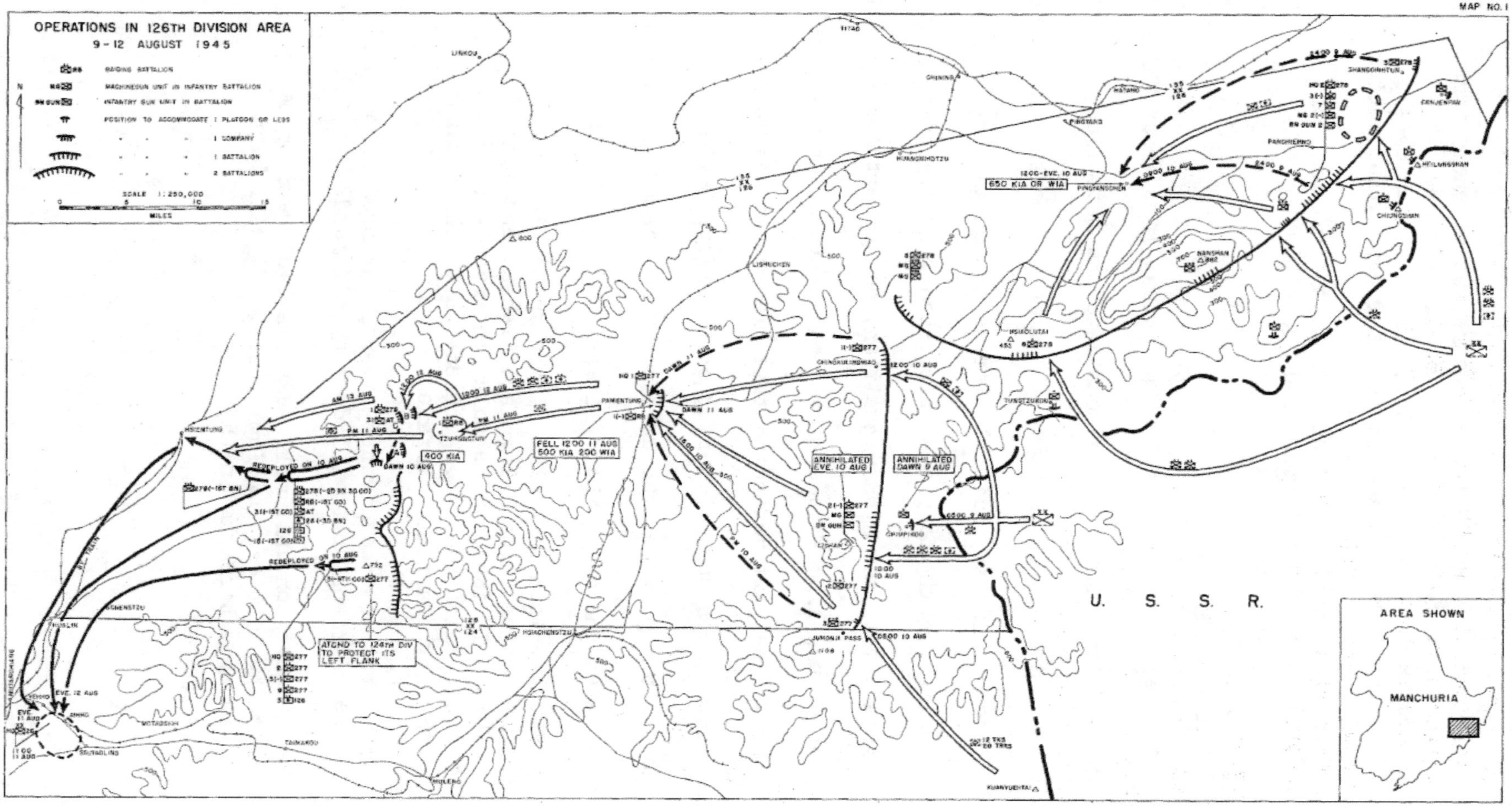

> In order to prevent the penetration of enemy tanks, one unit will be detailed immediately upon the opening of hostilities to demolish the bridges north of Panchiehho and in the Pingyangchen sector.
>
> Movement after the retreat from the vicinity of Pingyang will be determined according to the developing situation.

The Pamientung Line

On the left extremity of the Pamientung line, near Chingkulingmiao, in positions that could accommodate one battalion, one company (less elements) was deployed. The most important position in this line was at Lishan, suitable for accommodating two battalions, but with only approximately one reinforced infantry company deployed there. Adjacent to the Lishan position, on the extreme right flank of the Pamientung line were deployed one platoon, approximately 5 miles apart. The unit defending this line consisted mainly of the 1st Battalion (less some elements) of the 277th Regiment.

The defense plan for the garrison unit responsible for the Pamientung area was along these lines:

> The garrison unit will firmly defend the line connecting Chingkulingmiao, Lishan, and Jumonji Pass. If the enemy should penetrate and infiltrate this line, the garrison unit will destroy them by guerrilla warfare.
>
> To obstruct the advance of enemy armored units, the garrison unit will destroy all roads.
>
> The garrison unit will make its last resistance at the hill east of Pamientung, and will burn the army barracks in the area.

The border area fronting this garrison was entirely covered with dense forests. Both Japanese and Soviet dispositions were light and were located at considerable distances from the border line. Although there had been no border disputes in this area, there had always been a brisk traffic of enemy spies.

The Lishan and Chingkulingmiao Positions

Construction of fortifications on the line connecting Lishuchen, Chingkulingmiao, Lishan, and Jumonji Pass had been started during the summer of 1944. These consisted of two fairly strong field-position type constructions, one in Lishan, the other near Chingkulingmiao, both of which had been completed. A plan to strengthen these positions during fiscal year 1945 had been formulated, with the work scheduled to begin in April, but was suspended by order of Fifth Army. The defense front was too wide in proportion to our defending force, and since terrain features favored the enemy, it was believed that a defensive engagement in this area would be difficult.

Opening of Hostilities

The night of 8-9 August, moonless and drizzling without a letup, was filled with an air of ghastliness at Panchiehho, when all of a sudden at midnight a strange light was seen and the drone of aircraft heard to the south. Soon thereafter enemy aircraft were sighted crossing the Soviet-Manchurian boundary. At about the same time several shots were heard from the direction of our border lookout positions; telephone communication with them was completely disrupted.

Recognizing the gravity of the situation, the garrison commander (commander of 2d Battalion, 278th Regiment) reported the above facts to Pingyang where the division maintained an intelligence liaison officer. At the same time he established contact with the Nanshan and Shangchihtun garrison units from whom he learned that although they themselves were not yet under attack their border lookout posts were believed to be engaging the enemy. The garrison commander concluded that the Japanese-Soviet war had at last broken out and ordered all garrison units under his command to prepare to meet the enemy in accordance with the garrison's prearranged defense plan.

At division headquarters in Pamientung, meanwhile, the division intelligence officer was awakened by the drone of enemy aircraft at midnight. By telephone he received reports from border garrison units in both the Pingyang and Pamientung area that they were being attacked by an overwhelmingly superior enemy. He immediately transmitted this report to Army Headquarters as well as to the division commander who was at Yehho participating in table-top maneuvers of Fifth Army Headquarters.

Meanwhile at the Panchiehho garrison positions continuous firing was heard in the distance. At 0200 a messenger brought in a report that the Chiungshan lookout unit had been annihilated.

The enemy who advanced to the front of the Pingyang line was believed to consist of one infantry division. His main force quickly overran the small lookout units at Heilingshan and Chiungshan, and advanced approximately 4 kilometers with lightning speed. Finding a wide gap in the Japanese line, a situation quite contrary to the results of his reconnaissance conducted in pre-war days, he feared that a trap had been laid by the Japanese Army. From about 1000 until 1500 he waited. Upon ascertaining that there were no Japanese troops deployed in the area, the enemy sent elements of his force to attack the left flank of the Panchiehho positions and assembled the main body of his force at a point east of Panchiehho on the evening of the 9th. (This information was revealed by the Soviet division commander after the war ended.)

Engagement in Pingyangchen

Until this time the positions at Panchiehho had not been attacked. But in view of the threats posed by the assembly of the enemy it was apparent to the battalion commander that his force would be isolated completely on the following day, the 10th. He therefore decided to withdraw to the vicinity of Pingyang at midnight of the 9th. Taking advantage of the darkness the force withdrew to Pingyangchen along a by-path. Because of the fact that the march was made at night, it did not reach Pingyangchen until 0900 of the 10th.

Meanwhile, an enemy column had broken through the Hsiaolutai garrison defenses and advanced to the sector west of Pingyangchen. The battalion commander was now confronted with two encroaching enemy columns. He decided to use elements to check the enemy that was pursuing him from the Panchiehho sector, and to employ his main force in an attack on the enemy that had broken through the Hsiaolutai sector and was now in the sector west of Pingyangchen. Beginning at about noon of the 10th a fierce engagement was fought in Pingyangchen. The enemy relying on his superiority in numbers and our force relying on resolution to stop him, the fighting became disorganized and confused. By about 1600 the battalion commander had been wounded, and majority of our officers killed. The force virtually lost its effectiveness. After dark, Second Lieutenant Ito, commander of Third Company, ordered the remaining men to assemble and led them in a withdrawal that broke through the enemy line.

Of the approximately 850 officers and men who took part in this engagement, 650 were either killed or wounded. Enemy casualties exceeded our's, although the total number could not be ascertained.

Engagement in the Pamientung Area

Upon sighting enemy aircraft flying west across the border before daybreak on 9 August, the battalion commander immediately alerted each unit of his defense force along the Pamientung line to prepare for an engagement. Like the Pingyang garrison commander, he then contacted division headquarters and adjacent garrison units, and from them learned that the enemy was attacking along the entire front. While continuing to maintain contact and to keep abreast of the enemy situation, he ordered all units to take their battle stations and to barricade roads and destroy bridges.

At 1000 hours on the 9th, a report came from the commander of the Lishan garrison to the effect that the Chiupikou lookout unit had been annihilated by one enemy battalion at day-break. As yet no trace of the enemy had been seen in Lishan or Chingkulingmiso, although at about 1200 hours there were indications that a powerful enemy unit was advancing westward through the dense forest.

On dawn of the 10th, the Lishan garrison telephoned a report to the effect that Lishan had been subjected to artillery fire and that an enemy force of at least two and possibly three battalions was attacking. The report added that the unit there was engaged in a fierce battle for its positions. On the heels of this report came another telephone call from the Chingkulingmiao stating that the garrison there was being attacked. At this point telephone communication with both of these positions was severed.

At about 0800 hours, the Jumonji Pass garrison telephoned that an enemy force of more than ten enemy tanks and twenty motor vehicles (carrying supporting foot troops) had advanced from the direction of Kuanyuehtai and was attacking. Shortly afterwards telephone communication with this unit also was severed. The battalion commander than dispatched mounted orderlies to frontline units to obtain information.

Engagements Along the Pamientung Line

The tanks appearing on the front of the Jumonji Pass garrison unit fired at the barracks and set them afire at about 1000 hours on 10 August. The fire spread to a nearby forest and temporarily halted the advance of the enemy tanks. But the enemy's infantrymen continued the attack. Infiltrating the forest and supported by fire from the tanks, they inflicted heavy losses on the garrison unit. The commander, Second Lieutenant Kawakami, realizing the disadvantage of engaging the tanks, directed his troops to make an orderly withdrawal toward Pamientung through the forest, meanwhile hindering the advance of enemy tanks by barricading the road leading to Pamientung.

At the Lishan positions, meanwhile, the enemy after subjecting the garrison to artillery fire at about 1000 hours on the 10th, infiltrated through gaps in the positions. Beginning at noon hand-to-hand engagements were fought in many places. The garrison's stubborn resistance repulsed the enemy several times. However, the enemy's repeated attacks by a numerically superior force finally succeeded in making steady inroads in the garrison's positions. By evening, almost all officers and men of the unit, including the commander, had been killed. The Lishan position thus fell completely into enemy hands.

The positions of the Chingkulingmiao garrison were located in terrain that made it difficult for the enemy to approach. This garrison fought well, and the enemy was able to occupy only the southern corner of the garrison's position by the evening of the 10th. But immediately after the fall of Lishan, enemy troops infiltrated the right flank and rear of the garrison's positions in rapid succession. That night the garrison commander decided to withdraw to Pamientung. He assembled his company and by taking a by-path which had been previously reconnoitered, arrived at the hills east of Pamientung before dawn of the 11th. There he joined the main force of the battalion.

Meanwhile, at about 1600 hours on the 10th, approximately ten enemy tanks appeared near Pamientung, to which front line units were withdrawing. Each individual of the main body of the 1st Company of the Raiding Battalion armed himself with explosives, and rushed the enemy tanks. Although minor damage was inflicted on a majority of them, the explosives were not of sufficient strength (3 to 7 kilograms) to halt the tanks.

Early in the morning of the 11th, enemy infantry forces supported by artillery appeared on the east and south sides of Pamientung, and launched a coordinated attack. The garrison resisted stoutly, but its equipment was inadequate to cope with enemy weapons. By noon of the 11th, after the garrison suffered increasingly heavy losses, Pamientung also fell into enemy hands. Total casualities sustained by the Pamientung garrison were estimated at 700, of which 600 were in the garrison unit, and 100 in the 1st Raiding Company. Of the 700 casualties 500 were KIAs. The enemy's losses, though estimated to be greater, could not be ascertained. However, two of his tanks were destroyed and seven were disabled.

Engagement Near Tzuhsingtun

When the division's main body was ordered to move toward Yehho on the night of 10 August, (see below) the remaining elements were assigned the mission of checking the enemy in the Tzuhsingtun area in order to facilitate the withdrawal of the division's main force and the 135th Division's main force. These elements, commanded by First Lieutenant Yamagishi, consisted of the 1st Battalion of the 279th Regiment, one company of the 31st Antitank Battalion, and one-third of the 1st Company of the Raiding Battalion.

The enemy armored column that had attacked Pamientung continued a westward advance and on the afternoon of the 11th arrived in the vicinity of Tzuhsingtun where it renewed its attack on our force. The Tzuhsingtun (Yamagishi) detachment's infantry elements were deployed atop the mountain, and its antitank guns and raiding unit in the foothills. Although our antitank guns and close-quarter combat teams engaged the enemy, neither achieved any measure of success. Meanwhile, the infantry held its position on the heights and prepared for an engagement with enemy infantry.

At about 1000 hours on the 12th, three or four enemy infantry battalions supported by twenty artillery pieces also appeared in the vicinity of Tzuhsingtun. At noon the artillery began to subject Hill B to intense, concentrated fire. (See Map) Enemy infantry elements then made successive flanking movements toward the north. The Yamagishi detachment met these movements by deploying some troops from Hill A north to Hill C. The enemy gradually shifted his artillery fire to Hill C while his infantry, taking advantage of the forest, moved towards the same hill. In order to minimize losses from enemy artillery fire our troops moved to the western slope and there exchanged fire with enemy infantry. The enemy's force was superior, however, and it gradually gained ground to the left rear of our positions. By evening the enemy occupied Hills B and C.

During the night Lieutenant Yamagishi regrouped the remaining troops and launched a counterattack on Hill C. Although the attack achieved temporary gains, the hill soon reverted to enemy control. Before daybreak of the 13th, the detachment moved to a position in the forest to the south. The enemy left small elements to observe our troops, and with his main force pushed on toward Hsientung.

Of the approximately 650 troops who participated in the engagement near Tzuhsingtun, approximately 400 were killed. Weapons lost included four antitank guns, two infantry battalion guns, and three machineguns.

The force remaining in the area had by now been reduced to one-third of its original strength. Lieutenant Yamagishi assembled the men and led them in a withdrawal towards the southwest in an effort to join the division's main force. The move was through a mountainous area, however, and hence was slow. On the evening of the 16th this force reached a hill northeast of Yehho, but on learning that the enemy was already near Mutanchiang, turned toward Tungchingcheng.

While en route to Tungchingcheng, moreover, our troops learned of the termination of the war. On the 20th they were disarmed in the vicinity of Tungchingcheng.

Plan for the Withdrawal of the Division's Main Force from Tzuhsingtun

At 1800 hours on 10 August, after learning that the main body of the enemy's mechanized force was proceeding along the Muleng-Motaoshih-Mutanchiang road, Fifth Army had ordered the withdrawal of the main body of the 126th Division and of 135th Division to the vicinity of Yehho. Accordingly, the 126th Division planned to withdraw during the night of the 10th, and issued the following withdrawal plan:

> The main body of the division will withdraw in two columns to the Yehho area on the night of 10 August. Elements of the division will remain at Tzuhsingtun and Hill 792.
>
> The main body of the left column will be commanded by Colonel Kikuchi, commander of the 279th Regiment. It will consist of the 279th Regiment (minus the 1st Battalion), the 126th Field Artillery Regiment (minus the 3d Battalion), the 31st Antitank Battalion (minus the 1st Company), the 126th Transport Unit, the 126th Engineer Unit, the 2d and 3d Companies of the 15th Independent Engineer Regiment, and the division Veterinary Depot and the Ordnance Duty Unit.
>
> The rear guard of this left column will consist of the 278th Regiment (minus the 3d Company and the 2d Battalion), and the division raiding battalion.
>
> The left column will leave Tzuhsingtun at 2000 hours on the 10th and move toward Yehho via the Hsientung-Hualin road. (Division headquarters will depart in advance by truck.) The 279th Regiment

will be transported by train from Hsientung and arrive at Yehho on the evening of the 11th. Other elements of the left column will proceed by foot and arrive at Yehho on the evening of the 12th.

The right column will consist of the 277th Regiment (minus the 1st and 3d Battalions but including the 3d Company of the 1st Battalion and the 9th Company of the 3d Battalion), and the 3d Battalion of the 126th Field Artillery Regiment. This column will leave its positions at 2000 hours and move toward Yehho via Hill 791-Chengtzu-Hualin road, and will arrive at Yehho on the evening of the 12th.

The Tzuhsingtun detachment will consist of the 1st Battalion of the 279th Regiment, the 1st Company of the 31st Antitank Battalion, one-third of the 1st Company of the Raiding Battalion (which will occupy positions west of Tzuhsingtun and cover the division's withdrawal), and the 3d Battalion (minus the 9th Company) of the 277th Regiment, which will secure Hill 792 and cover the left flank of the 124th Division. This latter unit will be placed under the tactical command of the 124th Division.

Plan for Occupying Positions Near Yehho

As soon as the division commander, General Nomizo, reached Yehho he reported to Fifth Army Headquarters. There at about noon of the 11th, he received orders regarding the redeployment of his division to what amounted to a new MLR in front of Yehho. The order follows:

> Fifth Army Order Issued at Yehho at 1200 hours on 11 August.

At present the enemy mechanized force is desperately engaging the 124th Division in the vicinity of Muleng.

The Army intends to crush the attack of the enemy mechanized force in the area east of the Mutanchiang River.

The 126th Division will occupy a position extending from the vicinity of Yingchitun to Hill 371 via the Freight Depot Hill and Ssutaoling and will crush the attack of the enemy mechanized force. One field heavy artillery battery, the raiding battalion of the 135th Division, the 2d and 3d Companies of the 15th Independent Engineer Regiment, and four tanks will be attached to the division.

General Nomizo at 1700 hours prepared the division order based on this, and directed that it be given orally to the commander of each unit as soon as the unit arrived in Yehho. After repeating the first paragraph of the Army's order, the division's order went on as follows:

The division intends to occupy a position extending from the vicinity of Yingchitun to Hill 371 via Freight Depot Hill and Ssutaoling and to crush the attack of the enemy mechanized force advancing from the direction of Muleng.

The 277th Regiment (less the 1st and 3d Battalions but including the 3d Company of the 1st Battalion) will become the Right Sector Unit and occupy a position on the hill east of Yingchitun facing southward. The Regiment will establish antitank obstacles, particularly along the stream south of Yingchitun.

The 278th Regiment (less the 3d Company and the 2d Battalion) with the Freight Depot Guard Unit under its command, will become the Central Sector Unit and will occupy a position on the hill south of the Freight Depot facing towards the southeast. The Regiment will establish antitank obstacles at the foot of the eastern slope of the hill.

The 279th Regiment (less the 1st Battalion) will become the Left Sector Unit and will occupy Ssutaoling Hill with its main body, and Hill 371 with its remaining elements. The regiment will cooperate closely with the division engineer unit deployed on the main road in the vicinity of Ssutaoling.

Boundaries between the sector units will be as follows: between the right and central sectors, the line connecting the southern tip of the Ordnance Depot and two houses southeast of the Yingchitun Hill; between the central and left sectors, the line connecting the southern tip of the tank unit's former barracks, the northern tip of the Freight Depot, and the stream on the east side of the Freight Depot.

The artillery unit (the 126th Artillery Regiment reinforced with one field heavy artillery battery) will deploy its main force in the vicinity of the former tank unit barracks and some elements the low ground on the west side of Hill 371. The unit will make firing preparations so as to direct its entire fire-power on the eastern slope of Ssutaoling Hill, especially in the sector along the main road. It will direct a part of its firepower in front of the central sector and the front of Hill 371.

The engineer unit (the 126th Engineer Unit reinforced with the 2d and 3d Companies of the 15th Independent Engineer Regiment) will station its troops in Ssutaoling village in order to construct tank obstacles in the area extending from the stream west of Ssutaoling to the narrow stream 2 kilometers east of Ssutaoling as well as prepare foxholes for close-quarter attack against tanks.

The Raiding Unit (composed of the raiding battalions of the 126th and 135th Divisions and commanded by the 135th Division's raiding battalion commander) will prepare as many foxholes as possible for close-quarter attacks in the area extending from the narrow stream west of Ssutaoling to the east end of Yehho.

The 126th Transport Unit, the Veterinary Hospital, and the Ordnance Duty Unit will take positions in Yehho village, under the command of the Transport Unit commander. The close-quarters combat teams organized by the Transport Unit will be stationed in front of division headquarters.

The Pamientung Army Hospital commandant will command both the Pamientung and Pingyangchen Army Hospitals and will establish a temporary field hospital at the Yehho infantry barracks.

Each unit will pay special attention to concealing from observation by enemy aircraft, all construction work in its position as well as troop movements.

I am at the barracks formerly occupied by the tank unit in Aiho. - 126th Division Commander, Kazuhiko Nomizo.

The 279th Regiment arrived at its new station on the night of 11 August and immediately started construction work; other units arrived on the following night and occupied positions according to the plan. Each unit worked continuously, night and day, concealing itself from enemy aircraft observation. By the evening of the 13th, construction of standing trenches and several communication trenches was nearing completion.

Engagements Near Hill 371 and Ssutaoling Hill

On the 13th a battalion of enemy tanks, the vanguard of the tank division that had overrun Motaoshih, advanced towards Ssutaoling, encountering several of our close-quarters combat teams enroute. In the evening it came to within 2 kilometers of Ssutaoling, and was soon joined by the division's main body. There the enemy armored division prepared for the assault on Fifth Army's new resistance line in front of Yehho, including the positions on Hill 371 our artillery positions north of Ssutaoling Hill, and on Ssutaoling itself.

At about 1000 hours on the 14th enemy artillery took positions on both sides of the road approaching Ssutaoling. An hour later it opened fire, initially selecting our artillery positions north of Ssutaoling Hill as targets. While continuing this fire, the enemy at 1300 began laying a concentration of fire on Ssutaoling Hill itself.

On the division's left flank, meanwhile, another enemy force, consisting of about seven tanks, attacked positions in a salient southeast of Hill 371, held by the 3d Battalion of the 279th Regiment. Outpost troops, concealing themselves in trenches, made desperate efforts to hold their positions, but by 1500 hours all of them, about thirty in number, had been annihilated by enemy tank fire. Immediately thereafter, enemy infantry advanced and occupied the Hill 371 positions, and hence gained a favorable observation post. That night our troops launched several night attacks in an attempt to recapture it, but failed mainly because the enemy was able to reinforce his positions repeatedly.

Meanwhile, the regiment's main body was locked in an infantry-tank-artillery struggle in the Ssutaoling Hill positions. Enemy tanks were unable to move to the upper part of this hill. The enemy therefore began a four-hour concentration of fire on the summit and finally destroyed our positions there completely. With the summit positions out, about thirty enemy tanks then attacked the road at the slopes and at the same time fired on the northern slope of the Hill. Infantry troops near the road concealed themselves in firing trenches and let the enemy tanks pass over them. When the enemy infantry following the tanks came close our men opened fire. The enemy was put to route in great confusion.

Immediately afterwards enemy tanks in reserve to the rear moved up and fired upon our troops one by one. By sunset the Ssutaoling positions, but not the village of Ssutaoling, were in enemy hands. In an attempt to recapture them, heroic close-quarter combat teams organized by the Engineer Unit repeatedly engaged the enemy, and succeeded in destroying eight tanks. Artillery units concentrated their fire on the enemy tanks without giving thought to the counter-battery fire being placed on their positions; sixteen enemy tanks were destroyed by our battery of the 20th Heavy Field Artillery Regiment and ten by the 126th Artillery Regiment.

After sunset the division continued its attempts to recapture Ssutaoling Hill. Taking advantage of the brief lull at night in the enemy's use of tanks and artillery, the division sent out close-quarter units of the raiding battalion. The enemy's security measures around his newly-won positions were very effective, however, and prevented our elements from gaining measureable success. The division also directed the 279th Regiment to launch a night assault. This assault failed for the same reason. The enemy suspended his attacks during the night and concentrated on strengthening the security of his position.

The enemy, apparently because of heavy tank losses he suffered on the 14th at the hands of our artillery and close-quarter raiding units, decided to attack these two elements ferociously. For eight hours, from 0800 to 1600 hours, on the 15th he conducted continuous artillery bombardment, concentrating his fire power on our artillery unit and on our close-quarter raiding units in positions astride the road. As a result of this destructive fire, all but one of the twenty-four pieces of our artillery unit were completely destroyed and our four tanks and all antitank guns were disabled.

As soon as our antitank guns had been silenced, approximately thirty enemy tanks appeared in front of the main positions of the 278th Regiment. They opened fire immediately and inflicted heavy damage, picking off the defenders one by one and disabling our heavy weapons. As a result of this enemy tank attack, the regiment moved its headquarters to a kaoliang farm. At about 1600 hours its telephone communication with division headquarters was completely disrupted. During this engagement, the 278th Regiment destroyed four enemy tanks and disabled five.

Shortly afterwards, fifteen enemy tanks appeared in front of the division command post. One squad of fire men of the Transport Unit, each armed with a 15 kilogram explosive, attacked the leading five tanks in a suicide charge, one tank per man, and successfully demolished all five tanks. The succeeding tanks, after witnessing this scene, retreated hurriedly toward Ssutaoling. Enemy infantry following the tanks on foot were also put to route.

On receipt of the first report concerning the advance of enemy tanks in the immediate front of the command post, division headquarters concluded that the fighting had entered its final stages. When the chief of staff asked the division commander "What shall we do?" the commander answered calmly: "Since I entrust you with everything, you can do as you see fit." Then the chief of staff said: "Then, I will order a final charge." He immediately announced this to all personnel of the headquarters and directed that preparations be made. The time was about 1800 hours.

Meanwhile, however, the destruction of the five leading enemy tanks and the route of the others had taken place, and upon learning of this heroic act, the chief of staff decided that the headquarters did not have to resort to the final charge. The enemy artillery discontinued firing and the battlefield became rather quiet. At 1830, Major Maeda, staff officer of Fifth Army Headquarters arrived with the following Army order for withdrawal:

> The Army intends to cross the Mutanchiang River tonight and retreat towards Hengtaohotzu to formulate a plan for the future.
>
> The 126th Division will withdraw at 2400 hours tonight, cross the Hsinglung Bridge, and move towards the sector southwest of the city of Mutanchiang. The main road south of Yehho Village will be used by the 126th Division. The 135th Division will cross the bridge west of Yehho via the road north of Yehho and move to the northwest sector of Mutanchiang City. The Reserve Officer Candidate Unit will become the cover unit of the Army and will cross the bridge west of Yehho after both divisions have crossed the Mutanchiang River.

Couriers will be dispatched at 0800 hours on the 16th to the building formerly occupied by First Area Army Headquarters to receive further orders.

In accordance with this Army order, the division alerted the necessary couriers from each unit at 2000 on the 15th. Meanwhile, it issued the following plan for the withdrawal of the division:

The 277th Regiment will evacuate the present position at 2300 hours, advance to Hsinglung, occupy Hsinglung as well as the vicinity of the airfield south thereof, and cover the division in crossing the Hsinglung Bridge.

Under the command of the Transport Unit commander, the Field Hospital, the Transport Unit, the Veterinary Hospital, and the Ordnance Duty Unit will depart Yehho at 2300 hours and withdraw toward the west side of the Mutanchiang Freight Depot via the Hsinglung Bridge.

Under the command of the Artillery Regiment commander, the 135th Division Raiding Battalion, the 126th Division Raiding Battalion, the 31st Independent Antitank Battalion, and the 126th Artillery Regiment (with the attached battery of heavy field artillery) will depart the vicinity of Aiho Station at 2300 hours and withdraw toward the south side of the Mutanchiang Freight Depot via the road linking Yehho and the Hsinglung Bridge.

The 7th Company of the 277th Regiment, the division headquarters, the Engineer Unit, and the 279th Regiment will depart the vicinity of the former tank unit barracks at 2400 hours in the order mentioned and withdraw toward the south side of the city of Mutanchiang via the road linking Yehho and the Hsinglung Bridge.

The 278th Regiment will evacuate its present position at 2400 hours and withdraw to the area north of the Hsinglung Bridge via the road linking Yingchitun and Hsinglung Bridge.

The withdrawal of the 126th Division was carried out smoothly, and according to schedule. By approximately 0800 of the 16th, all elements except the 278th Regiment, which was unaware of the withdrawal order, had crossed the Hsinglung Bridge.

The regimental liaison officer who had received the withdrawal order at division headquarters directed a noncommissioned officer and private to carry the order to the 278th Regiment. At that time regimental headquarters was located in a kaokiang farm, about 1 kilometer from the position it had occupied during daytime. The two enlisted couriers failed to locate the new site of regimental headquarters in spite of the fact that they searched until dawn. They concluded that the order must have been transmitted to regimental headquarters by other means, and returned to the west bank of the Mutanchiang River without conveying the order. Meanwhile, the commander of the 3d Battalion, Major Ueda, visited regimental headquarters before dawn of the 16th and told the commander that the division's main body had withdrawn. The regimental commander, however, declared: "I am ready to die here. I will not withdraw until I receive a definite order to do so."

At about 1000 hours, while still in position near the Kaoliang farm, the 278th Regiment was completely enveloped by a powerful enemy force consisting of infantry, tank, and artillery units. The regiment fought bravely and in the face of rapidly mounting casualties. At 1200 the officers and men of the regiment assembled under the regimental colors. Being determined to die at the position, the regimental commander, Colonel Hajime Yamanaka, respectfully bowed to the east, burned the regimental colors, rallied the assembled men and led a last charge toward the south. Then together with Major Ueda, the 3d Battalion Commander, he committed hara-kiri in the presence of the enemy.

The losses suffered by the 126th Division during the eight days of hostilities totaled approximately 2,050, broken down as follows:

277th Regiment	100
278th Regiment	800
279th Regiment	600
Artillery Regiment	150
Engineer Unit	100
Raiding Battalions	250 (incl 135th's)
Others	50

Principal weapons lost included 23 field pieces, four tanks, eighteen infantry guns, and sixteen heavy machine guns.

Enemy casualties are not known. However, approximately sixty Soviet tanks were destroyed and a great many more damaged.

Monograph No 154-I

CHAPTER XVIII

The 135th Division's Preparations[79]

Organization

Although not organized until July 1945, the 135th Division was formed principally from units already in existence, particularly the 77th Independent Mixed Brigade. The latter unit had been organized provisionally in February from the 3d Cavalry Brigade.

Aside from the 77th Independent Mixed Brigade, the division's source of personnel included the 3d and 4th Border Garrison Units, as well as recruits obtained during the July mass-mobilization in Manchuria. The division was in the last bloc of divisions organized by Kwantung Army, and was the last to be assigned to the Fifth Army.

In May 1945, the 77th Independent Mixed Brigade (predecessor of the 135th Division) was deployed in two major areas constructing fortifications. Two of its infantry battalions (plus three Manchurian Army infantry battalions) though stationed at the Linkou barracks were constructing positions near Mashan, slightly forward of the Area Army's MLR. The brigade's main body, consisting of four infantry battalions, two artillery battalions, and major elements of the engineer unit, was constructing fortifications at Chihsing, on the left flank of

---

79. The information in this chapter was furnished by Colonel Toshisuke Inouye, operations officer of 135th Division.

the Area Army's MLR. The brigade elements remained in place and continued their construction projects while being reorganized into the 135th Division.

Headquarters elements of the new division were formed between 5 and 10 July, followed by tactical elements, most of which were transferred intact. By the 30th, nine days before hostilities began, almost all major divisional elements had been formed. The organization of the division was never actually completed, however, since by the time the war broke out it lacked about one-fourth of its authorized personnel.

The commander of the division was Lieutenant General Yoichi Hitomi, and his headquarters was at Tungan.[80] Although the 368th Regimental Headquarters was at Hulin, two of its battalions were in the Chihsing positions. The headquarters of the 369th Regiment was at Tungan, while one of its battalions was at Chihsing, two of its companies at Paoching, and smaller elements at Jaoho near the frontier. The main body of the 370th Regiment, including its headquarters, was at Linkou, while one of its battalions was at the Chihsing construction site. Supporting elements of the division were in the Tungan area, except that the Engineer Unit (battalion size) was principally at Chihsing, as were also two battalions of the Artillery Regiment. The division's strength was augmented by a raiding battalion organiz-

---

80. General Hitomi had been the commander of the 1st Border Garrison Unit until its disbandment in July 1945.

ed at about the same time as the division and stationed near Linkou.

Division elements were therefore scattered. Some were garrisoning the border; some were in the vicinities of their normal stations--Hulin, Tungan, and Linkou; some were constructing forward defense position near Mashan, and others were engaged in major construction projects in the MLR near Chihsing. (See Map No 2, Monograph 154-F) This disposition was recognized to be disadvantageous. A redisposition in the shortest possible time was planned and was to be carried out on orders from the Army. But before the plan could be implemented, the Soviet Union attacked. Consequently approximately one-third of the division was unable to take part in combat operations. Since the division had only three-fourths of its authorized personnel, this meant that the division's operations against the enemy had the effect of only half a division. Furthermore, the division's incomplete status of training, reduced its combat effectiveness to only about 10 per cent.

Operational Planning

Pursuant to Fifth Army instructions, the division, in formulating its operations plan, merely modified the plan drafted earlies by the 77th Independent Mixed Brigade. The outline of the plan was:

> The division will establish an advance position on the Mashan line (20 kilometers east of Linkou) and a main defensive zone on the Chihsing line, and will crush the combat strength of the enemy. Major defense emphasis will be placed on the sector along the Linkou-Chihsing road; the enemy's mechanized units will be the main target. The main defensive zone will be formed in depth.

The troop strength in the advance position at Mashan will be one infantry battalion, one artillery battery, and an element of engineers. The mission of this force will be to destroy the enemy's strength as much as possible without becoming involved in a decisive battle. The troop strength in the main defensive zone at the outset will be eight infantry battalions, the main body of the artillery, and the main body of the engineers; following the withdrawal of the force in advance positions, the troop strength of the main defensive zone will be the division's main body.

The Manchurian Army Unit (three infantry battalions) now cooperating in the construction of advance positions at Mashan will be the reserve unit.

In the event Fifth Army orders the transfer of two or three infantry battalions from the division, such transfer will be made from troops in the main defensive zone.

When it becomes difficult for border garrisons to hold their positions, they will endeavor to exhaust the enemy's fighting strength by guerrilla warfare.

Status of Fortification Construction

The construction of positions at Mashan and Chihsing was begun about the middle of May by the 77th Independent Mixed Brigade. Emphasis was placed on underground installations such as caves. The work did not progress satisfactorily because of the shortages of materials. On 30 July, a meeting of unit commanders was held to study the results obtained, and to formulate new plans concerning the acquisition of materials and methods of accelerating the work. Although a program was agreed upon, the Soviet Union entered the war before it could get under way. By this time, the construction of obstacles against tanks and infantry had not been started; other work was about half complete.

Signal and Road Communication

An adequate signal communication network had been completed throughout the division's area for executing both garrison duties and operations in the border areas and in the rear.

The major road network consisted of the following gravel or dirt roads which permitted the passage of trucks but required the exercise of caution during the summer months because of numerous soft shoulders:

        Tungan-Hulin-Hutou
        Tungan-Hsingkai-Paoching-Jaoho
        Tungan-Mishan-Miaoling
        Tungan-Poli-Linkou
        Tungan-Chining-Linkou

Other roads were in fairly good condition. The section between Tumuho and Hutou permitted the passage of trucks. The Linkou-Chushan-Chihsing-Hsientung-Hualin-Yehho road (along the Tumen-Chiamussu railway), important for operations, had some very bad spots near Chushan which precluded the passage of motor vehicles. Repair work on this section of the road was under way at the time of the outbreak of war. The incompleteness of repairs was to prove a serious hindrance to the execution of operations. On the other hand, the newly-constructed Pamientung-Tzuhsingtun-Hsientung road was to be used to good advantage by the enemy, ironically enough, in the attack on our left-wing front positions near Yehho, particularly by an armored unit.

Training

While the division was still the 77th Independent Mixed Brigade, an inspection of the status of training was held. This revealed that although the brigade had keenly felt the importance of giving adequate infantry training to the many conscript reservists and troops transferred from the cavalry, artillery, and other branches of service, it could not do so because of the overriding importance of employing its forces in construction work. It was only after the division was organized that a policy was adopted, pursuant to an Army directive, of giving proper infantry training at the fortification sites concurrent with construction work. However, this program was begun just ten days before hostilities opened, and the results achieved were negligible.

The degree of preparedness reached by each type of unit was relatively low. Approximately only 50 per cent of men assigned to infantry units were qualified to fight as infantrymen; the remainder had to be led into combat with difficulty. The bulk of officers and men in these infantry units had been transferred from the cavalry. In reference to the raiding battalion, the individual training of the soldier was observed to be good, but only a small number of officers had received group training, and even these had only the barest outline knowledge of guerrilla warfare. Such being the case, it was out of the question to expect them to fulfill the proper mission of the battalion. As regards the artillery unit, the men were capable merely of conducting squad drill. As for the engineer unit, although some of the officers were engineers, the others were engineers in name only. However, the division had at least one advantage. The majority of its officers and men had been living in Manchuria as ordinary residents or military men, and hence were well acquainted with the terrain features. This particularly applied to soldiers formerly assigned to the 77th Independent Mixed Brigade and to men who had lived in Tungan province.

Intelligence

The intelligence section of the 135th Division gathered information on the Soviets from three principal sources: border garrison units, the Tungan Special Service (intelligence) Agency, and Fifth Army. Particularly observed were the movements of Japanese residents, Manchurians, Koreans, and White Russians. In this connection close liaison was maintained with Manchurian Government agencies.

During July and early August the Soviets along the border engaged in several unlawful acts and adopted an insulting attitude towards the Japanese. There were frequent instances of Soviet spies infiltrating Manchuria and making contact with Manchurians and Koreans. In spite of all the Soviet provocations, our border garrisons and observation units were patient and observed instructions of higher headquarters to avoid incidents.

Japanese residents, in general, harbored a certain degree of uneasiness, but most of them believed that Japan would not be defeated.

On the other hand, Manchurians believed that Japan would be defeated in the near future, and their contempt for Japan became increasingly evident. The uneasiness of Japanese families increased when many of the young males were conscripted either into munition factories or military service. This steady loss caused some families to be reduced to old men, women, and children. The feeling of uneasiness gradually mounted, especially with the worsening attitude of the Manchurians, so that some families began to feel they were in danger. This feeling became so widespread that many families were provided temporary quarters in the vacant Army barracks at Tungan.

Border Garrisoning

The division's border garrison mission extended from Miaoling (13 kilometers south of Tungan) eastward through Tangpichen (on the northwestern shore of Lake Hanka), then northward through Hutou to Jaoho. The 369th Regiment stationed in Tungan was responsible for garrisoning the Miaoling and Tangpichen sectors. The 368th Regiment, with headquarters in Hulin, was responsible for the area extending from the northeastern shore of Lake Hanka, through Hutou, to Tumuho (50 kilometers north of Hutou). The 369th Regiment also deployed some elements in Paoching, and these elements guarded the Jaoho border sector. Within the 135th Division's boundary, furthermore, the 15th Border Garrison Unit, under Fifth Army's direct control until hostilities began, was deployed in the Hutou area.

Status of Preparations

The combat effectiveness of the 135th Division was estimated to be one of the lowest of the divisions in Manchuria. Equipment was extremely inferior. Infantry units used the old Model 31 mountain guns (75-mm) instead of the new infantry regimental guns (75-mm), and had no battalion guns (37-mm). It possessed only one-half the authorized number of light and heavy machineguns. Two of the three artillery battalions were equipped with three field pieces per battery, the other battalion with four trench mortars per battery. The division's water supply and purification unit consisted of personnel but no equipment. The division had its full quota of horses.[81]

Most company commanders were second lieutenants; some were warrant officers. The quality of noncommissioned officers was generally poor, as was also the quality of the men. Both in training and in the condition of their equipment they were at a disadvantage.

The troops which could take positions in an emergency were the two infantry battalions at Mashan forward of the MLR, and the main body of the division at Chihsing. Only a fraction of the heavy weapons for infantry, field pieces for artillery, and implements for engineers had been brought to the construction sites from the Tungan

---

81. Normally, a division in Manchuria was authorized 6,000 horses. Those operating in mountainous areas were authorized 8,000.

barracks. Almost no ammunition had been brought with them. The units stationed at Hulin, Tungan, and Paoching for garrison duty were to be withdrawn to the Chihsing positions according to a prearranged plan, but their concentration would require several days unless railway transportation was available. The units garrisoning the border were to fight in their positions.

On 5 August, General Hitomi and his chief of staff left Tungan to attend table-top maneuvers at Headquarters Fifth Army in Yehho, and Lieutenant Colonel Haruo Shimakawa, operations officer, was left in charge of division headquarters.

At noon of the same day the Soviets created an incident near Kanhsiatun, about 40 kilometers south of Hutou. (This incident is described in First Area Army's monograph.) Fifth Army Headquarters sent Staff Officer Kashiwada to division headquarters in Tungan to investigate the incident. Since the incident was not prolonged, however, he returned to Army Headquarters on the 6th. There he reported the situation to the Army Commander as well as to each division commander attending table-top maneuvers. Staff Officer Kashiwada estimated that

> --as had often been the case, this incident appears to be nothing more than the usual Soviet tactics to cause a feeling of uneasiness on our part. It will not lead to a serious incident so long as we ignore it--

The incident, however, was graver than those experienced in the past in view of the fact that two days later the Soviet Army launched an all-out war. The incident was later considered to have been provoked either to pave the way for a Japan-Soviet war or to sound out the reaction of the Japanese Army. At any rate, it is quite evident that it was a preliminary step for an over-all offensive of the enemy.

CHAPTER XIX

135th Division Operations

Opening of Hostilities

While the division commander and the chief of staff were at Yehho, they were summoned to Army Headquarters at about 0300 hours and given a copy of Fifth Army's first operational order. (See Fifth Army Monograph, "Opening of Hostilities.")

As soon as General Hitomi, 135th Division Commander, received the order he telephoned to Staff Officer Shimakawa in Tungan instructing him as to the measures to be taken, and then proceeded to the airfield intending to return to Tungan by air. Arriving at the airfield he saw enemy planes above the field. On the advice of the officer in charge that air travel was difficult and that he should go by train, he immediately went to Mutanchiang Station and departed by a special gasoline car of the railway line with the chief of staff and his party. The time was about 0600 hours. (The 134th Division Commander and his party also departed on a similar car at the same time for Chiamussu). The Mutanchiang Station was crowded with many Japanese, and there was great confusion.

General Hitomi, while returning by rail to join his headquarters at Tungan, detrained at several stations along the route and using the railway telephone sent piecemeal instructions to his headquarters. At the Chihsing Station he telephoned the following instructions:

> Elements of each unit will return to Tungan and Hsitungan to retrieve the unit's weapons and other materiel. The division's main body will make immediate preparations for engaging the enemy.

At the Linkou Station he was met by liaison officers of the 370th Regiment. General Hitomi transmitted the following order through them:

> A battalion of the 370th Infantry Regiment will immediately occupy the Mashan advance position. The Infantry Regimental Headquarters, a battalion of the regiment, and the Raiding Battalion will promptly entrain for Chihsing.

As the gasoline car proceeded from Linkou towards Pingyang, the party observed that each station was crowded. Upon arrival at Pingyang Station, they heard various alarming rumors, including one to the effect that an enemy tank unit had cut the railroad west of Tungan. While the party was still at the Pingyang station, the 0700 train from Mutanchiang arrived, filled with Japanese civilians and troops. All civilians not having urgent business were ordered to get off. The division commander and his party boarded the train, and after division troops aboard were given instructions on what to do in an emergency the train departed Pingyang. It arrived at Tungan Station at about 1800 hours without incident.

Like the station in Mutanchiang, the Tungan Station was crowded with Japanese and was in great confusion. General Hitomi and his party detrained and went immediately to division headquarters to hear Staff Officer Shimakawa's report on the tactical situation.

Engagements of Border Garrison Units

At dawn of the 9th, Colonel Shimakawa explained, all border garrisons had been subjected to surprise attacks. The border garrison unit at Miaoling (one battalion of the 369th Regiment) had lost contact with its front-line elements, which were believed to have been annihilated. At noon enemy elements had advanced to the front of the main positions of the Miaoling garrison, but did not attack. The garrison began to assemble its troops in preparation for a withdrawal in accordance with orders from division. At about 1900 hours, without engaging the enemy, it began to withdrew to Tungan to join the main body of the regiment. The enemy in the Miaoling and Mishan areas, initially estimated to consist of one or two battalions, was being reinforced to an estimated strength of one division.

Between the sector south of Tachiao and Hutou, all observation units and forward garrison units (each with twenty to thirty men) along the border were believed to have been annihilated by surprise attacks and their positions completely enveloped. Communication with them had been disrupted during the morning.

At Tachiao itself, one company of the 368th Regiment was attacked at noon by an enemy force of about two or three battalions. Communication with this garrison was severed during the evening, and its personnel were believed to have been annihilated.

Enemy troops who had crossed the Ussuri River at a point north of Jaoho at daybreak on the 9th steadily approached that town. Although the Jaoho garrison engaged them, it was outnumbered and retreated toward the Paoching area under cover of darkness.

Sketchy information from the 15th Border Garrison Unit indicated that it was completely enveloped and that, together with Japanese residents who had thrown in their lot with the garrison, the defenders were fighting desperately in an isolated and helpless situation under heavy enemy pressure. The exact situation there was unknown however.

After listening to the situation report, General Hitomi summarized his orders since the beginning of hostilities and added new instructions. The general purport of his orders was to redeploy almost the entire division to the Chihsing area promptly, and to send some elements to the Mashan positions. Details of the orders were:

> The division's main body in the Chihsing positions will immediately prepare for an engagement with the enemy. (Two battalions of the 368th Regiment, one battalion each of the 369th and 370th Regiments, two battalions of the 135th Artillery Regiment, and the main strength of the Engineer Unit.)
>
> Of the units at Linkou, regimental headquarters and one battalion of the 370th Regiment plus the Raiding Battalion will proceed to Chihsing by railway. One battalion of the 370th Regiment together with the Manchurian Army Unit will immediately occupy the Mashan positions.
>
> Of the units at Tungan and Hsitungan, the main body of the 369th Regiment (less the battalion already in Chihsing) will immediately proceed to Chihsing via the Tungan-Poli-Chihsing road. An element of the regiment will occupy positions in Tungan and cover the withdrawal of the main body. The 135th

Artillery Regimental Headquarters and one of its battalions (less a battery) will proceed to Chihsing. The remaining battery plus an element of the 135th Engineer Unit will proceed by train to Mashan where it will be placed under the command of the Mashan position commander. Other elements of the division (Signal, Transport Ordnance Duty, Medical, Water Supply and Purification, and Veterinary Hospital) will proceed to Chihsing by train if possible, if not via the Tungan-Poli-Chihsing road.

Of the Units at Hulin, regimental headquarters and one battalion of the 368th Regiment will proceed to Chihsing.

The 15th Border Garrison Unit at Hutou (placed under the 135th Division on 9 August) will continue to carry out its mission as outlined by the Fifth Army order.

Division Headquarters will depart Tungan at midnight of the 9th via the Tungan-Poli-Linkou road.

The Army Commander Revises the Defense Plan

Division Headquarters departed Tungan for Poli in approximately ten motor vehicles at midnight of 9 August as prearranged. Due to frequent motor troubles and bad road conditions, travel was very slow. While the vehicles were halted on a height northwest of Tungan, bomb explosions were heard far to the south. On turning toward Tungan, members of the convoy saw pillars of blazing flame rising into the sky. The convoy continued and arrived at Poli at about 1400 hours of the 10th, and at Linkou after sunset. At Linkou division headquarters immediately established contact with Army Headquarters by telephone. From the Army Commander it received the following information and instructions:[82]

> The superior enemy armored unit which invaded the front of Suifenho at dawn on the 9th pushed across Suiyang on the same day, and on the evening of the 10th, today, advanced to the vicinity of Hsiachengtzu. The Army intends to change the prearranged plan and to occupy a position in the vicinity of Yehho with the 126th and 135th Divisions. The division commander is ordered to present himself at Army Headquarters in order to reconnoiter the position.

At that time the division commander was in no condition to travel, being confined to bed with dysentery. Consequently, he instructed the chief of staff to act on his behalf. The chief of staff instructed Colonel Shimakawa to move all units of the division to Yehho, and on the following day (the 11th) entrained for Yehho accompanied by one officers and one noncommissioned officer.

Mutanchiang Station had been bombed and was in a turmoil. Since the train could not enter the station, the chief of staff and his party detrained near a farm outside the station. He then proceeded to Army headquarters where at about 1600 hours on the 11th he was given a copy of the Army order issued at 1200, 11 August. (The text of this order is reproduced in Fifth Army sub-monograph, page 202)

Meanwhile, division elements from Chihsing and Linkou began

---

82. See page 190. The Army Commander, unable to reach the division commander, directed two battalions of the 135th Division to reinforce the 124th Division on 9 August.

arriving at Yehho. The first to arrive were the Raiding Battalion, and one battalion each of the 368th and 370th Regiments. The arrival of headquarters and one battalion of the 370th Regiment, another battalion of the 368th, one of the 369th, and one battalion of the 135th Artillery Regiment was expected on the afternoon of the following day, the 12th.

During the early morning of the 12th, the chief of staff accompanied by Major Takikawa, a battalion commander of the 370th Regiment, reconnoitered new positions from a hill northwest of Yehho.

Army intelligence reported at this time that an enemy armored element was advancing along the Pamientung-Tzuhsingtun-Hsientung road, and was capable of reaching the vicinity of Hsientung at about 1700 hours on the 12th. Troops which arrived in Yehho on the evening of the 12th were therefore ordered to occupy their assigned positions immediately.

In the meantime, the chief of staff dispatched First Lieutenant Takase to the Army ammunition depot to pick up a supply of rifle and artillery ammunition (high-explosive shells only), and explosives (picric acid and powder from 15-kilogram aircraft bombs), and to transport these munitions to the rear of the new positions.

The units expected to arrive in Yehho by the afternoon of the 12th, actually arrived by the evening of that day. The Raiding Battalion and one battalion of the 368th Regiment were attached to the 126th Division. The 370th Regiment and its two battalions had their regular commanders. The battalions of the 368th and 369th Regiments had acting commanders, holding the rank of first lieutenant; only one of the commanders of the batteries of the 135th Artillery Regiment was its regular commander.

Immediately upon arriving at their new areas for the defense of Yehho, each unit began constructing positions. By the evening of the 13th, construction of standing fire trenches and a few communication trenches had been completed. However, the positions were not continuously linked. Fortifications such as wire entanglements and antitank ditches were totally non-existent.

Engagement of Division's Main Body Near Yehho (see Map No 1)

The enemy armored force which had advanced to the vicinity of Hualin via Pamientung, Tzuhsingtun, and Hsientung, turned up in front of the 135th Division's positions early on the morning of the 13th, and began making preparations to attack. The force, perhaps regimental in size, was equipped with the much vaunted T34 tank, and also with about ten artillery pieces. No infantry troops were observed in the force.

At about 1000 hours, the enemy began attacking with a column of about ten tanks along the Hualin-Yehho road. Our left sector battalion, commanded by Major Takikawa counterattacked with close-quarter combat squads hidden on both sides of the road, and succeeded in disabling

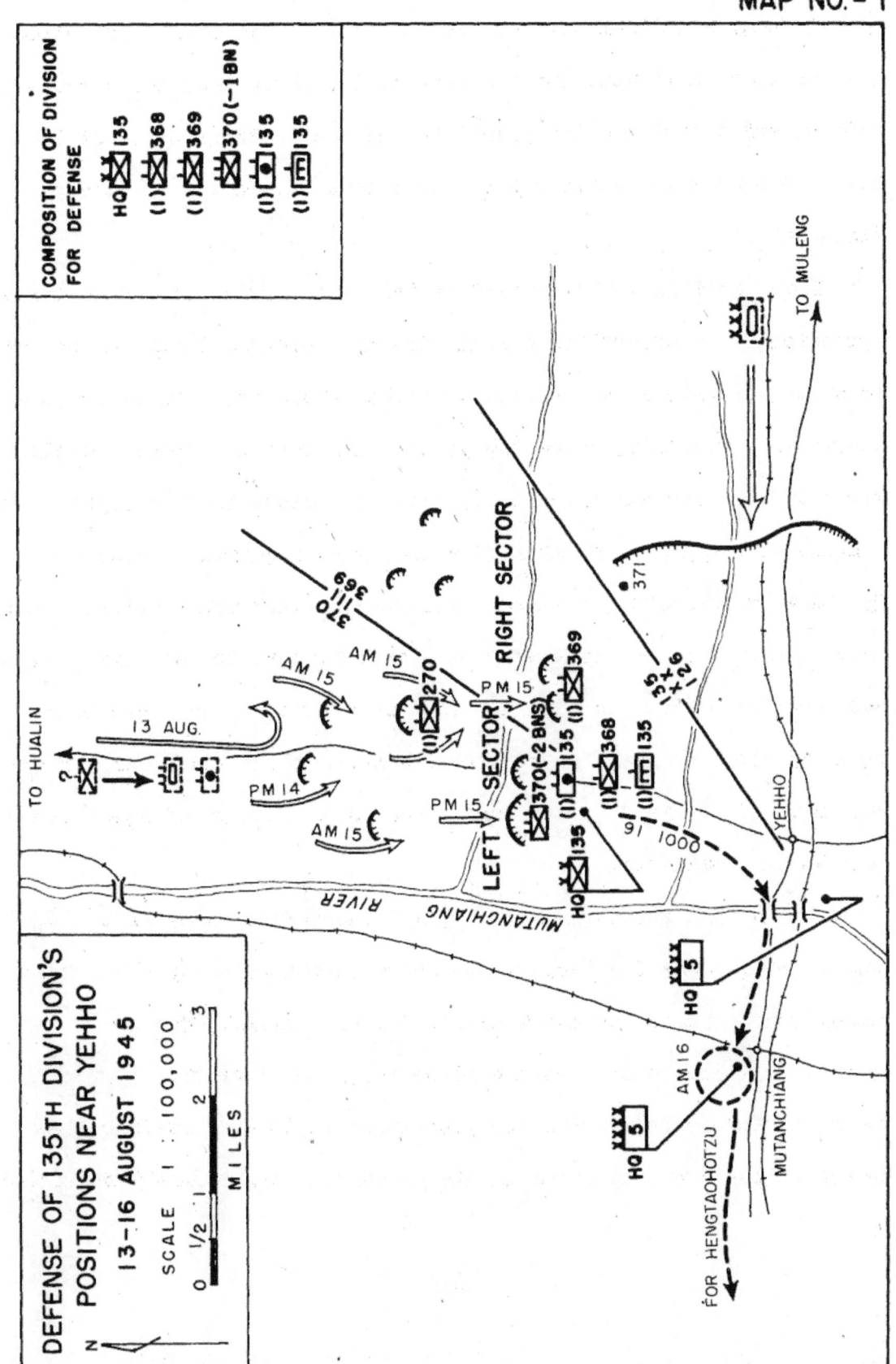

the leading tank. Although this momentarily slowed down the speed of the enemy's initial advance, he continued to push on. Our close-quarter teams next attacked the rear tanks, which then abandoned the attack, and turned and disappared behind the northern slope of the hill. Attempts to repair the stranded tank failed and the enemy abandoned it.

Enemy artillery then opened up and began firing on our positions sporadically. Our artillery laid fire on the enemy tanks in the rear in order to obstruct the repair of tanks. However, even though the enemy tanks were hit, since the projectiles were not armor piercing, the actual damage was practically nil. (In close quarter fighting a minimum of 1 kilogram of explosive charge is required to render a T34 tank inoperative. Any less amount is totally ineffective.) The enemy calmly repaired his tanks on a spot exposed to us. His behavior was arrogant and insolent in the face of our impotence. His tanks remained along the road in column, and avoided the swampy ground near-by. Some of the tanks crews were observed to consist of female as well as male soldiers.

During that morning, the 13th, and thereafter enemy aircraft, most of which were fighters, were very active in the sky above the combat zone. There was not a single friendly plane. Our rifle fire brought down one reconnaissance plane which had been flying low over the division's sector. The occupant appeared to be a staff officer. An operations document found in his possession was promptly forwarded to Army Headquarters.

In the afternoon ten enemy tanks mounted two attacks against our positions. The method of attack was much the same as that used in the morning. Each attack was repulsed by our close-quarter suicidal teams. Two enemy tanks were disabled.

Engagement on 14 August

On the morning of the 14th, the enemy tanks disabled in the previous day's action were no longer observed on the battlefield, and it was presumed that they had been removed for repairs. Hence we determined that in the future it would be necessary to demolish tanks completely and beyond repair. Later in the morning enemy tanks launched several attacks, this time with infantry support, and in coordination with aircraft. Though our officers and men checked the rushing tanks temporarily, late in the afternoon the positions of the left sector of the front line position were breached.

By the end of the day, three enemy tanks had been disabled. One of them had penetrated our position so deeply that it lay on the road on the west side of the hill where the front line battalion headquarters was located. When details were reported to Army Headquarters, it dispatched a staff officer to investigate. The tank was determined to be the T34 type. Its turret was equipped with a 75-mm gun with a very long barrel. The tank was also equipped with four traversing machineguns, two each in front and rear.[83] Although we tried to open the tightly shut turrent doors, we failed. We then decided to abandon the tank since it rested at the center of the road which the enemy had to use to attack and would obstruct the passage of enemy tanks in the following day's engagement. We assumed that its entire crew had been blasted to death.

However, in the evening our observers discovered a change in the position of the tank and decided to approach it but were prevented by machinegun fire from the tank. The tank had been shifted at an unguarded moment to the side of the road in such a way that the tank stood against the foot of a hill. Taking advantage of the dead space to its rear we approached the tank and with gasoline set fire to it. As the flames rose, the tank crew suddenly opened the turret doors, jumped out and began firing pistols. We surrounded the crewmen, numbering six, and finally killed them. Besides the T34 tanks, several light tanks were seen in this day's action.

The enemy made no attacks whatsoever in the hilly area on the right sector adjacent to the 126th Division, either on this day or the day before. He seemed to concentrate on both sides of the main road in the left sector. Judging from the enemy pressure on this day,

---

83. This appears to be the old model T-34, which however was equipped with a 76-mm (not 75-mm) gun until 1943. No explanation of the four (instead of two) machineguns is available.

it was realized that it would be difficult to hold the position of the front line battalion in the next day's engagement if we confined ourselves to close-quarter tactics. In some respects we feared that the positions of the second line battalion might be penetrated by the enemy.

Engagement of 15 August

On the 15th, the enemy repeated the pattern of the attacks of the preceding day. In the morning he launched an attack using tanks as the spearhead, coordinated with infantry, artillery, and air. By noon most of the positions of the front line battalion had been seized, although battalion headquarters itself continued to hold out. Enemy tanks then advanced to a small stream between the first and second line battalions and, with close support from his infantry and artillery, attempted such a determined penetration of the division's position that a major battle began.

While this engagement was developing, Staff Officer Tada arrived from Army Headquarters at about 1500 with orders to withdraw the division across the Mutanchiang River. (See Page 211 Fifth Army's monograph for the text of the Army order issued at 1200 hours, 15 August at Yehho.) Instructions to the 135th Division Commander were to withdraw at 2400 hours on the 15th, via the road on the northern side of Yehho village, and to proceed to the northwestern side of Mutanchiang City. These orders were based on Area Army orders transmitted to Fifth Army earlier.

General Hitomi immediately issued a division order directing that preparations be made for the withdrawal, and sent messengers to each unit with a copy of the order.

Meanwhile, the battle in the 135th Division positions continued, with the enemy's attacks mounting in fury. Several of his tanks got as far as the vicinity of division headquarters. Our close-quarters combat teams continued their suicidal attacks and amid the bursting shells and the shouts of both sides the twilight engagement took on a ghastly appearance. Night fell before the battle reached the decisive stage. The enemy's front line troops retired to the line of the small stream, and the battlefield gradually became quiet.

Engagement of Division Headquarters Near Hualin

Division Headquarters, which on the night of the 10th had arrived at Linkou from Tungan, remained there until the 12th, devoting its efforts to controlling and transporting troops en route to Yehho. On the 13th, it entrained for Yehho, together with remaining elements of the 370th Regiment and one battalion of the 20th Heavy Field Artillery Regiment (which had come from Feite). General Hitomi, having recovered sufficiently from his attack of dysentery, accompanied these troops.

Before departing Linkou, headquarters was informed that an enemy tank force had invaded the Hsientung area and was pushing on towards Hualin. During the journey, therefore, it exercised strict caution. It intended to force its way if attacked by enemy tanks in Hualin.

When the train was nearing Hualin on the evening of the 13th, headquarters personnel observed that the railroad bridge as well as the vehicular bridge across the Mutanchiang River had been destroyed (apparently by First Area Army units which had withdrawn earlier). The train stopped and was immediately fired upon by an enemy tank unit. Our troops quickly got off the train and endeavored to engage the tanks, but were thrown into great confusion. Some were killed by tank shells, some sought cover in the forest, and others jumped into the Mutanchiang River and attempted to swim across it. The scene was disastrous beyond description. General Hitomi, accompanied by some of his officers and men, narrowly escaped danger and took shelter in a mountain side along the right bank of the River.

On the 14th, this incident was reported to the chief of staff who had gone to Yehho on the 11th to reconnoiter new positions. Although he was engaged in a battle on a hill northwest of Yehho when word reached him, he nevertheless dispatched a small element of the division to rescue the division commander and his party. Although the division commander escaped, there were numerous casualties. Among them were Colonel Shimakawa, who was killed, and two adjutants, listed as missing. Lieutenant Colonel Tanimura, chief of the Medical Section, Major Kono, senior medical officer, and Lieutenant Colonel

Saito, chief of the Veterinary Section escaped into the hills disguised in Manchurian clothes and arrived at Tunhua a few days later.

During this tank attack against the train, the battalion of the 20th Heavy Field Artillery Regiment attempted to remove field pieces from the train in order to engage the enemy, but failed. The guns were destroyed and many of the men were killed in action or were listed as missing.

Meanwhile, the enemy tanks turned south and began attacking a division position south of Hualin, but were routed and returned to Hualin to re-assemble.

Withdrawal of the 135th Division Toward Hengtaohotzu

In the division's main positions, where the engagement was entering a decisive stage, a distance of 700 to 800 meters separated the front lines of the friendly and enemy forces. Although the battlefield became quiet, the enemy frequently fired illuminating shells and pyrotechnics. The division began withdrawing in the following order: the Reserve Unit, the Artillery Unit, the Right Sector Unit (369th Regiment), and the Left Sector Unit (370th Regiment). The withdrawing units followed the prescribed route. The division's main body crossed the bridge west of Yehho by dawn of the 16th and assembled northwest of Mutanchiang. The withdrawal was executed smoothly, and no pursuing enemy troops were sighted. Meanwhile, the Takikawa Battalion was still engaging the enemy, but upon learning belatedly of the division's withdrawal, its members dispersed by two's and three's.

After assembling at the prearranged place, the division continued withdrawing toward Hengtaohotzu. Although no enemy ground pursuit troops were seen, enemy aircraft bombed and straffed the retreating column without opposition beginning in the morning. This interrupted the column's movement, and the ranks of all units of the division were broken. A state of complete disorder and confusion prevailed. Nevertheless, assembly at Hengtaohotzu was completed by the evening of the 17th.

After arriving in the area and performing necessary reconnaissance, the division reorganized its elements and assigned positions to each. Division positions assigned by the Army were located in the sector north of the main road and approximately 6 kilometers east of the town. (The positions of the 126th Division were south of the road.) In this area were several positions which had been constructed by the 11th Independent Engineer Regiment.

Disarmament of the Division's Main Body

Shortly after 2300 hours on the 17th, the division chief of staff, Colonel Inouye, was summoned to Army Headquarters where he was shown a message concerning the unconditional surrender of Japan, which had been broadcast by the Emperor. That this was not a rumor was verified by the Area Army. On the following morning, the division received an Army order concerning disarmament, and on the same day

Soviet forces entered Hengtaohotzu.

The disarmament of elements of the division which had fought in the border areas took placed in various localities. The units near Hulin, under the command of Colonel Iizuka (commander of the 368th Regiment) departed the border area at midnight on 9 August, and withdrew toward Yehho on foot, crossing the Wanta mountain range north of Tungan. While withdrawing it had to fight off attacks by rebellious Manchurian Army troops. It finally arrived at a sector northeast of Linkou where it learned of the cessation of hostilities. Its disarmament took place there in late August.

The units in and around Tungan, Feite, and Hsitungan, after being informed on the 9th by railway telephone that an enemy column had invaded the area between them and the rear, departed Tungan at midnight on orders from the division. They retreated to Poli along the Tungan-Poli road, organized an entraining movement, and departed for Yehho. Those elements whose assembly at Poli was delayed, entrained for Yehho on the 17th, but on receipt of a report that the enemy had already invaded Linkou, detrained along the way. Under the command of Colonel Nakayama (commander of the 369th Regiment) they marched westward north of Linkou. After crossing the Mutanchiang River by a bridge west of Linkou (constructed years earlier for transporting lumber) they proceeded to Lengchuan (east of Yapuloni) via the area north of Hengtaohotzu. The majority of them were disarmed in that vicinity in late August or early September. One element appears to have escaped to Tunhua or Kirin and to have been disarmed there in mid-September.

Losses on Both Sides

Estimates of 135th Division losses are difficult to make because elements were scattered and also because the Soviets prohibited liaison among units. Roughly, it is estimated that the division lost 3,000 men killed in action. Of this number, 1,000 were killed during the Yehho engagement or the retreat to Hengtaohotzu, 1,500 were killed in action in the border areas, and approximately 500 members of elements of the division were killed in scattered actions. In addition, approximately 1,000 were listed as missing. Materiel losses included eighteen field artillery pieces, twelve trench mortars, and approximately fifteen motor vehicles. Approximately 3,000 horses were captured by the Soviets. Enemy losses during the engagement near Yehho were approximately 1,000 killed. About ten enemy tanks were disabled.

Post Hostilities Status

The abruptness of the Soviet entry into the war prevented the Army as well as the division from carrying out unified operations. At the war's end, the units that had succeeded in retreating to Hengtaohotzu were:

> Division Headquarters
> 1 Battalion, 368th Regiment
> 1 Battalion, 369th Regiment
> Regimental Headquarters, 370th Regiment

       1 Battalion, 370th Regiment
       Raiding Battalion
       2 Battalions, 135th Artillery Regiment
       1 Company, 135th Engineer Unit

These units, however, were by no means intact. The total strength of these remnants was approximately 5,000. Equipment in their possession at the time of disarmament was negligible. Infantrymen had only their rifles, close-quarter combat teams had only several kilograms of explosives, the artillery had only two field pieces and four trench mortars.

Key members of division headquarters who survived were the division commander, the chief of staff, one acting adjutant (first lieutenant), the chief of the Medical Section, the senior medical officer, the chief of the Veterinary Section, three duty officers, and three noncommissioned officers. Except for the commander of the 370th Regiment, no regimental or battalion commanders of the division survived. However, the Raiding Battalion still had its commander. The artillery had one battalion commander and the engineers one company commander. The division's fighting capacity was estimated at less than one-third of what it had been before hostilities began.

Negotiations with Soviet Forces

On 17 August, Army headquarters dispatched a delegate to Soviet Army Headquarters in Mutanchiang to open negotiations. Our division intended to act in accordance with the result of the Army's negotiations. But on the 18th a Soviet lieutenant colonel arrived at division headquarters and, utterly disregarding negotiations then under way at Army Headquarters, opened negotiations directly with the division, giving unilateral orders.

The disarmament of the division was completed on the 18th. On the 19th the division commander, along with other generals of Fifth Army, was taken by the Soviets as a prisoner of war. Other members of division headquarters were held in house detention in Mutanchiang. Units were marched from Hengtaohotzu to Hailin and Laku on the 19th, and reached internment camps there on the following day.

While the division commander was en route to Mutanchiang by car, his sword was confiscated by an officer of the Soviet Army on the pretext of propriety. Officers and men of each unit, while en route to Kalu, were stripped of their watches, boots, shoes, map cases, and waist belts by Soviet officers and men encountered on the way. They reached Hailin and Laku without sleep or rest.

The buildings of the internment camps consisted of hangars, warehouses, official residences which had survived war destruction, and improvised shanties which barely sheltered the internees from the rain. Food for internees was obtained from the Mutanchiang Branch Freight Depot, and because of low stocks, the food ration per person was less than the standard amount. There was no supply of vegetables. Many internees suffered from diarrhea and malnutrition.

Late in August, the Soviets organized Japanese troops in the internment camps into units of approximately 1,000 each, and marched them one after another to Soviet territory, via Suifenho. On 6 November most of the officers were transferred by train from Mutanchiang to Rada, south of Moscow in European Russia for internment.

Monograph No 154-J

CHAPTER XX

The 128th Division[84]

Organization

The organization of the 128th Infantry Division was begun in the Tungning area during January-February 1945. It was the successor to the 120th Division then being reorganized for transfer.[85] The initial source of personnel for the new division was the remnants of the 120th Division. Subsequent sources were principally recruits, Japanese and Korean, obtained during the succeeding months.

Division Headquarters was at Chengtzuhou, on the outskirts of Tungning. The division commander was Lieutenant General Yoshishige Mizuhara. The first elements to be formed were the 283d and 284th Infantry Regiments, one at Chengtzuhou the other at Shihmentzu. These regiments deployed squad size elements at observation points along the border. Two such elements were deployed near the fortified strong points in the Tungning sector then under the jurisdiction of the 1st Border Garrison Unit, and four farther south along the border. To control and supply these squads, one company of the 284th Regiment was deployed near Paitaoshantzu.

---

84. Information in this chapter was furnished by Lieutenant General Yoshishige Mizuhara, Commander of the 128th Division.

85. Orders to transfer the 120th Division to the Seventeenth Area Army in Korea were issued on 31 March 1945.

On 26 February, when the formation of some major elements was well under way, the division was assigned to Third Army, and was given responsibility for the area on the left flank of Third Army, adjacent to Fifth Army. In its area and deployed in the Tungning strong points was the 1st Border Garrison Unit, also assigned to Third Army.[86]

By early April, the division had completed a major part of its organization. However, the 285th Infantry Regiment, the 128th Field Artillery Regiment, and the division Raiding Battalion were not completely organized until late July. By that time several major changes had taken place or were under way: Kwantung Army's plan for delaying operations had been announced; the 1st Border Garrison Unit was being reorganized into the 132d Independent Mixed Brigade and was scheduled to be assigned to the division; and the First Area Army announced that upon the outbreak of hostilities the division would be placed under its direct control.

From the beginning of the organization of the division until the outbreak of hostilities in August the division was kept quite busy. In an atmosphere of restlessness and uneasiness among the troops, it had to organize new units; undertake extensive training programs for officers and men in accordance with Kwantung Army instructions;

---

86. The relationship between the division commander and the border garrison unit commander is not clear. It appears, however, that the former could issue commands to the latter only in matters relating to the maintenance of peace and order.

cope several times with the enrollment of Japanese and Korean recruits; transfer its elements from their barracks areas to the site of fortification construction, simultaneously disposing of the many complicated matters that invariable accompany such transfers; and carry out the construction work itself.

Redeployment

In accordance with Kwantung Army's adoption of the plan for delaying operations in the spring of 1945, the 128th Division was to redeploy to the rear. The garrisoning of the border, principally the strong points near Tungning, was to be left completely in the hands of the 1st Border Garrison Unit. The squads and supporting company which the division had deployed along the border were placed under the operational control of the commander of the 1st Border Garrison Unit.

In conformance with the new plan, the division headquarters moved to Lotzukou and directed the redisposition of division elements. The moves, carried out between late May and mid-June, placed the main body of the division along the Laomuchuho-Lotzukou-Taipingkou line and other major elements in the Tachienchang sector, as follows: (See Map No 1.)

Unit	Location	Remarks
283d Regiment	Mountains east of Tachienchang	One battalion deployed in mountains about 10 kilometers west of Tachienchang.

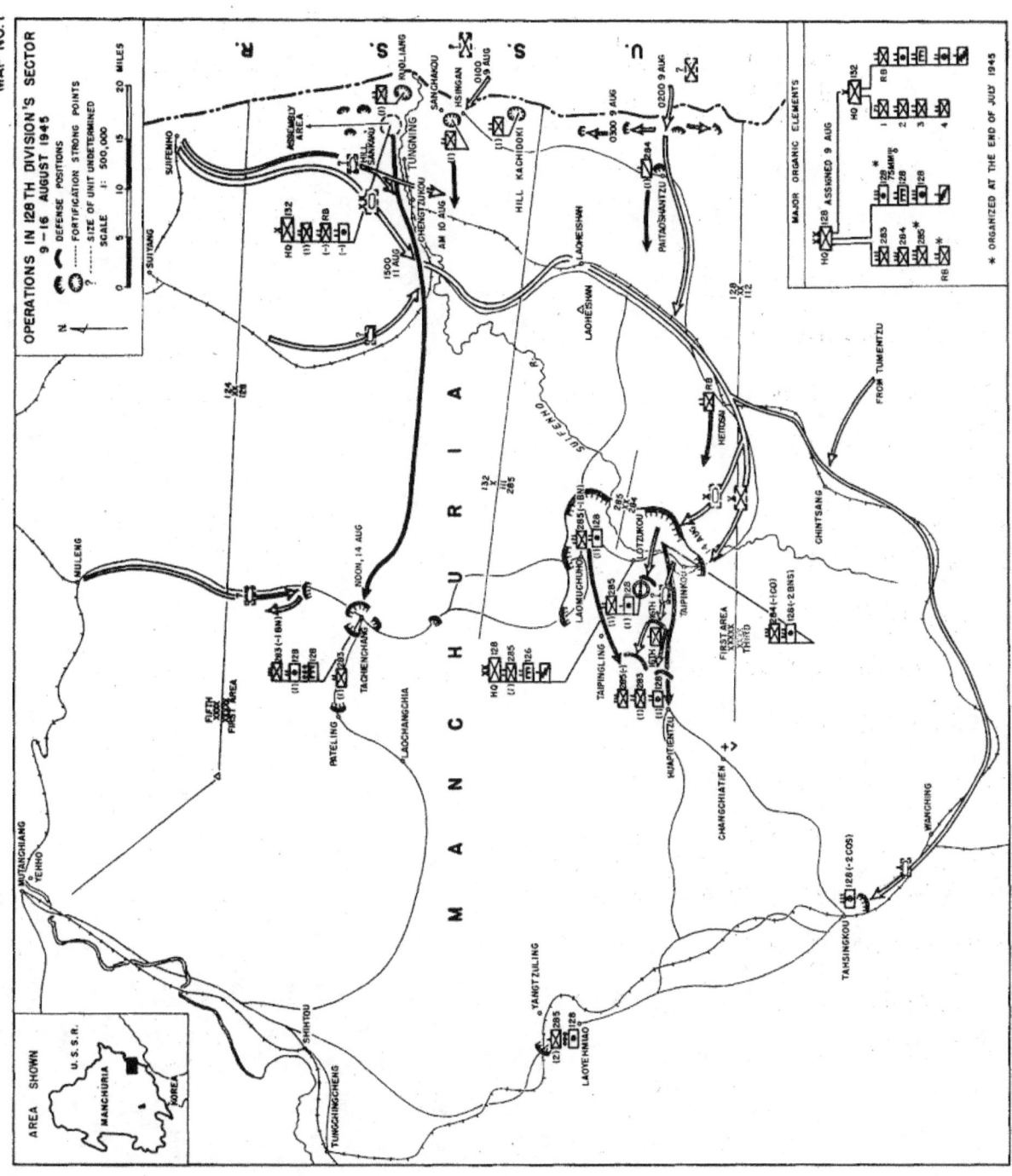

284th Regiment	Mountains east of Taipingkou	One battalion deployed in mountains northeast of Lotzukou
Engineer Unit	Mountains southeast of Lotzukou	One platoon attached to each infantry regiment
Signal Unit	Plain north of Loamuchuho	Established telephone lines between Lotzukou and Tachienchang; the main force of the wire platoon maintained these lines. Two sections of wireless telegraph platoon attached to division headquarters and one section to the 283d Regiment
Transport Unit	Tahsingkou (Railhead)	Main force transported supplies between Lotzukou and Tahsingkou, elements between Muleng and Tachienchang, and between Lotzukou and Laoheishan
Veterinary Hospital	Lotzukou	
Field Hospital	Lotzukou	Elements at Tachienchang

In conjunction with this redisposition, the Third Army Commander directed the 128th Division to construction new strong points in the Lotzukou and Tachienchang areas for the division's main elements. These positions would place the 128th Division in the center of the Area Army's main line of resistance.

After the completion of the organization of the 285th Regiment, the 128th Artillery Regiment, and the division's Raiding Battalion in July, they were deployed as follows:

Unit	Station	Remarks
285th Regiment	Mountains east and northeast of Laomuchuho	Three companies deployed in mountains southwest of Taipingling

128th Artillery Regiment	Mountains east of Taipingkou	One battalion attached to each infantry regiment
Division Raiding Battalion	Laoheishan	Underwent training in the former barracks area of the 284th Regiment

Status of Preparations

In transmitting the new plan, the Area Army had set September 1945 as the deadline for the competion of the fortifications required in conjuction with the new plan. The 128th Division was unable to accomplish its work according to schedule, particularly as regards cave type fortifications, because of various adverse conditions. Although work at important points was pushed forward day and night on the two-shift system, the situation at the beginning of August was such that underground caves in the fortifications could not possibly be completed until October 1945, and surface defense works not until the following spring (1946) after the thawing of the winter snows.

The adverse conditions which most particularly hindered construction were: 1) an insufficient supply of dynamite and rock-drilling implements for use in rocky terrain, 2) lack of officers able to supervise and men able to construct the special type fortfications required, 3) difficulty in supplying units far from the railroad line (at one time the nutrition standard had to be lowered because of a reduction in food rations), 4) cold-proof living quarters had to be prepared for the troops constructing fortifications. These difficulties were aggravated by the fact that the selection of positions had been based on a survey conducted early in 1945 while the ground was covered with snow and the trees bare. With the disappearance of snow and the beginning of foliation it became clear that the field of fire in almost every position was too short, and that in summer the foliage on trees a short distance from each position could afford concealment to the enemy's approach. Consequently, it became necessary to strengthen facilities for flanking and oblique fire.

The division's actual strength at the opening of hostilities was approximately 12,623, compared with an authorized strength of 23,000. In addition, the division had about 8,000 horses. It had its authorized number of field pieces and heavy and light infantry weapons, but lacked about one-third of the number of authorized heavy grenade launchers. The number of rifles was insufficient; some men were equipped with bayonets only. The division had no close-quarters antitank weapons.

The command ability of the division's officers left much room for improvement, as did also the esprit de corps of troops. The combat effectiveness of the division was estimated to be about 20 per cent.

Opening of Hostilities

As early as the spring of 1945, Soviet aircraft had flown across the border several times. Furthermore, Soviet officers were often seen near our frontier positions. In spite of these signs of enemy aggressiveness, we believed that the invasion by Soviet forces would not commence in the near future. Meanwhile, however, the division commander issued orders to tighten the border garrison defenses, and to accelerate construction work in main positions.

On midnight of 8-9 August, an unidentified aircraft flew above Lotzukou. At about 0100 hours the first ground attack by Soviet forces was made--against the Hsingan Village Detachment in the Tungning area. Between 0200 and 0300 hours, the observation posts along the border in front of Paitaoshantzu were apparently overrun by the Soviet forces. Communication with these observation posts was severed after the initial report of attack, and their subsequent fate was never learned.

Beginning before dawn, the streets of Tungning were subjected to concentrated fire from giant guns of the enemy. Key points in all positions of the 132d Independent Mixed Brigade were brought under fierce fire by enemy artillery and machineguns before daybreak. When the enemy ground forces attacked after daybreak the brigade promptly engaged them, and with utmost effort stopped their advance.

On the basis of the reports obtained one after another from the border areas, the division commander ordered all division elements in the rear to take their positions in the fortifications then under construction. At the same time, he ordered the accumulation of ammunition, provisions, and forage at these positions. He then instructed the commanders of all units to assemble at the Lotzukou command post for orders.

With the commencement of hostilities, the Tungning Army Hospital was evacuated to Tachienchang, and the Laoheishan and Chengtzukou Army Hospitals to Lotzukou. All these hospitals were placed under the 128th Division Commander.

At about 1000 hours, the division received orders from the First Area Army Commander placing it under his direct command. At the same time the 132d Independent Mixed Brigade was placed under the division's command. The mission given to the division was to resist the enemy by occupying the existing line of fortifications, and at the same time to protect the flanks of the Third and Fifth Armies.

At noon the division commander issued his first operational order to all unit commanders then assembled at Lotzukou. (All had assembled except General Onitake, the Independent Mixed Brigade Commander.) The order is outlined below:[87]

> The Commander of the 132d Independent Mixed Brigade will divide his force. With two infantry battalions, two field artillery batteries, two heavy field artillery batteries, and two engineer platoons he will form

---

87. The transmission of this order to the 132d Independent Mixed Bridged was delayed. The brigade had no wireless telegraph and the message had to be encoded and transmitted by telephone. It did not reach the brigade commander until 1400 hours. The 2d and 3d paragraphs of the message were transmitted by phone to the company commander at Paitaoshantzu.

the Tungning Detachment and leave it at its established positions to resist the enemy. He will then redeploy the main strength of the brigade as quickly as possible to Tachienchang where it will take command of the 283th Infantry Regiment (less one battalion) stationed there, plus one artillery battalion and two transport companies. Together these units will become the Tachienchang Detachment, and will cover the left flank and rear of the main body of the division, and at the same time cover the right flank and rear of the Fifth Army's right wing group (the 124th Division) by securing the Muleng-Tachienchang road.

The border observation units will continue with their present duties.

The company at Paitaoshantzu, if pressed by the enemy, will withdraw toward the Laoheishan area while carrying out a rear guard action, and then will check the advancing enemy tanks on the Laoheishan-Heitsai-Lotzukou road. It will cooperate with the Division Raiding Battalion at Laoheishan.

The division's main body will be divided into two sector units. The Right Sector Unit under the commander of the 284th Infantry Regiment (Colonel Matsuyoshi), and composed of the 284th Infantry Regiment (less the company stationed at Paitaoshantzu) and 128th Field Artillery Regiment (less two battalions), will firmly hold its present positions along the line of construction works, and will check the advance of the enemy both along the Laoheishan-Heitsai-Lotzukou road and in the sector on both sides of the road. In particular, it will hinder the advancing enemy tanks, while supporting the Division Raiding Battalion. It will transfer the position north of Lotzukou to the Left Sector Unit. The Left Sector Unit under the commander of the 285th Infantry Regiment (Colonel Akutogawa), and composed of the 285th Infantry Regiment (less one battalion) and one battalion of the 128th Field Artillery Regiment, will occupy the positions northeast of Lotzukou and east of Laomuchuho, and will check the enemy advancing frontally, while hindering the advance of enemy tanks on the road between Tachienchang and Lotzukou.
It will also neutralize the front of the Right Sector Unit with its firepower.

The Raiding Battalion (with its attached wireless telegraph section) will hinder the advance of enemy tanks especially those advancing along Laoheishan road in front of the Right Sector Unit.

The Engineer Unit (less one platoon) will complete the construction of the division's ammunition and fuel storage dumps in the area southeast of Lotzukou, and then await orders at Tachienchang.

The Signal Unit (less elements attached to other units) will take position at Lotzukou with its main force and continue its present duties.

The Transport Unit will change the supply route for the Tachienchang area to the Tachienchang-Tungchingcheng road and, by suspending transportation on the Laoheishan-Lotzukou road, will strengthen the transportation capacity between Lotzukou and Tahsingkou.

The division reserve will consist of one battalion of the 283d Infantry Regiment (now engaged in construction work at a point approximately 10 kilometers west of Tachienchang) and one battalion of the 285th Infantry Regiment. It will be stationed at the northern tip of the airfield southwest of Lotzukou.

Operations of the 132d Independent Mixed Brigade

After forming the Tungning Detachment as directed, the commander of the 132d Independent Mixed Brigade ordered it defend to the last the position at Kachidoki Hill and north of it. Under cover provided by this detachment the brigade commander at sunset on the 9th assembled the main force in the rear of the Kuoliang position for the withdrawal to Tachienchang. The assembled units departed at midnight in two columns, the left column, (the main strength) along the road connecting Tungning, Hoyen, and Tachienchang, and the right one along the road south and parallel to it. While withdrawing toward Tachienchang they were attacked thrice between 10 and 12 August by an enemy tank unit advancing south from Suifenho, and were also bombed by enemy aircraft. The columns repulsed each of the attacks. The brigade commander arrived at Tachienchang on the evening of the 13th, and the troops on the morning of the 14th, and immediately assumed their task as the Tachienchang Detachment.[88]

The Division Commander visited Tachienchang on the evening of the 13th, and conferred with Major General Onitake who gave an account of the situation since the outbreak of hostilities. He approved General Onitake's plan of holding the Tachienchang positions by concentrating rather than despersing troops, in view of the terrain and also because of reduced strength resulting from the engagements while withdrawing. However, the division commander pointed out that the Detachment was confronted with two threats, one from the southeast and one from the north; on the morning of the 13th the enemy advancing frontally was threatening Laoheishan and, from the Muleng area the roar of artillery was increasing. He therefore directed General Onitake to take strict precautions over the roads approaching Tachienchang from Muleng and from Lotzukou, and to make special preparations for the destruction of enemy tanks. The division commander departed early in the morning of the 14th and returned to Lotzukou at noon that day.

---

88. See Monograph No 154-K.

Divison Operations

The enemy tank unit which had engaged the 132d Independent Mixed Brigade during its withdrawal from the 10th to the 12th, attacked the Laoheishan area on the evening of the 13th. Almost at the same time an infantry division carrying two or three (regimental) colors invaded the same area. The subsequent situation near Laoheishan was obscure.

Before daybreak on the 14th, however, came reports that several enemy light tanks were reconnoitering in front of the Right Sector Unit position. It was concluded, therefore, that efforts to check the enemy tanks in front of the Lotzukou position had been ineffective. The Right Sector Commander dispatched two raiding companies to the forward area, but they were overwhelmed by the enemy. At daybreak, the Right Sector Unit was attacked by an enemy infantry force supported by tanks and artillery. Although the unit threw its entire strength into a defensive battle, its casualties mounted and its key gun and heavy and light weapon positions were destroyed one after another by the concentrated fire of the enemy's 150-mm guns. Nevertheless, the officers and men of the unit fought hand-to-hand engagements here and there both in front of and within the position, and finally succeeded in repulsing the enemy.

In preparation for the inevitable, however, the Right Sector Unit commander, Colonel Matsuyoshi, sent his regimental colors to to division headquarters so that the headquarters might look after the future affairs of the colors. The standard-bearer was accompanied by an escort. Three times the colors changed hands due to deaths in action. At about 1400 hours Colonel Matsuyoshi was killed in action inside the position. As soon as the artillery regiment commander, Major Katsumata, learned that all field pieces had been knocked out of action, he dashed into the enemy and died a heroic death almost at the same time as Colonel Matsuyoshi.

Wireless telegraph communication with the Right Sector Unit and with the Tachienchang Detachment were disrupted around noon, and thereafter the division had difficulty directing operations.

At 1500 hours, on orders from First Area Army, two companies of the 285th Infantry Regiment and a mountain gun platoon were rushed to the vicinity of Laoyehmiao (south of Yangtzuling) in order to hold the Mutanchiang-Tahsingkou road and check the southward advance of enemy tanks that had broken through the 124th Division's positions.

At 1600 hours the division commander toured the left bank of the Suifenho River and observed the battle situation in the area of the Right Sector Unit. As a result of his observation and of reports received from various units, he concluded that there was no alternative but to abandon the plan of reinforcing the Right Sector Unit position, and to fall back to second line positions southwest of Taipingling. He then reported the battle situation to the Area Army Commander and asked approval for the decision to to withdraw to Taipingling. After receiving approval he issued the following order:

> One battalion (reinforced with one field artillery battery), now in divisional reserve, of the 285th Infantry Regiment will depart immediately and occupy a position in the vicinity of the southern end of the airfield southwest of Lotzukou in order to cover the division's withdrawal and occupation of new positions. It will then hinder the advance of the enemy as long as possible. If forced to withdraw from their position, the battalion and the artillery battery will withdraw along the road and assemble at Huapitientzu to await orders.
>
> The Left Sector Unit will withdraw immediately from its present position, and will occupy established positions in the mountainous district southwest of Taipingling, where it will check the advance of the enemy from the direction of Lotzukou. Efforts will be made to conceal new position from the enemy particularly after daybreak. The Left Sector Unit commander will rush one field artillery battery to the southern end of the airfield and place it under the command of the battalion covering the division's withdrawal. (Said artillery battery is expected to return to the Left Sector Unit command after the completion of its mission.)
>
> One battalion of the 283th Infantry Regiment, now in division reserve, together with the Right Sector Unit will defend present positions stubbornly until sunset, and will then withdraw and assemble at Huapitientzu via the airfield, under the command of the senior officer of each unit.
>
> All units in the Lotzukou area will be prepared to depart at 2100 hours tonight.

At 2100 hours, the division departed Lotzukou. While withdrawing, its movements were hindered by the heavy traffic of ox and horse carts owned by people (mostly Koreans) fleeing from the vicinity of Lotzukou toward Tahsingkou. Furthermore, due to delay in transmitting orders to the Right Sector Unit, only 200 troops or so had assembled at Huapitientzu by noon of the 15th. Some of them retreated to Tahsingkou by mistake during the night, and motor vehicles had to be used to bring them to Huapitientzu.

Divisional units arrived in the vicinity of Huapitientzu by daybreak of the 15th. After a one-hour rest, all units were given new assignments. Fortunately, there was no enemy pursuit, and the division was in relatively good shape.

After the arrival at Huapitientzu the division commander issued orders to the following effect:

> Both the Field Hospital and the Veterinary Hospital will be stationed at Changchiatien. The Chief of Laoheishan Army Hospital will assume command because of his seniority.
>
> The Signal Unit will be stationed at Huapitientzu and establish a new telephone line between the division headquarters at Huapitientzu and the 285th Infantry Regiment Headquarters at southwest of Taipingling in addition to its previous mission.
>
> The Reserve Unit will be composed of the former Right Sector Unit and the Engineer Unit (less one platoon) and will be stationed at Huapitientzu.

Operations Near Huapitientzu and Taipingling

Early in the morning of the 15th, the Division Commander at Huapitientzu received an Area Army order to the effect that the 128th Division would continue to carry out its former mission by having its main body occupy already constructed positions southwest of Taipingling, and the Tachienchang Detachment occupy the Pateling area.

On the morning of the 16th, an enemy tank unit approached our forward positions in front of Huapitientzu. Enemy artillery in the vicinity of the northeastern end of the airfield concentrated heavy fire on these positions, under cover of which enemy infantry advanced with the apparent intention of enveloping both flanks. Our force neutralized the enemy infantry from afar, chiefly with artillery. Since we attained our objective on the whole, the forward units were ordered to evacuate their positions at 0800 hours. The forest in this neighborhood, however, was thickly wooded and overgrown with weeds and brambles which slowed their withdrawal considerably. Furthermore, they lost their bearings and found it extremely difficult to maintain contact with the main force of the division. Such being the case, there were very few who assembled at Huapitientzu by the time the war ended.

About 0830 hours, several enemy tanks came rushing to the front of our elaborately masked main position. By concentrating our artillery fire, we disabled five of them and put the rest to route. However, our artillery fire disclosed our artillery position, which was promptly subjected to concentrated fire by enemy tank guns. Almost all of our guns on the south side of the road were destroyed. There were many casualties among our men including officers and non-commissioned officers. Since our main position was well masked from enemy eyes and fire, however, it was not subjected to enemy artillery fire till the war's end. The enemy infantry merely wandered about the forest aimlessly and fired blindly. Although the battle situation became static temporarily, shots were heard ceaselessly in all directions.

Battle Near Tahsingkou

Prior to this, a report was received stating that approximately 1,500 enemy troops supported by 10-odd tanks, which had penetrated the right flank from the direction of Chintsang, were advancing toward Tahsingkou on the evening of the 15th. Major Ada, the Transport Unit commander, decided to check the enemy at a point south of the town by using both the tactical troops in the vicinity and the troops of his Transport Unit. He spent the night strengthening defenses and reconnoitering the enemy situation. The total numerical strength of this force was approximately 600.

Beginning in the early morning hours of the 16th, the enemy infantry-tank force gradually closed in and from about 0900 hours on the battle trend became increasingly unfavorable to us. Although Major Ada's force had no field pieces and was very poorly equipped, it held on to Tahsingkou till the cease-fire and thus kept the rear of the division safe.

Situation Near Tachienchang

The Tachienchang Detachment on the division's left flank, meanwhile, had not received the order to withdraw to Pateling, and hence remained at Tachienchang. (The order was received after the cease-fire.)

Although there was no new enemy attack in the area, the two threats remained. That from Lotzukou was intensified when, according to a report brought to the Detachment by a mounted messenger, the town was invaded by enemy tanks on the 15th. The other was from Muleng from which the sound of big guns was heard intermittently. In view of these threats, the Detachment reinforced the roads approaching from both directions. On the morning of the 16th, the detachment made a surprise attack with preparatory artillery fire on the enemy tanks advancing southward from the direction of Muleng, knocked out three, and routed the rest.

Estimated Losses to Both Sides

The size of the enemy force thrown against the 128th Division's sector was estimated to be at least one armored division with powerful artillery support, plus three infantry regiments. Casualties inflicted upon the enemy by the division and units under its command were estimated as 1,000 killed or wounded and twenty-two tanks destroyed or disabled, as shown in the following table:

Date (August)	Area	Enemy Personnel	Enemy Tanks
14	Lotzukou	500	10
16	Huapitientzu	150	2
16	Tahsingkou	150	2
10-12	Tungning to Tachienchang	200	5
16	Tachienchang	?	3

Estimated casualties suffered by the Division (excluding the 132d Independent Mixed Brigade) in the engagements from the 14th to the 16th are: approximately 4,500 killed or missing, and approximately 2,000 wounded. A breakdown of these figures is shown below:[89]

Date (August)	Unit	Area	Killed or Missing	Wounded	Equipment
14	Right Sector Unit (284th Regt, -1 Co) 128th Fld Arty Regt (-2 Bns)	Lotzukou	30% of strength	30% of strength	All artillery pieces and heavy machine-guns were completely demolished
16	285th Regt (-2 Cos) 1 Bn, 283d Regt 1 Bn, (-1 Plat), 128th Fld Arty Regt	Huapitientzu	20% of strength	1% of strength	About 1/3 of artillery pieces destroyed
16	Transport Unit	Tahsingkou	2% (of 600)	5% of strength	

Information concerning the casualties of the Raiding Battalion, which operated in the forward area of the Right Sector Unit, and the Paitaoshantzu Garrison Company is unavailable. The border observation squads in all likelihood were annihilated.

---

89. It is certain that Colonel Matsuyoshi, commander of the 284th Infantry Regiment, Captain Hayakawa and Captain Fukumoto, two of his battalion commanders, and Major Katsumata, commander of the 128th Artillery Regiment, were killed in action.

Although nothing had been heard from the units which shared the fate of the positions at Tungning, it was believed that about 150 troops had continued to fight stubbornly until 27 or 28 August.

Negotiations with the Soviet Army

Informed around 1100 hours on the 16th by the Area Army that the Imperial order concerning a cease-fire had been issued on the 15th, we were filled with trepidation at the unexpected turn of events. On receipt of the order stating "Each commanding officer will make immediate arrangements with the Soviet Army commander in his area and cease firing; he shall comply with the Soviet commander's instructions," we regretfully followed the order and tried every possible way to transmit it.

At 1300 hours on the 16th when our truce-bearer party was dispatched along the Huapitientzu-Lotzukou road to open negotiations with the Soviets, it was caught in enemy fire. As a result one officer and one interpreter were killed. Thereupon the party was told to return.

With determination to wage a decisive battle in case the enemy should attack, we moved the division command post to the site of the 285th Regimental Headquarters southwest of Taipingling, strengthened defenses, and studied the situation. As soon as the sun had set, the enemy attempted to remove the disabled tanks in the area of the main road. To conceal his action, he tried to draw our attention by firing wildly at our positions on both sides of the main road. We patiently avoided an engagement, and continued to strengthen our defense, and maintain strict watch. After midnight, when the enemy had removed all tanks, silence prevailed on the battlefield. Before the following dawn the command post was moved back to its former location.

At 0900 hours on the 17th, an enemy delegation arrived at the 285th Regimental Headquarters and ordered the commander to cease fire and disarm. In reply, the division commander stated that he would draw up an agreement on disarmament after meeting the Soviet supreme commander for this area. However, when he learned that the order had come from the Soviet armored division commander for the area, he promptly instructed the various units under his command to gather ordnance and ammunition for delivery to the Soviet Army and cautioned his officers and men against taking reckless action. Just before noon a Soviet major-general (the armored division commander) came and ordered our division commander to go to Wangching to receive instructions from the Soviet supreme commander for this area who was expected there soon. In the meantime our division commander secretly burned the colors of the 284th Infantry Regiment. At 1400 hours two officers who understood the Russian language were sent to Wangching to receive instructions. On the afternoon of the following day, the 18th, they returned with an order from the 25th Soviet Army Commander that the division commander himself should promptly go to Wangching.

The Transport Unit Commander at Tahsingkou drew up an agreement with the local Soviet commander for a cease-fire at about 1500 hours on the 16th, and was then taken away to Wangching. He was allowed to return to division headquarters on the 18th with the above-mentioned two officers sent by the division headquarters. At 1400 hours on the 18th, the division commander and his chief of staff accompanied a Soviet lieutenant colonel to Wangching where they met with the Commander of the 25th Soviet Army. The gist of the conference was as follows:

> General Chushchakov: Have you executed the order given yesterday, the 17th?
> General Mizuhara: It is being carried out gradually. I do not know the time of completion because of difficulties in assembling the troops
>
> General Chushchakov: How were your troops disposed at the time of the cease-fire?
> (General Mizuhara replied by referring to a map)
>
> General Chushchakov: Has the cease-fire order been transmitted to each unit?
> General Mizuhara: I have quickly transmitted it to the unit commanders in the area of the division main force, but to those in the distant areas mounted liaison officers have been dispatched because of the interruption of electric communication lines.
>
> General Mizuhara: I ask you to grant proper facilities for our search for Japanese casualties left on the battlefield since the 14th.
> General Chushchakov: The search will be carried out by the Soviet Army. (Despite repeated requests, the Soviet commander did not consent).

On departing, the Soviet commander once again demanded faithful and rapid execution of the order dated the 17th.

After General Mizuhara returned to Huapitientzu at noon of the 19th and bade farewell to the officers and men under his command, he was again taken, together with Adjutant Sasaki by a Soviet officer, this time to Yenchi (via Wangching) and was interned there at noon of the 20th. At the end of the month he was transferred to the camp at Voroshilov, and after a month of internment there, he was transferred to the camp at Khabarovsk.

On about 20 August the main body of the division, including Chief of Staff Ishibashi, was sent from Huapitientzu, some to Chintsang and others to Yenchi. In early November they were interned in Soviet territory.[90]

Civil Affairs

When the division moved back to the fortified zone in early June, the division commander, in view of the number of Japanese civilians in forward areas, asked General Murakami, Commander of the Third Army, at a conference, "In view of the possible invasion of the Soviet forces, isn't it necessary to give a hint of it to the Governor of Tungning Prefecture and the chief of the Japanese Residents' Association?" General Murakami replied that it was impossible because military secrets were involved. As a result, this problem was shelved.

---

90. Some members of the division were repatriated after the war. Others are still believed to be detained by the Soviets.

The division transferred only the dependents of military personnel and civilian employees from the area within its jurisdiction, most of them to the Tunhua area or to Japan. This was done in compliance with a directive from higher headquarters. The division did not force the dependents of the 1st Border Garrison Unit to evacuate, however, because most of them decided to share the fate of the Garrison Unit.

Japanese civilian residents under the division's jurisdiction were estimated at 3,000, of whom approximately 2,000 lived in and around Tungning, approximately 400 at Laoheishan, approximately 300 at Tatutzuchuan, and a small number in other areas. At daybreak on 9 August when several heavy bombs were dropped on the streets of Tungning, and the sound of rifles and guns was heard in the border area, and flights of Soviet aircraft were seen, Japanese residents were alerted, and preparations were begun for their immediate evacuation. Despite considerable confusion, by evening most of them had been evacuated to Kirin or Tumen, principally by train, although some by motor vehicle, and others on foot.

There were three Japanese agriculture cultivating parties in the division's area before hostilities began, with a total of about 500 personnel. Two groups were located east of Tungning,(one west of the area of 1st Border Garrison Unit Headquarters), and one group east of Chengtzukou. Their evacuation is believed to have been carried out in the same manner as other civilian residents.

At the beginning of hostilities most Manchurian government officials, including the Governor of Tungning Prefecture (a Japanese national), evacuated the division area by automobile to the Kirin area through Tachienchang.

There were no Manchurian Army troops stationed within the division's jurisdictional area. The Manchurian police force was under the jurisdiction of the Japanese Kempei-tai. Police stations were located in Tungning, Tatutzuchuan, Laoheishan and Lotzukou, with substations in other major communities. The chief of the Lotzukou Police Station, a Japanese, had been reassigned prior to outbreak of the war, but his successor had not yet arrived. The former chief had kept very close liaison with the Army. The Lotzukou Police Station officials evacuated the town on the evening of the 14th when the troops were retreating.

Monograph No 154-K

CHAPTER XXI

The 132d Independent Mixed Brigade[91]

Organization

The 132d Independent Mixed Brigade was organized near Tungning beginning on 10 July 1945 from the disbanded 1st, 2d, and 11th Border Garrison Units. It consisted principally of four infantry battalions and three artillery batteries. A raiding battalion organized at about the same time was assigned to the brigade. On 30 July the brigade was assigned to Third Army.

On 2 August Major General Onitake, appointed to command the brigade, arrived at his post. On the following day he was briefed by an intelligence officer concerning the situation in front of Tungning. The essentials points of the briefing were as follows:

> That a considerable concentration of enemy armored divisions, infantry divisions, and air force units were reported to be in front of Tungning.
>
> That the Soviet Army has been moving its troops to the frontier area. (Higher authorities concluded that these were troops returning from joint air and ground maneuvers conducted in the rear.)
>
> That new roads leading to the frontier had been constructed by the Soviets.

---

91. The information in this chapter was furnished by Major General Goichi Onitake, Commander of the 132d Independent Mixed Brigade.

> That the Soviets were constructing fortifications near the frontier.
>
> That many Soviet officers had periodically come to the vicinity of the frontier in motor vehicles in order to conduct observation.

From this information the brigade commander concluded that the Soviet forces were preparing for operations and would start an invasion in the near future. He felt the necessity for establishing counter-measures, and immediately ordered subordinate commanders to prepare for operations, emphasizing that he wanted the brigade to take the following emergency measures:

> Strengthen key points of defense, and alter troop dispositions accordingly.
> Repair field fortifications.
> Conduct training exercises in the emergency occupation of position.
> Complete firing preparations and training for defensive action.
> Request higher headquarters to provide weapons and materials needed immediately for emergency measures.

Although the organization of the brigade was completed at the end of July many deficiencies existed; for example, there were shortages of weapons and ammunition, and the quality and training of soldiers was poor.

Although the total member of men was approximately at the authorized 5,000, the quality was low. The competence of officers was, in general, unsatisfactory; except for the headquarters staff officer the brigade had no Military Academy graduates. The post of raiding battalion commander was vacant. The brigade commander did not arrive at his post until 2 August and the staff officer not until the 6th. One battalion commander was absent from the unit, participating in training exercises being held by higher headquarters.

The brigade consisted of the following elements: four infantry battalions, each consisting of four infantry companies, one machinegun company, and one infantry gun company (75-mm); one raiding battalion (three companies); one artillery unit (three batteries[92]); one signal unit; one engineer unit (three platoons), and one transport unit (two horse-drawn companies and one motor transport company).

Status of Supplies and Training

Supplies of weapons and ammunition were seriously short, particularly, light and heavy machineguns, and infantry guns. One of the artillery batteries was equipped with only six light mortars. Signal apparatus was inadequate. Moreover, the brigade had no wireless set capable of establishing communications with higher commands. The quantity of engineer equipment was very small. There were only thirty antitank mines. The transport unit was not supplied with any motor vehicles. Horses and carts were insufficient.

Although the brigade's zone of responsibility was in Tungning Prefecture, it was supplied with only a few maps of that area.

---

92. It is not known whether one of these batteries belonged formerly to the Tungning Heavy Artillery Regiment.

Telephone and telegraph facilities between the headquarters and the local government agencies were incomplete.

Since the mixed brigade was organized from units which had performed garrison duties only, it lacked field training. Furthermore, the raiding battalion because of its recent formation had been given no specialized training.

In summary, it may be said that higher headquarters, in directing the organization of the brigade, had overlooked the fact that organizing a unit for border operations differs in one major respect from organizing a unit for operations in the rear. Organizing and equipping a border unit must be accomplished in a short period of time and on a priority basis, in order that garrison duties might be carried out uninterruptedly. Since this point was overlooked, preparations for operations as well as actual operations were seriously handicapped.

Opening of Hostilities

At about 2300 hours on 8 August, enemy aircraft crossed the border. At about 0100 hours, 9 August, the lookout post at Hsingan village south of Sanchakou (old Tungning), was attacked. Upon receiving this report, brigade headquarters alerted units deployed in first line defense positions along the border, and at the same time reported to Third Army Headquarters.

Judging that a war between Japan and the USSR had broken out, General Onitake placed the brigade's emergency defense plan into effect, the gist of which was:

The brigade will break up the attack of the enemy at the closest range (mainly because of the lack of long-range weapons and the scarcity of ammunition) and, at the same time, will carry out surprise attacks with our raiding unit (lack of long-range weapons forced us to resort to this measure).
The brigade will particularly check the enemy invading along the Voroshilov-Tungning road in order to facilitate rear groups' preparations for operations and, at the same time, will cover the withdrawal of the Japanese residents.[93]

To reinforce front line units, brigade headquarters then issued instructions to units in the second line positions to the following effect:

One company of the raiding battalion stationed at Shihmentzu will reinforce the Kachidoki position.

The Kachidoki and Kuoliang positions will each be reinforced by one artillery battery and one engineer platoon.

Wireless telegraph communication will be established between brigade headquarters and lookout positions at Kachidoki, Sanchakou, Kuoliang and Ichinotani.

The Transport Unit will supply ammunition and provisions from the rear.

Other units in second line positions will assemble at Hill Sankaku.

Antitank ditches between Kuoliang and Sanchakou will be enlarged.

---

93. The author's insistence that there was a lack of long-renge weapons appears not to be borne out by statements of other participants which generally agree that the Tungning defenses had four 280-mm emplaced howitzers. (See also Sketch No 1, First Area Army monograph)

As soon as day broke, the enemy launched violent artillery attacks against our first line positions and against the Hill Ikkan (Ikkansan) position, the road connecting Kuoliang, Sanchakou, and Tungning, and simultaneously fired upon the family dwellings of military personnel, and the town of Tungning in general. At about noon an element of the enemy force infiltrated the Kachidoki position. Meanwhile enemy aircraft constantly flew over our positions.

At about 1000 hours, First Area Army orders were received assigning the brigade to the 128th Division.

At about 1400 hours, an encoded order was received by telephone from the 128th Division Commander directing General Onitake to take his main force to Tachienchang, and to leave other elements at Tungning. (see Monograph 154-J for the text of this order.) Immediately after this order was received, the wire communications system was destroyed by heavy enemy shelling. Since no wireless telegraph equipment for contacting the rear had been issued to the brigade, this caused a complete interruption of liaison with the division.

Pursuant to the 128th Division's order, a Tachienchang Detachment and a Tungning Detachment were formed, as follows:

Tachienchang Detachment	Tungning Detachment
General Goichi Onitake	Major Komai

Right Column

  1 Inf Battalion[94]   2 Inf Battalion
                  2 Field Arty Btries
                  2 Heavy Arty Btries
                  2 Engineer platoons

Left Column
  Brigade Headquarters
  1 Inf Battalion
  1 Raiding Battalion
  1 Arty Bn (-2 Btries)
  1 Provisional 105-mm Howitzer Btry
  1 Engineer Bn (-2 Platoons)
  1 Signal platoon
  Main body, Transport Bn

  A withdrawal plan for the Tachienchang Detachment was drawn up and distributed immediately (see Map No 1). It contained the following provisions:

> The Tachienchang Detachment will arrive at the new position with a minimum loss of time and fighting power, in order to fill the gap between the Fifth and the Third Armies and also to cover the flanks of both Armies.
>
> The march will be carried out in several stages and only at night in order to keep the plan of withdrawal secret and to avoid attack by armored forces or aircraft. Before each dawn the detachment will bivouac in an area favored by terrain features so that it will be difficult for the enemy to attack either with armored forces or aircraft.
>
> The detachment will destroy all roads that might be of use to the enemy.
>
> During the withdrawal the detachment will make use of every road that will facilitate the march.

  By 1700 hours all arrangements for the withdrawal had been completed. The brigade commander then took leave of Major Komai, commander of the

---

94. Upon receipt of orders to move his main body to Tachienchang, General Onitake decided to abandon the Sanchakou position and to withdraw the infantry battalion (plus signal elements) as the Right Column. His reasons were: 1) Insufficient strength to defend all key points, 2)

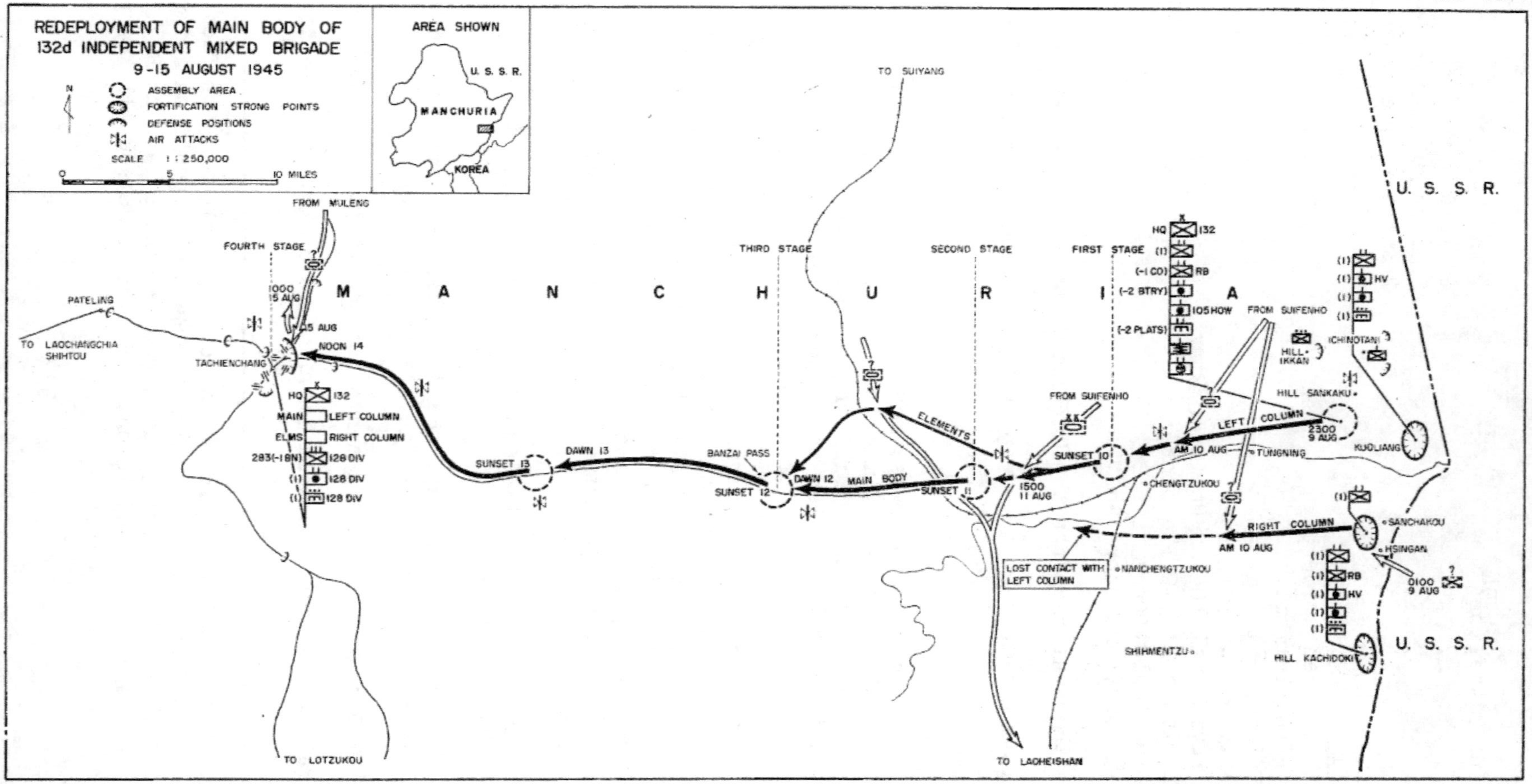
REDEPLOYMENT OF MAIN BODY OF
132d INDEPENDENT MIXED BRIGADE
9-15 AUGUST 1945
N
ASSEMBLY AREA
FORTIFICATION STRONG POINTS
DEFENSE POSITIONS
AIR ATTACKS
SCALE 1 : 250,000
0
5
10 MILES
AREA SHOWN
U. S. S. R.
MANCHURIA
KOREA
M A N C H U R I A
U. S. S. R.
U. S. S. R.
FOURTH STAGE
THIRD STAGE
SECOND STAGE
FIRST STAGE
FROM MULENG
TO SUIYANG
TO LAOCHANGCHIA SHIHTOU
PATELING
TACHIENCHANG
TO LOTZUKOU
TO LAOHEISHAN
1000 15 AUG
15 AUG
NOON 14
HQ 132
MAIN LEFT COLUMN
ELMS RIGHT COLUMN
283(-1 BN) 128 DIV
(1) 128 DIV
(1) 128 DIV
SUNSET 13
DAWN 13
BANZAI PASS
DAWN 12
SUNSET 12
MAIN BODY
SUNSET 11
ELEMENTS
1500 11 AUG
SUNSET 10
FROM SUIFENHO
HQ 132
(1)
(-1 CO) RB
(-2 BTRY)
105 HOW
(-2 PLATS)
FROM SUIFENHO
HILL IKKAN
ICHINOTANI
(1) HV
(1)
(1)
(1)
HILL SANKAKU
LEFT COLUMN
2300 9 AUG
AM 10 AUG
TUNGNING
KUOLIANG
CHENGTZUKOU
RIGHT COLUMN
AM 10 AUG
SANCHAKOU
HSINGAN
0100 9 AUG
LOST CONTACT WITH LEFT COLUMN
NANCHENGTZUKOU
(1) RB
(1) HV
SHIHMENTZU
HILL KACHIDOKI

Tungning Detachment, at the command post at Kouliang with these parting words: "I hope you will fight bravely for the sake of the Japanese Empire." He then went up Hill Sankaku where brigade headquarters was located. A glance toward the west showed the sun setting behind Hill Ikkan, which was covered with the dark red smoke of bursting shells fired by the infiltrating enemy forces and by long-range guns beyond the border. It was a wretched spectacle.

During the preparations for withdrawal, the brigade appropriated four 105-mm howitzers (and 30 rounds of ammunition) which had been dismantled from border fortifications and allocated to a rear force but which because of the lack of transporting facilities had remained in the brigade's position. The brigade formed a provisional artillery battery and allocated it to the Tachienchang Detachment.

Although the withdrawing force intended to depart at dusk, its departure was delayed unexpectedly by the failure of the Raiding Battalion to assemble on schedule. At dawn of that day it had been ordered to assemble with other units of the withdrawal force at the Hill Sankaku position, but due to the persistent hindrance of enemy aircraft and heavy fire by enemy artillery during the day, it had been forced to move one platoon at a time.

Engagements During the Withdrawal (See Map No 1).

The 45-mile march was to be made in five stages, with all movements limited to the hours of darkness. The force was to with-

---

the Kuoliang guns were capable of restraining the enemy in Sanchakou, and 3) the Sanchakou positions were in terrain unsuitable for delaying operations. (Letter, General Onitake to Mil. His. Sec. HQ AFFE, 25 Apr 54, MHS files.)

draw in two parallel columns, with the main body in the Left (north) Column. Stations were designated for stopping before dawn of each day.

At 2300 hours, 9 August, the withdrawal began. The night weather was fair. The march was much slower then expected due to the heat and the weak marching power of the men who were primarily garrison troops and unaccustomed to long marches. Consequently the withdrawal force did not arrive at the line designated for the first stage on schedule, that is before dawn.

Forced to continue the march after daybreak of the 10th, it was hindered by enemy aircraft. A part of the Left Column and the Right Column were attacked by enemy tank units. Since the Right Column had hardly any antitank weapons and materials, it suffered great losses. It became confused and finally lost contact with the main force. An adjutant was sent by truck to establish contact but failed.

During the daylight hours, the Left Column finally arrived at the projected line and waited there until sunset, when the force started the second stage of the march.

On the night of 10-11 August the main force of the Raiding Battalion, the Signal Platoon and the Transport Battalion led the withdrawal. They lost their way and headed in the direction of Muleng. The columns had to be halted temporarily and reorganized.

It was not until dawn that the units learned their whereabouts. The march was resumed in the proper direction and, although the columns were subjected to attack by enemy aircraft, they reached the position designated for the second stop. At about noon contact was restored with elements of the Right Column, which was immediately ordered to catch up with the main force.

Prior to noon, the vanguard of an enemy tank unit reconnoitered our bivouac position, and at about 1500 hours the unit's main body, equipped with 150-mm guns, charged our outer perimeter defense. Our units, with only a limited number of antitank weapons and explosives, had no alternative but to fight a defensive battle relying mainly upon skillful use of terrain.

Soon after sunset the enemy withdrew. The troops (infantry, signal and transport) in the perimeter positions had borne the brunt of the enemy attack. They were so confused as a result of the day's battle that they could not be readily reorganized. Thereupon, staff officers were sent to each of the units concerned to transmit orders to start the withdrawal as planned as soon as the troops could be assembled. After dark the third stage of the withdrawal was begun. (The enemy which attacked the brigade on this day was presumed to be part of the armored division which had penetrated the Suifenho gap. It moved on to Laoheishan after attacking the brigade.)

Soon after dawn of the 12th the withdrawing troops arrived at the line scheduled for the third day. The morning was cloudy, with occasional rain. During the night march, the Signal Unit and the main force of the Transport Battalion were brought under control, but the greater part of the infantry battalion remained in disorder all day. Although an element of the enemy tanks overtook and attacked our left flank and rear on this day, it gave up the attack and turned back. Soon after sunset, the fourth stage of the journey was begun.

On 13 August--the weather was fair--the withdrawing column had to halt after dawn because the artillery unit was anable to keep up, having had difficulty during the night getting through Banzai Pass. The halt was necessary also to control troops, and to take precautions against enemy aircraft. But by this time, the threat of an enemy in pursuit had diminished, and the brigade commander decided to leave the column and hasten to Tachienchang. He arrived at the disignated main position around noon and, escorted by Colonel Ishimaru, the 283d Infantry Regiment commander, immediately inspected the key points of the new position.

On the basis of his inspection, and considering the remaining strength of the brigade and the enemy situation--specifically the enemy tank units that had given pursuit--the brigade commander decided upon his troop disposition including that of the 283 Regiment which was now under his command. (See Map No 1). At the same time he ordered regimental troops to continue the construction of emergency field positions, but to stop work on cave positions.

In his order, the brigade commander outlined the following objectives:

    To lay stress on antitank defense.

    To curtail the frontage of the position now under construction since it was too extensive in proportion to the surviving strength of the brigade.

    To construct additional defense installations against a possible enemy attack from the rear in order to carry out protracted resistance in the event of isolation.

    To avoid long-range battles as much as possible in view of the limited artillery strength. To employ artillery, during the decisive stages of the battle, principally against tanks, at short distances, for short periods, to achieve surprise, and for flank defense.

    To dispose troops in depth and construct obstacles in depth, both in front of and within the position, for antitank defense purposes.

    To construct emergency field positions instead of cave positions.

By noon of 14 August the withdrawing column arrived at the main position. Units were given assignments in accordance with the new disposition, and began construction work. By this time, approximately half of the units which had fallen into confusion during the encounter with enemy tanks had also arrived. However, the Right Column failed to catch up except for small elements.

The supply of ammunition and provisions from Shihtou (south of Mutanchiang) which had been continued by the Transport Unit up to that time was suspended because Fifth Army had destroyed the supply depot near Shihtou by fire. (The Soviet Army invaded that sector immediately thereafter.) The brigade dispatched one unit to Laochangchia, a defile east of Shihtou, to cover its rear.

Meanwhile, the brigade was ordered by the 128th Division to rush one infantry battalion to Laoyehling to cover the division's left flank. (Before this battalion was able to leave, the cease-fire order was received.)

In the afternoon, all contact with the 128th Division was disrupted. On the following day, the 15th, a liaison party headed by an officer was dispatched to the division but was unable to make contact. Also on 15 August, the enemy tank unit which had been zigzagging since the previous day rushed in from the direction of the Muleng-Tachienchang Road. We repulsed its leading element of approximately one company by means of close cooperation between the frontline infantry and artillery, and by the courageous fighting of officers and men.

From 16 to 21 August each unit was absorbed in the construction of positions for an engagement. Beginning on the 18th, enemy troops began assembling far to our rear. The frequency of sorties conducted by enemy aircraft decreased considerable by this time.

On 22 August we received a division order concerning a cease-fire. It was brought by a team of mounted messengers. We later learned that the division at intervals had dispatched two teams of mounted messengers; the first team never arrived. Simultaneously, we received the Imperial Rescript. Confronted suddenly by an unprecedentedly sad fate, we were filled with deep emotion.

Although there was some dissension at that time, we behaved properly and took necessary measures in accordance with the orders of higher headquarters, considering also the eternal existence of the nation. At this juncture, we also burned the colors of the 283d Infantry Regiment which was under our command.

Losses

Brigade losses (excluding the Tungning Detachment) were estimated at 200 killed, 150 wounded, and 600 missing. In addition, all machine guns and all infantry guns were lost or destroyed.

Enemy casualties were estimated at 200. Eight of his tanks and a few of his vehicles were disabled.

Civil Affairs

By the night of the 9 August most of Japanese residents had fled by train or car and some by foot in the direction of Mutanchiang, Tumen and Tungchingcheng. Those who fled on the last train leaving Tungning were attacked by enemy tanks in the vicinity of Suiyang at dawn 10 August, and were forced to scatter and take to the mountains. Having almost nothing to eat, they experienced indescribable hardships while retreating to the rear.

Some members of the cultivating groups throw in their lot with the brigade and cooperated in the construction of antitank ditches; others seemed to have taken refuge to the rear.

Immediately after the commencement of hostilities, the dependents of military personnel were quartered within the Tungning position. On the afternoon of the 9th they were transferred by truck to Tungning Station and entrained there for points west and south.

Since the Koreans in the years before the war had taken advantage of their rights as Japanese and had been rather arrogant and high-handed toward the Manchurians, they feared that the latter would take revenge. Although most of them remained in Manchuria, it is very likely that some of them sought refuge in Korea.

The Manchurian government officials and police learned of the outbreak of hostilities relatively early, and they escaped rather quickly by motor vehicles and other means of transportation.

Situation at the End of the War

The strength of the brigade had dropped by about one-third during the series of engagements fought while withdrawing. After occupation of the position at Tachienchang, the brigade's morale was restored and it took on a determination to defend the position to the death. Its morale rose considerably after it defeated the enemy tank unit on 15 August.

The cease-fire order delivered by the team of mounted messengers on 22 August directed the brigade to withdraw to the vicinity of Wangching (midway between Tumen and Tungchingcheng), to leave its arms behind, and await further instructions from the division. Accordingly, the brigade left the bulk of its arms at the Tachienchang position (with some officers and men to watch over these arms and to negotiate if necessary), evacuated the position on the 24th and, after four days of marching, arrived at an area north of Wangching where it found that the division had already been disarmed and interned. Consequently, on the 27th, the brigade at its own discretion opened negotiations with a nearby Soviet division. In accordance with instructions from the Soviet commander, the brigade marched to the vicinity of Tungchingcheng, where it was divided into nine battalions of approximately 1,000 men each and interned on 30 August. (This numerical increase resulted from the fact that the brigade successively absorbed surviving troops of adjacent units.) The subsequent movements of brigade troops are unknown, but it is believed that the men were transferred to Soviet territory in September and November, either in Central Asia or the Maritime Province.

INDEX

Acheng: 81, 83, 85
Ada, Maj: 322
Aerhchinshan: 183
Agochi: 95, 103
Aiho: 67, 206, 266, 271
Aihun: 15
Air
  bombardment: 46
  fields: 12, 48, 191, 285
  force: 10
  raids
    on Hailar: 9
    on Hsinking: 3
    on Mutanchiang: 3
  support: 10
  units: 19, 99n
Air Army
  Second: 5, 16, 19, 22 99n
Airfields
  Dokhodskoi: 74
  Hunchun: 127
  Shahoyen: 74
  Tunhua: 73
  Wenchun: 204
Air Training Brigade: 101st: 16, 18
Akutogawa, Col: 314
Ammunition: 8, 46, 48, 55-56, 58, 68, 84, 91, 114, 117, 144, 146, 166, 176, 178, 185, 198, 218, 234, 250, 283
  depot: 291
Antitank Battalion, 31st: 260, 262-63
Antu: 35, 46, 48-49, 89
Araki, Maj: 63, 65
Area Armies
  First: 1n, 3, 5, 9n, 15, 22, 26, 30-35, 38-42, 45-46, 48, 50-53, 55-56, 57, 57n, 59-61, 63, 67-69, 71, 74, 77, 80-81, 86n, 89, 93-94, 99n, 103-05, 120, 150, 153n, 155-56, 164, 194, 196, 201, 209-11, 217, 283, 298, 307, 313, 318, 325, 336
    Headquarters: 63, 72, 75, 80, 209, 214, 271
    Operational Order No 1: 59
  Third: 1n, 5, 10, 12, 17-19, 22, 44
  Fifth: 6, 8, 22, 63, 77
  Sixth: 149
  Twelfth: 151
  Fifteenth: 151
  Sixteenth: 151
  Seventeenth: 6-8, 22, 25, 26n, 37n, 43-44, 84, 86, 110, 112-13, 142n, 152, 306n
  Korea: 26n, 110
Arinuma, Lt Col, Genichiro: 1n
Armies (See also Army, General, and Area Army)
  Third: 1n, 9, 14, 30, 34-39, 41, 43-45, 48-52, 59-60, 62, 64-65, 70, 72-73, 80-84, 86-88, 90-94, 99n, 102, 105, 111, 112, 115, 117-20, 122, 127, 133, 136, 139-41, 142n, 146, 149-50, 156, 163-64, 168, 225, 307, 309, 313, 328, 331, 337
    composition of: 80
    Headquarters: 82, 84-85, 95-100, 105, 123, 126, 132
    issued Operational Order No 1: 94
  Fourth: (see also Monograph No 155) 1n, 5, 17, 22, 220
  Fifth: 1n, 2, 8, 14, 16, 30, 36, 38-39, 41-42, 44-45, 48-52, 54, 59-62, 65-70, 72-73, 78, 80-84, 87, 148-51, reach a peak 150-60, 153-66, 168, 209-21, 225-35, 239n, 249, 253, 262-63, 266, 276-77, 280-81, 285, 289, 296-97, 304, 307, 313-14, 337, 343,

    commander: 62-63, 65, 159
    Headquarters: 63, 240, 254, 263, 270, 283 (see also detachments, Kobayashi and Sasaki)
  Twelfth: 39n
  Fourteenth: 149
  Twentieth: 149
  Thirtieth: (see also Monograph No 155) 1n, 14, 16-17, 24, 94
  Thirty-second: 149
  Thirty-fourth: 1n, 30, 85n
  Thirty-sixth: 151
  Forty-fourth: (see also Monograph No 155) 1n, ordered to Manchuria 11-12, 16, 97n
  Korea Administrative District: 110
Armies, General
  China Expeditionary: 6-8, 10, 13, 22, 25, 85n
  Southern: 25
Armored column: 17-18, 58, 61, 64
Army General Staff: 39n
Army Map Service: 32n
Army Hospitals
  Chengtzukou: 313
  Chining: 154
  Haicheng: 103
  Hulin: 154
  Hunchun: 104
  Hutou: 154, 183, 190
  Laoheishan: 104, 313, 320
  Muleng: 154
  2d and 3d Mutanchiang: 154
  Ningan: 103
  Pamientung: 154, 265
  Paoching: 154
  Pingyangchen: 154, 265
  Suiyang: 154
  Tumentzu: 104
  Tungning: 313
  Yenchi: 104
Army Officers Club
  of Yenchi: 96, 105, 181
  of Yehho: 232

Arshaan: 15
Artillery Battalions
  12th-13th Hv, (150-mm guns): 80
Artillery Command, 8th: 151
Artillery Intelligence Regiment
  1st: 149, 151
Artillery Regiments
  2d Hv (240-mm how): 81, 85-87, 140
  3d Hv (240-mm how): 81, 84, 86-87, 118, 124, 133, 137
  12th Hv (150-mm guns): 80
  Mutanchiang Hv (240-mm how): 66, 81, 84-85n, 183, 193-94, 198, 227, 229
  Tungning Hv (240-mm how): 72, 81, 84, 86-87, 118, 124, 135, 183, 227-28, 333n
  1st: 158
  37th; 140, 144
  126th: 265, 268, 271
  128th: 309-10, 324
  135th: 288, 291-92, 303
  10th Hv Fld (150-mm how): 151
  12th Hv Fld (150-mm how): 149
  20th Hv Fld (150-mm how): 66, 152, 154, 158, 183, 196, 198, 201, 227, 229, 238, 247, 268, 297, 299
  126th Fld: 246, 262-63
  128th Fld: 307, 314, 324
Assaults: 19
  amphibious: 14
  landing: 18, 97n, 146
  units: 40n
  aircraft: 99n
Asu, Col, Takehiko: 185, 233
Borders
  Eastern Manchurian: 2
  Korea: 13, 43, 85, 141
  Korea and Soviet: 141
  Korea-Manchuria: 43, 48, 67, 81, 112, 118, 210
  Manchurian: 53, 67, 210
  Manchukuoan-Soviet-Mongolian: 5
  Soviet: 141

Soviet-Japanese: 6, 6n
Soviet-Manchukuoan: 6
Ussuri River: 54
Border Garrison Units
  1st: 39, 44, 80, 86n, 275n, 306-08, 329, 331
  2d: 39, 44, 80, 82, 151-53, 226, 331
  3d: 39, 45, 153, 246-47, 274
  4th: 39, 45, 153, 173, 274
  9th: 39, 80-81, 86n, 139
  11th: 39, 44, 80, 82, 151-53, 226, 246, 331
  12th: 39, 173, 246
  15th: 44-45, 52, 56, 152, 154, 158, 176, 180-81, 183-84, 190-91, 233, 281, 288-89
  Hutou: 161
Boundary
  Soviet-Manchurian: 253
Bridges
  Kyonghung: 60, 95, 97, 123
  Hsinglung: 211-12, 270-72
  Yehho: 212
Broadcast
  Moscow: 4
  Tass: 4, 6
Camps
  (No 79) Yerabuga: 137n
  A, G: 137n
  Lada: 137n
  Sub-Camp No 14: 137
Casualty Clearing Platoon
  47th: 154
Casualty Clearing Unit
  9th: 95, 103
Cavalry Brigade, 3d: 148, 150, 173
Cavalry Regiment: 86
  79th: 113, 116, 124
Cease-fire orders: 19, 24, 69, 71-72, 74, 133-35, 147, 214, 217, 220, 241-42, 325
Central Asia: 231
Chalaitochi: 24
Changchiatien: 104, 320
Changpyong: 116, 123, 140

Chaoyangchuan: 89, 102-03
Chengtzukou: 83, 102, 104, 306, 329
Chiamussu: 9, 29, 36, 51, 61, 63, 77, 158, 172
Chiaoho: 36, 77, 222
Chientao: 26, 81, 150
  Province: 64-65, 106
Chihsi: 30, 49, 62
Chihsing: 34, 157-58, 182, 187-90, 200, 222, 226, 274-77, 282-83, 286, 288-90
  Station: 285
Chilin: 26, 49-50
China: 1, 11, 13, 39, 148-49, 163, 176-77n
Chingkulingmiao: 61, 176, 186, 250, 252-53, 257-58
Chining: 163, 166, 172, 189, 248
Chinhsien: 10, 17
Chintsang: 60, 322, 328
Chiulungping: 99-101, 103-04, 128
Chiungshan: 54, 248, 254-55
Chiupikou: 186, 257
Chonghak: 44, 86, 100, 141, 142n, 146
Chongjin: 18-19, 87, 96-97, 99, 141, 146
Chongsong: (See also roads), 116, 133, 140
Chushan: 158, 167, 278
Chushchakov, Gen: 105, 327
Close-quarter
  attack: 142, 205-06, 208, 260, 265-67, 292, 297
  counterattack: 206
  fighting: 143, 194, 197, 230, 293
  suicidal teams: 294
  tactics: 296
  units: 268
Communications: 5, 23-24, 50, 61, 62, 64, 166, 177, 180, 183-84, 213, 229, 239, 241, 278, 312
  between Manchuria and Korea: 85
  network: 38, 50, 52-53
  overhead wires: 50-51

telephone: 209, 254, 257, 269
trenches: 46, 58, 162, 203, 228, 266
underground cable: 50
wireless (telegraph): 51-52, 168
Conferences: 90
  Hsinking: 83, 88
  Kwantung Army staff: 12, 19
  Potsdam: 2
Construction Duty Companies
  19th: 152
  32d: 103
Construction Units
  45th Fld Road: 154, 167
  46th Fld Road: 103
Continental Railway Command: (see also Monograph No 138) 16
Cultivating Groups: 138n, 191, 221, 224, 245
  Kutami: 244
Dairen: (see also railroads) 3, 5, 11, 14, 18, 34
Depots
  Air Supply: 143
  Freight (general supplies): 264-65
    Mutanchiang: 271, 304
  Ordnance: 265
Depot (Training) Division
  19th: 43, 110-11, 122
Detachments:
  Kobayashi: 196-97, 203-04, 239n
  Komusan: 115, 117, 124, 141-42
  Sasaki: 190, 195-97, 239n
  Tachienchang: 65, 314, 316, 318, 321-23, 336
  Taipingling: 321
  Tungning: 314-15, 336-38, 344
  Yamagishi: 260-61
Diphtheria: 108
Disarmament: 22-23, 72-73, 105, 134, 213, 217, 243, 300-01, 303-04

Dispensary: 133
District
  16th: 137n
Divisional District Units
  2d: 110
  Kuangju: 111n
  Nanam: 88, 111-14, 129, 136, 138, 143
  Pyongyang: 111n
  Seoul: 111n
  Taegu: 111
Dokhodskoi: (see airfields)
Emperor: 20, 21n, 22, 71, 140, 213, 300; broadcasting: 19, 100; signed orders: 6, 12n
Engineer Commands, 1st: 152, 154, 159
Engineer Companies
  1st: 116
  2d: 116, 120, 130
  3d: 116, 120, 136
Engineer Construction Unit: 125
Engineer Regiments
  79th: 113-14, 116-17, 121, 135
Engineer Units
  126th: 246, 262, 265, 271
  135th: 289, 303
Erhjenpan: 250-51
Erhtaohotzu: 189, 221
European Russia: 137, 305
Fangcheng: 9, 34, 36, 52, 61, 63, 70, 72
Feite: 163, 189, 297, 301
Fengmishan: 161
Field Freight Depots
  17th (First Class): 154
  Mutanchiang: 220
Field Hospital: 309, 320
Field Transport Headquarters, 7th: 151
Flood season: 181
Formosa: 21, 149
Fortifications: 27-29, 32-33, 35, 41, 46-47, 53-54, 78-88, 91, 112,

121-25, 142, 156, 159-62, 171,
174-75, 179, 185, 248, 250-51,
253, 277, 292, 308, 310, 312,
313, 332, 338, (see also
Sketch No 1, Monograph 154-B)
  at Chihsing: 274
  border: 55, 87
  Headquarters: 114
  in the MLR: 227
  over-the-border: 248
  underground: 57
Fortification Units, 3d Fld:
  152, 154, 196
Fortress Garrison Unit (see
  Najin Fortress Garrison Unit)
Fuel: 48, 56, 68, 90
Fujimoto, Lt Col: 93, 104
Fukumoto, Capt: 324n
Garrison Units
  Fuchin, Najin: 44
Gas Control Unit: 113, 116, 120,
  124, 133
Germany: 53, 173-74
German church in Yenchi: 108
Getsumeisan: 116, 125, 131
Ground Survey Company: 149
Guard Units
  46th: 45
  77th-80th: 42
  Freight Depot: 264
Guerrilla warfare: 10-11, 147,
  252, 277, 279
Guides (see plans)
Hailar: 9-10, 15, 18
Hailin: 219-20, 304
Hamhung: 138, 193
Hamyong
  Province: 82, 84, 112
  Pukto: 26n, 36
Harbin:(see also railroads) 17,
  22, 50, 61, 77, 219, 227, 244
Hata, Gen, Hikosaburo: 20, 71
Hataho: 248
Hattori, Province Councillor: 107
Hayakawa, Capt: 324n
Heiho: 9

Heilingshan: 250-255
Hengtaohotzu: 66-67, 70, 189, 200,
  209-14, 216-19, 221, 223-24,
  270, 300-02, 304
Highway: 61
Hills
  371-Meter: 66, 203, 205-06,
    264-67
  792: 262-63
  800-Meter: 183
  1,115-Meter: 182
  A: 260
  B: 239, 260-61
  C: 261
  Freight Depot: 264
  Ikkan (Ikkansan): 336, 338
  Kachidoki: 315, 335-36
  Kuanyuehtai: 231, 233
  Sankaku: 335, 338
  Ssutaoling: 264-67
  Yingchitun: 265
Hitomi, Lt Gen Yoichi, CG, 135th
  Div: 45, 184, 190, 200-01, 275,
  283, 285-86, 288, 297-98
Hoeryong: 34-35, 70, 95, 100, 114,
  117, 120-21, 123-24, 126, 137-
  38, 142-43, 146
Hohsi: 245
Hokkaido: 6
Hosokawa, Lt Col, Naotomo: 80n,
  93-94, 98, 106
Hospitals
  71st Zone of Comm: 152
  97th Zone of Comm: 103
  Field: 271
  Veterinary: 271, 289
Hoyen: 315
Hsiachengtzu: 30, 62, 81, 83-85,
  155-56, 183, 185, 193-94, 227,
  229, 290
Hsientung: (see also roads) 158,
  163, 164-67, 199, 261, 263, 291-
  92, 297
Hsingan: 24, 334
Hsingkai (Khanka): 165
Hsinglung: 68, 182, 271

Hsinking: (see also railraods, conference) 3, 5, 11, 13-20, 22-24, 34, 50-51, 71, 73, 77, 83, 88, 136, 159, 227, 244
Hsitungan: 163, 189, 286, 288, 301
Hualin: 66, 168, 183, 201, 203, 207-08, 292, 297-99
Huangnihotzu: 183
Huapitientzu: 64, 70, 89, 319, 320-21, 323-24, 328
Hujipyong: 116
Hulin: 30, 32n, 148, 161, 163, 166-67, 188, 231, 249, 276, 281, 283, 289, 301
Huma: 9
Hunchun: 15, 34-35, 43, 49, 52, 60, 65, 70, 80-81, 83, 85-89, 95-98, 101, 105, 118, 125, 127, 133n, 136-37, 139-40, 147, 157
Hunjen: 18
Hunyung: 116, 124, 126-27, 129-30, 137
Hutou: 2, 9, 31-32, 45, 52, 54, 59, 61, 153, 158, 161, 163, 167, 172-76, 181, 184, 188, 190-91, 233, 278, 281, 283, 287, 289
Hwangpa: 130
Hyesanjin: 138
Ichinotani: 335
Iizuka, Col: 188, 301
Iketani, Maj Gen, Hamjiro: 93, 105
Iman: 45, 158, 161, 183, 190-91, 247
Imienpo: 36, 49, 221
Imperial command: 242
Imperial General Headquarters: 6-8, 12-14, 19, 21, 23, 25, 35, 83, 110, 155-56
  Army Department Orders
    No 1130, 1131, 1245, 1338, 1339, 1340: 37n; 1374: 6n, 37n; 1378: 12n; 1381: 21n; 1382: 21; 1385: 23n

  Special Order No 3: 25n
  Army Directives
    No 2164: 26n, 37n; 2539: 13n; 2544: 22
  Army General Staff: 11n
  Deputy Chief: 11n
  issued emergency orders: 6
  War Office Order No 105: 152
Imperial Palace: 140
Imperial Rescript Terminating the War: 19-20, 21, 23, 71
Incidents
  Border: 5
  Kanhsiatun: 174n
  Mongoshile: 5n
  Wuchiatzu: 5n, 39n
Independent Battalions
  1st Hv Arty (150-mm guns): 152, 183
  5th and 8th Hv Arty (300-mm how): 152, 154
  11th Hv Arty (150-mm guns): 151
  52d Transport (packhorse): 102
  64th, 70th-71st Transport: 154
  70th Motor Transport: 152
  113th Motor Transport: 101-02
  31st Antitank: 150, 152, 154, 158, 183, 199, 227, 247, 271
Independent Batteries
  1st Hv Arty (150-mm guns): 154, 158, 198, 227, 229
  2d Hv Arty (240-mm how): 80, 85-87, 140, 234
Independent Companies
  69th Transport: 102
  72d, 74th Transport: 152
Independent Mixed Brigades
  77th: 45, 150, 152-53, 274, 276-77, 279-80
  78th: 42
  80th: 9, 15
  128th: 9n
  132d: (Chapter XXI) 38, 41, 43, 56-57, 64, 85-87, 92, 104, 153n, 307, 312-13, 315, 317, 324, 331

composition of: 44, 60
Tungning Detachment: 60
Independent Regiments
  3d Engineer: 152
  11th Engineer: 300
  12th Engineer: 213
  15th Engineer: 262, 264-65
  18th Engineer: 154, 203
  20th Mountain Arty: 113
Infantry Divisions
  2d: 110n
  8th: 45n
  10th: 42n
  11th: 39, 45, 148, 151, 161, 169, 173, 246
  12th: 39, 43n, 179
  19th: 110, 122
  24th: 148-49, 169, 173
  25th: 39, 45n, 149-51, 161, 169, 246-47
  63d: 11
  71st: 39, 42n
  79th: (Chapter VIII) 36, 40-41, 43-44, 52, 57, 65, 84, 86-87, 93, 99, 101, 105-16, 118-29, 131, 134
  107th: 15, 24
  108th: 10, 17
  111th: 39, 45n, 80, 82-83, 225
  112th: 15, 39-40, 43, 52, 57, 60, 65, 70, 72, 80-81, 83, 86-88, 92, 94-98, 101, 104-05, 110n, 118-20, 125, 127, 130, 139, 143, 145
  117th: 11
  119th: 9, 16, 18
  120th: 43n, 80, 83-84, 306n
  122d: 36, 40n-42, 47-48, 57, 60, 65, 70, 72, 80-81, 83, 86-88, 92, 94-98, 101, 104-05, 11n, 118-20, 125, 127, 130,
  124th: (Chapter XVI) 40n, 44, 45n, 52, 57, 61-62, 65-66, 70, 82, 151-52, 154, 158, 168, 170, 175, 178-79, 182-85, 190, 193-200, 202, 208-09, 216, 225-27, 239n, 243, 246-47, 263, 290n, 314, 318
  126th: (Chapter XVII) 40n, 44-45, 52, 57, 61-62, 67, 150-52, 154, 158-59, 168, 170, 177, 179, 182-83, 186, 199-205, 210-13, 229, 246-50, 262, 264-66, 270-71, 273, 290, 292, 295, 300, Tzuhsing-tun (Yamagishi) Detachment: 260-61, Raiding Battalion: 271
  127th: (Chapter IX) 40n, 43, 52, 57, 60, 82, 85-88, 91-94, 99-103, 105, 112, 117, 125-26, 139-43, 146
  128th: (Chapter XX) 8, 9n, 35, 38, 40n-41, 43, 51, 57, 59-60, 62, 64, 70, 77, 82, 85-87, 89, 92, 94, 102, 104, 153n, 157, 182, 229, 306, 308, 309, 310, 313, 320, 323, 324n, 336, 343, Hsingan Village Detachment: 312 (see also Tachienchang, Taipingling, and Tungning Detachments)
  134th: 9, 30, 36-37, 42, 51-52, 57, 59, 61, 63, 70, 72, 170, 183, 285
  135th: (Chapter XIX) 44-45, 52, 56-57, 61-62, 152, 154, 158-59, 168, 170-71, 176-58, 179, 182-84, 187-88, 190-91, 194-95, 199-200, 202-04, 207-08, 211-13, 217, 249, 260, 262, 264-65, 270-71, 274-75, 280-82, 285, 289-90, 292, 296-97, 299, 302, Raiding Battalion: 271, Takikawa Battalion: 207, 212, 299
  136th: 56
  137th: 117, 123
  139th: 36, 42, 56-57, 59, 62, 68, 70-71, 74, 122
  148th: 14
Infantry Regiments
  3d: 98
  101st: 100
  271st: 185, 193, 225-26, 228, 233, 239, 299
  272d: 225-26, 228, 235, 242

273d: 225-26, 228, 235, 237-38, 242
277th: 176, 186, 246-47, 263-64, 271, 273
278th: 176th, 187, 212, 246-47, 251, 254, 262, 264, 269, 271-73
279th: 199, 246, 252, 260, 262-64, 266-68, 271, 273
280th: 93, 95, 129, 139, 141, 145-47
281st: 106-07, 139, 141, 147
282d: 139, 141, 147
283d: 64, 306, 308-09, 314-15, 319, 341, 344, Tachienchang Detachment: 65
284th: 64, 306, 309, 314-15, 318-20, 324
289th: 113, 116, 130, 132-33
290th: 113-14, 116-17, 121
291st: 113, 116, 124, 126, 129, 131, 136
368th: 176, 188, 190, 275, 281, 287-89, 291-92, 301-02
369th: 187-89, 281, 287-88, 291-92, 301-02
370th: 200, 207, 217, 275, 286, 288, 291-92, 297, 299, 302-03
371st: 190
Inouye, Col, Toshisuke: 274n, 300
Ishibashi, Col, C/S, 128th Div: 328
Ishimaru, Col: 341
Isoko, Kenzo, Governor of Mutanchiang Province: 222
Ito, Second Lt: 256
Iwasaki, Col Toyoharu, C/S, 124th Div: 225n
Izeki, Lt Gen, Jin, CG, 134th Div: 42
Jaoho: 161, 171-74, 176, 182, 184, 188, 275, 281, 287-88
Jumonji Pass: 61, 176, 182-83, 186, 250, 252-53, 257
Kachidoki-yama: 106

Kangpallyong: 146
Kanhsiatun: 2, 54, 174, 249, 283
Kantoho: 86
Kashiwada, Col, Akiji: 54, 66-67, 148n, 195, 209-10, 217-18, 235, 283
Katsumata, Maj: 318, 324n
Kawagoe, Maj Gen, Shigesada, C/S Fifth Army: 217-18, 233
Kawakami, Second Lt: 258
Kazan: 137n
Kempeitai building: 108
Khabarovsk: 27, 137, 213, 328
KIA: 147, 259
Kikuchi, Col: 262
Kinoshita, Col, Hideki: 87
Kirin: 44, 73, 77, 98, 189, 222, 302, 329, 330
Kita, Gen, Seiichi, CG, First Area Army: 39, 62-63, 66-67, 105
Kobayashi, Col: 196, 205
Koga, Lt Gen, Ryutaro, CG, 127th Div: 43, 87
Koketsu, Col: 66, 194, 198, 237
Komai, Maj: 336-37
Komatsu, Col: 68, 73
Komusan: 95, 115-17, 124
Kono, Lt Col: 106
Kono, Maj: 298
Korea: (see also borders) 6-8, 12-13, 21, 29-30, 32, 36, 43-44, 84, 110-11, 141, 147, 152, 217
  north: 8, 14, 19, 26n, 36n, 46-47, 60, 64, 81-82, 84-85n, 86, 88-89, 96, 103, 111, 117, 138, 140, 142n, 194, 306n
  south: 7, 84
  Youth League: 109
Koreans: 77, 107, 109, 136, 221-22, 224, 248, 280, 306
  territory: 123, 138n
Kraskino: 137
Kuanchengtzu: 3
Kuanyuehtai: 61, 80, 151, 181-82, 185-86, 195, 226, 246, 257

Kuoliang: 315, 335-36, 338
Kusaji, Col, Teigo: 20
Kwantung Army: 1-8, 10-26, 30, 33-35, 36n, 38n, 41n, 43-44, 61, 63, 67, 82, 84-86, 91, 99, 112, 139, 143-44, 148, 153, 155-56, 164-65, 168, 173, 179, 210, 225-26, 246, 248, 274, 307-08
  2d Noncommissioned Officer Candidate Unit: 61-62, 65, 68, 73
  Combat Guide: 91, 169
  combat manual: 53
  Commander in Chief: 3, 5n, 7, 12, 20, 22, 24-25, 26n, 71
  estimate of enemy force: 8, 14
  Fortification Department: 161
  General Headquarters: 2-5, 8, 12, 17, 19, 20n, 21, 23-24, 44, 48, 50, 59, 71, 74, 83, 159, 171, 175, 177
    Operations (First) Section: Operations Division, Logistics Division, Railway Division, Signal Communications Division: 20
    Intelligence (Second) Section: 1-2, 13-16, 20n, 24
    Training (Third) Section: 20n
    Civil Affairs (Fourth) Section: 15, 20n
  jurisdiction: 47, 81
  Kempei-tai Training Unit: 14n
  regulations: 55
  "special maneuver": 148, 153, 168, 176-77n
  standing order: 3
  Reserve Officer Candidate Training Unit: 196, 270
    Intendance: 65, 196
    Shihtao: 203, 211
Kyodaiho: 85, 126
Kyonghung: 95, 123, 145
Kyongsong: 114
Kyongwon: 116, 124, 126, 133, 137
Lada: 137
Lakes
  Baikal: 31n
  Chingpo: 34, 36, 42, 47-48, 62-63, 66, 68-70, 73, 216
  Hanka: 171-73, 281
  Hasan: 141
  Taerhhu: 7
Laku: 219-20, 304
Land Duty Companies
  64th, 92d: 154
  84th, 95th: 103
Langchi: 89
Langer, W. L.: 175n
Langtungkou: 104
Laochangchia: 343
Laoheishan: (see also roads) 86, 96, 99, 102-04, 309-10, 314, 316-17, 329, 330, 340
Laomuchuho: 309, 314
Laoyehling: 343
Laoyehmiao: 318
Lengchuan: 189, 301
Lichuan: 15-16, 18
Linchiang: 13, 14n
Lines, Railroad
  Chongsong-Changpyong: 140
  Harbin-Suifenho: 277n
  Hsiachengtzu-Pamientung-Chihsi: 62
  Hunchun-Tumen: 118, 140
  Laomuchuho-Lotzukou-Taipingkou: 308
  Muleng-Pamientung-Linkou: 164
  Pamientung: 252, 257
  Pingyang: 250-51, 254
  Tungning-Suifenho: 156
Linhsi: 16
Linkou: 30, 34, 51, 155-58, 160, 167-68, 182, 189, 200, 216, 221, 246-47, 274-76, 286, 288-90, 297, 301
  Station: 286
Lishan: 182, 186, 147, 252-53, 257-58

Lishuchen: 34, 155-57, 251, 253
Logistical plan: 89, 163
London: 96
Lotzukou: 34-35, 38, 43, 51, 64, 87, 89, 157, 308-09, 312-17, 319-20, 323-24, 330
    Police Station: 330
Lumingtai: 182, 184, 226
Lungching: 104, 140
Maeda, Col: 213-14, 270
Malanho: 183
Malik, Ambassador, Jacob: 6n
Manchouli: 9-10, 28n
Manchukuo: (see also Manchuria) 14, 214, 227n
Manchukuoan: (see also Manchuria)
    administrative authorities: 75
    Emperor: 14n
    Government: 14n, 16, 49, 175, 179, 222
        agencies: 77, 222, 280
    police: 78, 223
    troops: 78
    vice minister: 16
Manchukuoan Army (Manchurian National Army): 5n, 48, 78, 221, 223, 274, 277, 288, 301, 330
    1st Division: 223
    6th Unit: 47
    11th Army District: 223
Manchuria: 1-2, 6-7, 13, 22, 26-28, 30, 32n, 34-35, 37n, 39-40, 54, 57n, 59, 61, 67, 69, 76, 80, 83, 91, 103, 119n, 122, 137-41, 144-45, 148-50, 153, 155, 171-72, 175-78, 180-81, 189, 225, 227, 248-49, 274, 280, 282, 345
    Agriculture Development Company: 75-76
    Geography of Manchuria: 26-30
    police force: 330
    rations: 57
    territory: 123, 174, 181, 231

Manchurian Air Transport Company: 24
Manchurian Railroad Company: 106
Manchurian Telegraph and Telephone Company: 128, 209
    Harbin Office: 214
    Mutanchiang Office: 209, 222
Manchurians: 77, 79, 109, 221-22, 224, 280-81, 299
Maneuvers: 175
    "table top": 38, 232, 254, 283
    map: 153, 155
    No 11: 117
    Samsangsan area: 120
Manjengchuankou: 183
Manpower
    shortage: 47
    mass-mobilization: 55
Mashan: 155-57, 182, 223, 276-77, 282, 288-89
Mason's tools: 46
Matsumura, Col: 66, 198
Matsumura, Maj Gen, Tomokatsu: 24
Matsumoto, Col, Hiroshi: 26n, 66-68n, 209-10
Matsuyoshi, Col: 64
Mayusan: 127, 129-31, 134, 136
Meihokou: 17, 94
Miaoling: 29, 173, 176, 182, 184, 187, 246, 281, 287
Michiang: 96-98, 126, 130
Michiangtun: 43
Military Academy: 332
Mingyuehkou: 89, 103-64
Mishan: 78, 161, 163, 173, 187-88, 223, 287
Missions
    Kwantung Army: 7, 21
        cancellation: 23
        in northern Korea: 37n
    1st Mobile Brigade: 86
    15th Border Garrison Unit: 45, 289
    79th Division: 111
    127th Division: 142

128th Division: 313
134th Division: 36
285th Regiment: 320
Divisional District Units
   Kwangju, Pyongyang, Seoul: 111n
First Area Army: 35, 38
raiding parties in Soviet territory: 96
Seventeenth Army: 37n
Third Army: 35
Mizuhara, Lt Gen, Yoshishige, CG, 128th Div: 38, 43, 87, 327-28
Mixed Regiment, 101st: 36, 40, 43-44, 64, 86-87, 97, 112, 124, 126, 136, 141, 142n, 143, 146
MLR (main line of resistance):
   Fifth Army: 89 155-60, 162-64, 166-67, 175, 179, 182, 185, 193-94, 196, 199, 203, 222, 226-29, 233, 235-36, 247, 249, 263, 274-76, 282, 309
Mobile Brigade:
   1st: 40, 43-44, 52, 65, 70, 86-87, 89, 94, 97-98, 100, 106, 136
Mobile Regiment, 3d: 72
Mochizuki, Col, Masakichi: 217
Mongoshile: (see Incidents)
Mortar Battalions
   13th: 152, 154, 158, 183, 227
   14th: 151
Moscow: (see also broadcast) 4, 106
Motaoshih: 65-66, 172, 182, 194, 196-98, 203-05, 266
Motor Transport Depot, 17th Fld (First Class): 154
Mountains
   Changpaishan: 67
   Ikkoku: 234-35
   Hsiaotushan: 198
   Laohei (800-Meters): 64-65, 83
   Milinshan (Mitsurinyama): 195
   Paektu (Changpaishan): 210
   Shozo (Shozusan): 237-39
   Shuilinfeng: 95
Mountain Range, Wanta: 167, 189, 301
Mountain Artillery Battalions
   1st: 114, 116
   2d: 120
Mountain Artillery Company: 3d: 132
Mountain Artillery Regiment, 79th (75-mm guns): 113, 115-16, 120
Mukden: 11, 17-18
Muleng: 14, 16, 27, 34, 36, 38, 45, 52, 65-66, 85n, 156-58, 160, 162, 164, 168, 182-83, 185, 197-98, 202, 204, 209, 216, 222, 226-30, 232-35, 237-39, 263-64, 309, 316, 323, 339
Murakami, Lt Gen, Keisaku, CG, Third Army: 43, 80, 100, 104-05, 111, 114, 328
Musan: 64, 89, 121, 124, 126
Mutan: 27
Mutanchiang: (see also railroads and roads) 3, 18, 26, 29-30, 48-51, 53, 61-63, 65, 73-74, 77-78, 80-81, 93, 103, 150, 158, 163, 166, 182, 201-02, 204, 209-12, 217-21, 224, 227, 234, 242, 244, 261, 270-71, 286, 299, 303-05
   City: 41, 211, 270, 296
   Province: 151, 222
   Station: 285, 290
Najin: (see also ports) 14, 44, 87-88, 97, 99, 125, 141, 146-47
Najin Fortress Garrison Unit 36, 40, 43-44, 64, 86-88, 97, 112, 141, 142n
Nakamura, Lt Gen, Jikizo, CG, 112th Div: 43, 71, 87, 98
Nakayama, Col: 301
Namyang: 116, 128-29, 132-35
Nanam: 43, 88, 90, 110-11, 114, 117, 122-24, 126, 137-38
Nanling: 5
   Concentration Camp: 25
Nanshan: 251, 254
Negotiations

armistice: 22, 105
  with Russian Army: 22, 72-74, 78, 134, 147, 217, 243, 303-04
  with Koreans: 78
New Delhi: 96
News Agencies
  Domei: 6
  Manchuria: 18
  Tass: 4
Ningan: 38, 68, 124, 198, 205, 215-16, 243-44
Nishio, Vice Provincial Governor: 107
Nishiwaki, Col, Takeshi: 184
Nomizo, Lt Gen, Kazuhiko, CG, 126th Div: 45, 247, 263-64, 266
Nomonhan: 9
Okamura, Gen, Yasuji: 13
Oki, Capt, Masao: 191n
Okinawa: 149
Onitake, Maj Gen, Goichi, CG, 132d Independent Mixed Brigade: 87, 313, 316, 331, 334, 336, 337n, 338n
Onsong: 130, 133, 137
Ordnance Depot
  17th Fld (First Class): 154
Ordnance Duty Unit: 133, 143, 262, 265, 271
Ota, Lt Gen, Teisho: 43, 87, 123, 129-30, 132
Outer Mongolia: 99n
Pacific: 148, 176-77n, 223-24
  fighting: 91
  operation: 160
  War: 170, 173
Pacts, Neutrality (Soviet-Japanese): 175
Paegam: 138
Paichengtzu: 10, 15, 18-19
Paitaoshantzu: 60, 87, 94-95, 99, 306, 312, 313-14
Pamientung: 29, 31-34, 36, 45, 52, 62, 80-81, 155-58, 160, 164, 166, 168, 176, 182, 184, 186, 199, 201, 207, 247, 250-52, 254, 256-60, 292
Panchiehho: 29, 54, 61, 153, 172, 174, 176, 182, 186-87, 246-48, 250-56
Paoching: 78, 148, 161, 163, 176, 188, 223, 275, 281, 283, 288
Pataohotzu: 43, 52, 85-87, 89, 94, 100, 112, 140, 147
Pateling: 321, 322
Path
  Hulin-Tumen: 167
Philippines: 110, 148-49
Pillbox: 28
Pinchiang: 26
Pingyang: 149, 176, 247, 250-52, 254-56, 286
  Station: 286
Pingyangchen: 8, 187, 252, 255-56
Plans
  Defense of the Manchukuoan-Soviet-Mongolian Border: 5
  Hachi-go: 31n
  "Ichi-go": 149
  Kwantung Army Combat: 91
Plotting Company: 149n
Pokotu: 16
Pokrovka: 74
Poli: 78, 166-67, 172, 183, 189, 200, 216, 221, 223, 289, 301
Ports
  Unggi: 86, 95
  Najin: 86
Potsdam: (see also conferences)
  Declaration: 6n
POW: 39n
Prefectures
  Miyagi: 122
  Fukushima: 122
  Niigata: 122
Pungni: 116, 130
Rada: 106, 305
Radio: 51, 72, 96
Raiding Unit: 44, 260, 265
  9th: 152, 154

Raiding Battalion: 140, 226, 259-60, 263-65, 268, 271, 286, 288, 291, 303, 307, 309, 314-15, 324, 338-39
Raiding Company
  1st: 259-60
Raiding tactics: 240
Railroads: 29, 51, 76
  Chinese-Changchun: 227n
  Dairen-Hsinking: 11, 14-15, 18
  Eastern Chinese: 28
  Harbin-Suifenho: 30
  Manchouli-Suifenho: 227n
  Namyang-Chongsong: 135
  North-Manchurian: 227n
  Paichengtzu-Arshaan: 15
  Suifenho-Mutanchiang: 229
  Suifenho-Mutanchiang-Harbin: 61
  Trans-Manchurian: 227
  Trans-Siberian: 28n, 45, 227
  Tumen-Chiamussu: 167, 278
Reconnaissance: 5, 47, 118, 155, 160, 205, 255
  planes: 99
Reconnaissance Regiment
  79th: 95
Regimental Ammunition Train: 133
Regimental Headquarters
  285th: 325-26
Regulations
  Wartime Defense: 5
  Manchukuo Defense: 5
Resistance nests: 28-29, 32, 87
Rivers
  Amur: 9, 27, 31
  Haerhpatung: 129
  Muleng: 164, 185-86
  Mutanchiang: 66-69, 73, 189, 201, 210-11, 215-16, 221, 244, 263, 270-72, 296, 298, 301
  Suifenho: 318
  Sungari: 14, 27, 36, 61
  Tumen: 27, 95, 124-25n, 127-29, 132, 134-35, 141-42
  Ussuri: 27, 31, 54, 174, 188, 190, 287

Roads
  Hill 791-Chengtzu-Hualin: 263
  Hsientung-Hualin: 262
  Huapitientzu-Lotzukou: 325
  Hunchun-Tumen: 85
  Kuanyuehtai Hill-Hsiachengtzu: 235
  Laoheishan: 315
  Laoheishan-Heitsai-Lotzukou: 314
  Laoheishan-Lotzukou: 315
  Laoheishan-Wangching: 86
  Lishuchen-Chining: 248
  Linkou-Chihsing: 276
  Linkou-Chushan-Chihsing-Hsientung-Hualin-Yehho: 278
  Muleng: 196
  Muleng-Motaoshih-Mutanchiang: 262
  Muleng-Tachienchang: 314, 343
  Muleng-Taimakou: 196
  Muleng-Yehho: 195-96, 201, 203
  Mutanchiang: 240
  Mutanchiang-Hengtaohotzu: 212
  Mutanchiang-Tahsingkou: 318
  Pamientung-Tzuhsingtun-Hsientung: 278
  Panchiehho-Hataho: 248
  Suifenho-Hsiachengtzu-Muleng: 194
  Suifenho-Muleng: 235
  Suifenho-Mutanchiang: 62, 65, 227, 235
  Tachienchang-Tungchingcheng: 315
  Tumen-Onsong-Changpyong: 135
  Tumen-Onsong-Kyongwon: 135
  Tumen-Poli: 167, 189, 301
  Tumen-Samyanggok-Chongsong: 135
  Tumen-Yenchi: 132
  Tumentzu-Wangching: 86
  Tungan-Chining-Linkou: 278
  Tungan-Hsingkai-Paoching-Jaoho: 278
  Tungan-Hulin-Hutou: 278
  Tungan-Mishan-Miaoling: 278
  Tungan-Poli-Chihsing: 288-89
  Tungan-Poli-Linkou: 278, 289
  Voroshilov-Tungning: 335
  Wangching-Chiulungping-Yenchi: 101
  Wangching-Tumen: 132
  Yenchi-Chiulungping: 100

Yehho-Hualin: 207, 292
Russia: (see also Soviet) 227n
Russian: 109, 143, 336
   Army: 22
Saito, Col: 72
Saito, Lt Col: 299
Saito, President of Manchuria Agriculture Company: 76
Saizu, Superintendent, Shinzo: 222
Sakai, Maj, Masao: 139n
Sakhalin: 6n, 21
Sakurai, Maj Gen, Ryozo, C/S, First Area Army: 68n, 71, 73, 209
Sambondong: 118, 142
Samdongdong: 116
Samsangsan: 120, 124
Samyanggok: (see also roads) 120, 133, 136-37
Sanchiakou: 72, 80, 106, 334-37n, 338n
Sanchiang: 26, 37, 50, 150
Sanho: 9
Sasaki, Adjutant: 328
Sasaki, Col: 195
Sea of Japan: 27, 141
Sekimoto, Army Adjutant: 222
Senda, Capt: 136
Sendai: 110n
Seya, Lt Gen, Kei: 87
Shahoyen: 48, 74
Shangchiaoshan: 146
Shangchihtun: 176, 182, 184, 250-51, 254
Shanhaikwan: 7
Shengwutun: 15
Shentung: 104
Shibo, Col: 93
Shihliping: 44, 52, 65, 87, 89, 97, 102
Shihmentzu: 306, 335
Shihtou: 38, 49, 80, 83, 151, 166, 185, 193, 225-27, 233-35, 290, 342, 343

Shiina, Lt Gen, Masatake, CG, 124th Div: 45, 193, 195, 225-27, 232-37, 239
Shimakawa, Lt Col, Haruo: 283, 285-87, 290, 298
Shimizu, Lt Gen, Noritsune, CG, Fifth Army: 44, 63, 154, 159, 191, 200
Shinabe, Col, Takaharu: 110n
Shozusan: (see Mountain)
Shuiliufeng: 88, 145-46
Siberia: 27-28, 53, 174
   eastern: 2
Signal
   station: 63
   unit: 241, 309, 315, 320, 341
Signal Regiments
   7th: 151
   46th: 152, 154, 168
Sound Locating Company: 149n
Soviets: (see also USSR) 1-4, 6-7, 13, 29, 32, 53-54, 69, 72-76, 78, 97, 104-05, 107, 131, 135, 137, 141, 143, 146, 174, 193, 205, 218, 223, 231, 247-50, 280, 283, 302-05, 311
   aircraft: 311
   airplane: 24
   Army: 4, 12, 24-25, 72, 77, 93, 96, 108, 145, 159, 163, 180, 210, 215, 218, 224, 233, 244, 249, 284, 325, 326, 331
   25th Army: 105, 326-27, 343
   First : 217
   Headquarters: 217, 303
   supreme commander: 71
   supreme Headquarters: 23
   artillery: 59
   heavy: 145
   Consul-General: 22
   Far East Army: 22, 24, 27, 75
   Far East Commander: 218
   force: 9, 45, 53, 67, 22-73, 94-95, 123, 127, 129, 134, 136, 146, 153, 172, 218, 224, 301, 303

Guard Unit: 248
  infantrymen: 54, 174
  invasion: 3, 7, 39, 41, 46,
    80, 175
  officers: 54, 73
  Russia: 214
  tank: 273
    battalion: 73
    force: 273
  territory: 74, 96, 172-73,
    219-20, 305
  troops: 2, 23, 54, 75, 138
  Union: 4, 6-8, 12-13, 25, 46,
    180, 276-77
  withdraw: 2
Special Service (Intelligence)
  Agency
    Mutanchiang: 231
    Tungan: 280
Special Guard Battalion; 460th:
  142n
Special Guard Companies
  628th-630th, 641st: 154
Ssutaoling: (see also Hills) 66,
  163, 165-66, 203, 205, 207,
  264-68
  Heights: 205-06
Sugupo: 133, 135, 138
Suifenho: (see also roads and
  railroads) 3, 28-29, 31-32,
  61-62, 65, 74, 80, 150, 181-82,
  184-85, 195, 219, 226-27, 233,
  245, 290, 305, 316, 340
Suihsi: 225, 227
Suinan: 225
Suiyang: 34, 49, 80, 83, 151, 166,
  185, 193, 225-27, 233-35, 290,
  344
Sunwu: 9, 16
Supply bases: 48
Suwonshan: 102
Swiss: 21n
Tachengtzu: 7
Tachiao: 173, 176, 184, 188, 287
Tachienchang: 34-35, 64, 89, 157,
  308-09, 313-16, 322-23, 330,
  336, 337n, 341, 345-46

Tada, Staff Officer: 296
Taimakou: 163-66, 190, 194-98,
  237-37, 240
Tahsingkou: 309, 315, 320, 322-23,
  327
Taipingkou: 309-10
Taipingling: 309, 318-21, 325
Takahashi, ex-Lt Col, Ko: iii
Takase, First Lt: 291
Takasugi, Maj, Kyoji: 1n
Takeda, Prince, Tsunenori: 20-21
Takikawa, Maj: 291-92
Tahualienkou: 243
Tambov
  City: 137
  Oblast: 106
Tanaka, Col, Masashi: 246n
Tangpichen: 173, 281
Tanimura, Lt Col: 298
Tass: (see broadcast and news
  agencies)
Tatar Republic: 137n
Tatutzuchuan: 102, 329, 330
Timber Unit: 124, 126
Togo, Foreign Minister, Shigenori:
  6n
Tojo, Premier, Hideki: 11n
Tokyo: 4, 6, 19-20, 39n, 139
Tonggwan: 115-16, 118, 133
Training: 38, 53, 56-58, 90-91,
  121, 160, 162, 168-69, 171,
  179, 230, 279, 282, 332-34
  Construction of fortification:
    53
  excercise: 53, 145, 179-80
  near Acheng: 81
  planes: 99n,
Transport Battalion: 339, 341
Transport Companies
  2d-3d: 116
Transport Regiments
  79th: 113-14
  126th: 246, 265
Transport Units: 309, 315, 322, 327,
  333, 335, 342
  126th: 262
Tsitsihar: 17

Tsumori, Staff Officer: 214
Tuhuangtzu: 60, 103
Tumen: (see also railroads, lines, and roads) 34-35, 43, 50, 52, 60, 62, 65, 70, 84-87, 90, 94, 98, 100-02, 105, 113-16, 118, 122-23, 127-37, 140-41, 147, 329, 344
Tumentzu: 60, 86-87, 94-97
Tumuho: 167, 183, 278, 281
Tungan: 26, 29, 31-32, 45, 49, 51-52, 148, 163, 166-67, 137, 175, 184, 187-91, 200, 216, 221-22, 275-76, 281-83, 285-98, 297, 301
  City: 29, 41n
  Province: 148, 153, 280
  Station: 286
Tungancheng: 173
Tungchingcheng: 50-51, 60, 68, 70, 77, 200, 205, 215-16, 244, 261-62, 344, 346
Tunghua: 13-15, 19, 105, 150, 189
Tungning: 3, 8, 29-30, 34, 38, 44, 49, 60, 64, 80-81, 87, 89, 103-04, 106, 133, 135, 197, 236-37, 245, 306-08, 312, 323, 325, 329, 331, 333, 336, 344-45
  Detachment: 72
  Prefecture Governor: 328, 330
Tunhua: 34-36, 38, 42, 46, 48-53, 62-64, 66-68, 70-74, 77, 99n, 136, 209-10, 213-14, 216-18, 222, 299, 302, 329
Tzuhsingtun: 158, 168, 182, 199-20, 207, 250, 260-63, 292
Ueda, Maj: 272-73
Unggi: (see also ports) 95, 97, 126, 147
Unggidong: 127
Unggiryong: 97
United States: 12-13
  Army: 1n, 57n, 249
Unmurei: 85, 116, 118, 120, 125-26

Ushiroku, Gen, Jun, CG, Third Area Army: 10-12, 14-15, 17-18
USSR: (see also Soviets) 2-3, 27n, 30, 37n, 106, 230, 240, 334
Vassilievsky, Marshal, A.M.: 22
Veterinary Depot (Hospital): 113, 133, 135, 143, 262, 265, 309, 320
Veterinary Quarantine Stations
  15th: 104
  20th (Second Class): 154
Vladivostok: 28n, 213
Voroshilov: 74, 328
Wangching: 30, 86, 98-101, 103, 105-06, 129, 326, 327-28, 346
Wakamatsu, Lt Col, Mitsunori: 72, 98
Watanabe, Col: 72
Weapon: 55-56, 228, 250
  cavalry guns (75-mm): 178
  battalion guns (37-mm): 282
  heavy: 58, 61, 68, 88
  infantry regimental guns (75-mm): 282
  Model 31 mountain guns (75-mm): 282
  Model 38 field guns: 178
  Model 41 mountain guns (75-mm): 178
  Model 90 field guns: 178, 185
  T34 tank: 292-93, 295
  75-mm gun: 294
  76-mm gun: 295n
  105-mm howitzer: 335
  150-mm gun: 340, 317
  280-mm howitzer: 335
Wenchun: 204
White Russians: 79, 224, 280
Wire entanglement: 28, 204, 228
Wuchakou: 10, 15, 24
Wuchiatzu: (see also Incidents) 8, 59-60, 80-81, 88, 93, 95, 99, 103, 125-26, 129, 141, 144-46
Wunoerh: 9
Yamada, Gen, Otozo: 5, 12-13, 15, 18-19, 25 (see also Kwantung Army commander in chief)
Yamagishi, First Lt: 199, 260-61

Yamanaka, Col, Hajime: 273
Yamanouchi, Col, Shizuo: 87
Yangkang: 161
Yangtzuling: 318
Yano, ex-Col, Muraji: iii
Yaoshan: 82, 150
Yapuloni: 189, 216, 301
Yasuki, Col, Kaneji: 72
Yehho: 41, 50-53, 62, 67, 70, 80, 84, 94, 158, 164-68, 175, 180-81, 183, 188-90, 191n, 193-94, 198-205, 207-09, 211-13, 221-22, 232, 254, 260-66, 271, 278, 283, 285, 290-92, 296-99, 301-02
   Village: 270, 296
Yenchi: 41, 49-52, 73, 77, 84-85, 89-90, 93, 96, 99-108, 123, 128-29, 132, 136-37, 328
   City: 106
Yerabuga: (see camps)
Yingchitun: 66, 203, 264, 271
Yukujuru Mausoleum: 7
Zharkovo: 22
Zone of Comm Duty Companies
  46th, 80th: 154
  77th, 79th: 102
Zone of Comm Medical Companies
  19th: 154
Zone of Comm Medical Unit
  13th: 103

www.ingramcontent.com/pod-product-compliance
Lightning Source LLC
Chambersburg PA
CBHW081023240426
43671CB00029B/2888